The Bioarchaeology of Cardiovascular Disease

Cardiovascular diseases (CVDs) are the leading cause of death worldwide today, but are not just a modern phenomenon. To explore the deep roots of CVDs in human history, this book, for the first time, brings together bioarchaeological evidence from different periods, as old as 5000 BCE, and geographic locations from Alaska to Northern Africa. Experts in their fields showcase the powerful tool set available to bioarchaeology, which allows a more comprehensive reconstruction of the human past through evidence for disease. The tools include aDNA and histological analyses and digital imaging techniques for studying skeletal and mummified human remains. While the insights gained from these studies are of value to historical research, they also demonstrate how archaeological human remains can provide the long view of the history of disease, thereby contributing to modern biomedical research within the context of evolutionary medicine.

Michaela Binder is a bioarchaeologist who has conducted research and fieldwork projects in many different countries, including Austria, Sudan, Egypt, Italy and Saudi Arabia. Combining cultural and biological perspectives, her work focuses on the comprehensive reconstruction of living conditions of past human populations. She is Senior Project Manager at Novetus GmbH Archaeological Services and lectures at the University of Vienna, Austria.

Charlotte A. Roberts is Emeritus Professor of Archaeology at Durham University, UK. A bioarchaeologist and former nurse, she has conducted palaeopathological research for over 40 years. She has authored over 200 papers/book chapters, and authored/ edited a number of books, including *The Backbone of Europe* (Cambridge University Press, 2019) and *Palaeopathology and Evolutionary Medicine: An Integrated Approach* (Oxford University Press, 2022). She was elected a Fellow of the British Academy in 2014.

Daniel Antoine is the Keeper (Head) of the Department of Egypt and Sudan at the British Museum and an Honorary Senior Research Fellow at University College London, UK. He has published widely on bioarchaeology and palaeopathology, including *Regarding the Dead: Human Remains in the British Museum* and *Ancient Lives, New Discoveries: Eight Mummies, Eight Stories* (both British Museum Press, 2014).

Cambridge Studies in Biological and Evolutionary Anthropology

Consulting editors

C. G. Nicholas Mascie-Taylor, University of Cambridge
Robert A. Foley, University of Cambridge

Series editors

Agustín Fuentes, University of Notre Dame
Nina G. Jablonski, Pennsylvania State University
Clark Spencer Larsen, The Ohio State University
Michael P. Muehlenbein, Baylor University
Dennis H. O'Rourke, The University of Kansas
Karen B. Strier, University of Wisconsin
David P. Watts, Yale University

Also available in the series

53. *Technique and Application in Dental Anthropology* Joel D. Irish and Greg C. Nelson (eds.) 978 0 521 87061 0
54. *Western Diseases: An Evolutionary Perspective* Tessa M. Pollard 978 0 521 61737 6
55. *Spider Monkeys: The Biology, Behavior and Ecology of the Genus Ateles* Christina J. Campbell (ed.) 978 0 521 86750 4
56. *Between Biology and Culture* Holger Schutkowski (ed.) 978 0 521 85936 3
57. *Primate Parasite Ecology: The Dynamics and Study of Host–Parasite Relationships* Michael A. Huffman and Colin A. Chapman (eds.) 978 0 521 87246 1
58. *The Evolutionary Biology of Human Body Fatness: Thrift and Control* Jonathan C. K. Wells 978 0 521 88420 4
59. *Reproduction and Adaptation: Topics in Human Reproductive Ecology* C. G. Nicholas Mascie-Taylor and Lyliane Rosetta (eds.) 978 0 521 50963 3
60. *Monkeys on the Edge: Ecology and Management of Long-Tailed Macaques and their Interface with Humans* Michael D. Gumert, Agustín Fuentes and Lisa Jones-Engel (eds.) 978 0 521 76433 9
61. *The Monkeys of Stormy Mountain: 60 Years of Primatological Research on the Japanese Macaques of Arashiyama* Jean-Baptiste Leca, Michael A. Huffman and Paul L. Vasey (eds.) 978 0 521 76185 7
62. *African Genesis: Perspectives on Hominin Evolution* Sally C. Reynolds and Andrew Gallagher (eds.) 978 1 107 01995 9
63. *Consanguinity in Context* Alan H. Bittles 978 0 521 78186 2
64. *Evolving Human Nutrition: Implications for Public Health* Stanley Ulijaszek, Neil Mann and Sarah Elton (eds.) 978 0 521 86916 4
65. *Evolutionary Biology and Conservation of Titis, Sakis and Uacaris* Liza M. Veiga, Adrian A. Barnett, Stephen F. Ferrari and Marilyn A. Norconk (eds.) 978 0 521 88158 6
66. *Anthropological Perspectives on Tooth Morphology: Genetics, Evolution, Variation* G. Richard Scott and Joel D. Irish (eds.) 978 1 107 01145 8
67. *Bioarchaeological and Forensic Perspectives on Violence: How Violent Death is Interpreted from Skeletal Remains* Debra L. Martin and Cheryl P. Anderson (eds.) 978 1 107 04544 6
68. *The Foragers of Point Hope: The Biology and Archaeology of Humans on the Edge of the Alaskan Arctic* Charles E. Hilton, Benjamin M. Auerbach and Libby W. Cowgill (eds.) 978 1 107 02250 8

69. *Bioarchaeology: Interpreting Behavior from the Human Skeleton*, 2nd ed. Clark Spencer Larsen 978 0 521 83869 6 & 978 0 521 54748 2
70. *Fossil Primates* Susan Cachel 978 1 107 00530 3
71. *Skeletal Biology of the Ancient Rapanui (Easter Islanders)* Vincent H. Stefan and George W. Gill (eds.) 978 1 107 02366 6
72. *Demography and Evolutionary Ecology of Hadza Hunter-Gatherers* Nicholas Blurton Jones 978 1 107 06982 4
73. *The Dwarf and Mouse Lemurs of Madagascar: Biology, Behavior and Conservation Biogeography of the Cheirogaleidae* Shawn M. Lehman, Ute Radespiel and Elke Zimmermann (eds.) 978 1 107 07559 7
74. *The Missing Lemur Link: An Ancestral Step in Human Evolution* Ivan Norscia and Elisabetta Palagi 978 1 107 01608 8
75. *Studies in Forensic Biohistory: Anthropological Perspectives* Christopher M. Stojanowski and William N. Duncan (eds.) 978 1 107 07354 8
76. *Ethnoprimatology: A Practical Guide to Research at the Human–Nonhuman Primate Interface* Kerry M. Dore, Erin P. Riley and Agustín Fuentes (eds.) 978 1 107 10996 4
77. *Building Bones: Bone Formation and Development in Anthropology* Christopher J. Percival and Joan T. Richtsmeier (eds.) 978 1 107 12278 9
78. *Models of Obesity: From Ecology to Complexity in Science and Policy* Stanley J. Ulijaszek 978 1 107 11751 8
79. *The Anthropology of Modern Human Teeth: Dental Morphology and Its Variation in Recent and Fossil Homo Sapiens*, 2nd ed. G. Richard Scott, Christy G. Turner II, Grant C. Townsend and María Martinón-Torres 978 1 107 17441 2
80. *The Backbone of Europe: Health, Diet, Work, and Violence over Two Millennia* Richard H. Steckel, Clark Spencer Larsen, Charlotte A. Roberts and Joerg Baten (eds.) 978 1 108 42195 9
81. *Hunter-Gatherer Adaptation and Resilience: A Bioarchaeological Perspective* Daniel H. Temple and Christopher M. Stojanowski (eds.) 978 1 107 18735 1
82. *Primate Research and Conservation in the Anthropocene* Alison M. Behie, Julie A. Teichroeb and N. Malone (eds.) 978 1 107 15748 4
83. *Evaluating Evidence in Biological Anthropology: The Strange and the Familiar* Cathy Willermet and Sang-Hee Lee (eds.) 978 1 108 47684 3
84. *The Genetics of African Populations in Health and Disease* Muntaser E. Ibrahim and Charles N. Rotimi (eds.) 978 1 107 07202 2
85. *The Evolutionary Biology of the Human Pelvis: An Integrative Approach* Cara M. Wall-Scheffler, Helen K. Kurki and Benjamin M. Auerbach 978 1 107 19957 6
86. *Evolution, Ecology and Conservation of Lorises and Pottos* K. A. I. Nekaris and Anne M. Burrows (eds.) 978 1 108 42902 3
87. *The Biodemography of Subsistence Farming: Population, Food and Family* James W. Wood 978 1 107 03341 2
88. *Patterns of Human Growth*, 3rd ed. Barry Bogin 978 1 108 43448 5
89. *The Colobines: Natural History, Behaviour and Ecological Diversity* Ikki Matsuda, Cyril C. Grueter and Julie A. Teichroeb (eds.) 978 1 108 42138 6
90. *World Archaeoprimatology: Interconnections of Humans and Nonhuman Primates in the Past* Bernardo Urbani, Dionisios Youlatos and Andrzej T. Antczak (eds.) 978 1 108 48733 7

The Bioarchaeology of Cardiovascular Disease

Edited by
MICHAELA BINDER
Novetus GmbH, Vienna, Austria

CHARLOTTE A. ROBERTS
Durham University, UK

DANIEL ANTOINE
The British Museum, London, UK

Shaftesbury Road, Cambridge CB2 8EA, United Kingdom

One Liberty Plaza, 20th Floor, New York, NY 10006, USA

477 Williamstown Road, Port Melbourne, VIC 3207, Australia

314–321, 3rd Floor, Plot 3, Splendor Forum, Jasola District Centre, New Delhi – 110025, India

103 Penang Road, #05-06/07, Visioncrest Commercial, Singapore 238467

Cambridge University Press is part of Cambridge University Press & Assessment, a department of the University of Cambridge.

We share the University's mission to contribute to society through the pursuit of education, learning and research at the highest international levels of excellence.

www.cambridge.org
Information on this title: www.cambridge.org/9781108480345

DOI: 10.1017/9781108648561

© Cambridge University Press & Assessment 2023

This publication is in copyright. Subject to statutory exception and to the provisions of relevant collective licensing agreements, no reproduction of any part may take place without the written permission of Cambridge University Press & Assessment.

First published 2023

Printed in the United Kingdom by TJ Books Limited, Padstow Cornwall

A catalogue record for this publication is available from the British Library.

A Cataloging-in-Publication data record for this book is available from the Library of Congress.

ISBN 978-1-108-48034-5 Hardback

Cambridge University Press & Assessment has no responsibility for the persistence or accuracy of URLs for external or third-party internet websites referred to in this publication and does not guarantee that any content on such websites is, or will remain, accurate or appropriate.

To past and present people who have had CVD or have CVD or will have CVD, and to Tony Waldron and Don Brothwell. . .

Contents

List of Contributors	*page* xi
Foreword	xv
Keith Manchester	
Acknowledgements	xviii

1 The Bioarchaeology of Cardiovascular Disease: Introduction   **1**
Michaela Binder

2 Exploring the Sources of Indirect Evidence for Cardiovascular Disease in Bioarchaeology: Potential Impact on Understanding Its Evolution   **7**
Charlotte A. Roberts

Part I Evidence from Mummified Tissues

3 Atherosclerosis, Mummies and Histological Analysis: A Review   **41**
Gino Fornaciari and Raffaele Gaeta

4 Computed Tomography Evidence of Atherosclerosis in Ancient Mummies: The Horus Studies of Mummies from Five Continents   **66**
Randall C. Thompson, Ashna Mahadev, M. Linda Sutherland and Gregory S. Thomas

5 The Genetic Background of Atherosclerosis in Ancient Mummies   **81**
Albert Zink, Christina Wurst, Frank Maixner, Samuel Wann, Randall C. Thompson and Gregory S. Thomas

6 Cardiovascular Disease in Nile Valley Mummies: Exploring the Need for a More Systematic Approach That Accounts for Vessel Prevalence, Links to Oral Health and the Impact of Dual-Energy CT Scanning   **98**
Daniel Antoine, Marie Vandenbeusch, Rebecca Whiting and Benjamin Moreno

7 Atherosclerosis among the Elites: A Bioarchaeological Investigation of Seventeenth- to Nineteenth-Century Mummified Human Remains from Palermo, Sicily (Italy) and Vilnius (Lithuania)   **130**
Dario Piombino-Mascali, Rimantas Jankauskas, Albert Zink and Stephanie Panzer

x Contents

Part II Cardiovascular Diseases Associated with Human Skeletal Remains

8 Calcified Structures as Potential Evidence of Atherosclerosis Associated with Human Skeletal Remains from Amara West, Nubia (1300–800 BCE) 147
Michaela Binder and Charlotte A. Roberts

9 Intracranial Atherosclerosis in Medieval Scandinavia 164
Caroline Arcini and Elisabet Englund

10 Abnormalities of the Vertebral Artery: Are Cervical Pressure Defects Being Overlooked in Palaeopathology? 174
Daniel Antoine and Tony Waldron

11 A Heart of Stone: A Review of Constrictive Pericarditis and Other Calcified Tissues from the Pathologic–Anatomical Collection at the Narrenturm in Vienna, Austria 202
Karin Wiltschke-Schrotta, Eduard Winter and Michelle Gamble

12 'Absence of Evidence Is Not Evidence of Absence': Why Is There a Lack of Evidence for Cardiovascular Disease in the Bioarchaeological Record? 214
Michaela Binder and Charlotte A. Roberts

Part III Contemporary Perspectives

13 The Challenging Diagnosis of Cardiovascular Disease in Skeletal Remains: Identifying Atherosclerotic Calcifications from Modern Documented Individuals 229
Lucie Biehler-Gomez, Emanuela Maderna and Cristina Cattaneo

14 Atherosclerosis in Indigenous Tsimane: A Contemporary Perspective 246
Randall C. Thompson, Gregory S. Thomas, Angela D. Neunuebel, Ashna Mahadev, Benjamin C. Trumble, Edmond Seabright, Daniel K. Cummings, Jonathan Stieglitz, Michael Gurven and Hillard Kaplan

15 Reflections on Cardiovascular Disease: The Heart of the Matter 258
Charlotte A. Roberts, Michaela Binder and Daniel Antoine

Index 263

Colour plates can be found between pages 142 and 143.

Contributors

Daniel Antoine
Department of Ancient Egypt and Sudan, British Museum, London, UK

Caroline Arcini
National Historical Museums, Contract Archaeology Service, Lund, Sweden

Lucie Biehler-Gomez
LABANOF (Laboratorio di Antropologia e Odontologia Forense), Department of Biomedical Sciences for Health, University of Milan, Milan, Italy

Michaela Binder
Novetus GmbH, Vienna, Austria

Cristina Cattaneo
LABANOF (Laboratorio di Antropologia e Odontologia Forense), Department of Biomedical Sciences for Health, University of Milan, Milan, Italy

Daniel K. Cummings
Economic Science Institute, Argyos School of Business and Economics, Chapman University, Orange, California, USA

Elisabet Englund
Department of Clinical Sciences, Division of Pathology, University of Lund, Lund, Sweden

Gino Fornaciari
School of Specialization in Archaeological Heritage, Department of Civilisations and Forms of Knowledge, University of Pisa, Pisa, Italy

Raffaele Gaeta
Division of Paleopathology, Department of Translational Research and of New Technologies in Medicine and Surgery, University of Pisa, Pisa, Italy

Michelle Gamble
Heritage and Archaeological Research Practice, Edinburgh, UK

Michael Gurven
Department of Anthropology, University of California–Santa Barbara, Santa Barbara, California, USA

Rimantas Jankauskas
Department of Anatomy, Histology and Anthropology, Faculty of Medicine, Vilnius University, Vilnius, Lithuania

List of Contributors

Hillard Kaplan
Economic Science Institute, Argyos Schol of Business and Economics, Chapman University, Orange, California, USA

Emanuela Maderna
LABANOF (Laboratorio di Antropologia e Odontologia Forense), Department of Biomedical Sciences for Health, University of Milan, Milan, Italy

Ashna Mahadev
School of Medicine, University of Missouri–Kansas City, Kansas City, Missouri, USA

Frank Maixner
Institute for Mummy Studies, Eurac Research Bolzano/Bozen (EURAC), Bolzano/Bozen, Italy

Benjamin Moreno
IMA Solutions, Toulouse, France

Angela D. Neunuebel
Emory School of Medicine, Emory University, Atlanta, Georgia, USA

Stephanie Panzer
Department of Radiology, Trauma Center Murnau, Murnau, Germany

Dario Piombino-Mascali
Department of Anatomy, Histology and Anthropology, Faculty of Medicine, Vilnius University, Vilnius, Lithuania

Charlotte A. Roberts
Department of Archaeology, Durham University, Durham, UK

Edmond Seabright
School of Collective Intelligence, Mohammed 6 Polytechnic University, Rabat, Morocco.

Jonathan Stieglitz
Université Toulouse 1 Capitole, Toulouse, France

M. Linda Sutherland
MemorialCare Health System, Fountain Valley, California, USA

Gregory S. Thomas
Memorial Care Heart and Vascular Institute, Long Beach Memorial, University of California–Irvine, Orange, California, USA

Randall C. Thompson
Saint Luke's Mid America Heart Institute, University of Missouri–Kansas City, Kansas City, Missouri, USA

Benjamin C. Trumble
School of Human Evolution and Social Change, Arizona State University, Tempe, Arizona, USA

Marie Vandenbeusch
Department of Ancient Egypt and Sudan, British Museum, London, UK

Tony Waldron
Department of Archaeology, University College London, London, UK

Samuel Wann
Division of Cardiology, University of New Mexico, Albuquerque, New Mexico, USA

Rebecca Whiting
Department of Ancient Egypt and Sudan, British Museum, London, UK

Karin Wiltschke-Schrotta
Department of Anthropology, Natural History Museum, Vienna, Austria

Eduard Winter
Department of Anthropology, Natural History Museum, Vienna, Austria

Christina Wurst
Institute for Mummy Studies, Eurac Research Bolzano/Bozen (EURAC), Bolzano/Bozen, Italy

Albert Zink
Institute for Mummy Studies, Eurac Research Bolzano/Bozen (EURAC), Bolzano/Bozen, Italy

Foreword

A man is as old as his arteries.   Thomas Sydenham (1624–89)

Dr William Harvey was Physician in Charge to St Bartholomew's Hospital in the City of London. He was Physician Extraordinary to King James I and King Charles I of England. In 1628 he published his seminal work *Exercitatio Anatomica de Motu Cordis et Sanguinis*. This work pronounced the dynamic physiological entity of the heart and the circulation of the blood, or the cardiovascular system. Ironically William Harvey died from a probable haemorrhage from his middle cerebral artery. In 1785 Dr William Withering perchance discovered the value of foxgloves in the management of peripheral oedema due to congestive heart failure. The result was the introduction of the drug digitalis into the clinical therapeutic practice of treating cardiac diseases. It is probable that the patient in this first therapeutic administration of digitalis was suffering from atrial fibrillation, an abnormality of cardiac rhythm due to pathologically induced functional electrical abnormality of the cardiac conduction system. Thus commenced the effective therapeutic management of disease of the cardiovascular system. The understanding of cardiac dysrhythmia was first enabled in 1893 by the invention of electrocardiography that demonstrated the pathways of electrical physiological activity within the cardiac musculature. By the 1950s the introduction of echocardiography had demonstrated the dynamics of cardiac function, the muscle contraction patterns and forms, and the actions of the heart valves.

In palaeopathology, however, the dynamic functionality of the living cardiovascular system cannot be observed or determined. This is because palaeopathological evidence, in both mummified and skeletal tissue, is fixed at the moment of death. However, in current clinical experience, sudden unexpected death, without any soft tissue cardiac findings, is common. Nevertheless, it is often presumed that such occurrences are due to unpredicted cardiac arrest secondary to ventricular dysrhythmia, commonly ventricular fibrillation, although this cannot be determined after death. Clearly, in palaeopathological contexts this diagnosis is impossible, but absence of evidence is not evidence of absence.

The finding of stenotic arterial disease, commonly due to atherosclerosis, is certainly not diagnostic of acute cardiac arrest in palaeopathological contexts. Furthermore, symptoms of disease are subjective and specific to the affected living person and can only be inferred in palaeopathology from clinical experience of the living patient. Thus, the finding of chronic arterial insufficiency presumed due to atherosclerosis cannot be assumed a positive cause of death in earlier peoples. The arteries involved in the findings of atherosclerosis in mummies are likely to have been symptomatic in ensuing limb ischaemia, but not in the central cardiac vessels. Further, the findings of atherosclerotic vessels in skeletons found as inhumation burials, which are currently rare finds, cannot be definitively ascribed to acute cardiac death. All that can be said is that the person likely had cardiovascular disease.

This volume seeks to present the identification of pathological lesions in the extant cardiovascular system of mummies, and the sequelae of such lesions with the skeletons of inhumations of past peoples. The volume documents many examples of peripheral atherosclerosis of arteries in mummies from many periods and geographic locations in the world. The evidence consists almost entirely of preserved calcified arterial deposits. This represents a chronic phase in the progressive pathogenesis of the condition, and of course does not indicate the true extent or frequency of atherosclerosis during the periods in question. Early stages of atherosclerotic pathogenesis are unlikely to be recognised because of the minimal pathological changes that are present. Thus, the prevalence of atherosclerosis in antiquity is likely grossly underestimated.

Whilst possibly of long-term clinical significance to the afflicted individual, in isolation these lesions may not indicate symptomatic clinical disease, depending on the degree of pathologically induced arterial stenosis. The ischaemic sequelae of atherosclerotic arteries may be symptomatic and therefore indicative of disease. However, even in this situation, the symptoms may not be reflected in organic ischaemic tissue change, at least in the early stages of pathogenesis. Arterial and arteriolar dynamic insufficiency causes, even in the early stages, activity-related angina pectoris (chest pain due to reduced blood flow to the heart muscles) and intermittent activity-related symptoms such as intermittent claudication in the muscles of propulsion that is induced by exercise and relieved by rest. Symptom severity of both varies from mild to severe. Intermittent claudication occurs as a result of muscle ischaemia during exercise caused by obstruction to arterial flow. Demonstrable pathological change in the soft tissues supplied by narrowed arterial vessels is usually a late phenomenon and, in the absence of therapeutic endarterectomy (removal of deposits), arterial bypass surgery or vasodilatory drug therapy (to enlarge the vessels), is permanent and progressive. Clearly, in the context of skeletal palaeopathology, such in vivo ischaemic tissue changes will not be detectable, although may be histologically in mummified remains. These caveats apply to peripheral arterial disease in the limbs and in the arterial supply of viscera (e.g. the heart), but even in mummified remains it is unlikely that histological evidence of visceral ischaemia will be detected in the desiccated preserved tissues. In the cerebrovascular circulation, however, neurological ischaemia is associated with microscopic and macroscopic loss of neural tissue that does not regenerate. The clinical symptomatic sequelae of specific neural damage are sensory and/or motor dysfunction, weakness or partial paralysis, full paralysis, or psychological or intellectual deficit. Clearly, in palaeopathology there are no determinable features of psychological or intellectual dysfunction. There may, however, depending on the duration of the illness, be indicators of muscle dysfunction in skeletons or mummies, such as atrophy/wasting of limb bones.

This volume, with its in-depth examination of atherosclerosis in mummified and skeletal remains, has extended our knowledge regarding in vivo cardiovascular disease in past peoples, and its multifactorial aetiology. The final chapter considers reasons for the paucity of evidence of atherosclerosis in the archaeological record and proposes measures, archaeological and investigative, to rectify this. Of course, we have to remember that the true impact and prevalence of cardiovascular disease in antiquity will never be known, but as a starting point it is dependent on identifying and documenting palaeopathological evidence in mummified and skeletal tissues. However, as I have stated, atherosclerosis is only one aspect of cardiovascular disease that can be considered palaeopathologically. The wide range of cardiac physical abnormalities, and the wide and complex phenomena of nerve-controlled dysrhythmias, are all potentially immediately fatal but do not leave a physical palaeopathological record, and are completely beyond the scope of the evidence that can be captured in the study of mummies or skeletons. Therefore the prehistoric and historical record for cardiovascular disease is, ipso facto, incomplete, and contributes in a major way to the familiar osteological (palaeopathological) paradox in which palaeopathologists work. I also reflect as a general clinician of 60 years' experience that, in practice, longevity is a major factor in the development of arteriosclerosis and atherosclerosis, terms which are frequently used synonymously for 'hardening of the arteries', the sequelae of which are, in reality, often difficult to differentiate in the living patient. In palaeopathology, erudite studies such as those presented in this volume will continue to improve our knowledge and understanding of diseases and illnesses past people experienced, especially those that do not directly affect the skeleton.

Keith Manchester MB, BS, BSc, DSc (Hon)
Honorary Professor of Palaeopathology
Biological Anthropology Research Centre
School of Archaeological and Forensic Sciences
University of Bradford
Bradford, UK

Acknowledgements

The realisation of this book would not have been possible without the help and support of a number of people. At Cambridge University Press, Dominic Lewis guided us through the initial steps of getting the book published. After his departure, Olivia Boult became responsible and despite repeated delays on our part patiently led us through the process of publishing. Sheridan Strang at Novetus GmbH assisted with the editing of the book and other bits and bobs. At the 2015 Symposium, Niels Lynnerup acted as discussant, strongly supporting our efforts to raise awareness for this, as yet, neglected area of bioarchaeological research into past human morbidity. Finally, we would not have a book without the authors all willingly producing their chapters; we are extremely grateful to them, their patience and their tremendous work.

1 The Bioarchaeology of Cardiovascular Disease

Introduction

Michaela Binder

In February 2010, I was crouching down in a subterranean tomb chamber at the archaeological site of Amara West in modern Sudan, excavating the human skeletal remains of people that had lived some 3000 years ago. Suddenly, I came across fragile tubular objects made of a whitish substance arranged almost like a string of beads parallel to the femur of a middle-aged woman (Figure 1.1). The unassuming little tubes were carefully collected, wrapped in scraps of acid-free tissue paper, packed in cardboard boxes used for Sudanese matches and labelled 'calcified arteries?'. Together with the excavated skeletal remains, they were later – courtesy of the National Corporation for Antiquities and Museums of Sudan – shipped to the British Museum in London for further scientific analysis within the framework of my PhD research at Durham University under the supervision of Charlotte A. Roberts, the co-editor with myself of this book. Over the course of several more excavation seasons at Amara West, the number of little boxes containing these objects labelled 'calcified arteries?' grew, resulting in a first paper published in the *International Journal of Paleopathology* in 2014. Drawing on clinical knowledge, new evidence from mummy studies that had just been published (e.g. Allam et al., 2009; Thompson et al., 2013), anatomical data and three-dimensional modelling, they were presented as the first evidence of calcifications resulting from cardiovascular disease (CVD) associated with human skeletal remains from an archaeological site (Binder & Roberts, 2014).

When the paper was published in 2014, it created an unexpectedly large amount of public interest, including media coverage in the USA, Canada, the UK, Russia, Japan and continental Europe. Reporters were not so much interested in the archaeology of the site, but the fact that CVDs were clearly not a modern phenomenon related to twenty-first century living but had already plagued humans 3000 years ago. An equally extensive media response had already been observed when the Horus team evidence of atherosclerosis in mummies from four different archaeological populations had been released a year prior to our paper in the *International Journal of Paleopathology* . With CVDs rising to become the number one cause of death worldwide, these studies had apparently hit a nerve in Western societies. Within the context of the developing field of evolutionary medicine (Nesse & Stearns, 2008; Stearns et al., 2010; Alcock, 2012; Plomp et al., 2022), the potential relevance of results from palaeopathological studies became evident for discussions about CVDs today.

Figure 1.1 Remnants of a calcified artery in a burial at Amara West (Sudan) in situ upon recovery. Source: courtesy of the Trustees of the British Museum.

1.1 The 2015 AAPA Symposium

With the archaeological evidence from Amara West and increasing interest in studying CVDs in mummified human remains, Charlotte Roberts and I felt it timely to bring together experts from different areas to discuss current knowledge of CVDs in past human populations and thus we organised a half-day symposium 'The Bioarchaeology of Cardiovascular Diseases' at the 84th Meeting of the American Association of Biological Anthropology[1] in St Louis, Missouri on 26 March 2015.

The aim of the symposium was to bring together experts in palaeopathology, forensic anthropology, biomolecular archaeology and evolutionary medicine to discuss current knowledge of CVDs in past human populations, including new research perspectives, recovery strategies and taphonomy, and to highlight the modern relevance of the insights gained from the data. Additionally, with the presentation at the symposium of recent results from burials containing skeletal remains, the potential for preservation of evidence of CVDs was highlighted, with the aim of increasing awareness to the possibilities and research potential of detecting CVDs in and with archaeological human remains. The symposium featured seven invited papers as well as a discussion led by Niels Lynnerup (University of Copenhagen) and Albert Zink (EURAC, Bozen). The papers presented in the 2015 symposium form the basis of this

---

[1] Formerly the American Association of Physical Anthropology; the name was changed in 2020.

book. Several more researchers were also invited to contribute to provide as full a reflection as possible of the current spectrum of bioarchaeological research on CVDs in past human populations. Amidst two career changes, one retirement, one child and a global pandemic, its realisation took somewhat longer than anticipated. However, with an increasing interest in studying the occurrence of diseases in the past to understand their background and evolution, we feel it remains highly relevant to a range of disciplines, including clinical and evolutionary medicine, palaeopathology, forensic anthropology, fieldwork in archaeology, and medical history.

1.2 Organisation of This Volume

The papers in this volume are organised into three thematic sections: Evidence from Mummified Tissues, Cardiovascular Diseases Associated with Human Skeletal Remains, and Contemporary Perspectives (Figure 1.2). In order to provide a comprehensive medical, biological and evolutionary framework for the papers in this volume, Charlotte Roberts opens the volume with an outline of the complex clinical, pathophysiological and epidemiological background of CVDs and a review of the range of sources available to the study of CVDs in bioarchaeology, including both direct and indirect evidence.

The section on mummy studies starts with a review chapter by Gino Fornaciari and Raffaele Gaeta that summarises the developments in the study of CVDs in mummified human remains through the use of histological analysis of cardiovascular tissues. Drawing upon their extensive research experience, they present examples from different chronological and geographical backgrounds. Randall Thompson and colleagues present an updated version of the ground-breaking Horus study first published in 2009 (Allam et al., 2009) that set the path for the systematic study of CVDs in skeletal and mummified human remains. In their chapter, new evidence is presented, including a larger subset of Egyptian mummies, and confirms earlier observations that CVDs were present in humans regardless of their social status throughout the past 5000 years. Over the past decade, the team from the British Museum's Department of Ancient Egypt and Sudan led by Daniel Antoine has conducted an extensive multidisciplinary research programme including state-of-the-art CT scanning and three-dimensional visualisation of their collection of mummies to reveal the life histories of the individuals they once were. Naturally, this also led to the repeated discovery of evidence of CVDs in the majority of the mummies they were studying. In their contribution to the book, they summarise their results, discuss the differences between different generations of CT scanners and call for a more systematic approach when analysing the prevalence of CVDs in past human populations. The research group led by Albert Zink studying the 5300-year-old ice mummy Ötzi were the first to approach the topic from a palaeogenetic perspective, identifying genes linked to a genetic predisposition to CVD. In their contribution, their results are discussed within the context of host–environment interactions in order to add to our understanding of the genetic risk factors for CVDs.

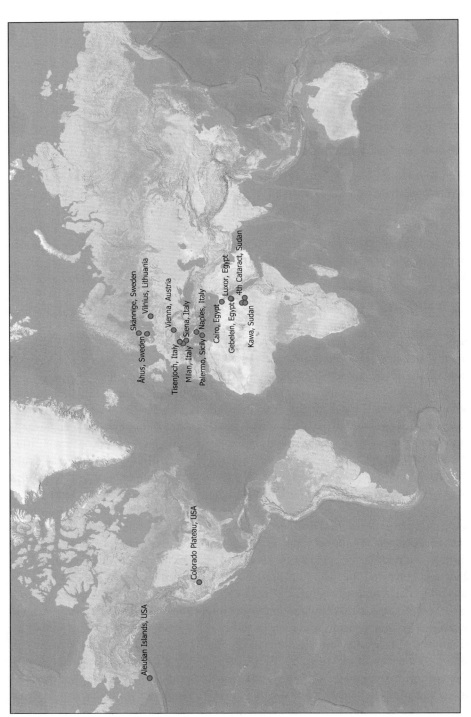

Figure 1.2 Map showing locations of sites discussed in this volume (basemap: ESRI World Physical Map). (A black and white version of this figure will appear in some formats. For the colour version, please refer to the plate section.)

The second section of the book is concerned with evidence related to CVDs recovered from and with human skeletal remains. In contrast to mummy studies, these have not been considered in bioarchaeological research until fairly recently due to difficulties in recognition, identification and recovery of pathological calcifications resulting from CVDs. This section for the first time brings together the small number of studies available to date. It hopes to raise awareness in the discipline of archaeology in general (e.g. excavators who are not bioarchaeologists), and particularly inspire bioarchaeologists. It also emphasises the need to look for the, often tiny, objects during excavation and analysis, and to use the data in bioarchaeological research as a means to broaden the spectrum of diseases considered when addressing morbidity and mortality in past human populations. In the first paper of this section, Michaela Binder and Charlotte Roberts present new calcified objects from the archaeological site of Amara West in Sudan alongside those already published in 2014. A second collection of calcifications related to CVDs from an archaeological context comes from medieval Sweden. Caroline Arcini and colleagues discuss their findings within the context of historical data from archival sources detailing dietary habits and living conditions, highlighting that the risk factors for developing CVDs were prevalent in medieval society just as much as in today's societies. Drawing upon one of the world's largest collections of historical pathological objects collected for teaching purposes in Viennese hospitals between the seventeenth and nineteenth century, the Narrenturm in Vienna, Karin Wiltschke-Schrotta and colleagues further present a selection of different calcified objects related to CVDs. These are intended as a visual guide for researchers to draw attention to the wide range of objects potentially arising from CVDs. In order to explore potential reasons for the lack of evidence of calcifications arising from CVDs, Michaela Binder and Charlotte Roberts summarise current knowledge about the biological background of arterial calcification and discuss it within the context of archaeological taphonomy. That evidence for CVDs in human skeletal remains is not only confined to calcifications within the cardiovascular system is outlined in the chapter by Daniel Antoine and Tony Waldron. They present examples of vertebral changes related to two abnormalities of the vertebral arteries, tortuosity and aneurysm.

The final section entitled Contemporary Perspectives combines contributions approaching the topic of this book from two very different angles. Providing a forensic perspective, Lucie Biehler-Gomez and colleagues examine calcifications from 72 individuals with a documented medical history from the twentieth-century Milano Cemetery Skeletal Collection. Their results, including macroscopic, histological and scanning electron microscopy/energy dispersive spectrometry, provide a tool for forensic anthropologists and bioarchaeologists alike to reconstruct individual biographies. Finally, even though the contributions in this volume show that CVDs were widespread throughout the world in a wide range of chronological periods, ethno-medical research by Randall Thompson and colleagues on the Tsimane people in the Bolivian Amazon provides evidence that populations with low levels of CVDs nevertheless do exist. With subsistence based on fishing, hunting, gathering and farming as well as a generally active physical life, the Tsimane lifestyle represents a counterpoint to many ancient and modern societies. Thus, overall, the insights gained from this project provide a deeper understanding of CVD data for both the past and present.

The editors hope that this volume will (1) establish a baseline of CVD data from human remains that ranges from forensic contexts to archaeological skeletons and mummies; and (2) emphasise that despite accepted wisdom that few diseases affect the bones and teeth of skeletons, with more nuanced and reflective approaches, including carefully excavating those remains, anything is possible!

References

Allam, A. H., Thompson, R. C., Wann, L. S., Miyamoto, M. I. and Thomas, G. S. (2009). Computed tomographic assessment of atherosclerosis in ancient Egyptian mummies. *Journal of the American Medical Association*, 302, 2091–4.

Alcock, J. (2012). Emergence of evolutionary medicine: Publication trends from 1991–2010. *Journal of Evolutionary Medicine*, 1(2), 1–12.

Binder, A. and Roberts, C. A. (2014). Calcified structures associated with human skeletal remains: Possible atherosclerosis affecting the population buried at Amara West, Sudan (1300–800 BC). *International Journal of Paleopathology*, 6, 20–9.

Nesse, R. M. and Stearns, S. C. (2008). The great opportunity: Evolutionary applications to medicine and public health. *Evolutionary Applications*, 1(1), 28–48.

Plomp, K., Roberts, C., Elton, S. and Bentley, G. R. (2022). *Palaeopathology and Evolutionary Medicine: An Integrated Approach*. Oxford: Oxford University Press.

Stearns, S. C., Nesse, R. M., Govindaraju, D. R. and Ellison, P. T. (2010). Evolutionary perspectives on health and medicine. *Proceedings of the National Academy of Sciences*, 107(Suppl 1), 1691–5.

Thompson, R. C., Allam, A. H., Lombardi, G. P., et al. (2013). Atherosclerosis across 4000 years of human history: the Horus study of four ancient populations. *Lancet*, 381, 1211–22.

2 Exploring the Sources of Indirect Evidence for Cardiovascular Disease in Bioarchaeology

Potential Impact on Understanding Its Evolution

Charlotte A. Roberts

2.1 Introduction

Cardiovascular diseases (CVDs) are a group of disorders of the heart and blood vessels and are classed as non-communicable diseases (NCDs) (World Health Organization, 2019). The four main CVD disorders are:

1. Coronary artery disease of blood vessels supplying the heart.
2. Cerebrovascular disease of the vessels that supply the brain, termed cerebrovascular accident (CVA) or 'stroke': the blood supply to the brain is cut off, caused by blockage of blood vessels in the brain or by bleeding into the brain.
3. Peripheral artery disease of the vessels that supply the arms and legs.
4. Disease of the largest blood vessel of the body (aorta).

The first two involve blockage of blood vessels to the heart and brain, usually due to fat build-up, leading to heart attacks and strokes, respectively, but blood clots (emboli) and bleeding from a blood vessel can also cause a stroke. Fat globules may also be released into the bloodstream following severe injuries to bones. They are caused by disruption of fat cells in fractured bones (especially the femur and pelvis), and can also cause blockage of the vessels (Rothberg & Makarewich, 2019). CVDs further include rheumatic heart disease, where the heart muscle and valves are damaged by streptococcal bacteria in rheumatic fever; heart malformation at birth (congenital heart disease; and deep vein thrombosis, which leads to blood clots usually being released from the leg veins into the bloodstream causing blockage of a pulmonary artery, known as an embolism (World Health Organization, 2019).

CVD is at the top of the global causes of death today, often as a result of heart attacks and strokes (World Health Organization, 2019). Nearly 18 million people died from CVDs in 2016 (around one-third of all global deaths), 85 per cent of which were due to heart attack and stroke. Most deaths occur in poorer people living in low- and middle-income countries. This is because the populations in those countries do not have healthcare systems that facilitate the detection of CVDs in their early stages and therefore treatment is delayed. In addition, the implementation of preventative measures via educational resources may not be available. In 2013 the World Health Organization (WHO) published a plan of action to prevent and control NCDs, which included six objectives:

1. Raising the priority for addressing NCDs globally, regionally and nationally.
2. Strengthening national capacity.

3. Reducing risk factors.
4. Strengthening health systems.
5. Supporting and promoting capacity for research and development.
6. Monitoring trends and determinants of NCDs and assessing success in prevention and control.

Emphasising the serious threat to human health posed by NCDs, the WHO estimated that 'the total annual number of deaths from non-communicable diseases will increase to 55 million by 2030 if "business as usual" continues' (World Health Organization, 2013: 7).

A varying combination of risk factors are linked to heart disease, including smoking, eating an unhealthy diet, being overweight (Figure 2.1), not taking enough

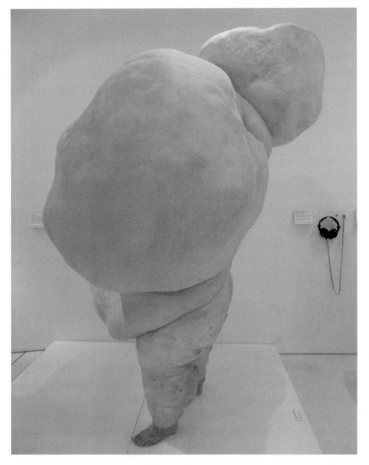

Figure 2.1 Sculpture by John Isaacs of an obese person with swollen legs and skin problems. Originally in a Wellcome Trust exhibition in London: Medicine Now (closed April 2019). Source: author's photo.

physical exercise, consuming harmful levels of alcohol, high blood pressure, diabetes and hyperlipidaemia (e.g. high cholesterol in the blood) (World Health Organization, 2019). Taking certain drugs, for example brufen and naproxen, can also increase risks for heart disease, and people being treated with radiotherapy are also more at risk (Arfè et al., 2016). High blood pressure damages blood vessels, smoking both damages and narrows vessels, and high cholesterol also narrows the vessels and increases the risk of blood clots. High blood sugar in diabetes can also narrow vessels, and being overweight increases the risk of diabetes and high blood pressure. Alcohol can increase cholesterol, raise blood pressure and contribute to weight gain (World Health Organization, 2019). South Asian, Caribbean or African ethnicities are more likely to have some risk factors for CVDs compared with other ethnicities, for example high blood pressure and type 2 diabetes. Furthermore, genomic studies are increasingly showing links between genes and susceptibility, as well as resistance, to CVDs. We are thus starting to appreciate the contributions a person's genetic profile (and environment) make to the occurrence of CVDs (Ewald, 2008; Bouchareychas et al., 2018; Musunuru et al., 2020). Heritability is a very important factor because of the interaction of multiple susceptibility alleles (Gluckman et al., 2009: 70). Furthermore, men tend to have an earlier age of onset of CVDs than women and although ill health and death from NCDs mostly affect adults, exposure to risk factors for CVDs can begin in early childhood (e.g. those who have type 1 diabetes or asthma).

CVDs may have been present prior to the second epidemiological transition (or period of change), which commenced in the early modern period with industrialisation (eighteenth/nineteenth centuries CE), although not all parts of the world experienced this at the same time; thus, it seems that CVDs were probably driven by risk factors associated with this transition (Barrett & Armelagos, 2013). Epidemiological transitions are shaped by patterns of population distribution in relation to changing patterns of mortality, fertility, life expectancy and leading causes of death. This second transition had followed the first, namely the transition from foraging for wild plants and hunting wild animals to farming our foods and living in settled communities, which promoted an increase in infectious and nutritional deficiency diseases (Roberts, 2015). In the second transition, a high frequency of infectious diseases was replaced by 'chronic' diseases that are not transmitted from human to human, namely NCDs (e.g. heart disease, stroke, cancer, chronic respiratory diseases and diabetes), conditions exacerbated by longer life expectancy. Rapid urbanisation, industrialisation and, later, globalisation brought about lifestyle changes that have promoted NCDs, including heart disease. Our bodies have been unable to keep pace with those changes as shown by the NCDs we are experiencing today. We currently face a mismatch (Figure 2.2) between our design and our environment: 'The design of our bodies is simultaneously extraordinarily precise and unbelievably slipshod' (Nesse & Williams, 1994: 5, 9; see also Gluckman & Hanson, 2006). This deep-time evolutionary perspective on the impact of epidemiological transitions on our health can help us to better understand who we are today, and importantly how we got there and what we need to do to preserve good health in the future.

Figure 2.2 An example of a modern-day mismatch (in this case footwear).

Clearly the problem of NCDs, and specifically CVDs, facing the global population today is well documented, but the actual antiquity of CVDs is relatively unknown. It has been suggested that CVDs and other NCDs (cancer, chronic respiratory diseases and diabetes) were much less common than they are today, possibly because the key risk factors were not present (Weil, 2008). CVDs primarily affect soft tissues (blood vessels), and therefore finding evidence associated with the most commonly excavated human remains in archaeology (i.e. skeletons) is challenging. Furthermore, the contemporary risk factors for CVDs were not likely to have been present in our ancestors' environment. Eating an unhealthy diet, being overweight, not taking enough exercise, having a high blood pressure, drinking lots of alcohol, diabetes and a high cholesterol level could have challenged people in the past, but they would not be the first risk factors we might think about in relation to ancient CVDs. For example, there is a strong possibility that exposure to particulate pollution, both natural (e.g. living in a place subject to volcanic eruptions) and human produced (e.g. open fires in homes), may have been more important in the development of CVDs in the past.

The aim of this chapter is to consider the direct and indirect evidence for CVDs in archaeological human remains and suggest some future directions. It starts with some thoughts on what people in the past knew about the cardiovascular system

(CVS) and associated diseases, briefly discusses previous work on CVDs in bioarchaeology, considers what direct evidence can be found and then focuses particularly on indirect evidence, including diseases that we can identify in skeletons and mummies that are clinically linked to CVDs.

2.2 Cardiovascular Disease in Bioarchaeology

The study of CVDs in palaeopathology has been relatively rare until recently, but knowledge of the CVS and some of its diseases are documented in early medical texts (see Sandison, 1967 for an overview: 474–9). For example, the Ebers Papyrus from Egypt (*c*. 1500 BCE) describes awareness of the heart's beating and 'transmission of impulses along vessels to the limbs' (Sandison, 1967: 476). Nunn (1996) also describes 'glosses' used in the Ebers Papyrus to define terms for pathological conditions affecting the heart (see table 4.2, p. 86; and see further examples from the Ebers Papyrus in Chapter 4). Whether CVD, as a condition that made people feel unwell in the past, was understood in any sense needs consideration. How early in time and where in the world was the anatomy and physiology of the CVS described, how widespread was this knowledge, and were the signs and symptoms of CVDs directly linked to an understanding of the CVS? Various sources highlight some valuable observations. For example, Aristotle, a fourth-century BCE Greek philosopher, believed the heart was key to the functioning of the body, although there was no knowledge of the brain at that time (Porter, 1997: 65), and in the *Corpus* of Hippocrates (460–377 BCE), a series of 70 treatises, one section provided anatomical details of the heart (Lloyd, 1983; Duffin, 2021: 72). By the time of Galen (second- to third-century CE physician, surgeon and philosopher), who promoted the idea that *pneuma* (air) was affected by the liver (nutrition and growth), the brain (sensation and reason) and the heart (vitality), knowledge of the CVS was increasing (Porter, 1997: 77). By the seventeenth century, the important work by William Harvey (1578–1657) entitled *De Motu Cordis* (1628) on the circulation of the blood and the function of the heart as a pump had become fundamental to modern anatomical and physiological knowledge about the CVS.

In terms of evidence for CVDs in archaeological contexts, atheromatous plaques and calcification, and other degenerative changes related to heart disease (e.g. affecting the elastic tissue forming the outermost part of the tunica intima of blood vessels), had been identified in the blood vessels of Egyptian mummies as early as the nineteenth century using radiology and histological analysis of blood vessel sections (Ruffer, 1911; Sandison, 1962, 1967). According to Sandison (1967), and assuming this is correct, the earliest report of vascular disease comes from a nineteenth-century laryngologist in Vienna, Austria, who found evidence for calcification of the aorta in an Egyptian mummy (Czermak, 1852 in Sandison, 1967). Indeed, there is much evidence of vascular disease in ancient Egypt both in literature and in mummies (for some recently reported evidence see Taylor & Antoine, 2014, and also the contributions by Antoine et al. in Chapter 6 and Zink et al. in Chapter 5).

Increasingly, more regions of the world where bodies are preserved are also reporting similar evidence (Aufderheide, 2000; Gaeta et al., 2013; see also Chapters 3 and 4). In addition, novel studies using ancient DNA evidence from preserved bodies is helping us to understand genetic predisposition for CVDs. For example, research on Ötzi, the Tyrolean 'Iceman' (c. 5300 years old), has revealed that he had a strong genetic predisposition for increased risk of coronary artery disease. He also revealed generalised atherosclerotic disease (Zink et al., 2014; see also Chapters 5 and 7).

However, most archaeological evidence for past people comes in the form of skeletons. Thus, the soft tissue changes of CVDs that may be seen in bodies in both archaeological (Bianucci et al., 2016; see also Chapter 4) and forensic contexts (Hugar et al., 2014; see also Chapter 13) have been considered essentially absent from archaeological contexts that have revealed skeletons. Nevertheless, Binder and Roberts (2014) have described calcified blood vessels associated with five skeletons from Amara West, Sudan, dated to 1300–800 BCE (see Chapter 8). Risk factors considered included exposure to poor air quality. Biehler-Gomez et al. (2018) also studied 24 skeletons from the Milano Skeletal Collection in Italy (12 with documentation indicating vasculopathy, i.e. disease of the blood vessels) and 12 control skeletons without any mention of vasculopathy (see also Biehler-Gomez et al., 2017). They reported 735 calcifications associated with 20 of the skeletons (in both the control and vasculopathy groups), noting that in forensic contexts clothing can help preserve the calcifications (e.g. in socks and tights). Independently known causes of death attributed to the people represented by the skeletons included cardiac and respiratory arrest, heart failure, and respiratory and hepatic failure. In some cases, the skeletal pathology noted included dental caries, periodontal disease, diffuse idiopathic skeletal hyperostosis (DISH, or Forestier's disease) and rheumatoid arthritis, all diseases that may be associated with heart disease and be seen in the skeleton (see Section 3.2). Most people were aged over 60 at their deaths. Again, this study shows that recovering CVD-related vascular calcifications associated with skeletons is possible in both forensic and archaeological contexts, but it is clear that care in the recovery process is needed to increase the amount of evidence identified (see Chapter 12). Indeed, in archaeological excavations, often in commercial environments, time and money are important factors, and the calcified blood vessels may be missed and excavators may not even be aware that they could exist in a grave.

2.2.1 Direct Evidence

Direct evidence for ancient CVDs includes calcified atheromatous plaques in blood vessels of preserved bodies (see Chapters 3–7) and calcified structures associated with atherosclerosis with skeletons (Binder & Roberts, 2014; see also Chapters 8 and 9), but also characteristic resorption of the bone of vertebral bodies and other bones as a result of aneurysms (see Chapter 10). Aneurysms occur as a result of a weakened artery wall and atherosclerosis can be a risk factor (Camm, 2002: 829). They particularly affect the main blood vessels of the body (e.g. aorta). In this case, the pressure of the blood pulsating through the weakened wall of the vessel leads to erosion of the surface of the vertebrae and loss of bone substance. This can also be related to other conditions such as tertiary syphilis, where cardiovascular and other complications occur (Kelley, 1979; Walker, 1983; Wakely & Smith, 1998; Waldron & Antoine, 2002; Castro et al., 2016; Byard, 2017). Here should also be mentioned strokes, which may also be recognised archaeologically, although the bone changes could have a number of causes. Strokes occur due to disease of the blood vessels of the brain, when the blood supply to part of the brain is restricted by haemorrhage through a weak vessel or by a blood clot in a vessel (Clarke, 2002). High blood pressure, a high cholesterol level, atrial fibrillation and diabetes are the key risk factors. Strokes can cause paralysis and subsequent bone atrophy but differentiating what actually caused atrophy in a skeleton or mummy can be very challenging (see Brothwell & Browne, 2002; Novak et al., 2014; Tesorieri, 2016). Collectively, and in recent years, evidence for CVDs has been found in an increasing range of preserved bodies, from Egypt to Europe and the Americas. Much evidence is reported in pre-industrial populations (Thompson et al., 2013, and chapters in this volume), suggesting that CVDs may not be characteristic of a specific diet or lifestyle. Indeed, the earliest evidence from archaeological contexts reported in preserved bodies and associated with skeletons represents populations who were far from industrialised (Czermak, 1852, in an Egyptian mummy; Binder & Roberts, 2014 and see Chapter 8, with skeletons from Sudan).

To a lesser extent, documentary or iconographic evidence (e.g. paintings, drawings, woodcuts, sculpture, reliefs, pottery) might also be considered direct evidence for a CVD if the evidence is very specific and unambiguous. Iconographic and documentary evidence is potentially more prolific than CVD evidence associated with archaeological human remains, albeit that it can only be found in periods where and when these sources were being produced. Nevertheless, documentary sources are not available in prehistory for the most part. However, other evidence might suggest a recognition of the heart and circulatory system or diseases associated with them. For example, Sandison (1967: 475) notes that 'man was aware of the importance of the heart as witnessed in his depicting for magical purposes the heart on cave paintings of animals'. However, it is unclear where this information originated. There are very few examples of Neolithic cave art (Paul Pettitt, 2020, pers. comm.), but in prehistoric Scandinavian rock (not cave) art there are depictions of internal organs that were created by hunter–gatherer–trapper societies from around 5000 BCE until around 100 CE. These include what appear to be hearts in a bear and a reindeer (Marta Diaz-Guardamino, 2020, pers. comm.; see also Helskog, 2014, and Figure 2.3). There is also Upper Palaeolithic evidence from Spain of a mammoth showing what has been interpreted as the heart inside its body (Alcalde del Río et al., 1911: El Pindal cave). Indeed, knowledge of animal anatomy would have increased through hunting wild animals and butchering both wild and domesticated animals. For example, Galen dissected a variety of animals and, although he had much influence in medicine, some of his observations do not stand up to scientific scrutiny now (Porter, 1997: 99). It was not until the mid-thirteenth-century CE that human autopsies became 'more regular' and the early fourteenth century (Bologna, Italy) saw the

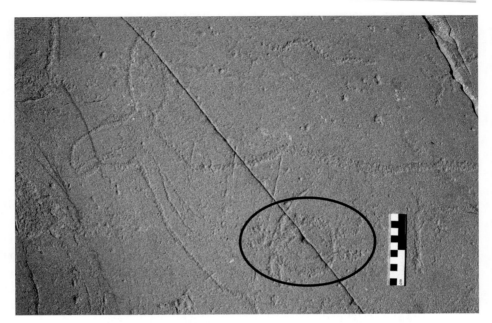

Figure 2.3 Rock art showing a young female reindeer with a depiction of its heart. From the panel Apanes I in Jiebmaluokta, Alta, Norway, dated to approximately 4000 ± 200 BCE. Source: Knut Helskog, The Arctic University Museum of Norway, Tromsø.

first human dissection undertaken by Mondino de' Luzzi (Porter, 1997: 132). His *Anatomia* became available in print from 1478. Of course, artists such as Andreas Vesalius (*De Humani Corporis Fabrica*, 1543) and Leonardo da Vinci (fifteenth to sixteenth century) were great anatomical illustrators, and both depicted the CVS in their anatomical art. We should also remember that bloodletting for various ailments was practised in the past (e.g. in Graeco-Roman medicine to balance the humours; Jackson, 2016), a treatment method to which knowledge of the anatomy and physiology of the CVS must have contributed.

However, the interpretation of documentary evidence can be challenging. In various publications, Mitchell (2011, 2012, 2017) provides criteria that need to be met for such evidence to be credible, criteria that anybody using such evidence should try to follow. For example, the London Bills of Mortality recorded the number of people who died weekly and their causes of death (Boyce, 2020) (Figure 2.4). The Bills are reported to have started as early as the sixteenth century. At first sight, many of the causes of death in these Bills make some sense to us, especially if some are still used in modern parlance (e.g. plague; see Brend, 1908 for an overview). However, other causes, such as 'purples', 'rising of the lights' and 'suddenly' are not so easy to understand. Apparently, 'lights' were the lungs and this phrase may have referred to a number of lung conditions (Brend, 1908: 14). Added to this, we have to be certain when using the Bills of Mortality that the data hold true when we know that the recorders (or 'searchers') of the cause of death data were not qualified physicians.

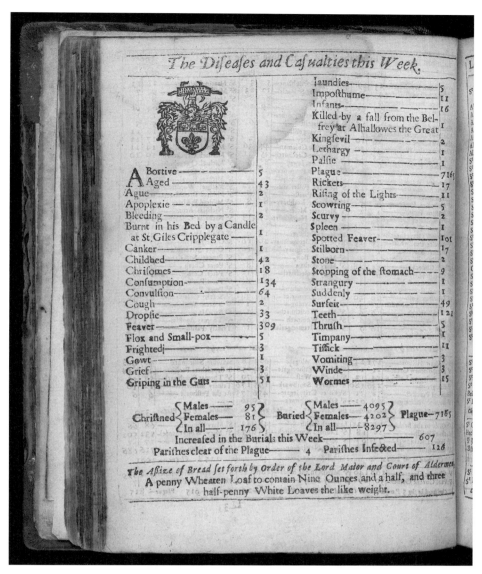

Figure 2.4 Example of a London Bill of Mortality, probably representing people who had died during that week of heart problems (e.g. 'aged'; 'dropsy'; 'suddenly'). Source: Wellcome Collection.

As Brend (1908: 8) says: 'Information collected in this manner was, of course, bound to be highly inaccurate' , and it is believed that data were deliberately altered to hide what was really happening and that searchers were bribed. A number of causes of death may be related to CVD with, for example, 'suddenly' possibly representing a heart attack or stroke. However, even today, the accuracy of cause of death data can be problematic (Johns et al., 2013).

In relation to artwork, evidence of CVDs is less visible when compared with written sources and is more difficult to interpret. Nunn (1996: 85), in his textbook on ancient Egyptian medicine, even went so far as to say that 'There is little to be learned about cardio-vascular disease in statues, reliefs and paintings, and the main sources of information are in the medical papyri, which are difficult to interpret in terms of modern concepts of cardiology'. For example, 'dropsy courting consumption', a nineteenth-century image depicting a thin and a fat person, has been interpreted as depicting (thin) people who had tuberculosis and overweight (obese) people with dropsy (Figure 2.5). Dropsy is believed to be oedema (swelling of parts of the body due to excess fluid) and is described as a fundamental cause of heart failure (Clark & Cleland, 2013). Another image, this time fourteenth century, supposedly depicts Gaston de Foix dying from an attack said to be due to coronary disease (Figure 2.6). The image is included in *The Chronicles of (Jean) Froissart* in a translation by John Bourcher, edited and reduced into one volume by G. C. Macauly and published in 1924. Froissart was a leading medieval historian who travelled widely, and he is considered to be a key source of information for the period. Both these images remind us that in using art and documentary sources as information about the presence of past disease, it is important to be sure that the signs and symptoms being described or depicted can be specifically attributed to a CVD before using such evidence. It is well known that some symptoms specifically associated with CVDs are also found in other medical conditions; for example, shortness of breath (dyspnoea), chest pain and fatigue can also be experienced by a person with tuberculosis.

The most common diseases recorded in palaeopathology tend to be those affecting the teeth and jaws, and joints, alongside injuries due to trauma (Roberts & Manchester, 2005). However, even the less commonly recorded diseases are more frequently documented than CVDs, for example neoplastic disease. The simple fact is that, when compared with other pathological conditions that affect both the soft tissues and the bones of the body, direct evidence for CVDs is rarely recorded. This is because these diseases directly affect the heart and blood vessels, which are of course not normally preserved with the most commonly recovered human remains (skeletons), or at least the evidence is not normally recovered during excavation or post-excavation processing.

Therefore, beyond using historical texts or iconographic evidence, we need to think 'outside the box' (i.e. explore the subject in creative and unusual ways) and try to access information that might broaden our perspectives on how frequent CVDs might have been in the past. While the perception today is that CVDs were uncommon in the past compared to their preponderance in populations today, in part because there is relatively little evidence in the archaeological record, some findings show that CVDs have been with us for a long time. However, alongside making particular efforts to recover the evidence with skeletons that are excavated, by thinking outside the box and considering indirect evidence for CVDs, we may be able to broaden the potential evidence beyond what is currently known.

Sources of Indirect Evidence for Cardiovascular Disease

Figure 2.5 An obese man wooing a tall lean woman outside a mausoleum, representing dropsy and consumption. Coloured etching by T. Rowlandson, 1810. Source: Wellcome Collection. (A black and white version of this figure will appear in some formats. For the colour version, please refer to the plate section.)

Figure 2.6 A fourteenth-century image of Gaston de Foix dying from a coronary attack, as described in Froissart's *Chronicles*, said to be due to coronary disease. Source: Wellcome Collection.

2.2.2 Indirect Evidence

In taking a proactive approach to exploring indirect evidence of CVDs, it is informative to consider diseases that can have cardiovascular consequences, with many such disorders affecting both the skeleton and soft tissues. While it would not be appropriate to say that a person whose skeleton has signs of any of these diseases had related CVD, because this could not be proved, the likelihood of this being the case could be assessed through consideration of the clinical literature (e.g. by looking at the probability of people with specific bone diseases linked to CVD actually developing CVD). For example, pericarditis has been noted in 30–40 per cent of people with rheumatoid arthritis who are 'strongly seropositive RA' based on echocardiographic or post-mortem studies (see Shipley et al., 2002: 542). Zhou and Byard's (2017) forensic study also reported that the principal cause of death in people with type 1 diabetes included CVD (44.7 per cent of those studied); for people with type 2 diabetes, it was 56.6 per cent.

This section documents a number of health problems, including examples of pathological conditions that can affect the skeleton, that can be related to CVD. This is not an exhaustive list, but the aim is to illustrate how indirect evidence for CVD might be identified in the bioarchaeological record, thus adding to what we know from the direct evidence. These are divided into congenital and acquired conditions. First, it should be noted that infectious disease as a comorbidity for CVD per se is not detailed in full as a separate section, but it should be acknowledged that infections are increasingly being linked to CVDs in the clinical record (see Bekkering et al., 2019). Second, in order to emphasise this association, and at relevant points throughout the acquired diseases section, if infection has been shown to be a comorbidity for CVD this is mentioned (e.g. in the section on dental diseases).

2.2.2.1 Congenital Anomalies

The WHO defines congenital anomalies as 'birth defects, congenital disorders or congenital malformations [...] structural or functional anomalies (e.g. metabolic disorders) that occur during intrauterine life and can be identified prenatally, at birth or later in life [...] can be caused by single gene defects, chromosomal disorders, multifactorial inheritance, environmental teratogens and micronutrient deficiencies ' (World Health Organization, 2021a). Of course, with the advent of ancient DNA analysis over the last 30 years, and recalling the first report of DNA being found in bones (Hagelberg et al., 1989), it is now becoming possible to positively identify genetic related diseases in archaeological skeletons (Traversari et al., 2019). The most common severe congenital anomalies today are heart defects, neural tube defects and Down syndrome (World Health Organization, 2021a). Three congenital conditions are considered here that may affect the skeleton: cyanotic congenital heart disease, Down syndrome and Marfan syndrome.

How might we detect congenital heart disease in skeletal remains? Today it may be caused by rubella infection, alcohol and drug abuse in mothers, and genetic related conditions (Camm, 2002). Should a person in the past have survived with cyanotic congenital heart disease, one of the related signs, although rare, is secondary hypertrophic osteoarthropathy (HOA) with periostitis of bones being the key feature (Resnick & Niwayama, 1995a, and references therein). The radii, ulnae, tibiae, fibulae and the terminal phalanges are the main bones affected. A variety of pulmonary diseases tend to be the most common cause of HOA, hence the term hypertrophic pulmonary osteoarthropathy (HPOA) is often used. A study of skeletons from the early twentieth-century Coimbra Identified Skeletal Collection in Portugal curated at the University of Coimbra has shown that the risk of developing HPOA is higher in people with tuberculosis (Assis et al., 2011). In another study from Sudan, a second- to third-century CE skeleton with this condition also had periosteal reaction on the internal surfaces of the ribs, suggesting that a pulmonary disease had led to the HOA (Binder & Saad, 2017). While not a pathognomonic condition that can be used to indicate a survivor of congenital heart disease in the past, this may be a sign.

Down syndrome is the most common chromosomal abnormality in infants (1 in 700 live births globally; see Iles, 2002), and there is a high chance (40–60 per cent) that those affected have associated congenital heart disease (Morrison & McMahon, 2018). This is commonly an atrioventricular septal defect, with holes between the chambers of the right and left sides of the heart and the valves that control the blood flow between them not forming correctly (World Health Organization, 2021a). Down syndrome, or trisomy 21, is caused by faulty cell division resulting in a baby having three copies of chromosome 21 instead of two. Bone changes of Down syndrome include hip dysplasia and flared iliac wings, along with hypoplasia of the mid phalanx of the fifth finger, short metacarpal bones, accessory epiphyses, cube-shaped vertebral bodies, 11 pairs of ribs, microcephaly, a short and arched palate, delayed cranial suture closure, under or incomplete development of the sinuses, and instability of the joints between the atlas and axis and between the atlas and occipital condyles (McAlister & Herman, 1995). None of these bone changes alone is pathognomonic and their occurrence will vary between affected individuals. In addition, there is little published evidence on Down syndrome in the archaeological record (Brothwell, 1960; Rivollat et al., 2014). Nevertheless, in addition to the need to identify more evidence of this syndrome archaeologically, it is worth noting when investigating CVDs due to the high risk of congenital heart disease linked to Down syndrome.

Marfan syndrome is an inherited familial condition of connective tissue and is much rarer than Down syndrome (1 in 5000 of the global population; Goldman, 1995; Camm, 2002). It is associated with the Marfan syndrome gene (*FBN1*) and primarily involves the eye, skeleton and the CVS. People affected tend to be taller than normal for their population and have a notable increase in the length of their extremities (arms and fingers). They can also have pectus carinatum/excavatum (respectively, pigeon/sunken chest due to involvement of the sternum, accompanied by protrusion of the sternum and ribs), a dolichocephalic (long) skull, a high arched palate, scoliosis, angular deformities of the joints (the joint ligaments are 'loose') and eye abnormalities (Goldman, 1995). As there is a high CVD risk, people tend to die young in their twenties (see Hugar et al., 2014). All adults with Marfan syndrome have an abnormal CVS (Stuart & Williams, 2007: table 2). Cardiovascular involvement includes necrosis of the aorta or pulmonary artery, aortic and mitral valve insufficiency, and aortic aneurysm. As with Down syndrome, there is sparse archaeological evidence. However, of particular interest is a report of Marfan syndrome and aortic dissection in a nineteenth-century mummy from the Capuchin Catacombs of Palermo in Sicily (Panzer et al., 2018). Aortic dissection can be defined as an injury to the inner layer of the aorta, whereby blood flows between the layers of the aortic wall and forces them apart. Similarly to Down syndrome, the infrequency with which Marfan syndrome is identified in the archaeological record perhaps reflects the large number of potential bone changes that can occur in this syndrome, many of which may appear in other conditions. However, Panzer et al.'s study of the Sicilian mummy further corroborates a direct association between the syndrome and heart disease.

2.2.2.2 Acquired Conditions
Metabolic Syndrome
Today, an individual with metabolic syndrome has a strong risk for developing type 2 diabetes and atherosclerosis (Grundy, 2016). The syndrome comprises raised blood pressure and blood sugar, excess body fat and high levels of low-density lipoprotein (LDL, the so-called 'bad' cholesterol) and low levels of high-density lipoprotein (HDL, the 'good' cholesterol); lipoproteins consist of protein and fat and transport choles-terol in the blood. The body of a person with metabolic syndrome develops a prothrombotic and a proinflammatory state (Vykoukal & Davies, 2011). The former is an abnormality of blood clotting that increases the risk of blood clots in blood vessels, while the latter is where a person is exposed to a risk factor that is capable of promoting inflammation in the body (e.g. air pollution). As a consequence of excess body fat and inflammation, metabolic syndrome and osteoarthritis tend to occur together (Rahman et al., 2013; Wang et al., 2016), and there is increasing evidence for gout to also occur (Roddy & Choi, 2014), with Swinson et al. (2010) suggesting that gout may be a useful marker of metabolic syndrome in the archaeological record. What might we deduce from this brief summary of metabolic syndrome and its relevance for the skeletal record?

Diabetes Mellitus
Firstly, we may wish to look for evidence of diabetes mellitus, a disease due to deficient production of insulin in the pancreas or to a resistance to insulin, insulin being the hormone that controls blood sugar levels (Gale & Anderson, 2002). According to the WHO, globally there are 422 million people who have diabetes, a steady rise having been seen over the past few decades. Diabetes increases mortality risk by 30–50 per cent and those affected can develop atherosclerosis, with strokes and coronary artery disease much more likely to occur than in a non-diabetic person (Johansson et al., 2018). In a study of autopsy reports from South Australia between 2005 and 2009, CVD was the leading overall cause of death across all ages, except in those under the age of 30, with metabolic complications more common in the latter group (Zhou & Byard, 2017). In addition, people with diabetes may develop gangrene in their feet due to disease of the peripheral arteries. This can lead to a narrowing of blood vessels, reducing blood flow to the legs and feet and subsequently leading to ulcers and

gangrene that may result in the need for amputation. Half of people today who undergo lower limb amputations have diabetes (Zhou & Byard, 2017), and people with diabetes are 20 times more likely to experience this operation on the toes, feet or lower leg (World Health Organization, 2020). People with diabetes are also more prone to developing infections, including tuberculosis (McNicol & Foulis, 2008). In terms of the skeleton, diabetes causes reduced bone formation and increased bone destruction, with the result that fracture healing is impaired (Jiao et al., 2015). Thus fragile bones are more susceptible to fractures but they heal poorly. A prolonged inflammatory response in diabetes may also lead to osteoporosis and osteoarthritis, and DISH has been clinically linked to diabetes (Resnick & Niwayama, 1995b). Reported evidence of diabetes in the palaeopathological literature is limited to one publication (Dupras et al., 2010), once again most probably because of the non-specific nature of the suite of bone changes linked to diabetes. A male skeleton dated to 2050–1911 BCE from Dayr al-Barsha, Egypt, displays potential evidence for bilateral amputation of the toes through the metatarsophalangeal joints, DISH, severe dental disease (which can be related to heart disease; see Choudhury et al., 2016), a reduction in cortical bone thickness in the foot bones (with low bone density seen as a risk for CVD; see Farhat & Cauley, 2008), and signs of degeneration of one of the elbow joints. Dupras et al. (2010) also note that the 1500-year-old Egyptian Ebers Papyrus describes polyuria (increased frequency of urination, with the passing of excessive or abnormally large amounts of urine), which is a common symptom of diabetes. Further, Binder and Roberts (2014) report evidence of bilateral medial calcification of the femoral arteries associated with a skeleton from Amara West, Sudan, a calcification particularly associated with diabetes today (see Edmonds, 2019).

Joint Disease

Along with dental disease and trauma, joint disease is one of the most common pathological conditions visible in the skeletal record both globally and temporally (Roberts & Manchester, 2005: 133), and has been noted to co-occur with CVD (Rahman et al., 2013; Wang et al., 2016; see also Chapter 6). Moreover, currently 'Degenerative joint disease is the most common articular affliction' (Resnick & Niwayama, 1995c: 1263). One joint disease with a clear co-occurrence with CVD is osteoarthritis (OA), a disease of the synovial joints and noted as the 'most common joint disease today' (Waldron, 2019: 719). It is not only linked to metabolic syndrome but can also lead to high blood pressure, heart disease, stroke, diabetes and obesity, with the latter defined by a body mass index (BMI) of over 30 (where BMI represents an adult's weight in kilograms divided by their height in metres squared). Osteoarthritis tends to affect the hip and knee joints most, which is very much related to obesity causing pressure through the weight-bearing joints (Elia, 2002; Reyes et al., 2016). Essentially, reduced exercise and general mobility due to (painful) OA can underlie CVD, as can chronic inflammation, muscle weakness, and the use of non-steroidal anti-inflammatory drugs today (Rahman et al., 2013). Further, in their study of over 32 million patients, Hall et al. (2016) identified that 38.4 per cent had OA and CVD. Could the presence of OA, as seen in the classic (late-stage) changes on and round synovial joints (e.g. a combination of porosity, osteophytes, eburnation and/or sclerosis), and indeed body weight, be used to infer heart disease? It is certainly the case that variation in OA frequencies in different joints may be variously explained by age, stature, body mass and habitual use. However, in their study of these relationships in documented Portuguese skeletal collections, Calce et al. (2018) found that age was the strongest predictor for OA in the joints of the knee and pelvic and lumbosacral regions. Perhaps these associations simply reflect that if people in the past lived to old age, they would have been more likely to have CVDs.

Diffuse Idiopathic Skeletal Hyperostosis

A systemic non-inflammatory condition, DISH, causes soft tissue and bone changes in the spine and extra-spinal regions of the skeleton. The spine calcifies and ossifies along the anterolateral aspects of at least four adjacent vertebral bodies (Resnick & Niwayama, 1995b). In the thoracic region, this change is usually along the right side due to pulsation of the aorta down the left side preventing ossification. It is also characterised by entheseal new bone formation on post-cranial bones, such as the shoulder, elbow and knee joints, and on the calcaneus (symmetrically and bilaterally), with new bone 'bridging' also occurring in some at the sacroiliac joints. It has been suggested that DISH 'may represent not a disease per se but rather a vulnerable state in which extensive ossification results from an exaggerated response of the body in some patients to stimuli that produce only modest new bone formation in others' (Resnick & Niwayama, 1995b: 1439). Common in older men, DISH has been found to be associated with metabolic syndrome which, as discussed above, puts people at a higher risk for developing CVDs (Grundy, 2016). Therefore, can we use the evidence of DISH in a skeleton as a potential indicator of metabolic syndrome-related CVD? It would certainly be interesting to see if there is any evidence of CVD in archaeological mummified remains with associated DISH as a first step. Of interest here, DISH in skeletal remains has been associated with calcified blood vessels in an older first-century CE male skeleton from Roman Droitwich, Worcestershire, England (see Manchester, 1980). In addition, DISH is commonly found in skeletal remains, particularly from medieval Europe, including from cemeteries linked to monastic institutions. It has also been linked to the monastic diet and way of life (Rogers & Waldron, 2001), although there is earlier evidence (Faccia et al., 2006) and evidence in non-monastic contexts. There are further reports in people of higher social status (Jankauskas, 2003) but the skeletons of lower-status people also show evidence of DISH. Mader et al. (2009) also recorded that patients with DISH are significantly more likely to develop metabolic syndrome than those without DISH and have a significantly higher CVD risk. A condition that can become confused with DISH during diagnosis in palaeopathology is ankylosing spondylitis. The latter is a chronic inflammatory condition that affects young adults, primarily in their spines (Shipley et al., 2002), and is also called a seronegative spondyloarthropathy. Men are more than twice as likely to have the disease, and the human leukocyte antigen (HLA) B27 is often present in the blood (Shipley et al., 2002). Genetic and/or environmental factors are believed to be part of its aetiology (Resnick & Niwayama, 1995d; Brown et al., 2016). For example, by 2016 more than 40 genetic variants had been identified as influencing the risk of a person having ankylosing spondylitis (Brown et al., 2016). The bone changes start in the sacroiliac joints (a hallmark that is bilateral and asymmetrical in occurrence) and move up the spine. Enthesitis affects the tendon and ligament attachments to the bones, and the synovial and cartilaginous peripheral joints may be involved (Resnick & Niwayama, 1995d). There is also ossification and calcification of the spinal ligaments, which can lead to fusion of the vertebrae. Uveitis (inflammation, blurred vision and pain in the middle layer of the eyeball) can also occur (Shipley et al., 2002). In terms of its association with CVD, there may be cardiac enlargement, pericarditis, inflammation of the aorta and aortic valve, and aortic aneurysm (aortic insufficiency). Thus, we should think of potential heart disease affecting people in the past who have the skeletal pathological changes of either ankylosing spondylitis or DISH.

Gout

Gout (raised uric acid levels) may also be an indicator of a person having CVD in the past. Gout is a systemic disease that affects men more than women, and today it tends to be more frequent in developed countries and is rising in frequency (Shipley et al., 2002). Ancestral origin and a hereditary predisposition play their part in its occurrence (Buckley, 2011: 107; 'modern Pacific Island populations have the highest frequencies in the world'). It is linked to excess production of uric acid and may be due to eating cooked or processed foods that are rich in the chemical compounds called purines. It can also be caused by reduced excretion of uric acid. Alcohol is further linked to gout, especially the consumption of beer (Ragab et al., 2017). While there are relatively few reports of gout in archaeological human remains (see table 2 in Buckley, 2011; also Fornaciari et al., 2019, and an Egyptian Christian mummy described in Elliot-Smith & Dawson, 1924), the bone changes are caused by the deposition of uric acid in the form of urate crystals within and around a joint, which cause erosive lesions (Resnick & Niwayama, 1995e). The first metatarsophalangeal joint is affected in the majority of people. Gout is related to diabetes and high blood pressure, and of course is part of the metabolic syndrome (Swinson et al., 2010). In their study, Huang et al. (2020) also support the theory that it is linked with an increased risk for CVD.

Vitamin D Deficiency

The metabolic disease caused by vitamin D deficiency has also been specifically connected with CVDs. Although not part of the metabolic syndrome, it needs mention here, especially since more evidence of vitamin D deficiency is recognised in the bioarchaeological record due to recent developments in its diagnosis (see summary in Brickley & Mays, 2019). Vitamin D deficiency is currently considered a global pandemic, and has been associated with many illnesses including coronary artery diseases, stroke and infectious diseases (Wang, 2016; Holick, 2017; Kheiri et al., 2018) and their associated risk factors. Synergisms with infections have also been noted in the bioarchaeological record (see Roberts & Brickley, 2019). The human body synthesises this vitamin in the skin as a response to exposure to ultraviolet light. Most of the vitamin is acquired in this way, with a relatively small proportion coming from the diet (e.g. oily fish). Of particular interest in relation to CVDs is that low levels of vitamin D are associated with obesity (Walsh et al., 2017). This is because the vitamin is fat soluble and can be found in fat, muscle, the liver and the serum of the blood. When a person is obese all these parts of the body experience an increase in volume, which leads to lower levels of the vitamin due to its dilution across these larger volumes. Of course, if the body lacks vitamin D, calcium and phosphorus are not absorbed and therefore the bones are not mineralised and can subsequently suffer deformation in children (rickets) and adults (osteomalacia), with characteristic signs (Pitt, 1995; Brickley & Mays, 2019). Perhaps vitamin D deficiency is another route to exploring CVD in the past, and it should be noted that chronic kidney disease is also associated with vitamin D deficiency (Jean et al., 2017; see also section Autoimmune, Endocrine, Idiopathic and Renal Diseases) and hyperparathyroidism, due to problems maintaining normal levels of calcium, phosphate and vitamin D in the body (Mays et al., 2007).

Dental Disease

Poor oral health, commonly identified in skeletons from archaeological sites, can predispose to CVD in later life (Sanz et al., 2020; see also Chapter 6), and a link between dental disease and congenital heart disease has also been identified (Pourmoghaddas et al., 2018). The dental diseases identified as risks for CVD include caries, plaque (or calcified plaque, i.e. calculus) and periodontitis (Carrizales-Sepúlveda et al., 2018; Kim et al., 2019). Pathogens from these conditions can enter the bloodstream and cause cardiovascular problems. Pathogens originating from the periodontal tissues may lead to endothelial injury due to an inflammatory response. They also play a role in the development and progression of atherosclerosis and may even be present in the atherosclerotic plaques that develop (Haraszthy et al., 2000; Dhadse et al., 2010). Therefore, it is possible that calcified arteries found with skeletons or preserved bodies may encapsulate the DNA of pathogens responsible for oral diseases. Indeed, two Egyptian mummies (Tamut and Padiamenet) dated to several hundred years BCE were reported to have atherosclerosis and poor dental health (Taylor & Antoine, 2014; see also Chapter 6), as was Ötzi, the Neolithic Iceman (Seiler et al., 2013). Of course, establishing a direct link from dental disease to CVD is challenging.

Patients with CVDs further show an increased frequency of dental pulp calcification/stones compared with patients without CVD (Khojastepour et al., 2013), pulp stones being described as 'discrete islands of calcified masses that may be found in dental pulp tissue' (Tomczyk et al., 2017: 563). They are identified on radiographs as radiopaque structures that may fill the whole pulp cavity. The cause of pulp stones is still debated, although associations with dental disease (e.g. caries) and heavy attrition, and an increase with age, have been noted. In a study of radiographs from 55 dental patients in an age group not expected to have pulp stones, Edds et al. (2005) also concluded that the presence or absence of pulp stones may possibly be used to detect people with underlying CVD. In their study, there was a relationship between pre-existing CVD and pulp stones; 74 per cent ($n = 14/19$) of patients with CVD had pulp stones, although 39 per cent ($n = 14/36$) of those with pulp stones had no history of CVD. This raises the question of why some people with no history of CVD have pulp stones.

In recent years, archaeological evidence for pulp stones has been identified on radiographs of the teeth of skeletons dated to as early as 5900 ± 100 BCE (Tomczyk et al., 2014, 2017, 2020; Cooper, 2016; see Figure 2.7). Tomczyk et al. (2017) studied dental radiographs of eighteenth- to nineteenth-century skeletons from Poland and found that 94 of 121 individuals (and 273 of 780 molars) had evidence of pulp stones. Tomczyk et al. (2014) also found a high prevalence rate in individuals from Syria, dating from the early Bronze Age (2650–2350 BCE) through to the modern Islamic period (1850–1950 CE), with 99 of 117 individuals having pulp stones affecting 271 of 529 teeth. Dental wear and a high calcium diet were said to be associated with pulp stones in this study.

As mentioned at the start of this section, dental calculus is included in a suite of dental conditions that are risks for CVDs. Calculus is commonly seen on the teeth of skeletons and has often been the focus of research in bioarchaeology, particularly in recent years as scholars have realised its potential for studying inclusions preserved within this calcified plaque, including oral and respiratory pathogens (Blatt et al., 2011; Preus et al., 2011; Weyrich et al., 2015; Hardy et al., 2016; Fiorin et al., 2018; Huynh et al., 2018). The human oral cavity harbours microorganisms that live in or on the human body. They can be symbiotic (have a mutually beneficial relationship with each other) or pathogenic. Symbiotic relationships particularly include

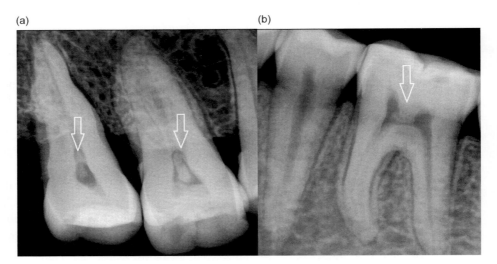

Figure 2.7 Pulp stones in eighteenth- to nineteenth-century individuals from Radom, Poland. (a) Upper posterior teeth (male, 30–35 years); (b) Lower posterior teeth (male, 20–21 years).
Source: Jacek Tomczyk, Institute of Biological Sciences, Cardinal Stefan Wyszynski Unversity, Poland.

commensalism, where one organism derives benefits from another without harming or helping it. Commensal bacteria are part of the normal flora in the mouth. There are also pathogenic microorganisms in the oral cavity that cause disease, including those that cause caries and periodontitis, but also some systemic diseases such as CVD and stroke (Dewhirst et al., 2010). The oral cavity harbours the second most abundant microbiota, with the gastrointestinal tract topping the table (Verma et al., 2018).

This is why dental calculus has become a focus for ancient research, with Warinner and colleagues leading the way forward in 2014. In this 'first detailed analysis to our knowledge of ancient oral microbiome ecology and function at the genus and species levels', the focus was on teeth from four medieval human skeletons with periodontal disease from Germany (c. 950–1200 CE), alongside modern dental calculus. A genome of a periodontal pathogen was reconstructed, with most of the sources of the sequenced DNA being bacterial, with contributions on a lesser scale from human DNA, and that of viruses, fungi, and DNA of dietary origin. Periodontal pathogen DNA and proteins (peptides) were identified, as were pathogens related to blood infection and infective endocarditis. Indeed, bacteria related to CVD (atherosclerosis) are specifically mentioned. The ancient human proteins in the calculus showed evidence of 'inflammation, innate immunity and host defense' (Warinner et al., 2014: 340). Of interest is that total DNA recovery in both modern and ancient calculus was comparable, thus confirming the remarkable potential for further analyses of this material.

Research on dental calculus from the teeth of seventeenth-century soldiers (Gerrard et al., 2018: 69–72, 98–99) found that it contained a range of microscopic inclusions such as the remains of foods these men had eaten. Macroscopic evidence of dental disease was also found (caries, abscesses and periodontal disease). Biomolecules such as DNA and proteins (peptides) associated with disease were further identified and some bacteria related to periodontal disease were found, thus correlating with macroscopic evidence of periodontal disease. Notably, the DNA of the organisms *Cardiobacterium hominis* and *Cardiobacterium valvarum* was identified in the dental calculus of three skeletons. Today, these are implicated in endocarditis (Millard et al., 2020), a serious disease that has a 100% mortality without treatment (Camm, 2002).

As can be seen, evidence of dental disease can realistically be used to infer CVD in the past, especially through research on dental calculus.

Inflammation of the Respiratory Tract

It is also relevant to mention the potential interpretation of lesions on the ribs (Eyler et al., 1994) and sinus walls (Tovi et al., 1992), accepted in bioarchaeology to reflect lower and upper respiratory tract inflammation, respectively (Lambert, 2002; Krenz-Niedbała & Łukasik, 2016; Davies-Barrett et al. 2019, 2021). Inhalation of poor-quality air, for example when air pollution is present, can lead to irritation of the mucous membranes of the respiratory tract and an inflammatory response on the bone surfaces (bone formation/destruction). Exposure to biomass and other sources of smoke-related air pollution have been linked to endothelial inflammation/atherosclerosis (Caravedo et al., 2016; Bourdrel et al., 2017; Rajagopalan et al., 2018). Like people today exposed to biomass smoke in their homes, their workplaces and their general environments, our ancestors were also subject to problems with air quality. This is of course not only a problem in developing countries, as developed Western societies are also exposed to air pollution (World Health Organization, 2021b). Thus, the identification of rib or sinus lesions in skeletal remains, or polluting particles in the respiratory tract of mummified remains, may be, indirectly, considered possible markers of high-risk factors for CVD. There is already some evidence for this in the archaeological record.

For example, Zink et al. (2014) not only identified atherosclerosis in the body of Ötzi the Neolithic Iceman, but dark staining on his lungs suggests exposure to smoke, perhaps from an open fire. Binder and Roberts (2014) also found evidence for lung inflammation (rib lesions) in five skeletons from Amara West, Sudan, along with calcified structures suggested to be evidence for atherosclerosis. These individuals also had periodontal disease. Together, this evidence suggests that exposure to burning biomass fuel in homes or workplaces may have been linked to lung inflammation and subsequent atherosclerosis, but periodontal disease pathogens may also have contributed to CVD in this population (see Chapter 6). Some of the seventeenth-century skeletons of soldiers described above also had different lines of evidence that suggested the possibility that they may have had CVD, in spite of no direct evidence being present (Millard et al., 2020). For example, an adolescent had maxillary sinusitis, and microscopic evidence of micro-charcoal and soot in his calculus. Through protein analysis of his calculus, the presence of peptides of *Streptococcus pneumoniae* and *Bordetella bronchialis*, which are linked to bacterial respiratory infections, were also found. Another person revealed evidence for sinusitis, pipe smoking, periodontal disease and the peptide of the periodontal pathogen *Porphyromonas gingivalis* in his dental calculus. Finally, a third person who had sinusitis was a pipe smoker, and had micro-charcoal and soot in his calculus.

Clearly, it is important to consider that evidence of respiratory inflammation in the past may be the result of poor air quality being experienced by the population of interest. The additional information from biomolecular analysis (e.g. peptides as indicators of respiratory infections, or DNA markers for a genetic predisposition to increased risk for coronary artery disease), in combination with macroscopic markers on or with the skeleton, or in mummified tissues, can strengthen arguments for CVD affecting people in the past. It may also help identify the main drivers of CVD in the past.

Autoimmune, Endocrine, Idiopathic and Renal Diseases
Even though exploring the possible indirect evidence for CVDs in archaeological human remains may be viewed as "clutching at straws", other potential pathological conditions that might be considered include rheumatoid arthritis (RA), acromegaly, idiopathic Paget's disease and renal disease.

RA is an autoimmune disease that affects the bone and soft tissues of the synovial joints of the appendicular skeleton in a symmetrical manner, particularly the peripheral joints (Resnick & Niwayama, 1995f; Shipley et al., 2002). The cervical spine may also be affected. It has a genetic and environmental aetiology and, as a chronic inflammatory joint disease, it primarily damages the cartilage and bone of the metacarpophalangeal and proximal interphalangeal joints, and the bones of the wrist, shoulder and knees (Reid, 2008). The joints are affected by erosions of the bone centrally and marginally, and osteoporosis may be associated. The soft tissues associated with the joints are also involved (e.g. tendons, ligaments), as well as the lungs, blood vessels and heart. In around 30–40 per cent of 'strongly seropositive' people with RA, pericarditis can occur (Shipley et al., 2002: 542), and in some rare cases endocarditis and myocardial disease have also been noted. The nervous system, eyes and the spleen, lymph nodes and blood may further be involved. Despite the link between RA and CVD, there is not much evidence for RA in the bioarchaeological record (see Waldron et al., 1994; Mckinnon et al., 2013), probably due to difficulties in differentiating the disease from other joint diseases, especially if a skeleton is poorly preserved.

The endocrine disease acromegaly is a disorder of the pituitary gland, and is usually due to a tumour (adenoma) that causes overproduction of growth hormone by the gland (McNicol & Foulis, 2008). Overgrowth of the soft tissues and bones leads to enlarged hands and feet and if the overproduction of hormone occurs before the epiphyses are closed, the person can become abnormally tall (see Resnick, 1995 for details of bone changes; Lewis, 2019 for some albeit rare bioarchaeological evidence). It can be associated with an enlarged heart and high blood pressure, and heart failure.

Likewise, CVD can be a complication of Paget's disease, a condition where disordered remodelling of bone leads to high bone turnover, characterised particularly by bone destruction. However, as a rare complication, the heart muscle can undergo hypertrophy (enlargement) due to the need for a high cardiac output related to increased blood flow through affected bones, and cardiac failure may ensue (Shipley et al., 2002; Reid, 2008). In recent years, it has been established that people with the disease (usually men aged over 40 years; Resnick & Niwayama, 1995g) may have mutations in specific genes, thus indicating a genetic predisposition (Gennari et al., 2019). Risk factors in people's environments also play a part in its occurrence, including the viral respiratory infections caused by paramyxoviruses. The remodelled bone tends to be less strong and may fracture or become deformed. The skull, pelvis, thoracic and lumbar spine, sacrum and tibia are the most commonly affected bones (Shipley et al., 2002; see also Grauer & Roberts, 2019). Osteoarthritis is also common (Reid, 2008), and osteosarcoma may be another complication. However, Paget's disease tends to be an uncommon condition diagnosed in bioarchaeology (see some examples in Wells & Woodhouse, 1975; Aaron et al., 1992; Boylston & Ogden, 2005; Rossetti et al., 2018; Grauer & Roberts, 2019).

Finally, while heart disease can lead to kidney disease (the kidneys filter the blood), the latter can also cause heart disease (Haynes et al., 2020; Tuegel & Bansal, 2017), and they share two key causes: high blood pressure and diabetes. If the heart is failing, it becomes congested with blood, as does the main vein to the kidneys and the kidneys themselves, with the kidneys receiving insufficient oxygenated blood. If the kidneys are damaged, the body (hormones) tries to increase blood supply to them and the heart has to work even harder against higher pressure in the blood vessels, and eventually is damaged itself. This is a classic example of comorbidity. Furthermore, there is clear evidence that coronary artery calcification is related to the risks of CVD, myocardial infarction and heart failure in people who have chronic kidney disease (Chen et al., 2017). Therefore, it is relevant to think about evidence of kidney disease in archaeological human remains in two ways: therefore, we might look for evidence of kidney stones and calcified arteries associated with both skeletons and preserved bodies. Although kidney stones are not commonly reported in the archaeological record, they can cause kidney failure (see examples of kidney stones modern and ancient in Steinbock, 1985, 1989; Jaskowiec et al., 2017; Aufderheide, 2000: 470–3 and table 8.2 for evidence in mummies and with skeletons reaching back to 3100 BCE).

Some of the conditions surveyed in this section that can be related to CVD are clearly rare in both the archaeological and current records. Therefore, there may be limitations in our ability to explore how frequent CVD was in the past. However, while they are worth considering, it is perhaps the more common acquired pathological conditions within the metabolic syndrome, and also dental disease and inflammatory conditions such as those detected in the respiratory tract that may be more helpful.

2.3   Conclusions

As Swynghedauw (2016: 138) says, 'Evolutionary medicine and evolutionary cardiology take the view that illness is linked to incompatibilities between the environment in which humans currently live and their genome which has been shaped by successive environmental conditions during biological evolution'. This, of course, is the case for CVD and our bodies continue to adapt to changes in our environment that create risks for CVDs, as for many other diseases. In fact, Danziger (2016: 156) maintains that 'the selective forces that have acted on the cardiovascular system are now being replaced by new forces to which the cardiovascular system is not adapted'. It is clear that the evidence for CVDs goes back several thousands of years. This includes insights gained from archaeological human remains, but also historical documents. Today, CVD can be found across the world and significantly increased as a major health problem in the second epidemiological transition as NCDs emerged onto the scene.

Our ancestors did not live as long as we do today, but clearly experienced the impact of CVDs on their lives. However, our evidence in the archaeological record is likely to be a gross underestimate of frequency rates. This is the result of the archaeological evidence always being a fragmentary record for the history of our health. The particular challenges archaeologists have in finding the evidence for CVDs include a lack of ability to identify and/or recover the evidence, poor awareness and/or training of bioarchaeologists, taphonomic challenges, and the fact that most human remains are skeletonised. However, we do know that potential risks existed within people's environments, including an unhealthy diet, tobacco/alcohol use and low physical activity, especially in higher status people, so one would expect the evidence for CVD to be present. Additionally, CVD-related susceptibility genes may have been an added risk factor, an area of archaeological investigation that is increasing today as methods improve, and one that has potential for understanding past CVDs via ancient DNA analysis.

Evidence for CVDs in archaeological human remains will never be as common as, for example, joint or dental diseases, but by thinking outside the box we can begin to provide suggestions as to how we might, via direct and indirect evidence, achieve a better understanding of the impact of CVDs on our ancestors' lives. A long-term evolutionary perspective is also important and potentially contributes to our understanding of the drivers of CVDs today. This chapter thus closes with some recommendations for future work in identifying CVDs in the archaeological record. These include (1) generally improving knowledge of CVDs in bioarchaeology and what might be important to search for; (2) recognising that preserved bodies are not the only human remains that might show either direct or indirect evidence of CVDs; (3) using better recovery and processing techniques to identify and recover the evidence from excavations, including calcified blood vessels associated with skeletal remains; (4) using the appropriate analytical methods to identify the evidence (e.g. microscopy, imaging and DNA analysis); and (5) increasing the use of biomolecular techniques to detect susceptibility and resistance genes.

References

Aaron, J. E., Rogers, J. and Kanis, J. A. (1992). Paleohistology of Paget's disease in two medieval skeletons. *American Journal of Physical Anthropology*, 89, 325–31.

Alcalde del Río, H., Breuil, H. and Sierra, L. (1911). *Les cavernes de la Région cantabrique. (The Caves in the Cantabric Region)*. Monaco, France: Impr. Vve. A. Chéne Monaco.

Arfè, A., Scotti, L., Varas-Lorenzo, C., et al. (2016). Non-steroidal anti-inflammatory drugs and risk of heart failure in four European countries: nested case-control study. *British Medical Journal*, 354, i4857.

Assis, S., Santos, A. L. and Roberts, C. A. (2011). Evidence of hypertrophic osteoarthropathy in individuals from the Coimbra Skeletal Identified Collection (Portugal). *International Journal of Paleopathology*, 1, 155–63.

Aufderheide, A. C. (2000). *The Scientific Study of Mummies*. Cambridge, UK: Cambridge University Press.

Barrett, R. and Armelagos, G. J. (2013). *An Unnatural History of Emerging Infections*. Oxford: Oxford University Press.

Bekkering, S., Miller, J. E. and Burgner, D. P. (2019). Childhood infection may mediate the relationship between suboptimal intrauterine growth, preterm birth, and adult cardiovascular disease. *European Heart Journal*, 40, 3273–4.

Bianucco, R., Loynes, R. D., Sutherland, M. L., et al. (2016). Forensic analysis reveals acute decompensation of chronic heart failure in a 3500-year-old Egyptian. *Journal of Forensic Sciences*, 61, 1378–81.

Biehler-Gomez, L., Cappella, A., Castoldi, E., Matrille, L. and Cattaneo, C. (2017). Survival of atherosclerotic calcifications in skeletonized material: forensic and pathological implications. *Journal of Forensic Sciences*, 63, 386–94.

Biehler-Gomez, L., Maderma, E., Brescia, G., et al. (2018). Distinguishing atherosclerotic calcifications in dry bone: implications for forensic identification. *Journal of Forensic Sciences*, 64, 839–44.

Binder, A. and Roberts, C. A. (2014). Calcified structures associated with human skeletal remains: possible atherosclerosis affecting the population buried at Amara West, Sudan (1300–800 BC). *International Journal of Paleopathology*, 6, 20–9.

Binder, M. and Saad, M. (2017). Hypertrophic osteoarthropathy in a young adult male from Berber, Sudan (2nd–3rd century CE). *International Journal of Paleopathology*, 18, 52–62.

Blatt, S. H., Cassman, V. and Sciulli, P. W. (2011). Dirty teeth and ancient trade. Evidence of cotton fibres in human dental calculus from Late Woodland, Ohio. *International Journal of Osteoarchaeology*, 21, 669–78.

Bouchareychas, L. and Raffai, R. L. (2018). Apolipoprotein E and atherosclerosis: from lipoprotein metabolism to microRNA control of inflammation. *Journal of Cardiovascular Development and Disease*, 5(2), 30. doi: 10.3390/jcdd5020030

Bourdrel, T., Bind, M.-A., Béjot, Y., Morel, O. and Argacha, J.-F. (2017). Cardiovascular effects of air pollution. *Archives of Cardiovascular Diseases*, 110, 634–42.

Boyce, N. (2020). Bills of mortality. Tracking disease in early modern London. *Lancet*, 395, 1186–7.

Boylston, A. and Ogden, A. (2005). A study of Paget's disease at Norton Priory, Cheshire. A medieval religious house. In S. R. Zakrzewski and M. Clegg, eds., *Proceedings of the Fifth Annual Conference of the British Association for Biological Anthropology and Osteoarchaeology*. British Archaeological Reports International Series 1383, pp. 69–76.

Brend, W. A. (1908). *Bills of Mortality*. London: Baillière, Tindall and Co.

Brickley, M. B. and Mays, S. (2019). Metabolic disease. In J.E. Buikstra, ed., *Ortner's Identification of Pathological Conditions in Human Skeletal Remains*, 3rd ed. London: Academic Press, pp. 531–66.

Brothwell, D. R. (1960). A possible case of mongolism in a Saxon population. *Annals of Human Genetics*, 24, 141–50.

Brothwell, D. and Browne, S. (2002). Skeletal atrophy and the problem of the differential diagnosis of conditions causing paralysis. *Antropologia Portuguesa*, 19, 5–17.

Brown, M. A., Kenn, T. and Wordsworth, B. P. (2016). Genetics of ankylosing spondylitis: Insights into pathogenesis. *Nature Reviews Rheumatology*, 12, 81–91.

Buckley, H. (2011). Epidemiology of gout: perspectives from the past. *Current Rheumatology Reviews*, 7, 106–13.

Byard, R. W. (2017). Syphilis: Cardiovascular manifestations of the great imitator. *Journal of Forensic Sciences*, 63, 1312–15.

Calce, S. E., Kurki, H. K., Weston, D. A. and Gould, L. (2018). The relationship of age, activity, and body size on osteoarthritis in weightbearing skeletal regions. *International Journal of Osteoarchaeology*, 22, 45–53.

Camm, A. J. (2002). Cardiovascular disease. In P. Kumar and M. Clark, eds., *Kumar and Clark Clinical Medicine*, 5th ed. Edinburgh: W.B. Saunders, pp. 701–832.

Caravedo, M. A., Herrera, P. M., Mongilardi, N., et al. (2016). Chronic exposure to biomass fuel smoke and markers of endothelial inflammation. *Indoor Air*, 26, 768–75.

Carrizales-Sepúlveda, E. F., Ordaz-Farías, A., Vera-Pineda, R. and Flores-Ramirez, R. (2018). Periodontal disease, systemic inflammation and the risk of cardiovascular disease. *Heart, Lung and Circulation*, 27, 1327–34.

Castro, M. M., Benavente, M. A., Ortega, J., et al. (2016). Thoracic aortic aneurysm in a pre-Columbian (210BC) inhabitant of Northern Chile: implications for the origins of syphilis. *International Journal of Paleopathology*, 13, 20–6.

Chen, J., Budoff, M. L., Reilly, M. P., et al. (2017). Coronary artery calcification is independently and significantly related to the risks of cardiovascular disease, myocardial infarction, and heart failure in patients with CKD. *Journal of the American Medical Association Cardiology*, 2, 635–43.

Choudhury, A. R., Choudhury, K. N. and Islam, S. M. S. (2016). Relationship of dental diseases with coronary artery diseases and diabetes in Bangladesh. *Cardiovascular Diagnosis and Therapy*, 6, 131–7.

Clark, A. L. and Cleland, J. G. (2013). Causes and treatment of oedema in patients with heart failure. *Nature Reviews Cardiology*, 10, 156–70.

Clarke, C. R. A. (2002). Neurological disease. In P. Kumar and M. Clark, eds., *Kumar and Clark Clinical Medicine*, 5th ed. Edinburgh: W.B. Saunders, pp. 1123–224.

Cooper, N. (2016). *Putting your heart into it: a study into the prevalence rates of pulp stones in two British archaeological populations, and their possible relevance to cardiovascular disease.* Unpublished MSc Palaeopathology dissertation, Durham University.

Czermak, J. (1852). Beschreibung und mikroskopische Untersuchung zweier agyptischer Mumien [Description and microscopic studies of two Egyptian mummies]. *Sonderberichte Akademie Wissenschaft Wien,* 9, 427–69.

Danziger, R. S. (2016). Evolutionary imprints on cardiovascular physiology and pathophysiology. In A. Alvergne, C. Jenkinson and C. Faurie, eds., *Evolutionary Thinking in Medicine: From Research to Policy and Practice.* Cham, Switzerland: Springer International Publishing, pp. 155–63.

Davies-Barrett, A., Antoine, D. and Roberts, C. A. (2019). Inflammatory periosteal reaction on ribs associated with lower respiratory disease. A method for recording prevalence from sites with differing preservation. *American Journal of Physical Anthropology,* 168, 530–42.

Davies-Barrett, A., Antoine, D. and Roberts, C. A. (2021). Time to be nosy: Evaluating the impact of environmental and sociocultural changes on maxillary sinusitis in the Middle Nile Valley (Neolithic to Medieval periods). *International Journal of Paleopathology,* 34, 182–96.

Dewhirst, F. E., Chen, T., Izard, J., et al. (2010). The human oral microbiome. *Journal of Bacteriology,* 192, 5002–17.

Dhadse, P., Gattani, D. and Mishra, D. (2010). The link between periodontal disease and cardiovascular disease: How far we have come in last two decades? *Journal of the Indian Society for Periodontology,* 14, 148–54.

Duffin, J. (2021). *History of Medicine. A Scandalously Short Indication.* Toronto: University of Toronto Press.

Dupras, T. L., Williams, J., Willems, H. and Peeters, C. (2010). Pathological skeletal remains from Ancient Egypt: The earliest case of diabetes mellitus? *Practical Diabetes International,* 27, 358–63.

Edds, A. C., Walden, J. C., Scheetz, J. P., et al. (2005). Pilot study of correlation of pulp stones with cardiovascular disease. *Journal of Endodontics,* 31, 504–6.

Edmonds, M. (2019). Vascular disease in the lower limb in type 1 diabetes. *Cardiovascular Endocrinology and Metabolism,* 8, 39–46.

Elia, M. (2002). Nutrition. In P. Kumar and M. Clark, eds., *Kumar and Clark Clinical Medicine,* 5th ed. Edinburgh: W.B. Saunders, pp. 221–51.

Elliot-Smith, G. and Dawson, W. R. (1924). *Egyptian Mummies.* New York: Dial Press.

Ewald, P. W. (2008). An evolutionary perspective on the causes of chronic diseases. Atherosclerosis as an illustration. In W. R. Trevathan, E. O. Smith and J. J. McKenna, eds., *Evolutionary Medicine and Health: New Perspectives.* Oxford: Oxford University Press, pp. 350–67.

Eyler, W. R., Monsein, L. H., Beute, G. H., et al. (1996). Rib enlargement in patients with chronic pleural disease. *American Journal of Radiology,* 167, 921–6.

Faccia, K., Waters-Rist, A., Lieverse, A. R., et al. (2016). Diffuse idiopathic skeletal hyperostosis (DISH) in a middle Holocene forager from Lake Baikal, Russia: potential causes and the effect on quality of life. *Quaternary International,* 405, 66–79.

Farhat, G. N. and Cauley, J. A. (2008). The link between osteoporosis and cardiovascular disease. *Clinical Cases in Mineral and Bone Metabolism,* 5, 19–34.

Fiorin, E., Sáez, L. and Malgosa, A. (2018). Ferns as healing plants in medieval Mallorca, Spain? Evidence from human dental calculus. *International Journal of Osteoarchaeology,* 29, 82–90.

Fornaciari, G., Marinozzim, S., Messineom, D., et al. (2019). A remarkable case of gout in the Imperial Rome: Surgery and diseases in antiquity by osteoarchaeological, paleopathological, and historical perspectives. *International Journal of Osteoarchaeology,* 29, 797–807.

Gaeta, R., Giuffra, V. and Fornaciari, G. (2013). Atherosclerosis in the Renaissance elite: Ferdinand I King of Naples (1431–1494). *Virchows Archiv,* 462, 593–5.

Gale, E. A. M. and Anderson, J. V. (2002). Diabetes mellitus and other disorders of metabolism. In P. Kumar and M. Clark, eds., *Kumar and Clark Clinical Medicine,* 5th ed. Edinburgh: W.B. Saunders, pp. 1069–121.

Gennari, L., Rendina, D., Falchetti, A. and Merlotti, D. (2019). Paget's disease of bone. *Calcified Tissue International*, 104, 483–500.

Gerrard, C. M., Graves, P., Millard, A., Annis, R. and Caffell, A. (2018). *Lost Live, New Voices: Unlocking the Stories of the Scottish Soldiers from the Battle of Dunbar 1650.* Oxford: Oxbow Books.

Gluckman, P. and Hanson, M. (2006). *Mismatch: The Lifestyle Diseases Timebomb.* Oxford: Oxford University Press.

Gluckman, P., Beedle, A. and Hanson, M. (2009). *Principles of Evolutionary Medicine.* Oxford: Oxford University Press.

Goldman, B. (1995). Heritable diseases of connective tissue, epiphyseal dysplasias, and related conditions. In D. Resnick, ed., *Diagnosis of Bone and Joint Disorders.* London: W.B. Saunders, pp. 4095–162.

Grauer, A. L. and Roberts, C. A. (2019). Infectious diseases 4: Fungal, viral, multicelled parasitic and protozoan infections, and malaria. In J. E. Buikstra, ed., *Ortner's Identification of Pathological Conditions in Human Skeletal Remains*, 3rd ed. London: Academic Press, pp. 441–78.

Grundy, S. M. (2016). Metabolic syndrome update. *Trends in Cardiovascular Medicine*, 26, 364–73.

Hagelberg, E., Sykes, B. and Hedges, R. (1989). Ancient bone DNA amplified. *Nature*, 342, 485.

Hall, A. J., Stubbs, B., Mamas, M. A., Myint, P. K. and Smith, T. O. (2016). Association between osteoarthritis and cardiovascular disease: Systematic review and meta-analysis. *European Journal of Preventive Cardiology*, 23, 938–46.

Haraszthy, V. I., Zambon, J. J., Trevisan, M., Zeid, M. and Genco, R. J. (2000). Identification of periodontal pathogens in atheromatous plaques. *Journal of Periodontology*, 71, 1554–60.

Hardy, K., Radini, A., Buckley, S., et al. (2016). Dental calculus reveals potential respiratory irritants and ingestion of essential plant-based nutrients at Lower Palaeolithic Qesem Cave Israel. *Quaternary International,* 398, 129–35.

Haynes, R., Zhu, D., Judge, P. K., et al. (2020). Chronic kidney disease, heart failure and neprilysin inhibition. *Nephrology Dialysis Transplantation*, 35, 558–64.

Helskog, K. (2014). *Communicating with the World of Beings: The World Heritage Rock Art Sites in Alta, Arctic Norway.* Oxford: Oxbow Books.

Holick, M. F. (2017). The vitamin D deficiency pandemic: Approaches for diagnosis, treatment and prevention. *Reviews in Endocrine and Metabolic Disorders*, 18, 153–65.

Huang, W.-S., Lin, C.-L., Tsai, C.-H. and Chang, K.-H. (2020). Association of gout with CAD and effect of antigout therapy on CVD risk among gout patients. *Journal of Investigative Medicine*, 68, 972–9.

Hugar, B. S., Praveen, S., Kainoor, S. K. and Shetty, A. R. S. (2014). Sudden death in Marfan syndrome. *Journal of Forensic Sciences*, 59, 1126–8.

Huynh, H. T. T., Verneau, J., Levasseur, A., Drancourt, M. and Aboudharam, G. (2018). Bacteria and archaea paleomicrobiology of the dental calculus: A review. *Molecular Oral Microbiology*, 31, 234–42.

Iles, R. K. (2002). Cell and molecular biology, and genetic disorders. In P. Kumar and M. Clark, eds., *Kumar and Clark Clinical Medicine*, 5th ed. Edinburgh: W.B. Saunders, pp. 153–90.

Jackson, R. P. J. (2016). Roman medicine: The practitioners and the practices. In W. Hasse, ed., *Band 37/1. Teilband Philosophie, Wissenschaften, Technik. Wissenschaften (Medizin und Biologie).* Berlin: De Gruyter, pp. 79–101.

Jankauskas, R. (2003). The incidence of diffuse idiopathic skeletal hyperostosis and social status correlations in Lithuanian skeletal materials. *International Journal of Osteoarchaeology*, 13, 289–93.

Jaskowiec, T. C., Grauer, A. L., Lee, M. and Rajnic, S. (2017). No stone unturned: The presence of kidney stones in a skeleton from nineteenth century Peoria, Illinois. *International Journal of Paleopathology*, 19, 18–23.

Jean, G., Souberbielle, J. C. and Chazot, C. (2017). Vitamin D in chronic kidney disease and dialysis patients. *Nutrients*, 9, 328.

Jiao, H., Xiao, E. and Graves, D. T. (2015). Diabetes and its effect on bone and fracture healing. *Current Osteoporosis Reports*, 13, 16–25.

Johansson, I., Dahlström, U., Edner, M., et al. (2018). Type 2 diabetes and heart failure: Characteristics and prognosis in preserved, mid-range and reduced ventricular function. *Diabetes and Cardiovascular Research*, 15, 494–503.

Johns, L. E., Madsen, A. M., Maduro, G., et al. (2013). A case study of the impact of inaccurate cause-of-death reporting on health disparity tracking: New York City premature cardiovascular mortality. *American Journal of Public Health*, 103, 733–9.

Kelley, M. A. (1979). Skeletal changes produced by aortic aneurysms. *American Journal of Physical Anthropology*, 51, 35–8.

Kheiri, B., Abdalla, A., Osman, M., et al. (2018). Vitamin D deficiency and risk of cardiovascular diseases: A narrative review. *Clinical Hypertension*, 24, 9.

Khojastepour, L., Bronoosh, P., Khosropannah, S. and Rahimi, E. (2013). Can dental pulp calcification predict the risk of ischemic cardiovascular disease? *Journal of Dentistry (Tehran)*, 10, 456–60.

Kim, K., Choi, S., Chang, J., et al. (2019). Severity of dental caries and risk of coronary heart disease in middle-aged men and women: A population-based cohort study of Korean adults, 2002–2013. *Scientific Reports*, 9, 10491.

Krenz-Niedbała, M. and Łukasik, S. (2016). Prevalence of chronic maxillary sinusitis in children from rural and urban skeletal populations in Poland. *International Journal of Paleopathology,* 15, 103–12.

Lambert, P. (2002). Rib lesions in a prehistoric Puebloan sample from Southwestern Colorado. *American Journal of Physical Anthropology,* 117, 281–92.

Lewis, M. (2019). Endocrine disturbances. In J. E. Buikstra, ed., *Ortner's Identification of Pathological Conditions in Human Skeletal Remains*, 3rd ed. London: Academic Press, pp. 567–84.

Lloyd, G. E. R., ed. (1983). *Hippocratic Writings.* Translated by J. Chadwick, W. N. Mann, I. M. Lonie and E. T. Withington. London: Penguin Books.

McAlister, W. H. and Herman, T. E. (1995). Osteochondrodysplasias, dysostoses, chromosomal aberrations, mucopolysaccharidoses, and mucolipidoses. In D. Resnick, ed., *Diagnosis of Bone and Joint Disorders.* London: W.B. Saunders, pp. 4163–244.

Mckinnon, K., Van Twest, M. S. and Hatton, M. (2013). A probable case of rheumatoid arthritis from the middle Anglo-Saxon period. *International Journal of Paleopathology,* 3, 122–7.

McNicol, A. M. and Foulis, A. K. (2008). The endocrine system. In D. A. Levison, R. Reid, A. D. Burt, D. J. Harrison and S. Fleming, eds., *Muir's Textbook of Pathology*, 14th ed. London: Hodder Arnold, pp. 449–73.

Mader, R., Novofestovski, I., Adawi, M. and Lavi, I. (2009). Metabolic syndrome and cardiovascular risk in patients with diffuse idiopathic skeletal hyperostosis. *Seminars in Arthritis and Rheumatism*, 38, 361–5.

Manchester, K. (1980). An ossifying diathesis of 1st century AD date. Abstracts of the 4th European Meeting of the Paleopathology Association, Caen, France, 16–19 September, p. 8.

Mays, S., Brickley, M. and Ives, R. (2007). Skeletal evidence for hyperparathyroidism in a nineteenth century child with rickets. *International Journal of Osteoarchaeology,* 17, 73–81.

Millard, A. R., Annis, R. G., Caffell, A. C., et al. (2020). The Scottish soldiers from the Battle of Dunbar 1650: A prosopographical approach to a skeletal assemblage. *PLoS One*, 15, e0243369.

Mitchell, P. D. (2011). Retrospective diagnosis and the use of historical sources for investigating diseases in the past. *International Journal of Paleopathology*, 1, 81–8.

Mitchell, P. D. (2012). Integrating historical sources with paleopathology. In A. L. Grauer, ed., *A Companion to Paleopathology.* Cambridge: Cambridge University Press, pp. 310–23.

Mitchell, P. D. (2017). Improving the use of historical written sources in paleopathology. *International Journal of Paleopathology*, 19, 88–95.

Morrison, M. L. and McMahon, C. J. (2018). Congenital heart disease in Down syndrome. In S. Dey, ed., *Advances in Research on Down Syndrome.* Rijeka, Croatia: Intech, pp. 95–138.

Musunuru, K., Quasim, A. N. and Reilly, M. P. (2020). Genetics and genomics of atherosclerotic cardiovascular disease. In R. Pyeritz, B. Korf and W. Grody, eds., *Emery and Rimoin's Principles and Practice of Medical Genetics and Genomics: Cardiovascular, Respiratory, and Gastrointestinal Disorders*, 7th ed. London: Academic Press, pp. 209–30.

Nesse, R. M. and Williams, G. C. (1994). *Why We Get Sick: The New Science of Darwinian Medicine.* New York: Vintage.

Novak, M., Čavka, M. and Šlaus, M. (2014). Two cases of neurogenic paralysis in medieval skeletal samples from Croatia. *International Journal of Paleopathology*, 7, 25–32.

Nunn, J. F. (1996). *Ancient Egyptian Medicine.* London: British Museum Press.

Panzer, S., Thompson, R. C., Hergan, K., Zink, A. R. and Piombino-Mascali, D. (2018). Evidence of aortic dissection and Marfan syndrome in a mummy from the Capuchin Catacombs of Palermo, Sicily. *International Journal of Paleopathology*, 22, 78–85.

Pitt, M. J. (1995). Rickets and osteomalacia. In D. Resnick, ed., *Diagnosis of Bone and Joint Disorders.* London: W.B. Saunders, pp. 1885–992.

Porter, R. (1997). *The Greatest Benefit to Mankind: A Medical History of Humanity from Antiquity to the Present.* London: Fontana Press.

Pourmoghaddas, Z., Meskin, M., Sabri, M., Tehrani, M. H. M. and Najafı, T. (2018). Dental caries and gingival evaluation in children with congenital heart disease. *International Journal of Preventive Medicine*, 9, 52.

Preus, H. R., Marvik, O. J., Selvig, K. A. and Bennike, P. (2011). Ancient bacterial DNA (aDNA) in dental calculus from archaeological human remains. *Journal of Archaeological Science,* 38, 1827–31.

Ragab, G., Elshahaly, M. and Bardin, T. (2017). Gout: An old disease in new perspective. A review. *Journal of Advanced Research*, 8, 495–511.

Rahman, M. M., Kope, J. A., Cibere, J., Goldsmith, C. H. and Anis, A. H. (2013). The relationship between osteoarthritis and cardiovascular disease in a population health survey: A cross-sectional study. *British Medical Journal Open*, 3, e002624.

Rajagopalan, S., Al-Kindi, S. G. and Brook, R. D. (2018). Air pollution and cardiovascular disease: JACC state-of-the-art review. *Journal of the American College of Cardiology*, 72, 2054–70.

Reid, R. (2008). The locomotor system. In D. A. Levison, R. Reid, A. D. Burt, D. J. Harrison and S. Fleming, eds., *Muir's Textbook of Pathology*, 14th ed. London: Hodder Arnold, pp. 330–72.

Resnick, D. (1995). Disorders of other endocrine glands and of pregnancy. In D. Resnick, ed., *Diagnosis of Bone and Joint Disorders.* London: W.B. Saunders, pp. 2076–104.

Resnick, D. and Niwayama, G. (1995a). Enostosis, hyperostosis, and periostitis. In D. Resnick, ed., *Diagnosis of Bone and Joint Disorders.* London: W.B. Saunders, pp. 4396–466.

Resnick, D. and Niwayama, G. (1995b). Diffuse idiopathic skeletal hyperostosis (DISH): ankylosing hyperostosis of Forestier and Rotes-Querol. In D. Resnick, ed., *Diagnosis of Bone and Joint Disorders.* London: W.B. Saunders, pp. 1463–95.

Resnick, D. and Niwayama, G. (1995c). Degenerative disease of extraspinal locations. In D. Resnick, ed., *Diagnosis of Bone and Joint Disorders.* London: W.B. Saunders, pp. 1263–371.

Resnick, D. and Niwayama, G. (1995d). Ankylosing spondylitis. In D. Resnick, ed., *Diagnosis of Bone and Joint Disorders.* London: W.B. Saunders, pp. 1008–74.

Resnick, D. and Niwayama, G. (1995e). Gouty arthritis. In D. Resnick, ed., *Diagnosis of Bone and Joint Disorders.* London: W.B. Saunders, pp. 1511–55.

Resnick, D. and Niwayama, G. (1995f). Rheumatoid arthritis and the seronegative spondyloarthropathies: Radiographic and pathologic concepts. In D. Resnick, ed., *Diagnosis of Bone and Joint Disorders.* London: W.B. Saunders, pp. 807–970.

Resnick, D. and Niwayama, G. (1995g). Paget's disease. In D. Resnick, ed., *Diagnosis of Bone and Joint Disorders.* London: W.B. Saunders, pp. 1923–68.

Reyes, C., Leyland, K. M., Peat, G., et al. (2016). Association between overweight and obesity and risk of clinically diagnosed knee, hip, and hand osteoarthritis: A population-based cohort study. *Arthritis and Rheumatology*, 68, 1869–75.

Rivollat, M., Castex, D., Hauret, L. and Tillier, A.-M. (2014). Ancient Down syndrome: An osteological case from Saint-Jean-des-Vignes, northeastern France, from the 5th–6th century AD. *International Journal of Paleopathology*, 7, 8–14.

Roberts, C. A. (2015). What did agriculture do for us? The bioarchaeology of health and diet. In G. Barker and C. Goucher, eds., *The Cambridge World History, Volume 2: A World with Agriculture, 12,000 BCE–500 CE.* Cambridge: Cambridge University Press, pp. 93–123.

Roberts, C. A. and Brickley, M. (2019). Infectious and metabolic diseases: A synergistic bioarchaeology. In A. Katzenberg and A. Grauer, eds., *Biological Anthropology of the Human Skeleton*, 3rd ed. Chichester: Wiley-Blackwell, pp. 415–46.

Roberts, C. A. and Manchester, K. (2005). *The Archaeology of Disease*. Cheltenham: The History Press.

Roddy, E. and Choi, H. K. (2014). Epidemiology of gout. *Rheumatic Disease Clinics of North America*, 40, 155–75.

Rogers, J. and Waldron, T. (2001). DISH and the monastic way of life. *International Journal of Osteoarchaeology*, 11, 357–65.

Rossetti, C., Pasquinelli, L., Verzeletti, A., et al. (2018). A case of Paget from a Northern Italy medieval necropolis. *International Journal of Paleopathology*, 20, 104–7.

Rothberg, D. L. and Makarewich, C. A. (2019). Fat embolism and fat embolism syndrome. *Journal of the American Academy of Orthopaedic Surgery*, 27, e346–e355.

Ruffer, M. A. (1911). On arterial lesions found in Egyptian mummies. *Journal of Pathology and Bacteria*, 15, 453–62.

Sandison, A. T. (1962). Degenerative vascular disease in the Egyptian mummy. *Medical History*, 6, 77–81.

Sandison, A. T. (1967). Degenerative vascular disease. In D. Brothwell and A. T. Sandison, eds., *Diseases in Antiquity*. Springfield, IL: Charles C. Thomas, pp. 474–88.

Sanz, M., del Castillo, A. M., Jepsen, S., et al. (2020). Periodontitis and cardiovascular diseases: Consensus report. *Journal of Clinical Periodontology*, 47, 268–88.

Seiler, R., Spielman, A., Zink, A. and Rühli, F. (2013). Oral pathologies of the Neolithic Iceman, c. 3,300 BC. *European Journal of Oral Sciences*, 121, 137–41.

Shipley, M., Black, C. M. and O'Gradaigh, D. (2002). Rheumatology and bone disease. In P. Kumar and M. Clark, eds., *Kumar and Clark Clinical Medicine*, 5th ed. Edinburgh: W.B. Saunders, pp. 473–586.

Steinbock, R. T. (1985). The history, epidemiology and paleopathology of kidney and urinary bladder stone disease. In C. F. Merbs and R. J. Miller, eds., *Health and Disease in the Prehistoric Southwest*. Anthropological Research Papers No. 34. Tempe, AZ: Arizona State University, pp. 177–90.

Steinbock, R. T. (1989). Studies in ancient calcified soft tissues and organic concretions II: urolithiasis (renal and urinary bladder disease). *Journal of Paleopathology*, 3, 39–59.

Stuart, A. G. and Williams, A. (2007). Marfan's syndrome and the heart. *Archive of Diseases in Childhood*, 92, 351–6.

Swinson, D., Snaith, J., Buckberry, J. and Brickley, M. (2010). High performance liquid chromatography (HPLC) in the investigation of gout in palaeopathology. *International Journal of Osteoarchaeology*, 20, 135–43.

Swynghedauw, B. (2016). Evolutionary paradigms in cardiology: The case of chronic heart failure. In A. Alvergne, C. Jenkinson and C. Faurie, eds., *Evolutionary Thinking in Medicine: From Research to Policy and Practice*. Cham, Switzerland: Springer International Publishing, pp. 137–53.

Taylor, J. H. and Antoine, D. (2014). *Ancient Lives, New Discoveries: Eight Mummies, Eight Stories*. London: British Museum Press.

Tesorieri, M. (2016). Differential diagnosis of pathologically induced upper and lower limb asymmetry in a burial from late medieval Ireland. *International Journal of Palaeopathology*, 14, 46–54.

Thompson, R. C., Allam, A. H., Lombardi, G. P., et al. (2013). Atherosclerosis across 4000 years of human history: The Horus study of four ancient populations. *Lancet*, 381, 1211–22.

Tomczyk, J., Komarnitki, J., Zalewska, M., et al. (2014). The prevalence of pulp stones in historical populations from the middle Euphrates valley (Syria). *American Journal of Physical Anthropology*, 153, 103–15.

Tomczyk, J., Turska-Szbka, A., Zalewska, M. and Olczak-Kowalczyk, D. (2017). Pulp stones prevalence in a historical sample from Radom, Poland (AD 1791–1811). *International Journal of Osteoarchaeology*, 2, 563–72.

Tomczyk, J., Myszka, A., Regulski, P. and Olczak-Kowalczyk, D. (2020). Case of pulp stones and dental wear in a Mesolithic (5900 ± 100 BC) individual from Woźna Wieś (Poland). *International Journal of Osteoarchaeology*, 30, 375–81.

Tovi, F., Benharroch, D., Gatot, A. and Hertzanu, Y. (1992). Osteoblastic osteitis of the maxillary sinus. *Laryngoscope*, 102, 427–30.

Traversari, M., Serrangeli, M. C., Catalano, G., et al. (2019). Multi-analytic study of a probable case of fibrous dysplasia (FD) from Certosa Monumental Cemetery (Bologna, Italy). *International Journal of Paleopathology*, 25, 1–8.

Tuegel, C. and Bansal, N. (2017). Heart failure in patients with kidney disease. *Heart*, 103, 1848–53.

Verma, D., Garg, P. K. and Dubey, A. K. (2018). Insights into the human oral microbiome. *Archives of Microbiology*, 200, 525–40.

Vykoukal, D. and Davies, M. G. (2011). Vascular biology of metabolic syndrome. *Journal of Vascular Surgery*, 54, 819–31.

Wakely, J. and Smith, A. (1998). A possible eighteenth–nineteenth century example of a popliteal aneurysm from Leicester. *International Journal of Osteoarchaeology*, 8, 50–60.

Waldron, T. (2019). Joint disease. In J. E. Buikstra, ed., *Ortner's Identification of Pathological Conditions in Human Skeletal Remains*, 3rd ed. London: Academic Press, pp. 719–48.

Waldron, T. and Antoine, D. (2002). Tortuosity or aneurysm? The palaeopathology of some abnormalities of the vertebral artery. *International Journal of Osteoarchaeology*, 12, 79–88.

Waldron, T., Rogers, J. and Watt, I. (1994). Rheumatoid arthritis in an English post-Medieval skeleton. *International Journal of Osteoarchaeology*, 4, 165–7.

Walker, E. G. (1983). Evidence of prehistoric cardiovascular disease of syphilitic origin on the Northern Plains. *American Journal of Physical Anthropology*, 60, 499–503.

Walsh, J. S., Bowles, S. and Evans, A. L. (2017). Vitamin D in obesity. *Current Opinion in Endocrinology, Diabetes and Obesity*, 24, 389–94.

Wang, H., Bai, J., He, B., Hu, X. and Liu, D. (2016). Osteoarthritis and the risk of cardiovascular disease: A meta-analysis of observational studies. *Scientific Reports*, 6, 39672.

Wang, T. J. (2016). Vitamin D and cardiovascular disease. *Annual Review of Medicine*, 67, 261–72.

Warinner, C., Matias Rodrigues, J. F., Vyas, R., et al. (2014). Pathogens and host immunity in the ancient human oral cavity. *Nature Genetics*, 46, 336–44.

Weil, E. J. (2008). From ancient seas to modern disease. In W. R. Trevathan, E. O. Smith and J. J. McKenna, eds., *Evolutionary Medicine and Health: New Perspectives*. Oxford: Oxford University Press, pp. 382–98.

Wells, C. and Woodhouse, N. (1975). Paget's disease in an Anglo-Saxon. *Medical History*, 19, 396–400.

Weyrich, L. S., Dobney, K. and Cooper, A. (2015). Ancient DNA analysis of dental calculus. *Journal of Human Evolution*, 79, 119–24.

World Health Organization. (2013). *Global Action Plan for the Prevention and Control of Noncommunicable Diseases 2013–2020*. Geneva: World Health Organization.

World Health Organization. (2019). Non-communicable diseases. www.who.int/news-room/fact-sheets/detail/cardiovascular-diseases-(cvds) (accessed 25 November 2022).

World Health Organization. (2020). Diabetes. www.who.int/health-topics/diabetes#tab=tab_1 (accessed 25 November 2022).

World Health Organization. (2021a). Congenital anomalies. www.who.int/health-topics/congenital-anomalies#tab=tab_1 (accessed 25 November 2022).

World Health Organization. (2021b). Air pollution. www.who.int/health-topics/air-pollution#tab=tab_1 (accessed 5 October 2021).

Zhou, C. and Byard, R. W. (2017). An analysis of the morbidity and mortality of diabetes mellitus in a forensic context. *Journal of Forensic Sciences*, 63, 1149–54.

Zink, A., Wann, L. S., Thompson, L. C., et al. (2014). Genomic correlates of atherosclerosis in ancient humans. *Global Heart*, 9, 203–9.

Part I

Evidence from Mummified Tissues

3   Atherosclerosis, Mummies and Histological Analysis

A Review

Gino Fornaciari and Raffaele Gaeta

3.1   Background

Atherosclerosis, a disease with a multifactorial aetiology, is characterised by the accumulation and hardening of fatty materials in the arterial blood vessels that may cause obstruction (stenosis) of the lumen. Today, it is one of the most common diseases of the developed countries, and every year thousands of people die of the complications associated with atherosclerosis (Herrington et al., 2016). Indeed, the severe consequences include myocardial infarction (heart attack), stroke (cerebrovascular accident or CVA) and chronic kidney failure (Yusuf & McKee, 2014).

The aetiology of atherosclerosis includes modifiable (tobacco smoking, obesity, hypertension, diabetes, dyslipidaemia) and non-modifiable (male sex, advanced age, genetic predisposition, family history) risk factors (Roberts, 1992). Recent scientific research has linked the development of atherosclerotic plaques, composed of fat, cholesterol, calcium and other substances found in the blood, to inflammation, diet and environmental factors (Ding & Kullo, 2009; Farzan et al., 2021; Krupa et al., 2021). Over time, plaque hardens and narrows the arteries, leading to reduced oxygen delivery to the body. Many genes and proteins are also involved in the development of atherosclerosis, with a multiplicity of pathways (Novelli et al., 2010; Poznyak et al., 2020).

The accumulation of inflammatory-related 'response' lipids develops progressively in a number of arterial vessels such as the aorta, the coronary arteries and the carotid arteries, so that the histological changes become increasingly complex. Over the course of a lifetime these changes undergo gradual development. Initially, fatty (lipid) streaks appear in childhood and adolescence; these early alterations can only be detected microscopically, and are reversible. Next, early fibroatheroma occurs with the accumulation of macrophages, chronic inflammatory cells and fibroblasts (Insull, 2009). The physiological architecture of the vessel's intima is distorted and finally broken by the increasing accumulation of extracellular lipids and cellular necrosis. A fibrous tissue cap forms under the endothelium and overlies the lipid-rich necrotic core; this represents the typical alteration of atherosclerosis (i.e. the atheroma) (Virmani et al., 2000). Advancing atheroma might occur in individuals aged over 55 years. The thin fibrous cap may ulcerate, thus exposing the thrombogenic interior arterial wall and producing a thrombus that extends into the arterial lumen. Enlargement of the plaque can reduce the arterial lumen until complete obliteration occurs, which ultimately may cause ischaemia through flow restriction. Small aggregates or large deposits of calcium in the arterial wall can be detected throughout all these steps. Such changes are significantly influenced by the above-mentioned risk factors (Ding & Kullo, 2009; Farzan et al., 2021; Krupa et al., 2021).

Coronary atherosclerosis is the main cause of myocardial infarction (Feigin et al., 2009). When the disease involves the coronary arteries, possible reduction in the blood flow, or its total absence due to obliteration of the vascular lumen, can cause ischaemia of the myocardium. It is no coincidence that the occurrence of such lesions coincides with the peak incidences of stroke and myocardial infarction (Insull, 2009). Owing to its connection with dietary habits (rich intake of meat, sugar and fat) the disease has been considered distinctive of a modern sedentary and well-nourished society.

The documentation of atherosclerosis in past societies is already known thanks to macroscopic observation during autopsies. In fact, among the first to describe atherosclerosis was Leonardo da Vinci (1452–1519), who wrote: 'vessels in the elderly restrict the transit of blood through thickening of the tunics' (Slijkhuis et al., 2009: 140). In addition, the presence of atherosclerosis in human mummies excavated from different time periods and various geographic contexts (Thompson et al., 2013) suggests that the disease was already common in the past. This may seem unlikely given that dietary habits were very different from today in terms of quantity and 'quality', as food was less processed and more genuine. However, as atherosclerosis is a multifactorial disease determined primarily by chronic inflammation and diet as well as other environmental, biological and genetic factors (Campbell and Rosenfeld, 2015), we may assume a similar rate of atherosclerosis in the past as today.

3.2 Methods

The study of ancient mummified remains has taken advantage of the techniques available in modern pathology. Firstly, histology has proved to be a basic support for the diagnosis of diseases in antiquity but, as technology progresses, the tools made available to the palaeopathologist have gradually expanded. Modern radiographic techniques such as conventional X-ray (Ventura et al., 2020), computed tomography (CT) and cone beam CT scanning have become key tools, with palaeogenetic and ancient DNA analyses becoming more frequent (Pinhasi et al., 2019; Hagan et al., 2020).

Macroscopic analysis performed on a mummified body during autopsy can also be of great help in the diagnosis of atherosclerosis. However, the identification of small- and medium-calibre vessels, such as the arteries of the head and neck or the coronary arteries, is often problematic mainly because drying phenomena cause structural collapse of such small-diameter vessels. Nevertheless, the aorta has a large calibre throughout its entire course and is almost always 'easily' identifiable; it is also the most common site for atherosclerosis, especially in its abdominal tract (Kojima et al., 2019). In addition to problems associated with the identification of vessels, atherosclerosis may not always be diagnosed macroscopically. It is a progressive disease in which pathological changes range from the initial modifications that are only visible microscopically to the severe final-stage changes that involve obliteration of the lumen (Insull, 2009; Rafieian-Kopaei et al., 2014).

While the pathological changes in the vessel wall in advanced atherosclerosis are visible macroscopically, random sampling of vessels is the only possible technique that can diagnose early-stage atherosclerosis. In advanced atherosclerosis, a vessel may be partially or entirely calcified for a large part of its length. In some cases, it is even possible to identify a luminal thrombus (Gaeta et al., 2018). In other cases, when the anatomy of a mummy is in a poor state of preservation, with wide areas of skeletonisation, we can still detect calcified flakes that represent the remains of atherosclerotic vessels (Charlier et al., 2014). These minimal findings can easily be lost, so it is necessary to be extremely vigilant during the archaeological phases of a survey on a mummy that has become partly skeletonised. However, the most reliable technique is direct microscopic observation of the lesions on histological slides, as radiological imaging can be subject to false positives and negatives. Indeed, vascular calcification is related not only to atherosclerosis but also to other conditions such as disorders of calcium/phosphorus metabolism, diabetes, chronic microinflammation and chronic renal insufficiency (Palit & Kendrick, 2014; Grønhøj et al., 2016). Furthermore, the identification of atherosclerosis based on the presence of a calcification in the expected course of an artery can only be speculative as the anatomy can be strongly altered by post-mortem events, for example the walls of the vessels might collapse, dehydrate and have the appearance of calcific thickening (Gaeta et al., 2013).

Most mummified tissues, from skin to the internal organs, acquire a brownish colour and a hard or fibrous consistency as a consequence of the embalming and dehydration processes (Aufderheide, 2011). For these reasons, it is not possible to manage these tissues as normal histological samples. Before inclusion in paraffin, they must undergo rehydration, which is an indispensable step. The most delicate part of the whole process is to gradually introduce aqueous solutions in order to stretch the tissues, especially the connective tissue (Fulcheri & Ventura, 2001). Excessive and non-gradual rehydration at this stage can lead to lysis of the tissues and cells, swelling of the connective tissues and a loss of histo-architectural integrity. Conversely, inadequate and insufficient rehydration does not allow optimal diaphonisation, and consequently creates imperfect paraffin impregnation resulting in a hard and inelastic sample that is difficult to dissect with the microtome (Fulcheri & Ventura, 2001). First described by Sandison (1955), the predominant rehydrating solution consists of 95% alcohol (30%), 2% formalin (50%) and 5% sodium carbonate (Na_2CO_3) (20%).

The first approach to the histological study of paraffin-embedded tissues from atherosclerotic vessels is basic haematoxylin and eosin (H&E) staining. Haematoxylin has a deep blue-purple colour and stains nucleic acids (such as those found in the nucleus), while eosin is pink and non-specifically stains proteins such as those found in the cytoplasm and the extracellular matrix. Other useful histochemical stains are used for the identification and distribution of various chemical components in the tissues. The most commonly adopted stains for the evaluation of atherosclerotic changes are as follows (Relucenti et al., 2010; te Boekhorst et al., 2011; Leone et al., 2020):

- Weigert's elastic staining, useful for identifying the elastic fibres of the vessels.
- Oil Red O, for triglycerides, lipids and lipoproteins.
- Periodic acid–Schiff (PAS), used to detect glycogen, glycoproteins, glycolipids and mucins.
- Von Kossa's stain, used to detect microcalcifications in atherosclerotic plaques.

3.3 Review of the Literature

We conducted a review of the published literature in order to identify palaeopathological evidence of atherosclerosis in mummified remains that have been confirmed by histological analysis. To the best of our knowledge, atherosclerosis has been detected histologically in 33 mummies (Table 3.1), described in papers ranging from 1852 to the present day. In the last 20 years, publications have intensified and the histological data have been increasingly corroborated using sophisticated imaging techniques and molecular biology. Ancient Egypt is the country with the highest number of cases and at least one individual with atherosclerosis has been described on almost all continents (Africa, Europe, North and South America and East Asia), as we illustrate in Table 3.1. Individual mummies of different biological sex, age at death and dates have been studied.

The first published histological study on the vessels of an ancient mummified body dates back to the mid-nineteenth century. This pioneering study describes 'multiple considerably large and calcified plaques' in a descending aorta during the autopsy of a mummy of an elderly Egyptian woman (Czermak, 1852).

In 1911 M. A. Ruffer, who is considered the founder of palaeopathology, wrote about observations of pathological changes in the vessels of several Egyptian mummies covering a very large temporal range, from 1580 BCE to 525 CE (Ruffer, 1911). Of great importance, this paper included 16 microscopically investigated anonymous mummies presenting various degrees of atherosclerosis in different blood vessels (e.g. aorta, subclavian and carotid arteries). The mummies studied by Ruffer had variable degrees of preservation and derived from disturbed archaeological contexts devoid of any historical data, and the suggested temporal range (1580 BCE to 525 CE) was likely to be conjectural. Moreover, it was possible to specify the age and sex (one male and one female, both about 50–60 years old) for only two individuals, while the remaining 14 were classed as 'adults', 'indeterminable' or were not specified by the author. Ruffer enriched the work with broad and precise illustrations comprising drawings showing the macroscopic and histological aspects of some vessels (Figure 3.1). With extreme insight, the author stated that 'the old Egyptians suffered as much as we do now from arterial lesions identical with those found in the present time. Moreover, [. . .] such lesions were as frequent three thousand years ago

Table 3.1 Evidence of ancient atherosclerosis in mummies confirmed by histological analysis.

Number of individuals	Sex	Identification	Age at death	Country	Date	Affected vessels	Reference
1	Female	Unknown	Old	Egypt	Not specified	Descending aorta	Czermak (1852)
16	1 female; 1 male; 14 not specified or indeterminable	Unknown	2 adults; 14 not specified or indeterminable	Egypt	From 1580 BCE to 525 CE	Thoraco-abdominal aorta, subclavian, common carotid, common iliac, common femoral, posterior peroneal, anterior tibial, posterior tibial, brachial, ulnar, radial	Ruffer (1911)
1	Male	Pharaoh Merneptah	Old	Egypt	?–1203 BCE (19th Dynasty)	Aorta	Shattock (1909)
1	Male	Unknown	Adult	Peru	c. 700 CE	Right tibial artery	Williams (1927)
1	Female	Lady Teye	Old	Egypt	c. 1000 BCE (21st Dynasty)	Coronary arteries, mitral valve, renal arteries	Long (1931)
1	Male	Har-Mose	Old	Egypt	1490 BCE (18th Dynasty)	Superior mesenteric artery	Bernard Shaw (1938)
1	Male	Unknown	Adult	Alaska	18th century CE	Abdominal aorta, iliac artery	Zimmerman et al. (1971)
1	Male	Pum II	35–40 years	Egypt	c. 170 BCE	Thoracic aorta	Cockburn et al. (1975)
1	Female	Unknown	50–60 years	USA (Alaska)	c. 400 CE	Aorta, coronary arteries	Zimmerman & Smith (1975)
1	Female	Unknown	Adult	USA (Alaska)	18th century CE	Aorta	Zimmerman et al. (1981)
1	Female	Unknown	Adult (~40 years)	USA (Alaska)	1500 CE	Aorta, coronary arteries, mitral valve calcifications	Zimmerman & Aufderheide (1984)
1	Female	Lady Tai	Adult (~50 years)	China	168 BCE	Coronary arteries	Cheng (1996)
1	Male	Priest Nesyamun	Adult	Egypt	1100 BCE	Femoral artery	David et al. (2010)
1	Male	Ferrante I of Aragon, King of Naples	70 years	Italy	1424–1494 CE	Carotid artery	Gaeta et al. (2013)
1	Female	Unknown (nicknamed Mungyeong)	45–50 years	South Korea	17th century CE	Thoraco-abdominal aorta, left anterior descending coronary	Kim et al. (2015); Shin et al. (2017)
2	Two females	Unknown	(1) Adult (2) 30 years	(1) Chile (2) Peru	(1) c. 300 CE (2) c. 95 BCE	(1) Aorta and iliac arteries (2) Abdominal aorta	Gabrovsky et al. (2016)
1	Male	Girolamo Macchi	86 years	Italy	1648–1734 CE	Abdominal aorta, iliac arteries, carotid artery	Gaeta et al. (2018)

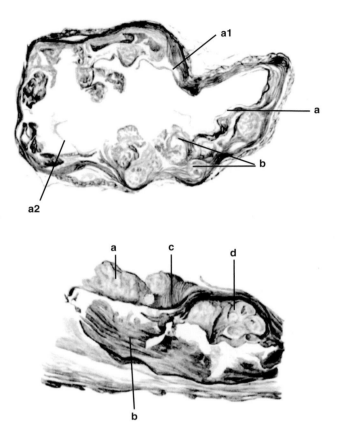

Figure 3.1 The upper figure shows a section through an almost completely calcified posterior peroneal artery (a, a1, a2, remnants of endothelium and fenestrated membrane; b, calcified patches). The lower figure displays a section of a calcified patch of an ulnar artery (a, d, calcified patches; b, partially calcified muscular coat; c, annular muscular fibre). Source: adapted from Ruffer (1911), figure 9-10, plate XLIV. (A black and white version of this figure will appear in some formats. For the colour version, please refer to the plate section.)

as they are today' (Ruffer, 1911: 460), even if at that time the aetiology of this disease was unclear. In addition to recognising that being exposed to tobacco smoke could have contributed to the atherosclerosis observed, Ruffer intuitively concluded that 'I cannot exclude a high meat diet as a cause with certainty, as the mummies examined were mostly those of priests and priestesses of Deir el-Bahari, who, owing to their high position, undoubtedly lived well' (Ruffer, 1911: 461).

A work of similar importance and detail was that of S. G. Shattock, who in 1924 performed histological analyses on tissues of the mummy of King Merneptah 13th, son of Ramesses II and the Great Royal Bride Isetnofret, who reigned from 1213 to 1203 BCE (Nineteenth Dynasty) (Shattock, 1924). His mummy, initially examined by G. Elliott Smith on 7 July 1907, is that of an elderly man (about 70 years old) measuring 1.74 m tall, with degenerative arthritis and hydrocele–swollen scrotum (Elliott Smith, 1912).

Shattock also described severe atherosclerotic disease on the basis of large calcified patches in the aorta, especially in its thoraco-abdominal sections.

In 1927 the pathologist H. U. Williams reported the macroscopic and microscopic results of an autopsy performed on a mummy from Lima (Peru), dating back to 700 CE. His diagnosis was calcific arteriosclerosis of the right posterior tibial artery, with the presence of a thrombus (blood clot) (Williams, 1927).

The pathologist A. R. Long described in 1931, for the first time, ancient evidence of atherosclerosis of the coronary arteries. The 'patient', the mummy of Lady Teye, was a middle-aged Egyptian woman of approximately 50 years of age who lived during the Twenty-first Dynasty (c. 1000 BCE). She also suffered from atherosclerosis of the aorta and the renal arteries, which may have caused atherosclerotic renovascular disease (ARVD), characterised by progressive chronic kidney disease (Woolfson, 2001).

In 1938, G. Bernard Shaw studied the canopic jar containing the internal organs of Har-Mose, an elderly Egyptian male singer of the Nineteenth Dynasty (c. 1490 BCE) (Bernard Shaw, 1938). He provided a detailed description of the state of preservation of the body, its macroscopic appearance and the histological picture of the lungs, liver, gallbladder, intestine and mesentery, which were remarkably well preserved. On account of the distribution and amount of adipose tissue in the organs, the author declared that Har-Mose was probably an obese individual, or at least a well-nourished man. Thickening of the innermost layer (intima) of the superior mesenteric artery, without clear evidence of atheroma, was also noted. The Egyptian man further suffered from acute bronchopneumonia and pleurisy which, owing to their extent, must have been the immediate cause of his death. Bernard Shaw's report is very detailed, in the modern sense, and documented iconographically with drawings reproducing the histological appearance on the slides.

In 1975, A. Cockburn and co-workers performed a complete autopsy on the mummy Pum II (Pennsylvania University Museum II), an Egyptian man who died around 170 BCE (Cockburn et al., 1975). Their work resulted in a cornerstone publication for the study of atherosclerotic disease in palaeopathology, as it combined for the first time radiographic and macroscopic investigations followed by histological study. The body, still wrapped in 12 layers of linen, was that of an adult male aged between 35 and 40 years at death, with a stature of approximately 1.62 m, in an excellent state of preservation. A complete autopsy was performed, and all the identified anatomical structures were analysed. The aorta and other major vessels of Pum II were in very good condition, but no coronary arteries were identified due to the small amount of cardiac tissue found in the chest. In the abdominal tract of the aorta, near the mediastinum and thoracic cavity, the authors found several large and small atheromatous plaques. Intimal fibrous thickening of the large and small arteries was also detected in the other organs sampled within the visceral (chest/abdomen) packages. The authors concluded that chronic arterial disease was common in antiquity, and its cause might have been one specific to past environments rather than to a modern one, such as stress or contemporary diet (Cockburn et al., 1975).

Between the 1970s and 1980s, M. R. Zimmerman described four ancient bodies with atherosclerosis from Alaska and the Aleutian Islands. The first paper concerned an adult male mummy from Kagamil Island, in the central part of the Aleutian chain, dating back to the eighteenth century (prior to 1740 CE) (Zimmerman et al., 1971). During a complete autopsy the thoracic aorta, oesophagus and trachea were identified and removed en bloc. The abdominal aorta and the iliac vessels were well preserved and easily identified. A firm yellow plaque, measuring 2×1 cm, was observed in the right iliac artery, but there was no other macroscopic evidence of atherosclerosis. Histological examination of the aorta revealed preservation of the three layers of its wall and of the elastic tissue, with the presence of a single atherosclerotic plaque formed by cholesterol crystals and containing minute calcific foci. However, gross findings and histological images suggested that the cause of death may have been lobar pneumonia caused by a Gram-negative bacillus, possibly complicated by septicaemia and diffuse metastatic abscesses.

Zimmerman's second paper concerned the discovery of the frozen body of a tattooed woman in October 1972 in the Bering Sea, at Kialegak Point on the Southeast Cape of Saint Lawrence Island. Using ^{14}C dating, Zimmerman and Smith (1975) dated this natural mummy to 405 ± 70 years BP. Both the body and the internal organs of this elderly woman were well preserved. Macroscopically, there was a moderate degree of coronary atherosclerosis but no evidence of myocardial infarction. Histological samples of the coronary arteries confirmed the atheromatous lesions, while the myocardium was normal, albeit poorly preserved. Microscopic fracture of the right temporal bone was also noted, with associated haemorrhage, indicating that this was a peri-mortem fracture and suggesting that a traumatic event had been responsible for the woman's death. Based on the archaeological context and the evidence of trauma, with haemorrhagic material found in the bronchi, it appears that 'this elderly woman had been trapped in her semisubterranean house by a landslide or earthquake, buried alive and asphyxiated' (Zimmerman, 1998: 142).

A third study (Zimmerman et al., 1981) described the pathological conditions of a middle-aged female Aleutian mummy who was wrapped in sea-otter and sea-lion skins and tied into a flexed position (preserved in the Peabody Museum of Archaeology and Ethnology, Harvard University). Archaeological dating placed the mummy in the early eighteenth century, and her age at death, determined by photon–osteon analysis, as 51 ± 6 years. Autopsy of the mummy showed poor preservation of the organs, but the lungs, liver, intestinal tract, kidneys and brain were identified and removed for histological examination that revealed minimal sclerotic changes of the larger renal arterioles and atherosclerosis of the aorta.

Finally, in a fourth study, Zimmerman and Aufderheide (1984) reported the autopsy findings of the remains of an entire frozen family found in a crushed winter house in the ancient village of Utqiagvik (Alaska) in the Arctic Ocean. The group included three completely skeletonised young people (a 20-year-old female, a 13-year-old male and an 8-year-old female) and two mummified females with fatal crushing chest injuries, one in her forties and the other in her mid-twenties. The elderly woman was found near the exit of the house with all her ribs fractured due to the roof collapsing on her. Examination of the lungs showed marked alteration of the architecture of the parenchyma and a significant volume of fluid in the chest cavities.

Atherosclerosis was observed in the coronary arteries and the aorta, while calcified plaques were found in the mitral valve of the heart. Based on radiocarbon dating, their deaths occurred around 1510 ± 70 CE, probably caused by the phenomenon of *ivu* (a type of hurricane that carried broken sea-ice), which caused the collapse of their dwelling and death by crushing and asphyxia.

Atherosclerotic disease has also been detected in ancient China. In 1972, a perfectly preserved mummy was found in a second-century BCE tomb in Mawangdui, Hunan Province (Cheng, 1996). Biomedical investigations identified the body as that of Lady Xin Zhui, wife of Li Cang and Marquis of Tai during the Western Han Period. At her death in 168 BCE, she was sealed inside several coffins and liquid around the body maintained the humidity and elasticity of the tissues and organs. Her preserved remains, 1.54 m tall and weighing 34.3 kg, underwent autopsy and histological analysis. Samples obtained from her heart showed that the left anterior descending coronary arteries were severely occluded by atherosclerotic plaques, composed of dense collagen fibres, which were likely responsible for her sudden death from a myocardial infarction affecting the anterior wall of the heart. Lady Tai was exposed to several risk factors. She was overweight, which possibly resulted in diabetes and hypertension and, as a noblewoman with many servants, she probably did not need to be very active physically. Finally, the tomb contained packets of cinnamon, magnolia tree bark and peppercorns that, according to Han medical canons, were prescribed for patients with angina pectoris (chest pain caused by reduced blood flow to the heart muscles). In addition, palaeoparasitology showed that she suffered from *Schistosoma japonicum* (a fluke), *Trichuris trichiura* (whipworm) and *Enterobius vermicularis* (pinworm) (Peng & Wu, 1998), which can cause a chronic inflammatory state.

Palaeopathological data and historical and archaeological evidence can be combined to generate a complete picture of an individual's lifestyle. A clear example was provided in 1990 by the well-known Manchester Egyptian Mummy Project (David et al., 2010). The mummy of a priest, which was brought to Leeds (UK) in the early nineteenth century, was the subject of a multidisciplinary investigation. The middle-aged man lay in a coffin bearing his name, Nesyamun, and was identified by his titles as a priest in the Temple of Montu. He was an incense-bearer and scribe at the ancient Egyptian temple complex at Karnak and died around 1100 BCE. These roles suggest that he may have participated in the temple offerings through preparing the foods and looking after the storehouse. For the performance of these tasks, he received a portion of the sacred food destined for the gods daily, and therefore he belonged to a high social elite that had access to large quantities of food that may have increased the risk of cardiovascular disease. Confirmation of these facts came from the histological examination of tissue samples from the femoral artery during endoscopic analyses of the mummy, which showed well-formed atherosclerotic plaques.

A useful example for an accurate understanding of the interaction between imaging and histology was published by Kim et al. (2015). In April 2010, a female mummy was discovered in a tomb linked to the Joseon culture (around 1650 CE) in Mungyeong County, South Korea. The so-called Mungyeong mummy was a middle-aged woman (around 50 years), whose stature was estimated to have been 1.53

m. The body underwent CT analysis, which revealed multiple aortic calcifications within the aortic wall. The authors obtained authorisation to perform a complete autopsy, which revealed ulcerated plaques of the aorta, haemorrhage and intimal thickening, with a necrotic core. Cross-sections of the lesions were taken to make a comparison with the corresponding calcifications on the CT images. Histological examination confirmed that ulcerated atheromatous plaques with necrotic cores were evident within the thoracic and abdominal aorta. The authors also performed a complete histological study of the coronary arteries, which showed intimal thickening in the lumen of the left anterior descending coronary artery, even if no evidence of myocardial fibrosis/scarring was observed. The final results confirmed that CT images of vascular calcification can be a useful diagnostic tool in formulating an initial diagnosis of ancient atherosclerotic disease, and a guide for the pathologist during the autopsy for targeted sampling, thereby reducing invasiveness (Kim et al., 2016).

More recently, the same mummy has been studied from a genetic point of view to supplement the diagnosis of atherosclerotic cardiovascular disease (ASCVD) (Shin et al., 2017). Ancient DNA was extracted from a brain tissue sample, amplified using polymerase chain reaction and then cloned and sequenced. The authors wanted to establish whether any genetic predisposition to atherosclerosis could be detected in this seventeenth-century Joseon mummy. Some single nucleotide polymorphisms (SNPs, i.e. a variation in a single nucleotide occurring at a specific position in the genome) have proved to be major risk loci for ASCVD in modern East Asian populations. The Mungyeong mummy was homozygous for the risk alleles of seven SNPs (rs10757274, rs2383206, rs5351, rs2383207, rs10757278, rs4380028 and rs1333049) among 10 different ASCVD-related SNPs, confirming that she had a strong genetic predisposition to an increased risk of several cardio-vascular diseases, such as coronary artery disease and myocardial infarction. The Mungyeong mummy represents the only ancient evidence of atherosclerosis studied with all the scientific techniques currently available. The body was initially subjected to non-invasive imaging examination (CT) – which led to a diagnosis of atherosclerotic disease – then to macroscopic autopsy investigation, followed by histological analysis; finally, palaeogenetic analysis confirmed that the woman had a predisposition to cardiovascular disease. Currently, no investigations of the woman's diet have been accomplished.

In 2016, Gabrovsky et al. published a very detailed paper concerning the palaeo-pathology of cardiovascular diseases in South American mummies. The authors reported evidence of cardiovascular diseases in South American mummies from southern Peru and northern Chile during the Inca period (approximately 1000 BCE to 1500 CE). Radiological images were acquired prior to the autopsies, which were performed by applying techniques similar to those used in modern pathology. Thickening of the intima and a lipid deposit in the sub-intimal layer of the coronary artery were observed histologically in an adult female mummy from the Atacama Desert in Chile (Cabuza culture, 300–1000 CE).

Mild atherosclerosis, comprising cholesterol crystals in the abdominal aorta near the lumbar spine, was also detected in a 30-year-old female mummy from the Ica

Valley, Peru (*c.* 95 BCE) (Gabrovsky et al., 2016). This pathological condition, generally associated with advanced age, did not correlate with her young age. Instead, the autopsy of the mummy also focused on the study of the thyroid, an endocrine gland that secretes hormones responsible for metabolism and growth. A healthy thyroid is composed of small follicles filled with a gelatin-like substance (i.e. colloid) and scarce fibrous tissue. The mummy's thyroid instead showed two large calcified areas surrounded by a large amount of fibrous tissue, compatible with a diagnosis of goitre (enlarged thyroid gland that is not functioning properly) with hypothyroidism. Recent studies have reported that a hypothyroid state is associated with atherosclerosis and ischaemic heart diseases (Ichiki, 2010). Accelerated atherosclerosis in patients with hypothyroidism have been traditionally ascribed to an 'atherogenic lipid profile', diastolic hypertension and impaired endothelial function.

The authors noted that, compared to previous palaeoradiological investigations on large populations of mummies worldwide (Thompson et al., 2013), the incidence of atherosclerosis in Peruvian and Chilean mummies was significantly lower. Genetic predisposition is certainly one of the most important factors and is obviously not modifiable. The significant difference in the incidence of stroke in different regions of the world is explained not only by lifestyle but also by the genetic background of populations. Currently, the highest age-standardised incidence of stroke is reported in Asia, especially China (354 per 100 000 person-years), followed by eastern Europe (ranging from 200 per 100 000 person-years in Estonia to 335 per 100 000 person-years in Latvia). The lowest incidence is in central Latin America, in particular El Salvador (97 per 100 000 person-years) (GBD 2016 Stroke Collaborators, 2019).

A specific dietary habit or cultural practice is likely to have been a protective factor against the development of extensive atherosclerosis. Gabrovsky et al. believe that the cultural practice of chewing coca leaves (*Erythroxylum coca*) might have contributed to reduced cardiovascular risk. Archaeological records in northern Chile show the regular use of coca, and some mummies cited in the paper were buried with pouches containing coca since it was considered a sacred substance for ritual offerings to the gods. Its beneficial effects could be explained not only by the user's perception of reduced fatigue, but also by the reduction of overall body fat resulting from increased lipolysis and a decline in fat deposition (Favier et al., 1996). Moreover, coca plants do not contain the damaging substances found in tobacco smoke. Gabrovsky et al. (2016: 106) concluded that 'if chewing coca enhances lysis of fatty acids and facilitates prolonged physical activity, such as that associated with the rigors of farming land in a harsh environment, the lifetime cardiovascular effects of the psychostimulant might have contributed to less atherosclerosis'. Spielvogel et al. (1997) provided evidence for a significant influence of chewing coca leaves on body fluid homeostasis and cardiovascular adjustments at rest as well as during submaximal exercise in modern chronic coca users, but clear differences between the acute and chronic effects of coca use have not been elucidated. The effects of oral intake of coca are significantly different from the effects of injection, insufflation or inhalation of alkaloid cocaine. This is because a single coca leaf contains less alkaloid and absorption is limited (Jenkins et al., 1996). Cocaine abuse undoubtedly adversely

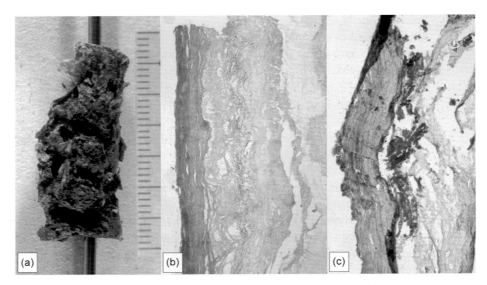

Figure 3.2 Atherosclerosis in the carotid artery of Ferrante I of Aragon. (a) Right common carotid artery: The wall is distorted but the lumen is open. (b) Histological section of the artery with foamy fatty material between the muscular layers (H&E, ×40). (c) Sub-intimal atheroma (Oil Red O, ×40). (A black and white version of this figure will appear in some formats. For the colour version, please refer to the plate section.)

affects the cardiovascular system, and numerous studies have linked it to atherosclerosis, cardiomyopathy, hypertension, aortic dissection, myocardial ischaemia and infarction, arrhythmias and strokes (Havakuk et al., 2017; Kim & Park, 2019).

Regarding evidence of atherosclerosis in Italy, Gaeta et al. (2013) reported evidence in two different historical periods. The most ancient mummy belonged to Ferrante I of Aragon (1424–1494), King of Naples and a key figure of the Italian Renaissance. He was exhumed in the monumental sacristy of the Basilica of San Domenico Maggiore in Naples (southern Italy). This mummy represents the unique histological evidence of atherosclerotic disease of the Renaissance age. Macroscopic examination showed that the right common carotid artery was calcified and had an irregular wall due to severe atherosclerosis, but the lumen was still patent (Figure 3.2a). The disease was confirmed by histological investigation since it was observed that an amorphous material (coloured intensely with Oil Red O histochemical stain) compatible with an atherosclerotic plaque was located within the well-preserved elastic wall (i.e. the artery wall) (Figure 3.2b,c). Some granular fragments of calcium were present at the periphery of the artery, with several empty spaces in the form of needle-like lacunae caused by crystals of cholesterol dissolved by routine histological methods. This complex plaque tends to ulcerate, with abundant foamy material circumferentially protruding into the lumen so that the artery becomes easily occluded. The smooth muscle of the wall appeared to have been largely replaced by fibrous tissue in the form of longitudinal stripes between the laminae. The intima was no longer present, probably because of post-mortem decay. This is a clear picture of sclerosis and elastosis (accumulation of abnormal elastic tissue), with disintegration of the elastic fibres. Furthermore, macroscopic examination showed that Ferrante was obese, despite his active lifestyle (horse-riding and hunting).

Previous studies have demonstrated that the king was affected by a mucinous (proteinaceous) adenocarcinoma infiltrating the soft tissues of his lesser (or true) pelvis (area enclosed by the pelvic girdle). DNA analysis revealed the presence of the *KRAS* codon 12 mutation, confirming that the tumour was a colorectal adenocarcinoma. Mutation of the *KRAS* gene is associated with exposure to chemical carcinogens, most likely to have been present in the diet, such as red meat and fatty foods (Marchetti et al., 1996; Ottini et al., 2011). According to contemporary historical data, the diet of the members of the Aragonese court was based on meat and wine, occasionally enriched with eggs, cheese and, on penitential occasions, fish. The consumption of vegetables was scarce, and fruit appears to have been almost totally absent from their menu. Palaeodietary analyses using carbon- and nitrogen stable isotope analysis (^{13}C and ^{15}N) performed on bone collagen from Ferrante revealed values of 11.9 parts per thousand for δ^{15}N and of –18.1 parts per thousand for δ^{13}C, indicating an intake of large quantities of meat with less marine fish (Fornaciari, 2008, 2016). Based on the historical and palaeonutritional data, it appears that the members of the elite Renaissance society were exposed to certain risk factors, namely diet and a sedentary lifestyle, for developing atherosclerosis and colorectal cancer.

Finally, evidence for severe atherosclerosis in a modern natural mummy was published in 2018. The mummy was found in the crypt of the SS. Annunziata Church inside the Medieval Hospital of Santa Maria della Scala in Siena, one of the first European examples of an orphanage and hospital. Thanks to the favourable microclimatic conditions of the crypt, a well-preserved naturally mummified male body, still wearing his original clothes, was discovered. The mummy was identified as the remains of Girolamo Macchi, who lived between 1648 and 1734 CE and worked in the Hospital as 'Archivist and Major Writer', being a sort of accountant for the hospital (Gaeta et al., 2018). The autopsy, accessed through his back to minimise the impact on the body, revealed the presence of severe and diffuse atherosclerosis in all his main arteries. The most impressive evidence affected the abdominal aorta up to the bifurcation of the common iliac arteries. Indeed, the wall of this very well-preserved 11-cm segment of the aorta was completely calcified, and the lumen appeared partially obstructed by a large atherosclerotic plaque of about 2 cm (Figure 3.3). Computed tomography showed calcification of the major arteries, in particular the femoral and popliteal arteries. Cone-beam CT of the sampled abdominal aorta led to the creation of a three-dimensional model of the artery and confirmed that the tissue had been completely substituted with hard-calcified material. Histological analysis showed that the elastic layers of the aorta wall appeared partially preserved, along with adipose tissue surrounding it. The lumen was partially stenosed due to two large calcified atherosclerotic plaques, with a central core composed of cholesterol crystals and necrotic material (Figure 3.4). Moreover, a sample obtained by cutting into the latero-cervical portion of the neck showed a

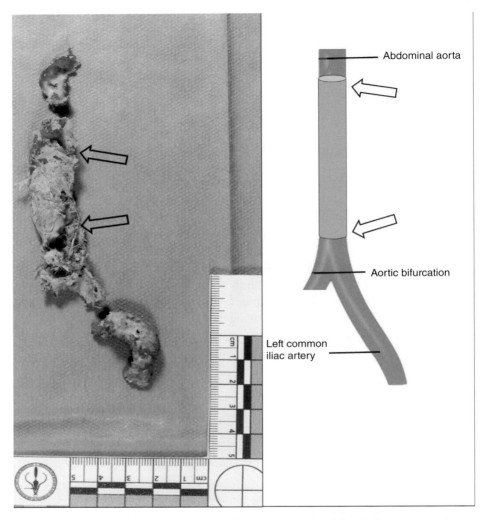

Figure 3.3 Atherosclerosis in the aorta of Girolamo Macchi. The abdominal aorta up to the bifurcation of the common iliac arteries (11 cm): The wall of this very well-preserved aorta is completely calcified, with the lumen partially obstructed by large plaques of about 2 cm in length (arrows). (A black and white version of this figure will appear in some formats. For the colour version, please refer to the plate section.)

collapsed mid-sized artery surrounded by abundant adipose tissue and striated muscular layers. The innermost layer of the artery appeared calcified for its entire circumference. Palaeonutritional data emphasised that Girolamo Macchi lived an elite life, typical of Sienese society of the seventeenth to eighteenth century, since the results of stable isotope analysis of a bone sample showed $\delta^{15}N$ values of 11.6 parts per thousand and $\delta^{13}C$ values of −18.5 parts per thousand, revealing a diet largely based on the consumption of animal protein. Our multidisciplinary approach showed that the aetiology of his extensive atherosclerotic disease was likely related to

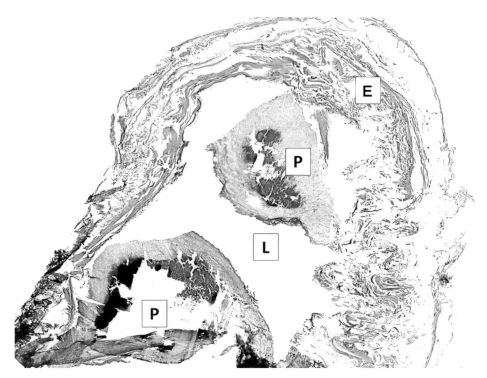

Figure 3.4 Histological section of the abdominal aorta of Girolamo Macchi: The elastic layers of the wall are partially preserved (E) along with the adipose tissue around the vessel; the lumen (L) appears partially stenotic, caused by two large calcified atherosclerotic plaques (P) with cholesterol crystals and necrotic material (H&E, ×25). (A black and white version of this figure will appear in some formats. For the colour version, please refer to the plate section.)

modifiable risk factors, such as a sedentary lifestyle with a diet rich in proteins and saturated fats, and to non-modifiable risk factors such as his advanced age (he died at 86) and being male.

3.4 Discussion

This literature review of evidence of ancient atherosclerosis in mummies confirmed by histological analysis allows some observations, although within the limits imposed by the low population size.

3.4.1 Sex

Considering the individuals whose sex has been identified (19 of 33), there is minimal higher prevalence of atherosclerosis in women (10 females; 9 males). These data are interesting since they clash with the literature on the incidence of the disease in modern society, where there is a clearly higher prevalence for men (Roger et al., 2010).

Therefore, a very interesting case is that of a 30-year-old female Chilean mummy presenting calcifications in the abdominal aorta, but with concomitant goitre and hypothyroidism that accelerate the atherosclerotic disease. Another important case is that of the female mummy Lady Tai, owing to its relatively young age (c. 50 years), although it probably showed all the comorbidities associated with atherosclerosis, including obesity, possible hypertension, diabetes and hypercholesterolaemia.

3.4.2 Age at Death

Regarding the age at death of the individuals reported, there is a clear predominance for adulthood and older ages, although the exact age of each mummy is not identified in most publications. This is because for individuals for whom we have neither biographical nor archival data, as for skeletons, we can only estimate an age range on the basis of standard anthropological methods (Jeong et al., 2008; Alterauge et al., 2017; Vasilyev et al., 2018). However, these assessments are closely linked to the state of preservation of the body, which must be as good as possible. Indeed, in some cases (14) it was not possible to even determine an age range because of the body's poor preservation. However, for two individuals (Girolamo Macchi and Ferrante I of Aragon) the numerous historical and archival data enabled the provision of an accurate biographical description. Interestingly, some evidence of atherosclerosis has been described in young adults, such as the aforementioned 30-year-old South American mummy, the mummy from Utqiagvik (c. 40 years), Pum II (35–40 years) and the Mungyeong mummy (45–50 years).

3.4.3 Geographic Origin

As shown in Table 3.2, the mummies included in this review come from most continents: Africa, Asia, Europe and North and South America. A total of 22 individuals, described in seven papers, derive from Egypt. This country frequently provides a very interesting picture of a past population because mummified bodies do not only

Table 3.2 Distribution of the evidence for ancient atherosclerosis by country.

Number of individuals	Country
22	Egypt
4	USA (Alaska)
2	Italy
2	Peru
1	Chile
1	China
1	South Korea

belong to a wealthy class; in fact the climate often preserves bodies from the lowest social group of the population. According to Abdelfattah et al. (2013), after accounting for perinatal complications and death from childhood infections, survivors into adulthood in ancient Egypt would still have a 50 per cent chance of surviving up to the age of 60, a sufficient length of life to produce atherosclerotic disease.

Only three South American mummies are included in our review (two Peruvians, one Chilean), although palaeopathological studies are numerous. In the important wide-ranging radiological investigation of several mummies from four regions of the world entitled the Horus study (Thompson et al., 2013), the authors reported that only 25 per cent of the 51 Peruvian mummies scanned had probable or definite signs of atherosclerosis, compared with 60 per cent in the Unangan (Aleutian Islands) sample, 40 per cent in the Ancestral Puebloan sample and 38 per cent in the ancient Egyptian sample. As previously described, while chronic infectious diseases are shared across all populations in antiquity (Fornaciari & Gaeta, 2014; Buzic & Giuffra, 2020; Henneberg et al., 2021), a specific diet or cultural practice might have been a factor mediating against the development of atherosclerotic disease in South America. As already noted, Gabrovsky et al. (2016) hypothesise that the practice of chewing the leaves of the coca plant might have led to beneficial cardiovascular effects in ancient South American populations; in particular it may have acted as a protective factor against plaque formation.

Finally, four North American (from Alaska and the Aleutian Islands), two Asian (one from China and one from South Korea) and two European (both Italian) mummies have been described. Obviously, the sample in the current study is considerably underestimated, and many mummies have already undergone a macroscopic or radiological diagnosis of atherosclerosis even though they lack histological confirmation, which we consider indispensable to avoid misdiagnosis due to artefacts, as previously mentioned. It should be noted that histological study is usually undertaken by pathologists, and currently few of them are involved in palaeopathological research. In addition, histological study of ancient tissues is not exactly the same as studying modern tissues. Essentially, practitioners need to have experience in both modern and ancient pathology.

3.4.4 Dating

The time range of the mummies in our review is very wide, covering a period of about 3300 years (Figure 3.5). Of the bodies for which we have dating, the oldest is from around 1580 BCE (Ruffer, 1911) but if we consider only mummies with a certain specific dating, the oldest individual is Har-Mose (Eighteenth Dynasty, 1490 BCE) (Bernard Shaw, 1938). The most recent mummy that has a precise autobiography is the Sienese Girolamo Macchi, who died in 1734 CE at the age of 86 years (Gaeta et al., 2018). Interestingly, all three South American mummies affected by atherosclerosis belong to the period before the Spanish colonisation, with the most recent dated to around 700 CE (Williams, 1927).

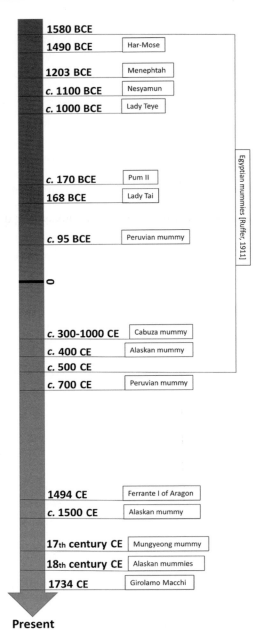

Figure 3.5 Time-frame of ancient atherosclerotic disease.

3.4.5 Affected Blood Vessels

The most affected vessel in the cases reviewed was the aorta, especially in the thoraco-abdominal tract. This has also been reported in the modern clinical literature (Davies & Hruska, 2001). Subsequently, atherosclerosis was diagnosed, in order of frequency, in the ilio-femoral and the coronary arteries, Finally, the following arteries have also been described as being affected: subclavian, common carotid, posterior peroneal, anterior tibial, posterior tibial, brachial, ulnar, radial, superior mesenteric and renal.

3.4.6 Techniques

It is now clear that for a complete and rigorous study of cardiovascular disease in antiquity the gold standard is the integration of imaging (in particular CT) with histological analysis, where possible. However, there is potential for palaeogenetics to contribute not only to phylogenetic studies (Pagès et al., 2012) and the sequencing of the gut microbiome (Santiago-Rodriguez et al., 2016), but also to the investigation of atherosclerosis itself, as already demonstrated in two studies (Zink et al., 2014; Shin et al., 2017). These currently represent the only publications that have studied this disease from a palaeogenetic point of view.

Zink et al. (2014) conducted a preliminary CT scan of the 5300-year-old Neolithic Iceman called Ötzi and highlighted major calcifications in the carotid arteries, the distal part of the aorta and the right iliac artery. These were not confirmed microscopically because of the restrictions on invasive investigations. However, the genome of this natural mummy displays several SNPs associated with cardiovascular disease in genome-wide association studies (McPherson et al., 2007; Luke et al., 2009; Roberts et al., 2013). Results show he was homozygous for the minor allele (GG) of rs10757274, located in the chromosomal 9p21 region. This polymorphism is considered among the strongest genetic predictors of myocardial infarction and has been confirmed in several studies as a major risk locus for coronary heart disease. This genetic predisposition may have contributed to the development of the arterial calcifications. The study by Shin et al. (2017) detected a genetic predisposition to atherosclerotic cardiovascular disease in the Mungyeong female mummy by analysis of SNPs using Sanger sequencing and SNaPshot techniques.

The demonstration that a genetic predisposition was also present in heterogeneous populations in the past may have important implications for the study of cardiovascular disease in current populations (Sazonova et al., 2017; Liu & Gutierrez, 2020). For example, studies could be done on large contemporary populations and compared with ancient populations (obviously extending palaeogenetic studies) to see how cardiovascular disease frequency has changed over time and whether a genetic background has affected its evolution. Despite the many complexities in the study of ancient DNA, due to various factors such as contamination, insufficiently preserved DNA and post-mortem alterations, future genetic studies of ancient populations from various geographic origins and time periods could provide a better understanding of the interaction between genes and the environment in the development of ancient atherosclerotic disease.

3.5 Conclusions

Based on this review of the histological analyses of mummies to diagnose atherosclerosis, the following summarises some final thoughts. Atherosclerosis has always been considered a disease of modern life, but we know that it is an inevitable condition of human ageing. In fact, arterial degeneration begins early in postnatal life and is progressive in all human populations, even if the severity of atherosclerosis can be delayed by lifelong avoidance of lifestyle risk factors (Wang et al., 2010). Among the modifiable risk factors, it is likely that populations in the past generally had limited access to fatty and well-seasoned food (except elite people), and had more physically active lives when compared with present populations due to a higher number of manual work activities. However, atherosclerotic disease has been identified in individuals from very different social contexts and with different standards of living (Zimmerman, 1998; Gabrovsky et al., 2016; Gaeta et al., 2018). For this reason, it is possible to speculate on the important role of infectious diseases and chronic inflammatory conditions in the development of atherosclerosis. In past populations, infections were very commonly encountered in everyday life and were one of the major causes of death (Shaw-Taylor, 2020). Bacteria on tooth surfaces are extremely numerous, and it is crucial that commensal bacteria are not overwhelmed by pathogenic strains. For example, Gram-negative bacteria have been reported to be significant predictors of coronary heart disease (Meurman et al., 2004). Some supposed mechanisms by which dental bacteria may contribute to atherosclerotic disease include the activation of innate immunity and direct involvement of mediators activated by dental plaque (Bartova et al., 2014).

For many years, bioarchaeological studies have focused on oral health, highlighting that past populations experienced different rates of oral disease as a result of diet, poor oral hygiene or the use of the teeth as a 'third hand' (Molnar, 2011; Krueger et al., 2019). Caries, for example, is a very old disease. It has been reported in several lineages of fossil hominins, such as *Homo habilis, H. erectus, H. heidelbergensis* and *H. neanderthalensis* (Lanfranco & Eggers, 2012). It also follows that an increased carbohydrate intake in human history occurred from the advent of agriculture to more recent dietary changes during the Industrial Revolution (Carrera-Bastos et al., 2011; Adler et al., 2013). Even if mechanisms involved in the association between dental caries and cardiovascular diseases are still unclear, it is hypothesised that severe dental caries may cause a chronic inflammatory response in coronary endothelial cells through bacterial invasion from carious teeth (Kim et al., 2019). Therefore, inflammation associated with a lack of oral hygiene (dental plaque and periodontal disease) is most likely to have played a part in the development of atherosclerotic disease (Haynes & Stanford, 2003; Bale et al., 2017; Mahalakshmi et al., 2017). For this reason, it would be interesting to investigate dental disease in mummies with atherosclerosis and analyse the oral microbiome encapsulated in dental calculus (Warinner et al., 2015; Neukamm et al., 2020).

Imaging as an initial diagnostic tool for the study of ancient atherosclerosis is essential. In some cases, invasive techniques such as those used in dissection or for sampling for histological analysis, cannot be performed on mummies owing to their high historical value or museum regulations. Therefore, CT could be the only option remaining for researchers seeking to diagnose atherosclerosis non-invasively. This approach, however, only detects plaques that have already been calcified, and histological examination is required to detect the early stages of the disease. Moreover, given the post-mortem changes observed in the vessel walls of a mummy, it is important to obtain histological samples in order to confirm the diagnosis of an atherosclerotic plaque.

Exposure to toxins (e.g. tobacco) and a modern lifestyle, characterised by inactivity and the intake of many calories, sugar and fats, have been shown to be responsible for the marked increase in cardiovascular disease in the twenty-first century (Boehme et al., 2017; Kopp, 2019). As described above, an alternative cause of atherosclerosis could be chronic microbial inflammation due to a lack of effective oral hygiene, periodontal diseases, the presence of poverty, and the absence of access to antibiotic and anti-inflammatory drugs, all of which might be expected in ancient populations. However, although the severity and speed of development of atherosclerosis now depend on environmental and dietary factors, humans may have a physiological genetic predisposition to atherosclerosis. For this reason, palaeogenetic study, which in recent years has been shown to be a reliable tool of research in palaeopathology, will be increasingly crucial in studying ancient cardiovascular disease. To date, only two mummies (Ötzi and Mungyeong; see previous sections) have been investigated for signs of genetic predisposition to developing atherosclerosis. Instead, a study on the role of bacteria or parasites as leading factors in the aetiology of atherosclerosis has not yet been published.

For these reasons, it is hopeful that in the future there will be an increase in multidisciplinary studies (imaging, histology and genetics) in order to further understand the mechanism underlying the onset and development of ancient and modern cardiovascular diseases.

References

Abdelfattah, A., Allam, A. H., Wann, S., et al. (2013). Atherosclerotic cardiovascular disease in Egyptian women: 1570 BCE–2011 CE. *International Journal of Cardiology*, 167, 570–4.

Adler, C. J., Dobney, K., Weyrich, L. S., et al. (2013). Sequencing ancient calcified dental plaque shows changes in oral microbiota with dietary shifts of the Neolithic and Industrial revolutions. *Nature Genetics*, 45(4), 450–5.

Alterauge, A., Kellinghaus, M., Jackowski, C., et al. (2017). The Sommersdorf mummies: An interdisciplinary investigation on human remains from a seventeenth–nineteenth century aristocratic crypt in southern Germany. *PLoS One*, 12(8), e0183588.

Aufderheide, A. C. (2011). *The Scientific Study of Mummies*. Cambridge: Cambridge University Press.

Bale, B. F., Doneen, A. L. and Vigerust, D. J. (2017). High-risk periodontal pathogens contribute to the pathogenesis of atherosclerosis. *Postgraduate Medical Journal*, 93(1098), 215–20.

Bartova, J., Sommerova, P., Lyuya-Mi, Y., et al. (2014). Periodontitis as a risk factor of atherosclerosis. *Journal of Immunology Research*, 2014, 636893.

Bernard Shaw, A. F. (1938). A histological study of the mummy of Har-Mose, the singer of the eighteenth dynasty (circa 1490 B.C.). *Journal of Pathology and Bacteriology,* 47(1), 115–23.

Boehme, A. K., Esenwa, C. and Elkind, M. S. (2017). Stroke risk factors, genetics, and prevention. *Circulation Research*, 120(3), 472–95.

Buzic, I. and Giuffra, V. (2020). The paleopathological evidence on the origins of human tuberculosis: a review. *Journal of Preventive Medicine and Hygiene* 61(1 Suppl 1), E3–E8.

Campbell, L. A. and Rosenfeld, M. E. (2015). Infection and atherosclerosis development. *Archives of Medical Research*, 46(5), 339–50.

Carrera-Bastos, P., Fontes-Villalba, M., O'Keefe, J. H., Lindeberg, S. and Cordain, L. (2011). The western diet and lifestyle and diseases of civilization. *Research Reports in Clinical Cardiology*, 2(2), 2–15.

Charlier, P., Wils, P., Froment, A. and Huynh-Charlier, I. (2014). Arterial calcifications from mummified materials: Use of micro-CT-scan for histological differential diagnosis. *Forensic Science, Medicine and Pathology*, 10(3), 461–5.

Cheng, T. O. (1996). Arteriosclerosis is not a modern disease. *Texas Heart Institute Journal*, 23(4), 315.

Cockburn, A., Barraco, R. A., Reyman, T. A. and Peck, W. H. (1975). Autopsy of an Egyptian mummy. *Science*, 187(4182), 1155–60.

Czermak, J. (1852). Description and microscopic findings of two Egyptian mummies. *Meeting of the Academy of Science (Beschreibung und mikrosko- pische Untersuchung Zweier Agyptischer Mumien, S B Akad Wiss Wien)*, 9, 27–69.

David, A. R., Kershaw, A. and Heagerty, A. (2010). Atherosclerosis and diet in ancient Egypt. *Lancet*, 375 (9716), 718–19.

Davies, M. R. and Hruska, K. A. (2001). Pathophysiological mechanisms of vascular calcification in end-stage renal disease. *Kidney International*, 60(2), 472–9.

Ding, K. and Kullo, I. (2009). Evolutionary genetics of coronary heart disease. *Circulation*, 119, 459–67.

Elliot Smith, G. (1912). *The Royal Mummies*. Cairo, Egypt: Institut Français d'Archéologie Orientale.

Farzan, S. F., Habre, R., Danza, P., et al. (2021). Childhood traffic-related air pollution and adverse changes in subclinical atherosclerosis measures from childhood to adulthood. *Environmental Health*, 20(1), 44.

Favier, R., Caceres, E., Koubi, H., et al. (1996). Effects of coca chewing on metabolic and hormonal changes during prolonged submaximal exercise. *Journal of Applied Physiology*, 80, 650–5.

Feigin, V. L., Lawes, C. C. M., Bennett, D. A., Barker-Collo, S. L. and Parag, V. (2009). Worldwide stroke incidence and early case fatality reported in 56 population-based studies: A systematic review. *Lancet Neurology*, 8, 355–69.

Fornaciari, G. (2008). Food and disease at the Renaissance courts of Naples and Florence: A paleonutritional study. *Appetite*, 51, 10–14.

Fornaciari, G. (2016). 'Tu sei quello che mangi': Le economie alimentari nelle analisi isotopiche di campioni medievali e post-medievali della Toscana. In *L'Alimentazione nell'Alto Medioevo: Pratiche, simboli, ideologie*, Vol. LXIII. Spoleto, Italy: Fondazione Centro Italiano di Studi sull'Alto Medioevo Fondazione, pp. 657–70.

Fornaciari, G. and Gaeta, R. (2014). Paleoparasitology of helminths. In F. Bruschi, ed., *Helminth Infections and their Impact on Global Public Health*. Wien: Springer-Verlag, pp. 29–47.

Fulcheri, E. and Ventura, L. (2001). Rileggendo tra antiche e nuove ricette per dare freschezza ai tessuti mummificati o disseccati. *Pathologica*, 93, 700–6.

Gabrovsky, A. N., O'Neill, K. D. and Gerszten, E. (2016). Paleopathology of cardiovascular diseases in South American mummies. *International Journal of Cardiology*, 223, 101–7.

Gaeta, R., Giuffra, V. and Fornaciari, G. (2013). Atherosclerosis in the Renaissance elite: Ferdinand I King of Naples (1431–1494). *Virchows Archiv*, 462(5), 593–5.

GBD 2016 Stroke Collaborators. (2019). Global, regional, and national burden of stroke, 1990–2016: A systematic analysis for the Global Burden of Disease Study 2016. *Lancet Neurology*, 18(5), 439–58.

Gaeta, R., Fornaciari, A., Izzetti, R., Caramella, D. and Giuffra, V. (2018). Severe atherosclerosis in the natural mummy of Girolamo Macchi (1648–1734), 'major writer' of Santa Maria della Scala Hospital in Siena (Italy). *Atherosclerosis*, 280, 66–74.

Grønhøj, M. H., Gerke, O., Mickley, H., et al. (2016). Associations between calcium–phosphate metabolism and coronary artery calcification: A cross sectional study of a middle-aged general population. *Atherosclerosis*, 251, 101–8.

Hagan, R. W., Hofman, C. A., Hübner, A., et al. (2020). Comparison of extraction methods for recovering ancient microbial DNA from paleofeces. *American Journal of Physical Anthropology*, 171(2), 275–84.

Havakuk, O., Rezkalla, S. H. and Kloner, R. A. (2017). The cardiovascular effects of cocaine. *Journal of the American College of Cardiology*, 70(1), 101–13.

Haynes, W. G. and Stanford, C. (2003). Periodontal disease and atherosclerosis: From dental to arterial plaque. *Arteriosclerosis, Thrombosis and Vascular Biology*, 23(8), 1309–11.

Henneberg, M., Holloway-Kew, K. and Lucas, T. (2021). Human major infections: Tuberculosis, treponematoses, leprosy. A paleopathological perspective of their evolution. *PLoS One*, 16(2), e0243687.

Herrington, W., Lacey, B., Sherliker, P., Armitage, J. and Lewington, S. (2016). Epidemiology of atherosclerosis and the potential to reduce the global burden of atherothrombotic disease. *Circulation Research*, 118, 535–46.

Ichiki, T. (2010). Thyroid hormone and atherosclerosis. *Vascular Pharmacology*, 52(3–4), 151–6.

Insull, W. Jr (2009). The pathology of atherosclerosis: Plaque development and plaque responses to medical treatment. *American Journal of Medicine*, 122(1 Suppl), S3–S14.

Jenkins, A. J., Llosa, T., Montoya, I. and Cone, E. J. (1996). Identification and quantitation of alkaloids in coca tea. *Forensic Science International*, 77(3), 179–89.

Jeong, K. H., Kim, H. K., Yoon, C. L., Lee, S. J. and Ha, S. Y. (2008). Age estimation of mummies by dental attrition: Application of three-dimensional CT images. *Korean Journal of Pathology*, 42(5), 299–305.

Kim, K., Choi, S., Chang, J., et al. (2019). Severity of dental caries and risk of coronary heart disease in middle-aged men and women: a population-based cohort study of Korean adults, 2002–2013. *Scientific Reports*, 9(1), 10491.

Kim, M. J., Kim, Y. S., Oh, C. S., et al. (2015). Anatomical confirmation of computed tomography-based diagnosis of the atherosclerosis discovered in a seventeenth century Korean mummy. *PLoS One*, 10(3), e0119474.

Kim, S. T. and Park, T. (2019). Acute and chronic effects of cocaine on cardiovascular health. *International Journal of Molecular Sciences*, 20(3), 584.

Kojima, K., Kimura, S., Hayasaka, K., et al. (2019). Aortic plaque distribution, and association between aortic plaque and atherosclerotic risk factors: an aortic angioscopy study. *Journal of Atherosclerosis and Thrombosis*, 26(11), 997–1006.

Kopp, W. (2019). How western diet and lifestyle drive the pandemic of obesity and civilization diseases. *Diabetes, Metabolic Syndrome and Obesity: Targets and Therapy*, 12, 2221–36.

Krueger, K. L., Willman, J. C., Matthews, G. J., Hublin, J. J. and Pérez-Pérez, A. (2019). Anterior tooth-use behaviors among early modern humans and Neandertals. *PLoS One*, 14(11), e0224573.

Krupa, A., Gonciarz, W., Rusek-Wala, P., et al. (2021). *Helicobacter pylori* infection acts synergistically with a high-fat diet in the development of a proinflammatory and potentially proatherogenic endothelial cell environment in an experimental model. *International Journal of Molecular Sciences*, 22(7), 3394.

Lanfranco, L. P. and Eggers, S. (2012). Caries through time: An anthropological overview. In L. Ming-Yu, ed., *Contemporary Approach to Dental Caries*. London: IntechOpen, pp. 3–34.

Leone, O., Corsini, A., Pacini, D., et al. (2020). The complex interplay among atherosclerosis, inflammation, and degeneration in ascending thoracic aortic aneurysms. *Journal of Thoracic and Cardiovascular Surgery* 160(6), 1434–43.e6.

Liu, M. and Gutierrez, J. (2020). Genetic risk factors of intracranial atherosclerosis. *Current Atherosclerosis Reports*, 22(4), 13.

Long, A. R. (1931). Cardiovascular renal disease: Report of a case of 3000 years ago. *Archives of Pathology*, 12, 92–4.

Luke, M. M., Lalouschek, W., Rowland, C. M., et al. (2009). Polymorphisms associated with both non-cardioembolic stroke and coronary heart disease: Vienna Stroke Registry. *Cerebrovascular Diseases*, 28 (5), 499–504.

McPherson, R., Pertsemlidis, A., Kavaslar, N., et al. (2007). A common allele on chromosome 9 associated with coronary heart disease. *Science*, 316(5830), 1488–91.

Mahalakshmi, K., Krishnan, P. and Arumugam, S. B. (2017). Association of periodontopathic anaerobic bacterial co-occurrence to atherosclerosis: A cross-sectional study. *Anaerobe*, 44, 66–72.

Marchetti, A., Pellegrini, S., Bevilacqua, G. and Fornaciari, G. (1996). K-RAS mutation in the tumour of Ferrante I of Aragon, King of Naples. *Lancet*, 347, 1272.

Meurman, J. H., Sanz, M. and Janket, S. J. (2004). Oral health, atherosclerosis, and cardiovascular disease. *Critical Reviews in Oral Biology and Medicine*, 15(6), 403–13.

Molnar, P. (2011). Extramasticatory dental wear reflecting habitual behavior and health in past populations. *Clinical Oral Investigations*, 15(5), 681–9.

Neukamm, J., Pfrengle, S., Molak, M., et al. (2020). 2000-year-old pathogen genomes reconstructed from metagenomic analysis of Egyptian mummified individuals. *BMC Biology*, 18, 108.

Novelli, G., Predazzi, I. M., Mango, R., Romeo, F. and Mehta, J. L. (2010). Role of genomics in cardiovascular medicine. *World Journal of Cardiology*, 2(12), 428–36.

Ottini, L., Falchetti, M., Marinozzi, S., Angeletti, L. and Fornaciari, G. (2011). Gene–environment interactions in the pre-Industrial era: The cancer of King Ferrante I of Aragon (1431–1494). *Human Pathology*, 42, 332–9.

Pagès, M., Chevret, P., Gros-Balthazard, M., et al. (2012). Paleogenetic analyses reveal unsuspected phylogenetic affinities between mice and the extinct *Malpaisomys insularis*, an endemic rodent of the Canaries. *PLoS One*, 7(2), e31123.

Palit, S. and Kendrick, J. (2014). Vascular calcification in chronic kidney disease: Role of disordered mineral metabolism. *Current Pharmaceutical Design*, 20(37), 5829–33.

Peng, L. X. and Wu, Z. B. (1998). China: The Mawangtui-type cadavers in China. In A. Cockburn, E. Cockurn and T. A. Reyman, eds., *Mummies, Diseases and Ancient Cultures*, 2nd ed. Cambridge: Cambridge University Press, pp. 328–35.

Pinhasi, R., Fernandes, D. M., Sirak, K. and Cheronet, O. (2019). Isolating the human cochlea to generate bone powder for ancient DNA analysis. *Nature Protocols*, 14(4), 1194–205.

Poznyak, A. V., Wu, W.-K., Melnichenko, A. A., et al. (2020). Signaling pathways and key genes involved in regulation of foam cell formation in atherosclerosis. *Cells*, 9(3), 584.

Rafieian-Kopaei, M., Setorki, M., Doudi, M., Baradaran, A. and Nasri, H. (2014). Atherosclerosis: Process, indicators, risk factors and new hopes. *International Journal of Preventive Medicine*, 5(8), 927–46.

Relucenti, M., Heyn, R., Petruzziello, L., et al. (2010). Detecting microcalcifications in atherosclerotic plaques by a simple trichromic staining method for epoxy embedded carotid endarterectomies. *European Journal of Histochemistry*, 54(3), e33.

Roberts, R., Marian, A. J., Dandona, S. and Stewart, A. F. (2013). Genomics in cardiovascular disease. *Journal of the American College of Cardiology*, 61, 2029–37.

Roberts, W. C. (1992). Atherosclerotic risk factors: Are there ten, or is there only one? *Atherosclerosis*, 97 (Suppl), S5–S9.

Roger, V. L., Go, A. S., Lloyd-Jones, D. M., et al. (2010). Heart disease and stroke statistics – 2011 update: A report from the American Heart Association. *Circulation*, 123(4), e18–e209.

Ruffer, M. A. (1911). On arterial lesions found in Egyptian mummies (1580 B.C.–525 A.D.). *Journal of Pathology and Bacteriology*, 15, 453–62.

Sandison, A. T. (1955). The histological examination of mummified material. *Stain Technology*, 30, 277–83.

Santiago-Rodriguez, T. M., Fornaciari, G., Luciani, S., et al. (2016). Taxonomic and predicted metabolic profiles of the human gut microbiome in pre-Columbian mummies. *FEMS Microbiology Ecology*, 92 (11), fiw182.

Sazonova, M. A., Ryzhkova, A. I., Sinyov, V. V., et al. (2017). New markers of atherosclerosis: A threshold level of heteroplasmy in mtDNA mutations. *Vessel Plus*, 1, 182–91.

Shattock, S. G. (1909). A report upon the pathological condition of the aorta of King Menephtah, traditionally regarded as the Pharaoh of the Exodus. *Proceedings of the Royal Society of Medicine*, 2 (Pathol Sect), 122–7.

Shaw-Taylor, L. (2020). An introduction to the history of infectious diseases, epidemics and the early phases of the long-run decline in mortality. *Economic History Review*, 73(3), E1–E19.

Shin, D. H., Oh, C. S., Hong, J. H., et al. (2017). Paleogenetic study on the seventeenth century Korean mummy with atherosclerotic cardiovascular disease. *PLoS One*, 12(8), e0183098.

Slijkhuis, W., Mali, W. and Appelman, Y. (2009). A historical perspective towards a non-invasive treatment for patients with atherosclerosis. *Netherlands Heart Journal*, 17(4), 140–4.

Spielvogel, H., Rodriguez, A., Sempore, B., et al. (1997). Body fluid homeostasis and cardiovascular adjustments during submaximal exercise: Influence of chewing coca leaves. *European Journal of Applied Physiology and Occupational Physiology*, 75(5), 400–6.

te Boekhorst, B. C., Bovens, S. M., Hellings, W. E., et al. (2011). Molecular MRI of murine atherosclerotic plaque targeting NGAL: A protein associated with unstable human plaque characteristics. *Cardiovascular Research*, 89(3), 680–8.

Thompson, R. C., Allam, A. H., Lombardi, G. P., et al. (2013). Atherosclerosis across 4000 years of human history: The Horus study of four ancient populations. *Lancet*, 381(9873), 1211–22.

Vasilyev, S. V., Galeev, R. M., Borutskaya, S. B., Yatsishina, E. B. and Kovalchuk, M. V. (2018). Anthropological study of the ancient Egyptian mummy based on the computed tomography method. *Anthropology*, 6, 203.

Ventura, L., Gaeta, R., Zampa, V., et al. (2020). Enostosis, hyperostosis corticalis generalisata and possible overlap syndrome in a 7000 years old mummy from Libya. *European Journal of Radiology*, 130, 109183.

Virmani, R., Kolodgie, F. D., Burke, A. P., Farb, A. and Schwartz, S. M. (2000). Lessons from sudden coronary death: A comprehensive morphological classification scheme for atherosclerotic lesions. *Arteriosclerosis, Thrombosis and Vascular Biology*, 20, 1262–75.

Wang, M., Monticone, R. E. and Lakatta, E. G. (2010). Arterial aging: A journey into subclinical arterial disease. *Current Opinion in Nephrology and Hypertension*, 19(2), 201–7.

Warinner, C., Speller, C. and Collins, M. J. (2015). A new era in palaeomicrobiology: Prospects for ancient dental calculus as a long-term record of the human oral microbiome. *Philosophical Transactions of the Royal Society B, Biological Sciences*, 370(1660), 20130376.

Williams, H. U. (1927). Gross and microscopic anatomy of two Peruvian mummies. *Archives of Pathology and Laboratory Medicine*, 4, 26–33.

Woolfson, R. G. (2001). Renal failure in atherosclerotic renovascular disease: Pathogenesis, diagnosis, and intervention. *Postgraduate Medical Journal*, 77, 68–74.

Yusuf, S. and McKee, M. (2014). Documenting the global burden of cardiovascular disease: A major achievement but still a work in progress. *Circulation*, 129(14), 1459–62.

Zimmerman, M. R. (1998). Alaskan and Aleutian mummies. In A. Cockburn, E. Cockurn and T. A. Reyman, eds., *Mummies, Diseases and Ancient Cultures*, 2nd ed. Cambridge: Cambridge University Press, pp. 138–53.

Zimmerman, M. R. and Aufderheide, A. C. (1984). The frozen family of Utqiagvik: The autopsy findings. *Arctic Anthropology*, 21, 53–64.

Zimmerman, M. R. and Smith, G. S. (1975). A probable case of accidental inhumation of 1,600 years ago. *Bulletin of the New York Academy of Medicine*, 51, 828–37.

Zimmerman, M. R., Yeatman, G. W., Sprinz, H. and Titterington W. P. (1971). Examination of an Aleutian mummy. *Bulletin of the New York Academy of Medicine*, 47(1), 80–103.

Zimmerman, M. R., Trinkaus, E., LeMay, M., et al. (1981). The paleopathology of an Aleutian mummy. *Archives of Pathology and Laboratory Medicine*, 105, 638–41.

Zink, A., Wann, L. S., Thompson, R. C., et al. (2014). Genomic correlates of atherosclerosis in ancient humans. *Global Heart*, 9(2), 203–9.

4 Computed Tomography Evidence of Atherosclerosis in Ancient Mummies

The Horus Studies of Mummies from Five Continents

Randall C. Thompson, Ashna Mahadev, M. Linda Sutherland and Gregory S. Thomas[*]

4.1 Introduction

Following the century-old landmark work by bacteriologist and experimental pathologist Sir Marc Armand Ruffer, who demonstrated the presence of atherosclerosis during autopsies of multiple Egyptian mummies (Ruffer, 1911), an international multidisciplinary group of physicians and scientists (the Horus Team, named for the Egyptian deity; Finch, 2011.) formed to evaluate the existence, extent and aetiology of atherosclerosis in ancient peoples. The Horus Team first described atherosclerotic calcifications on computed tomography (CT) scans in 2009 (Allam et al., 2009). The study was subsequently enlarged to include a total of 52 Egyptian mummies for the study 'Atherosclerosis in ancient Egyptian mummies' published in 2011 (Allam et al., 2011). This chapter describes the bioarchaeology findings of the Horus and other teams and explores potential causes of atherosclerosis. It concludes with a discussion of the implications for modern-day persons.

4.2 Material and Methods

The Horus Team CT scanned 52 mummies from the Museum of Egyptian Antiquities in Cairo, Egypt, systematically reviewing the images for signs of atherosclerosis. (For dating and sites, see Allam et al., 2009, 2011). While none of the 52 mummies were pharaohs, the Egyptologists on the team could often determine their social position and name through Museum record review and hieroglyphic inscriptions on the outer casings and coffins. Age and sex were estimated from the CT scans by biological anthropologist Muhammad Al-Tohamy Soliman of the National Research Centre of Egypt. He estimated age at death by an integrative assessment of the architectural changes of the clavicle, humerus and femur (Walker & Lovejoy, 1985; Buikstra &

---

[*] For the Horus Study Team. Horus Study Team Members (past and present): Adel H. Allam, Ibrahim Badr, Emily M. Clarke, Caleb E. Finch, Klaus O. Fritsch, Bruno Frohlich, Samantha I. King, Guido P. Lombardi, Gomaa Abd el-Maksoud, David E. Michalik, Michael I. Miyamoto, Jagat Narula, Francis M. Neunuebel, Abd el-Halim Nur el-Din (deceased), Sean J. Reardon, Chris J. Rowan, Muhammad Al-Tohamy Soliman, James D. Sutherland, Ian G. Thomas, Adam M. Thompson and L. Samuel Wann.

Ubelaker, 1994). If all of these bones were available, and each method resulted in the same age, he estimated a specific age. If only two of three methods were concordant, he estimated an age range. If bones were available for only two methods and were concordant, he also provided an age range. If only two methods were applicable and were discordant, he provided a larger age range. In retrospect, given the inherent imprecision of the method of measurement, larger age ranges may have been more appropriate.

The group consists of 33 males and 17 females, with two undetermined prepubescent mummies, neither of whom could be sexed using soft tissues. Seven experienced cardiologists and radiologists (A.H.A., M.I.M., J.D.S., M.L.S., G.S.T., R.C.T. and L.S.W.) reviewed the images and determined that 43 (83 per cent) of the 52 had identifiable vascular tissue and one had identifiable coronary arteries. Thus, 44 were used to evaluate the presence or absence of atherosclerotic plaques. The team defined definite atherosclerosis as calcification in the wall of a clearly identifiable artery, while calcification along the expected arterial course of a vessel was classified as probable atherosclerosis (see Allam et al., 2011). There were 25 mummies whose social status could be identified (see Allam et al., 2009, 2011).

4.3   Results

Of the 44 mummies, 12 were determined to have definite atherosclerosis and eight were determined to have probable atherosclerosis. In modern times, atherosclerosis is a disease that has increasing frequency with age (Tota-Maharaj et al., 2012). Although estimating age at the time of death from CT images of mummified skeletal remains has certain limitations (see below and Chapter 6), logistic regression analysis found the relative risk of having atherosclerosis at the time of death increased by 10 per cent per year of advancing age. Sex was not a significant factor in the frequency of atherosclerosis. (See further discussion of this issue below.)

The aorta was the most common site of atherosclerosis (32%) followed by the peripheral vessels (30%), and the carotid (18%), iliac (14%) and coronary (7%) arteries (Allam et al., 2011). One mummy was found to have calcifications in all five of these vascular beds (Figure 4.1). The mummy is that of Princess Ahmose-Meryet-Amon, who lived *c.* 1580–1550 BCE (Seventeenth Dynasty), during the Second Intermediate Period, and is thought to have died in her forties based on CT inspection of her skeletal remains. Princess Ahmose-Meryet-Amon is the earliest documented case of coronary artery disease and thus represents the most ancient human to be diagnosed with this disease (Allam et al., 2011; Finch, 2012; Clarke et al., 2013). Although royal mummies were not otherwise included in those selected to undergo CT scanning, the identity of Ahmose-Meryet-Amon as a Princess was discovered after she was imaged.

Of the 25 mummies in whom social status could be determined, 10 were priests or priestesses. Mummies with visible vascular tissue spanned all eras, with no obvious definitive predictors of atherosclerosis observed between each era. Allam et al. (2011) concluded that atherosclerosis was not more prevalent in any particular period. In view of the expense of the mummification process, they are all very likely to have

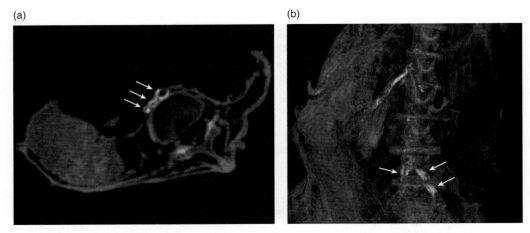

Figure 4.1 Atherosclerotic calcifications in the common iliac arteries on an axial view (a) and colorised three-dimensional volume coronal view (b) in the Egyptian mummy Ahmose-Meryet-Amon, a Princess who lived during the Second Intermediate Period (c. 1580–1550 BCE). (A black and white version of this figure will appear in some formats. For the colour version, please refer to the plate section.)

been from the upper classes of Egyptian society, and the findings presented do not offer an insight into the prevalence of atherosclerosis in the broader population. Subsequent CT scanning of individuals from other cultures have, nonetheless, found atherosclerotic lesions in the mummies of non-elite persons.

4.4 Discussion

Following these studies, the Horus team continued to image mummies, including 51 mummies in Peru, as well as collaborate with other investigators who had imaged Egyptian and non-Egyptian mummies. These results were published as a compendium of 137 mummies who had lived over a 4000-year period in four different ancient cultures (Thompson et al., 2013). The team found a similar frequency of atherosclerosis to that found in the Egyptian mummies in the studies described above. The compendium included CT scans of mummies from ancient Egypt ($n = 76$), ancient Peru ($n = 51$), ancestral Puebloans from what is currently the southwestern United States ($n = 5$) and the Unangans of the Aleutian Islands ($n = 5$). As in the earlier Horus studies (Allam et al., 2009, 2011), the same physicians reviewed the images for the presence or absence of arterial calcification.

Of the 121 mummies in which sex could be determined, including those described here, 44 were female and 77 male. Acknowledging the challenges of estimating age of death by CT imaging, the estimated mean age at death was approximately 36 years and did not differ significantly between men and women. Definite and probable atherosclerosis were observed in 25 and 22, respectively, yielding a combined total of 47 (34 per cent) of the 137 mummies with atherosclerosis among the four populations. Atherosclerotic calcifications were seen to varying degrees in five arterial

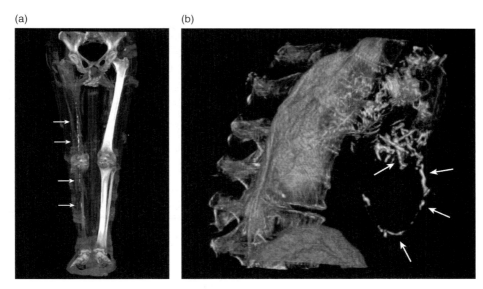

Figure 4.2 (a) Calcific atherosclerotic lesions (arrows) in the leg arteries of the Egyptian mummy of Hataiy, a scribe from the Eighteenth Dynasty (c. 1550–1295 BCE), coronal view, thick slab, right leg bones digitally removed. (b) Heavy coronary artery calcifications in a female Unangan, Aleutian Island mummy, three-dimensional reconstruction, sagittal view. (A black and white version of this figure will appear in some formats. For the colour version, please refer to the plate section.)

vascular beds: the aorta and the iliofemoral, popliteal/tibial,, carotid and coronary arteries. As previously observed, the aorta was the most frequent site, involved in 28 (20%) of the mummies. The iliofemoral and popliteal/tibial arteries were each affected in 25 (18%) of the mummies, with the carotid arteries involved in 17 (12%) and the coronary arteries in 6 (4%). Using an ordinal logistic regression model, increased age directly correlated with atherosclerosis severity (based on the number of involved vascular beds), with an increase in severity of 69 per cent per advancing decade of life (Thompson et al., 2013). Two mummies displayed particularly frequent atherosclerotic calcifications: an Egyptian scribe from the Eighteenth Dynasty who had substantial involvement of the carotid bifurcations and the arteries of the legs (Figure 4.2a) and a late nineteenth-century Unangan woman thought to be in her forties to fifties with heavy coronary artery calcifications (Figure 4.2b) (Thompson et al., 2013). These findings are consistent and demonstrate that atherosclerosis was common across four separate geographical regions spanning numerous time periods.

While the Egyptian mummies are from the elite and would have had access to domesticated animals and some may have had a diet rich in animal fat (David et al., 2010), ancient Peruvians relied predominantly on farming and fishing and had limited access to food derived from domesticated animals (Moseley, 2001; Horkheimer, 2004). Similarly, the ancestral Puebloans were forager-farmers (Downum, 2012) and the Unangans of the Aleutian Islands were true hunter-gatherers without any access to farming or domesticated animals (Jochelson, 1933; Houk, 2010; Frohlich et al., 2002).

Nonetheless, atherosclerosis seems to have afflicted people from all four groups regardless of social standing and not only those with sedentary wealthy elite lifestyles and diets that may have been rich in animal fat (Thompson et al., 2013).

The diet and lifestyles of these four populations appear to have varied greatly. As mentioned above, Unangans were hunter-gatherers, the Puebloans forager-farmers, and ancient Egyptians and Peruvians farmed and domesticated livestock. Thus, protein sources in their diets differed, as did the indigenous edible plants native to each region, which were dependent on the local environments. Ancient Egyptian people had domesticated animals while the Unangan hunter-gatherers relied on marine life including seals, whales, sea urchin and shellfish (Hrdlicka, 1945; Frohlich et al., 2002). Table 4.1 summarises the diets and lifestyles of these four pre-industrial populations. Despite many disparities in food sources and physical lifestyle, atherosclerosis was observed in individuals from all four populations (Thompson et al., 2013). Once again, these data lend support to the theory that atherosclerotic changes are linked to natural ageing and are not just a modern phenomenon. Rather, it is a condition that has existed for thousands of years across the globe (Figure 4.3).

4.4.1 Other Mummies with CT Evidence of Atherosclerosis

More recently, the Horus team has reviewed additional mummies, identifying atherosclerosis in Mongolians living in the fifteenth century (Thompson et al., 2014). Using the techniques of the Horus team or adopting new ones, other research groups have reported atherosclerosis in mummies from Korea and Europe by CT scanning and/or histological analysis (Gaeta et al., 2013; Piombino-Mascali et al., 2014; Kim et al., 2015; Shin et al., 2017; Gaeta et al., 2019). The most ancient mummy with CT scan evidence of atherosclerosis is the ice mummy found in the Tyrolean Alps (near the modern Austrian–Italian border) known as Ötzi, who lived approximately 5300 years ago. These studies from numerous investigators confirm that atherosclerosis has been present and may well have been ubiquitous across much of human history.

4.4.2 Evidence That the CT Findings Represent Atherosclerosis

In the field of palaeopathology, experts have learned to be circumspect as apparent abnormalities identified are sometimes later determined to be taphonomic or related to post-mortem processes. While atherosclerosis begins as a non-calcified plaque (lesion) in the arterial wall, as a plaque matures calcium hydroxyapatite is deposited in the plaque and its presence in an artery is pathognomonic (diagnostic) of atherosclerosis (Agatston et al., 1990; Stary et al., 1995). In mummies, CT scans can reveal dense calcium deposits identical to the atherosclerotic deposits seen in modern people, in terms of both appearance and location. These findings provide convincing evidence that the calcifications described on CT scan are indeed due to atherosclerosis. For example, the distal aorta, iliac bifurcations and the carotid arteries are

Table 4.1 Diet and lifestyle of the four cultures of the mummies studied.

	Egyptians (Ruffer, 1919; Ikram, 2010; Abdelfattah et al., 2012)	Peruvians (Moseley, 2001; Sutherland et al., 2014; Watson Jimenez, 2019)	Ancestral Puebloans (Sharrock, 1963; Daniels, 1976; Houk, 2010; Sedar, 2012)	Unangan/Aleuts (Jochelson, 1925; Hrdlicka, 1945; Laughlin, 1980; Frohlich et al., 2002)
Diet characterisation	Farmers, animal domestication	Farmers, animal domestication	Forager-farmers	Hunter-gatherers
Food examples	Farmed wheat, barley, dates, figs, olive, beans, pomegranates, radishes, onions, cucumber, lettuce, cabbage; made beer, wine	Farmed corn, potato, sweet potato, manioc, beans, bananas, hot pepper	Farmed maize (corn) and squash; collected pine nuts, seeds, amaranth, grasses	Marine (as below); collected berries; no agriculture
Protein sources	Domesticated cattle, sheep, goats, pigs, hyenas, ducks, geese; hunted quail, pheasants; fished	Domesticated alpaca, guinea pigs, ducks; hunted Andean deer and birds; collected crayfish; fished	Hunted rabbit, mice, bighorn sheep, mule deer with the Atlatl (ancient spear thrower); fished	Hunted (from kayak or baidarka) marine mammals (seal, sea lion, sea otter, whales); collected shellfish, sea urchins, eggs; fished
Landscape	Nile River within Sahara desert	Coastal desert valleys	Colorado Plateau, elevation 1524 m (5000 feet)	Volcanic islands with harsh cold, windy marine climate
Housing	Above-ground homes of mud bricks; a few elite had limestone homes	Above-ground mud homes	Subterranean single family homes (pithouses)	Subterranean homes (barabaras)
Smoke exposure	Cooked with wood or coal in yard or on roof	Those living along the coast cooked outside with wood and alpaca dung	Used fire for warmth and cooking in pithouses	Used fire for warmth and cooking in barabaras; used seal oil lamps for light in barabaras

Source: modified from Thompson et al. (2013) with permission from Elsevier.

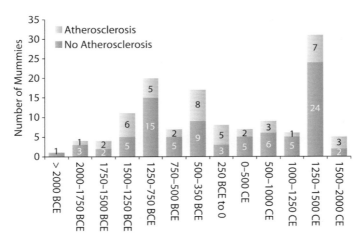

Figure 4.3 Atherosclerosis was seen in at least one mummy in each 250–500-year period over the past 4000 years. Source: modified from Thompson et al. (2013).

frequently involved in atherosclerosis in modern patients (Allam et al., 2018), the same areas where calcifications are commonly seen in the mummies.

Cardiologists and radiologists who review images from mummy CT scans concur that the pathological changes are the same as those observed in modern patients. As would be expected, the arterial calcifications are more often seen in longer-lived individuals. Autopsy results have also reported atherosclerosis, including calcific atherosclerosis, in ancient people (Ruffer, 1911; Kim et al., 2015). An autopsy of an Aleutian Island mummy found in the same cave as the Unangan/Aleut mummies reviewed by the Horus team also observed atherosclerosis (Zimmerman et al., 1981). Recently, Madjid and colleagues used a different technique, near-infrared spectroscopy, to demonstrate cholesterol-rich atherosclerotic lesions in samples obtained from Egyptian mummies (Madjid et al., 2019).

4.4.3 Cardiovascular Risk Factors in Ancient People

When comparing these data to modern atherosclerotic risk factors, certain similarities appear to exist among cultures. However, it can be difficult to accurately gauge ancient Egyptian risk factors. This is because data on the presence of conditions often linked to atherosclerosis, such as hypertension and diabetes mellitus, are unavailable. However, some dietary and lifestyle risk factors known today are evident. While it is known that tobacco was unavailable in ancient Egypt, historical records indicate that animal foods such as cattle, sheep, goat, lamb, birds, fish, as well as bread, oils, vegetables and dates were staples in their diet (see Ruffer, 1919; Darby et al., 1957; David et al., 2010). Additionally, as modern style transportation had yet to be invented, it can be inferred that ancient Egyptians lived a more active lifestyle.

Again, it is necessary to note that the lifestyle and diet of Egyptian elites likely differed from that of non-elite people of their time, leading to differing risk factors across the population.

4.4.4 The Iceman and Genetics of Atherosclerosis

In addition to remains of bodies that were mummified intentionally, either through natural or artificial means, another human who was preserved for millennia in a glacier also demonstrates that atherosclerosis was present in ancient times and offers insights into this condition. Europe's oldest mummy, named Ötzi or the Iceman, was discovered at the site of a melting glacier in 1991 in the Ötztal Alps. Despite his death long ago (c. 3300 BCE), his body was remarkably preserved in the ice. As discussed above, atherosclerotic calcifications were identified in his aorta and other vessels by CT imaging (Murphy et al., 2003).

The evaluation of the Iceman has been extensive, and much is known about his diet and lifestyle (Spindler, 1994; Zink, 2014). He does not appear to have experienced traditional risk factors for coronary artery disease in his life. The hunting gear he wore and his presence in the Alps suggests a very physically active man. Whole-genome analysis was applied to samples of his body. Several single nucleotide polymorphisms (SNPs) associated with coronary artery disease and atherosclerosis were identified (an SNP is a substitution of a single nucleotide that occurs at a specific position in the genome). He was homozygous for the minor allele rs10757274, a major SNP locus for coronary heart disease today. He was also homozygous for the minor allele rs2383206, a major coronary heart disease and ischaemic risk SNP today. His genome also harbours endothelin receptor type B, heterozygote variant rs5351, a risk factor for atherosclerosis in men today (see Keller et al., 2012). There were also SNPs in three other genes that have been associated with coronary heart disease in present-day humans (*VDR*, *TBX5* and *BDKRB1*). Thus, this uniquely detailed study provides evidence that modern-day genetic risk factors for atherosclerosis may have been relevant to the past prevalence of the disease (Murphy et al., 2003; Zink et al., 2014).

4.4.5 Non-traditional Cardiovascular Risk Factors: Infection and Inflammation

Bacterial infections and parasites were common in populations before the era of antibiotics and modern sanitation, resulting in high levels of chronic infection and inflammation among ancient peoples (Zink et al., 2003; Finch, 2012). There is also a plethora of circumstantial evidence associating infection and inflammation with the progression of cardiovascular disease in modern times (Ridker et al., 2009; Zebrack & Anderson, 2012; Schoepf et al., 2019). Thus, high levels of chronic infection and inflammation could also have promoted atherosclerosis in these ancient populations. Rheumatoid arthritis and systemic lupus erythematosus are both chronic inflammatory processes that lead to premature atherosclerosis in modern patients (Gartshteyn et al., 2019; Hansen et al., 2019; Katz et al., 2019). Acute infections such as influenza and chronic periodontal disease have also been suggested to play a role in the expression and/or manifestations of atherosclerosis (Clarke et al., 2013). An example of the infections that were likely common in ancient times is shown in the case of Nakht, an Egyptian weaver from Thebes, who died in his mid-teens around 1200 BCE. His 1974 autopsy performed at the University of Toronto, Canada was remarkable, revealing the presence of four different parasites: *Schistosoma haematobium, Tinea* species, *Trichinella spiralis* and *Plasmodium falciparum* (Clarke et al., 2013). 'If Nakht is at all representative of ancient Egyptians, and potentially other ancient cultures, a lifelong inflammatory burden analogous to modern day chronic inflammatory diseases, may represent a decisive risk factor in the development of atherosclerosis' (Clarke et al., 2013: 333).

Atherosclerosis may also have been accelerated by chronic smoke exposure from open fires used for cooking and heating (Painschab et al., 2013; Binder & Roberts, 2014). Anthracosis, the blackening and inflammation of the lung from chronic smoke exposure (Mirsadraee, 2014), is common in Egyptian and other mummies from other ancient cultures (Zimmerman et al., 1971, 1981; Montgomerie, 2012).

4.4.6 Atherosclerotic Cardiovascular Disease in Egyptian Women 1570 BCE to 2011 CE

While cardiovascular disease in the modern day afflicts men at an earlier age than women (Virani et al., 2021), the Horus team's studies did not reveal a major sex difference in ancient people, although several female mummies showed dramatic examples of atherosclerotic calcification on their CT scans. One such example is that of the famous and well-preserved Lady Rai, who shouldered significant responsibility during her life and experienced many of the stresses of managing career and family that are commonplace today (Figure 4.4; see Abdelfattah et al., 2012).

Currently curated in the Museum of Egyptian Antiquities in Cairo, Lady Rai lived from about 1570 to 1530 BCE (early Eighteenth Dynasty of the New Kingdom), and died when approximately 40–50 years of age. CT scanned in 2009, she was found to have calcified atherosclerotic plaques in her abdominal aorta, as well as evidence of a possible prior myocardial infarction (heart attack) (Figure 4.5). She was a nursemaid to queen regent Ahmose-Nefertari, caring for child Pharaoh Amenhotep I until he came of age. Her primary duties included the supervision of the household and organising Amenhotep I's activities (Abdelfattah et al., 2012).

As a member of the royal Egyptian court, Lady Rai's lifestyle was considerably more sheltered from the environmental and work-related stresses experienced by non-elite people. Additionally, she had access to a substantial nutrient-rich diet, although her probable indoor sedentary lifestyle may have increased her risk for atherosclerosis through low levels of exercise and possible exposure to smoke from cooking and heating. However, Lady Rai's role in caring for royalty may have also

Figure 4.4 Photograph of the face of the mummy of Lady Rai, 1570–1530 BCE, Cairo Museum of Antiquity. (A black and white version of this figure will appear in some formats. For the colour version, please refer to the plate section.)

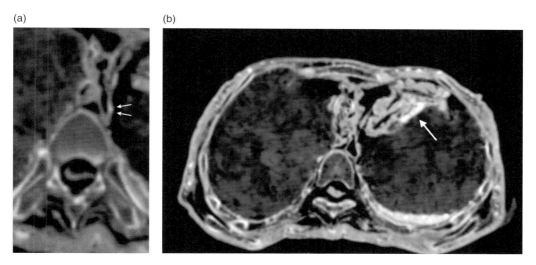

Figure 4.5 (a) Atherosclerotic calcifications on an axial CT in the aortic arch of the mummy of Lady Rai (arrows), 1570–1530 BCE. (b) Axial CT scan of the chest of Lady Rai demonstrating heavy calcification (arrow) in the area of the myocardium that could represent past myocardial infarction.

shielded her from several factors likely to have affected the length of an Egyptian's life, such as trauma, excessive physical labour, seasonal malnutrition, and periodic and lengthy famine. Although there is considerable uncertainty and such data are difficult to extrapolate, demographers believe that the likely range for average life expectancy was approximately 25–35 years throughout the ancient world (Roser et al., 2020). In addition, after taking into account common risk factors for childhood mortality, it is suggested that survivors into adulthood would have a 50 per cent chance of surviving to age 60 (Abdelfattah et al., 2012). Such estimates suggest that only a small fraction of the ancient Egyptian populations are likely to have survived to a very old age. However, there are obvious exceptions: Pharaoh Ramesses II is known to have surpassed 80 years of age, and Pepi II may have lived even longer (Clayton, 2006).

The complex progression of atherosclerosis has several contributory factors related to its aetiology, with a heterogeneous manifestation in each person (Virani et al., 2021). With regard to atherosclerosis, each person experiences a unique environment, diet, lifestyle and genetic profile. Given the numerous avenues that can lead to atherosclerosis, the preservation and study of Lady Rai's mummy serves as an important link between atherosclerosis in ancient and modern times. Women with a diet containing sufficient protein and a sheltered sedentary home life likely had the opportunity to live longer. Lady Rai, as a nursemaid and a modern 'career woman', had such a lifestyle. However, having a life with adequate nutrition and limited intense physical activity could have theoretically increased her chance of developing atherosclerosis.

4.4.7 Heart Disease in Ancient Egyptian Records

Did ancient Egyptians or ancient persons of other cultures have clinical heart or vascular disease; that is, did they develop myocardial infarction or stroke? The studies referenced above demonstrate that at least preclinical atherosclerosis was common in ancient people. Atherosclerosis was frequently present in the coronary and carotid arteries, the arteries that result in overt clinical events such as myocardial infarction and stroke, respectively. It is rarely possible, however, to determine an exact cause of death from a CT scan of an ancient body, or whether an individual suffered symptoms of heart or vascular disease. Nevertheless, archaeological excavation has uncovered evidence that suggests that clinical heart disease was indeed both present and recognised in the past.

The carved relief on the wall of the tomb of an Egyptian nobleman from the Sixth Dynasty (2625–2475 BCE) may be the oldest record of sudden death (Bruetsch, 1959). This carving from the Tomb of Sesi at Sakkara, Egypt depicts two servants busying themselves with the freshly, and apparently suddenly dead noble, while others show their grief with characteristic gestures and some try to revive the man's wife who has fainted. The actions characterised in the artwork suggest that the carvers were depicting an event of sudden death. Given the previous demonstrated presence of atherosclerosis in ancient Egypt (Ruffer, 1911), Bruetsch surmised that this sudden death may have occurred secondary to a coronary occlusion (Bruetsch, 1959). Most sudden deaths are indeed related to coronary artery disease, although ruptured cerebral aneurysms, cardiomyopathies, aortic dissections and other conditions cause a certain number of sudden deaths as well (Kuriachan et al., 2015).

Other evidence of symptomatic atherosclerosis in ancient times comes from the Ebers Papyrus, a document purchased by Georg Ebers in the winter of 1872–3. The papyrus had been found in a Theban tomb between the legs of a mummy (Von Klein, 1905). What became known as the Ebers Papyrus was written in the hieratic Egyptian script and remains one of the oldest surviving medical texts, dating to c. 1555 BCE. The Ebers Papyrus contains Egyptian remedies and incantations for countless ailments including gynaecological disorders, helminth infections, dental concerns and cardiac conditions. Regarding the symptom of chest pain, Ebbell's translation of the section of the Eber's Papyrus reads 'If thou examinist a man for illness in his cardia, and he has pains in his arms, in his breast and on one side of his cardia . . . it is death threatening him' (Ebbell & Banov, 1937). This description will be recognised by physicians today as classic symptoms of either myocardial infarction or acute angina pectoris (temporary lack of blood flow to the heart). Thus, symptomatic coronary heart disease must have been sufficiently prevalent prior to c. 1555 BCE for the writer of this section of the Ebers Papyrus to recognise the association between chest pain and near-term mortality, strong evidence that symptomatic coronary artery disease was not uncommon.

4.4.8 Limitations and Future Work

The use of CT scanning for the study of cardiovascular diseases in preserved bodies has obvious limitations. As mentioned above, it is rarely possible to determine the cause of death or whether an individual actually suffered symptoms of cardiovascular or other medical diseases. There are also known limitations to the accuracy of estimating the age at death from human remains. Despite these limitations, the Horus team continues to work to elucidate the origins of atherosclerosis and hopes that future advances will allow more accurate assessments, particularly by combining ancient DNA analysis with increasingly detailed anatomical evaluations of pathological changes.

4.5 Conclusion

Through the efforts of the Horus and other teams around the world, evidence has been uncovered confirming that atherosclerosis is not a disease simply of modern lifestyles, but a condition that has existed for many millennia. Atherosclerosis has been found in mummified remains across five different continents, spanning over 5000 years of human history. It has been noted among individuals of various periods with differing diets and lifestyles, and in men and women. The Horus and other teams have yet to find a culture that, if its individuals were mummified, does not exhibit evidence of atherosclerosis. Although risk factors such as an unhealthy diet (which promotes atherosclerosis, hypertension, hyperlipidaemia and diabetes mellitus), smoke exposure and a sedentary lifestyle influence the frequency and severity of atherosclerosis in people today, the presence of atherosclerosis in all cultures in which it has been studied suggests an inherent human predisposition for the disease. Given this predisposition, modern humans should do all they can to minimise their risk factors for atherosclerosis. This includes following a healthy diet, avoiding tobacco and minimising smoke exposure, while maintaining a low cholesterol, blood pressure and glucose as well as an active lifestyle. The presence of atherosclerosis in ancient populations, including those with a dearth of risk factors, also suggests the potential presence of novel as yet undiscovered causes of atherosclerosis.

References

Abdelfattah A., Allam, A. H., Wann, S., et al. (2012). Atherosclerotic cardiovascular disease in Egyptian women: 1570 BCE–2011 CE. *International Journal of Cardiology*, 167(2), 570–4.

Agatston, A. S, Janowitz, W. R., Hildner, F. J., et al. (1990). Quantification of coronary artery calcium using ultrafast computed tomography. *Journal of the American College of Cardiololology*, 15, 827–32.

Allam, A. H., Thompson, R. C., Wann, L. S., et al. (2009). Computed tomographic assessment of atherosclerosis in ancient Egyptian mummies. *Journal of the American Medical Association*, 302, 2091–3.

Allam, A. H., Thompson, R. C., Wann, L. S., et al. (2011). Atherosclerosis in ancient Egyptian mummies: The Horus study. *Journal of the American College of Cardiology Cardiovascular Imaging*, 4(4), 315–27.

Allam, A. H., Thompson, R. C., Eskander, M. A., et al. (2018). Is coronary calcium scoring too late? Total body arterial calcium burden in patients without known CAD and normal MPI. *Journal of Nuclear Cardiology*, 25, 1990–8.

Binder, M. and Roberts, C. A. (2014). Calcified structures associated with human skeletal remains: Possible atherosclerosis affecting the population buried at Amara West, Sudan (1300–800 BC). *International Journal of Paleopathology*, 6, 20–9.

Bruetsch, W. L. (1959). The earliest record of sudden death possibly due to atherosclerotic coronary occlusion. *Circulation*, 20, 438–41.

Buikstra, J. E. and Ubelaker, D. H. (eds.) (1994). *Standards for Data Collection from Human Skeletal Remains*. Arkansas Archaeological Survey Research Series No. 44. Fayetteville, AR: Arkansas Archaeological Survey.

Clarke, E. M., Thompson, R. C., Allam, A. H., et al. (2013). Is atherosclerosis fundamental to human aging? Lessons from ancient mummies. *Journal of Cardiology*, 63(5), 329–34.

Clayton, P. A. (2006). *Chronicle of the Pharaohs: The Reign-by-Reign Record of the Rulers and Dynasties of Ancient Egypt*. London: Thames & Hudson.

Daniels, H. S. (1976). *Adventures with the Anasazi of Falls Creek*. Durango, CO: Center for Southwest Studies.

Darby, W., Ghalioungui, P. and Grivatti, L. (1957). *Food: The Gift of Osiris*. London: Academic Press.

David, A. R., Kershaw, A. and Heagerty, A. (2010). Atheroslerosis and diet in ancient Egypt. *Lancet*, 375, 718–19.

Downum, C. E. (ed.) (2012). *Hisat'sinom: Ancient Peoples in a Land Without Water*. Santa Fe, NM: School for Advanced Research Press.

Ebbell, B. and Banov, L., Jr. (1937). *The Papyrus Ebers: The Greatest Egyptian Medical Document*. Copenhagen: Levin & Munksgaard.

Finch, C. E. (2011). Atherosclerosis is an old disease: Summary of the Ruffer Centenary Symposium, the paleocardiology of ancient Egypt, a meeting report of the Horus study team. *Experimental Gerontology*, 46(11), 843–6.

Finch, C. E. (2012). Evolution of the human lifespan, past, present, and future: Phases in the evolution of human life expectancy in relation to the inflammatory load. *Proceedings of the American Philosophical Society*, 156(1), 9–44.

Frohlich, B., Harper, A. B. and Gilbert, R. (2002). *To the Aleutians and Beyond: The Anthropology of William S. Laughlin.* Copenhagen: Department of Ethnology, National Museum of Denmark.

Gaeta, R., Giuffra, V. and Fornaciari, G. (2013). Atherosclerosis in the Renaissance elite: Ferdinand I King of Naples (1431–1494). *Virchows Archiv*, 462(5), 593–5.

Gaeta, R., Fornaciari, A., Izzetti, R., et al. (2019). Severe atherosclerosis in the natural mummy of Girolamo Macchi (1648–1734), 'major writer' of Santa Maria della Scala Hospital in Siena (Italy). *Atherosclerosis*, 280, 66–74.

Gartshteyn, Y., Braverman, G., Mahtani, S., et al. (2019). Prevalence of coronary artery calcification in young patients with SLE of predominantly Hispanic and African-American descent. *Lupus Science and Medicine*, 6(1), e000330.

Hansen, P. R., Feineis, M. and Abdulla, J. (2019). Rheumatoid arthritis patients have higher prevalence and burden of asymptomatic coronary artery disease assessed by coronary computed tomography: A systematic literature review and meta-analysis. *European Journal of Internal Medicine*, 62, 72–9.

Horkheimer, H. (2004). *Alimentación y obtención de alimentos en el Perú prehispánico.* Lima, Peru: Instituto Nacional de Cultura.

Houk, R. (2010). *Ancestral Puebloans.* Tucson, AZ: Western National Parks Association.

Hrdlicka, A. (1945). *The Aleutian and Commander Islands.* Philadelphia, PA: Wistar Institute of Anatomy and Biology.

Ikram, S. (2001). *Ancient Egypt: An Introduction.* New York: Cambridge University Press.

Jochelson, W. (1925). *Archaeological Investigations in the Aleutian Islands.* Washington, DC: Carnegie Institution of Washington.

Jochelson, W. (1933). *History, Ethnology and Anthropology of the Aleut.* Washington, DC: Carnegie Institution of Washington.

Katz, G., Smilowitz, N.R., Blazer, A. et al. (2019). Systemic lupus erythematosus and increased prevalence of atherosclerotic cardiovascular disease in hospitalized patients. *Mayo Clinic Proceedings*, 94(8), 1436–43.

Keller, A., Graefen, A., Ball, M., et al. (2012). New insights into the Tyrolean Iceman's origin and phenotype as inferred by whole-genome sequencing. *Nature Communications*, 3, 698.

Kim, M. J., Kim, Y.-S., Oh, C. S., et al. (2015). Anatomical confirmation of computed tomography-based diagnosis of the atherosclerosis discovered in seventeenth century Korean mummy. *PLoS One*, 10(3), e0119474.

Kuriachan, V. P., Sumner, G. L. and Mitchell, L. B. (2015). Sudden cardiac death. *Current Problems in Cardiology*, 40, 133–200.

Laughlin, W. S. (1980). *Aleuts: Survivors of the Bering Land Bridge.* New York: Holt, Rinehart and Winston.

Madjid, M., Safavi-Naeini, P. and Lodder, R. (2019). High prevalence of cholesterol-rich atherosclerotic lesions in ancient mummies: A near-infrared spectroscopy study. *American Heart Journal*, 216, 113–16.

Mirsadraee, M. (2014). Anthracosis of the lungs: Etiology, clinical manifestations and diagnosis: A review. *Tanaffos*, 13(4), 1–13.

Montgomerie, R. D. (2012). *The structural and elemental composition of inhaled particles in ancient Egyptian mummified lungs.* Unpublished PhD thesis, University of Manchester.

Moseley, M. E. (2001). *The Incas and Their Ancestors: The Archaeology of Peru.* New York: Thames & Hudson.

Murphy, W. A., Jr, zur Nedden, D., Gostner, P., et al. (2003). The Iceman: Discovery and imaging. *Radiology*, 226, 614–29.

Painschab, M. S., Davila-Roman, V. G., Gilman, R. H., et al. (2013). Chronic exposure to biomass fuel is associated with increased carotid artery intima–media thickness and a higher prevalence of atherosclerotic plaque. *Heart*, 99(14), 984–91.

Piombino-Mascali, D., Jankauskas, R, Tamošiūnas, A., et al. (2014). Atherosclerosis in mummified human remains from Vilnius, Lithuania (Eighteenth–nineteenth centuries AD): A computed tomographic investigation. *American Journal of Human Biology*, 26(5), 676–81.

Ridker, P. M., Danielson, E., Fonseca, F. A., et al. (2009). Reduction in C-reactive protein and LDL cholesterol and cardiovascular event rates after initiation of rosuvastatin: a prospective study of the JUPITER trial. *Lancet*, 373(9670), 1175–82.

Roser, M., Ortiz-Ospinam, E. and Ritchie, H. (2020). Life expectancy. Our World In Data. Available at https://ourworldindata.org/life-expectancy (accessed 2 January 2021).

Ruffer, M. A. (1911). On arterial lesions found in Egyptian mummies (1580 BC–535 AD). *Journal of Pathology and Bacteriology*, 16, 453–62.

Ruffer, M. A. (1919). *Food in Egypt*. Memoires présentés a l'Institut d'Egypte 1. Cairo: *French Institute of Oriental Archeology*, pp. 1–88.

Schoepf, I. C., Buechel, R. R., Kovari, H., Hammoud, D. A. and Tarr, P. E. (2019). Subclinical atherosclerosis imaging in people living with HIV. *Journal of Clinical Medicine*, 8(8), 1125.

Sedar, D. M. (2012). *Nevada's Lost City*. Charleston, SC: Arcadia Publishing.

Sharrock, F. W. (1963). *The Hazzard Collection*. Archives of Archaeology No. 23. Madison, WI: University of Wisconsin Press. Available at http://digital.library.wisc.edu/1711.dl/EcoNatRes.ArchivesArch23

Shin, D. H., Oh, C. S., Hong, J. H., et al. (2017). Paleogenetic study on the seventeenth century Korean mummy with atherosclerotic cardiovascular disease. *PLoS One*, 12(8), e0183098.

Spindler, K. (1994). The Iceman's last weeks. *Nuclear Instruments and Methods in Physics Research Section B: Beam Interactions with Materials and Atoms*, 92(1–4), 274–81.

Stary, H. C., Chandler, A. B., Dinsmore, R. E., et al. (1995). A definition of advanced types of atherosclerotic lesions and a histological classification of atherosclerosis: A report from the Committee on Vascular Lesions of the Council on Atherosclerosis. *Circulation*, 92, 1355–74.

Sutherland, M. L., Cox, S. L., Lombardi, G. P., et al. (2014). Funerary artifacts, social status, and atherosclerosis in ancient Peruvian mummy bundles. *Global Heart*, 9(2), 219–28.

Thompson, R. C., Allam, A. H., Lombardi, G. P., et al. (2013). Atherosclerosis across 4000 years of human history: The Horus study of four ancient populations. *Lancet*, 381, 1211–22.

Thompson, R. C., Allam, A. H., Zink, A., et al. (2014). CT evidence of atherosclerosis in the mummified remains of humans from around the world. *Global Heart*, 9(2), 187–96.

Tota-Maharaj, R., Blaha, M. J., McEvoy, J. W., et al. (2012). Coronary artery calcium for the prediction of mortality in young adults <45 years old and elderly adults >75 years old. *European Heart Journal*, 33 (23), 2955–62.

Virani, S. S., Alonso, A., Aparicio, H. J., et al. (2021). Heart disease and stroke statistics—2021 update: A report from the American Heart Association. *Circulation*, 143(8), e254–e743.

Von Klein, C. H. (1905). *The Medical Features of the Papyrus Ebers*. Chicago: Press of the American Medical Association.

Walker, R. A. and Lovejoy, C. O. (1985). Radiographic changes in the clavicle and proximal femur and their use in the determination of skeletal age at death. *American Journal of Physical Anthropology*, 68, 67–78.

Watson Jimenez, L. C. (2019). *Los gardos de Ancón-Perú (800d.C–1532d.C): Una perspectiva bioarqueológica de los cambios sociales en la Costa Central del Perú*. BAR International Series 2957. Oxford: BAR Publishing.

Zebrack, J. S. and Anderson, J. L. (2002). The role of inflammation and infection in the pathogenesis and evolution of coronary artery disease. *Current Cardiology Reports*, 4, 278–88.

Zimmerman, M. R., Yeatman, G. W., Sprinz, H., et al. (1971). Examination of an Aleutian mummy. *Bulletin of the New York Academy of Medicine*, 47, 80–103.

Zimmerman, M. R., Trinkaus, E., LeMay, M., et al. (1981). The paleopathology of an Aleutian mummy. *Archives of Pathology and Laboratory Medicine*, 105(12), 638–41.

Zink, A. (2014). *The World of Mummies from Ötzi to Lenin*. Barnsley, UK: Pen & Sword Books.

Zink, A. R., Sola, C., Reischl, U., et al. (2003). Characterization of *Mycobacterium tuberculosis* complex DNAs from Egyptian mummies by spoligotyping. *Journal of Clinical Microbiology*, 41(1), 359–67.

Zink, A., Wann, L.S., Thompson, R.C., et al. (2014). Genomic correlates of atherosclerosis in ancient humans. *Global Heart* 9(2), 203–9.

5 The Genetic Background of Atherosclerosis in Ancient Mummies

Albert Zink, Christina Wurst, Frank Maixner, Samuel Wann[*], Randall C. Thompson[*] and Gregory S. Thomas[*]

This chapter aims to outline current knowledge concerning the genetic background of cardiovascular disease (CVD) and its study in ancient human remains. This is demonstrated by the application of a palaeogenetic analysis to the mummy of the Tyrolean Iceman, who presented with both arterial calcifications and a strong genetic predisposition for heart disease. Further discussion highlights how the study of ancient humans can provide new insights into the genetic background of CVD and its intersection with risk factors related to lifestyle.

5.1 Palaeogenetics: Current Status, Limitations and Perspectives

Ancient DNA research, also referred to as palaeogenetics, emerged with the first studies on the retrieval of DNA from ancient human and animal remains more than 30 years ago (Higuchi et al., 1984; Pääbo, 1985). Initially, most studies on human remains focused on the detection of small DNA fragments from single individuals. Since then, the field has developed and a growing number of large-scale genome-wide studies of past human populations have been published (Skoglund et al., 2012; Mathieson et al., 2018). The application of modern sequencing technologies now allows for in-depth studies of the evolution of our species (Krause et al., 2010; Prüfer et al., 2014; Hajdinjak et al., 2018) and the molecular analysis of population dynamics and past migration patterns (Brandt et al., 2013; Sankararaman et al., 2014; Fernandes et al., 2020), as well as providing insights into past phenotypes such as those related to stature, skin and eye colour (Rasmussen et al., 2010; Cox et al., 2019). Palaeogenetic analysis also allows the detection of a wide range of pathogenic bacteria, viruses and parasites, revealing the occurrence and spread of infectious diseases such as tuberculosis, plague and malaria in ancient human populations (Zink et al., 2005; Hawass et al., 2010; Harbeck et al., 2013). In addition, advances in the application of DNA array capture and next generation sequencing (NGS) technologies have allowed full genome investigation of ancient pathogens, providing new insights into disease evolution through reconstruction of the genomes of *Yersinia pestis* and *Mycobacterium leprae* from medieval Europe (Bos et al., 2011; Schuenemann et al., 2013; Wagner et al., 2014; Keller et al., 2019) and the stomach pathogen *Helicobacter pylori* in the 5300-year-old Iceman mummy (Maixner et al., 2016).

---

[*] For the Horus Study Group.

Although the analysis of ancient DNA in mummies and skeletons has made substantial progress over the last decade, many factors affect the preservation and quality of the ancient genetic material studied. The degradation of DNA begins immediately following the death of an organism and, over time, enzymes and microorganisms cause significant DNA fragmentation. In addition, hydrolytic and oxidative processes can lead to destabilisation and miscoding of the DNA by deamination and depurination (Lindahl, 1993). Several parameters appear to have a negative impact on its preservation, particularly high temperature, ultraviolet radiation, fluctuating humidity and low pH (see Collins et al., 2002; Pääbo et al., 2004). A dry and cool climate, and rapid desiccation through mummification, may reduce ancient DNA degradation and increase its preservation. Thus despite the rapid development of palaeogenetics, the amount of endogenous DNA in ancient human tissue samples is often very low or may fall below detectable limits. Nevertheless, some studies have successfully recovered DNA from 800 000-year-old Pleistocene fauna buried in permafrost (Orlando et al., 2013) and 400 000-year-old hominin fossils from the Iberian Peninsula (Meyer et al., 2014). The risk of contamination of ancient by modern human DNA has also been a major hindrance to developments in this field and considerable efforts are made to avoid contamination (Cooper & Poinar, 2000; Hofreiter et al., 2001). Ancient DNA extraction requires the use of specially designated laboratories with physically isolated work areas that follow a workflow adapted to palaeogenetics, including specifically designed DNA extraction methods, control experiments and the exclusion of modern samples or positive controls. The latter would increase the risk of cross-contamination and the introduction of well-preserved genetic material into the ancient DNA laboratory. This contrasts with the mainly PCR-based approaches that were formerly used for ancient DNA research but which risked amplifying exogenous contaminant DNA instead of highly fragmented endogenous DNA (Pääbo et al., 2004). The widely used high-throughput sequencing technologies, including targeted enrichment strategies, now allow the reconstruction of full genomes, even from samples with mixed metagenomic information (Key et al., 2017). Furthermore, it is now possible to identify endogenous ancient sequences by analysing DNA degradation patterns that are known to accumulate over time, proving the authenticity of the ancient DNA (see Krause et al., 2010).

In 1984, DNA staining of histological samples from an Egyptian mummy was used for the first time (Pääbo, 1984). The following year, the study was extended by the extraction and amplification of a 3.4-kb DNA fragment using bacterial cloning (Pääbo, 1985). However, these findings were later attributed to modern DNA contamination, since it is highly improbable that such a fragment length derives from authentic ancient DNA (Kirsanow & Burger, 2012). In addition, early studies mainly focused on the detection of ancient DNA in single 'case studies', such as the first mitochondrial DNA analysis of the Tyrolean Iceman (Handt et al., 1994) or the PCR-based detection of *Mycobacterium tuberculosis* DNA in individual mummies from Peru, South America (Salo et al., 1994) and Egypt (Nerlich et al., 1997). In a few studies dealing with ancient pathogen DNA, a large-scale approach was used to analyse samples from several Egyptian mummies using molecular techniques such as spoligotyping and mutation analysis (Zink et al., 2003). During that time, Aufderheide and colleagues also worked on Chagas' disease in Chilean and Peruvian South American mummies that dated back to 9000 years BP (Aufderheide et al., 2004).

Early ancient DNA studies on mummies were received with considerable scepticism by parts of the scientific community. Some doubted that DNA could survive in ancient mummies from hot and dry climates such as Egypt (Marota et al., 2002). This led to a long-lasting debate (Zink & Nerlich, 2003; Gilbert et al., 2005) that was finally put to rest with the use of NGS applied to mummified remains, particularly from a hot dry climate. Keller et al. (2012) published the first and almost complete genome sequence from an ancient mummy, the 5300-year-old Tyrolean Iceman. In the following years, an increasing number of genomic studies on mummies (Gomez-Carballa et al., 2015) and the reconstruction of the genome of *M. tuberculosis* (Bos et al., 2014; Kay et al., 2015), hepatitis B virus (Kahila Bar-Gal et al., 2012; Patterson Ross et al., 2018) and *H. pylori* (Maixner et al., 2016) showed the feasibility of this approach in mummies. Finally, the publication of mitochondrial and nuclear genomic DNA from ancient Egyptian mummies (Molto et al., 2017; Schuenemann et al., 2017) clearly demonstrated that DNA can survive in mummified remains from hot climates.

5.2 Single Nucleotide Polymorphisms and Cardiovascular Disease

It is widely recognised that atherosclerotic cardiovascular disease (ASCVD) has a complex aetiology and multiple environmental risk factors that increase the potential for developing atherosclerosis, such as tobacco smoking, lack of physical activity and a high-fat diet. The influence of specific genetic regions linked to a predisposition to heart disease has long been understood and is estimated to account for 40–50 per cent of all people with the condition, even today (Myers et al., 1990, Marenberg et al., 1994). However, only through the implementation of genome-wide association studies (GWAS) has a growing number of single nucleotide polymorphisms (SNPs) been identified – substitutions of single nucleotides at specific positions in the genome associated with CVD. This work has significantly widened the spectrum of genetic factors that are related to the aetiology of ASCVD (Kessler et al., 2016). In 2007, the first GWAS identified SNPs at the chromosome 9p21 risk locus that showed a strong association with CVD (McPherson et al., 2007). In the following years, many additional SNPs were identified thanks to the formation of large GWAS consortia and major studies, including those with many thousands of participants (Samani et al., 2007; Loh et al., 2016). This led to the identification of new genetic risk variants (Erdmann et al., 2009) and additional loci associated with coronary heart disease (CHD) (Coronary Artery Disease (C4D) Genetics Consortium, 2011). Moreover, the genetic risk factors detected in earlier studies were confirmed by these large studies (Deloukas et al., 2013). In more recent studies, including an analysis of the UK Biobank (UKBB) with over 500 000 participants aged 40–69 years (Sudlow et al., 2015), the number of associated risk loci linked to CVD at a genome-wide significance level was further increased from 13 in 2009 to 163 (Erdmann et al., 2018).

Although the majority of loci could be assigned to specific pathophysiological pathways with a known influence on the development of ASCVD (e.g. lipid metabolism, blood pressure and vascular remodelling), little is known about the exact mechanisms that ultimately lead to the onset of the disease. One of the main reasons is the difficulty in understanding the function and specificity of a large number of SNPs located in non-coding regions. In addition, most of the associated loci contain several genes, hampering the detection of the causal gene. In only a few loci, such as the low-density lipoprotein receptor (*LDLR*) gene family, has a clear link between genes possibly related to ASCVD and the associated signal been demonstrated (Do et al., 2015). For the vast majority of risk loci, the responsible genes and the exact underlying pathological mechanisms remain to be uncovered through detailed and time-consuming investigations (Erdmann et al., 2018).

5.3 Atherosclerosis in Mummies

5.3.1 Radiological Evidence for Atherosclerosis in Ancient Humans

Histological and computed tomography (CT) investigations of ancient mummies have clearly shown that ASCVD has been affecting humans living in different environments and geographic regions for more than 5000 years. These include the CT scan detection of arterial calcifications in the 5300-year-old Tyrolean Iceman (Figure 5.1; Murphy et al., 2003; Gostner et al., 2011), the Horus study of four ancient populations from Egypt and North and South America spanning a period of 4000 years (Thompson et al., 2013; see also Chapter 4), Inuit mummies from Greenland

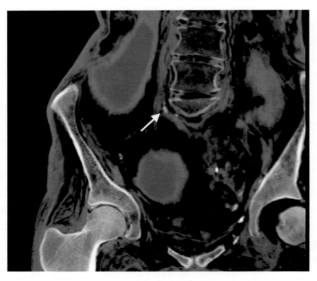

Figure 5.1 Oblique coronal CT scan image of the Tyrolean Iceman's pelvis showing a calcification in the distal abdominal aorta (arrow).

(Wann et al., 2019), naturally mummified human remains from South Korea (Kim et al., 2015) and 100-year-old mummies from crypts and churches in Europe (Piombino-Mascali et al., 2014; Gaeta et al., 2019; see also Chapter 7). The diagnosis of ASCVD in ancient mummies is usually based on the presence of arterial calcifications observed on CT scans that have the same appearance and similar Hounsfield unit densities as atherosclerotic lesions observed on scans of modern patients (Allam et al., 2009). The Hounsfield unit scale is a quantitative scale for describing radio-density on CT images, and ranges from −1000 (air) to 0 (water) to +3000 (metal). Arterial calcification is a late-stage process inherent to atherosclerosis (Stary et al., 1995) and, in mummified individuals, is found in the same locations in the body as in modern-day patients (e.g. the aortic bifurcation; Thompson et al., 2014). Observed in both intentionally and naturally mummified remains (Thompson et al., 2014), arterial calcifications are consistent in their appearance with autopsy studies of ancient Egyptian mummies performed more than 100 years ago (Ruffer, 1911). In several large-scale studies by the Horus team, the past prevalence of arterial calcification has ranged from 38 to 56 per cent of mummies with preserved cardiovascular tissue (Thompson et al., 2013).

The aorta appears to be the most affected region (32 per cent), with the coronary arteries showing fewer calcifications (9 per cent) (Allam et al., 2011). The data collected by the Horus team also showed that, as in modern studies, the presence and severity of atherosclerosis is correlated with age, although the estimated average age at death of the mummies that were studied was less than 40 years (Allam et al., 2011, Thompson et al., 2013).

5.3.2 Investigating Genetic Predisposition to Cardiovascular Disease in Ancient Humans

In order to study genetic predisposition for ASCVD in ancient humans, current approaches, mainly derived from large-scale GWAS, were adapted for ancient DNA studies. We considered the specificity of the associated SNPs, as well as the possible coverage of the SNP position in ancient genomes. As a first step, we selected a set of SNPs that have shown a clear association with CVD in clinical studies and/or GWAS investigations in modern populations (see above). Based on an extensive review of publications and studies, more than 700 SNPs were identified (see above; Erdmann et al., 2018). However, the *p*-values in different studies varied greatly, as did the association of several SNPs. Therefore, the SNPs were filtered based on a *p*-value with a genome-wide significance threshold of $p \leq 5 \times 10^{-8}$. This *p*-value was chosen as it is currently the most commonly accepted threshold in GWAS (Jannot et al., 2015). In addition, only SNPs showing a significant *p*-value in at least two independent cohorts, or newly discovered SNPs from relatively recent studies, were selected. Moreover, 11 SNPs that are only associated with CVD in Southeast Asian or Native American populations were added to the set of target SNPs for the analysis of ancient human mummies. Thereby it was considered that the SNP catalogue should be applicable in genome-wide studies of human remains from different geographic

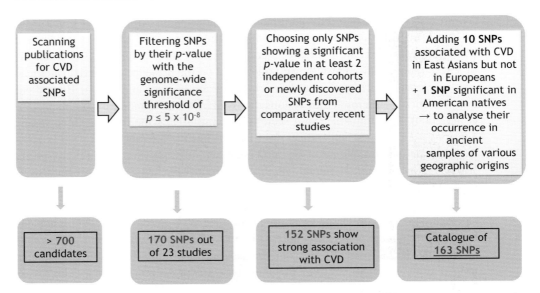

Figure 5.2 Workflow used to establish a catalogue of 163 target SNPs associated with CVD for the analysis of ancient human mummies.

origins, including mummies from Asia and the Americas. As a result, we were able to establish a catalogue of 163 strongly associated SNPs suitable for ancient DNA studies of ASCVD in mummified remains (Figure 5.2), including the Iceman (see Section 5.4).

5.4 The Tyrolean Iceman

The Iceman, commonly known as Ötzi, was found on 19 September 1991 by two German hikers 3210 m above sea level near Tisenjoch/Giogo di Tisa in the Schnalstal/Val Senales Valley in South Tyrol, Italy. His naturally mummified body is now housed at the South Tyrolean Museum of Archaeology in Bolzano, Italy, where he is on display together with his exceptionally well-preserved clothing and equipment (Figure 5.3). Initial investigations of the Iceman revealed that he lived c. 5300 years ago, died at an age of about 40–50 years and experienced several health problems (Gaber & Künzel, 1998). His body is covered with 61 tattoos divided into 19 groups of lines that are composed of two to seven linear markings arranged in parallel and in two cases form a perpendicular cross (Spindler & Osers, 1995, Samadelli et al., 2015).

Over the years, further discoveries have been made that have provided new information about his life and violent death, including analyses of the artefacts that were found with him (Barfield, 1992; Spindler, 2000). Therefore, the Iceman is likely one of the most intensively studied ancient human individuals in the world. A wide range of

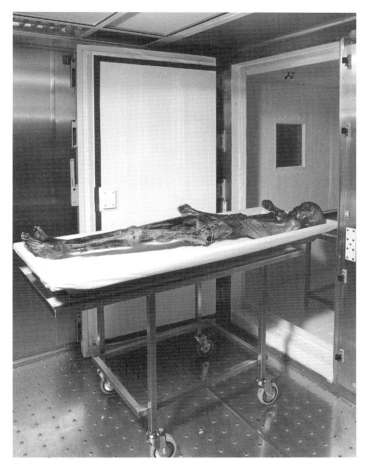

Figure 5.3 The Iceman is stored in a special cooling chamber at the South Tyrolean Museum of Archaeology. (A black and white version of this figure will appear in some formats. For the colour version, please refer to the plate section.)

methods has been applied to his body, providing detailed insights into his origin, diet, state of health and demise. Stable isotope analyses show that Ötzi grew up and most likely lived his whole life in the region of modern-day South Tyrol (Müller et al., 2003). Palaeobotanical studies, including pollen analyses, have enabled a detailed reconstruction of his last itinerary, providing information on what he ate and the possible reason behind his murder (Dickson et al., 2000; Oeggl et al., 2007). The Iceman further underwent a series of radiological investigations using CT and conventional radiography (X-ray) that revealed degenerative changes to his spine and several joints, healed rib fractures, arterial calcifications and an arrowhead in his left shoulder (Gostner & Egarter Vigl, 2002; Murphy et al., 2003). In later studies, it was shown that the arrowhead caused a severe laceration of his left subclavian artery, which would likely have led to massive extrapleural bleeding and, most likely, to rapid and deadly haemorrhagic shock (Pernter et al., 2007). In addition, areas of increased radiolucency in the posterior cerebral region of his brain showed that he had sustained a skull injury that had occurred shortly before death (Gostner et al., 2011). This was later confirmed by palaeoproteomic analyses of brain tissue samples using atomic force microscopy and gel-based and liquid chromatography/mass spectrometry-based proteomic technologies that showed clustered red blood cells and a significant accumulation of proteins related to stress responses and wound healing in the Iceman's brain (Maixner et al., 2013). Re-evaluation of his CT scans revealed that the Iceman also had dental disease, including periodontitis and several carious lesions (Seiler et al., 2013). Recently, radiological detection of gallstones and his completely filled stomach in this mummified body have enabled a thorough genetic study of the Iceman's stomach contents. Using NGS and targeted enrichment, the presence of the stomach pathogen *H. pylori* was detected. Genomic reconstruction revealed that it was a potentially virulent strain that could have caused gastric disease in the Iceman. The finding of the 5300-year-old *H. pylori* genome has significantly improved our knowledge of its ancestry and evolution, and how it may have affected the ancient European population (Maixner et al., 2016).

In a further study, the Iceman's last meal was reconstructed by applying a macroscopic, microscopic and multiomic approach to samples taken from his stomach contents. This analysis included isolating ancient DNA, proteins, metabolites and lipids, and revealed that he consumed an omnivorous diet rich in meat and fat originating from ibex and red deer, as well as cereals, such as an early domesticated wheat species (*Triticum monococcum*) (Maixner et al., 2018). Most interestingly, the stomach also contained traces of bracken (*Pteridium*) that Ötzi could have used as a medicine against intestinal parasites, or that he may have ingested unintentionally (Zink et al., 2019). However, bracken is toxic to humans and other animals and contains a highly carcinogenic compound, ptaquiloside, in all parts of the plant (Yujing et al., 2012). Despite the toxicity, ferns are still widely consumed today in China and other Asian countries, with the toxic components being removed by soaking the plant in water or an acidic or alkaline solution for a few hours before eating (Yujing et al., 2012).

5.4.1 The Iceman's Genome

In 2012, a whole sequencing of the Iceman's genomic DNA was initiated, expanding on previous studies that had targeted his mitochondrial DNA (Handt et al., 1994; Rollo et al., 2006; Ermini et al., 2008) and the excellent preservation of other biomolecules, such as collagen or blood that had been reported in other studies (Janko et al., 2012). Therefore, a successful reconstruction of his genomic DNA was expected, particularly as the preservation of ancient remains in cold environments, such as high alpine areas where his body was found, are particularly conducive to DNA preservation (Hofreiter et al., 2001). Following DNA extraction and sequencing library preparation, high-throughput sequencing revealed about 40 per cent reads that mapped to the human reference genome, with an overall coverage of 96 per cent of the complete genome (Keller et al., 2012). This study provided important new insights into the Iceman's ancestry, the diseases he had during life and physiological aspects of his body. Thereby, it was shown that he had brown eyes, was blood group O and was lactose intolerant, the latter an important genetic trait linked to the beginning of agriculture in Europe (Itan et al., 2009). The genomic data further showed a clear affinity to early European farmers, whereby the Iceman's Y haplogroup (G2a2b) is today encountered at a low frequency in Europe, but is more frequent in living Sardinians (Francalacci et al., 2013). However, his mitochondrial (mt)DNA lineage (K1f) has not been found in any modern or ancient populations, and may have disappeared during demographic events in Europe that were initiated by migrations of Early Neolithic people from the Near East through continental and Mediterranean routes around 8000 years BP (Coia et al., 2016). Ancient DNA studies suggest that both mtDNA haplogroup K1 and Y-chromosome G2a reached Europe with Neolithic farmers and spread across the continent (Brandt et al., 2015). Although the K1 mtDNA haplogroup was present in all parts of Europe at that time, our study suggests that the K1f branch most likely developed locally in the Eastern Alps and Ötzi's maternal lineage may have become extinct (Coia et al., 2016).

5.4.2   Genetic Risk Factors for CVD in the Iceman

The Iceman's genome was further screened for the presence of genetic risk factors, in particular SNPs known to be associated with specific diseases. Results showed a strong genetic predisposition for developing ASCVD or CHD (McPherson et al., 2007; Erdmann et al., 2018). This was an intriguing finding as it represented the first indication that genetic risk factors may have played a role in the development of ASCVD in ancient human populations. In addition, early CT studies had revealed calcifications in his carotid arteries, distal aorta, right iliac artery and coronary arteries (see Figure 5.1) indicating generalised atherosclerotic disease (Murphy et al., 2003; Pernter et al., 2018). Keller et al. (2012) focused on genetic risk factors shown to have a strong association with ASCVD and CHD in GWAS. These included two SNPs at the chromosomal locus 9p21, considered to have the strongest effects on coronary atherosclerosis risk (Erdmann et al., 2018). The homozygous minor allele of rs2383206 (GG) represents a major risk factor for CHD (Shen et al., 2008), while the minor allele (GG) of rs10757274 is considered a strong genetic predictor for myocardial infarction (heart attack) and has been shown to be a major risk factor for CHD (McPherson et al., 2007). Further, the presence of both SNPs significantly increases the risk for developing CHD (Chen et al., 2009).

In several large-scale GWAS investigations, such as the Copenhagen City Heart Study (CCHS) and the Atherosclerosis Risk in Communities Study (ARIC), a strong association between the 9p21 locus and CHD has been found. Whether or not other classic risk factors were present, an increased risk of developing clinical manifestations

Table 5.1 Number of SNPs related to CVD in the Iceman.

ASCVD SNPs	Diploid effective allele	Haploid effective allele	No effective allele	Not covered
163	58	46	58	1
		Total = 104		

of heart disease of up to 40 per cent was observed in different ethnic groups (McPherson et al., 2007). In addition, a meta-analysis of six different cohort studies revealed that the rs10757274 SNP found in the Iceman was a major risk locus for ischaemic stroke (blood clots at sites of arterial plaques/atherosclerosis), due to lack of blood flow, and sudden cardiac death (Luke, 2009; Newton-Cheh, 2009; Smith et al., 2009). Another SNP found to increase the risk for atherosclerosis (predominantly in men), the endothelin receptor type B heterozygote variant rs5351 on chromosome 13, was detected in the Iceman's genome. Additional SNPs that were observed in his genes are known to be associated with CHD, such as SNPs located in the start codon of the vitamin D3 receptor (*VDR*), T-box 1 (*TBX1*) and bradykinin receptor B1 (*BDKRB1*) genes .

In order to expand our understanding of the Iceman's susceptibility to ASCVD, we re-analysed his genome using the set of 163 SNPs described above. By applying the selected set of SNPs, we were able to identify 104 SNPs (58 homozygote and 46 heterozygote) with a clear association with ASCVD (Table 5.1). This result not only confirms his previously described strong genetic predisposition to an increased risk for ASCVD, but it also extends the number and significance of the identified related SNPs. In total, the Iceman had the risk allele in 104 out of the 162 covered loci (64.2%), with an allele frequency of 0.5 for all SNPs.

Considering the large number of genetic risk loci identified in the Iceman's genome, the previous assumption that a strong genetic predisposition to ASCVD significantly contributed to the development of arterial calcifications in his body is further substantiated (Keller et al., 2012; Zink et al., 2014). This is particularly relevant considering that other traditional cardiac risk factors may be ruled out at the time he was living, such as tobacco smoking, a lack of physical activity and a predominantly high-fat diet. Previous anthropological studies have clearly shown that the Iceman was used to walking over long distances in the mountainous area, had a slim and well-exercised body, and his overall diet appears to have been well balanced, although his last meal contained substantial amounts of animal proteins and fats (Ruff et al., 2006; Maixner et al., 2018). Tobacco was not available during the Neolithic, although it may be assumed that he was exposed to and inhaled some particulate matter from smoke during his life, most likely from open fires.

5.5 Conclusions

There exists strong radiological evidence for the presence of arterial calcification in ancient human mummies. However, the Iceman is still one of only a few ancient human mummies that have been studied where genome-wide analysis has revealed a genetic predisposition for CVD that could be linked to the physical appearance of calcified plaques. In their study of a seventeenth-century Korean female mummy with presumptive ASCVD signs, Shin et al. (2017) also found risk alleles of seven different SNPs that are known to be associated with ASCVD in East Asian populations. Although the authors used PCR-based techniques, Sanger sequencing and SNaPshot analysis that provide reproducible results, they limited their study to a set of 10 SNPs (Shin et al., 2017; see also Chapter 3). Nevertheless, this work represents an important contribution that broadens our knowledge of genetic susceptibility to ASCVD in ancient human populations. The application of our proposed set of 163 SNPs to the genome of the Korean mummy would provide a more detailed understanding of her genetic predisposition to ASCVD and enable us to compare our findings with those of Shin et al. (2017). We are also currently expanding our study of the Iceman to a wider range of mummies, including individuals that have a high incidence of arterial calcifications that were part of the Horus study (Allam et al., 2009; Thompson et al., 2013; see Chapter 4). Comparison of their phenotypes and genotypes, arising from differing lifestyles and environments over a broad geographic and temporal range, will provide an opportunity to gain unique insights into the role of genetic factors in the development and evolution of ASCVD. Detailed SNP analysis of a large number of cardiovascular risk factors will show us what risk factors were common to those we identify today and may also lead to the identification of new or currently unrecognised genetic polymorphisms that may no longer be present in modern-day humans.

However, such work clearly depends on the preservation and ability to retrieve ancient nuclear DNA in mummified remains. As noted above, the Iceman was preserved in a cold and, most likely, stable environment at high altitude in the Alps over a time period of more than 5000 years. This has led to exceptional preservation of his DNA, allowing the successful reconstruction of his full genome (Keller et al., 2012). In contrast, many other mummies were preserved in hot and dry climates, for example those found in the deserts of Egypt and South America, including the coastal area of Peru and the Atacama region in Chile (Marquet et al., 2012). In such mummies, the retrieval of ancient DNA could be significantly hampered by significant DNA degradation and genetic sequence modification that greatly impedes SNP analysis. Genome-wide studies of ancient mummies remain scarce, due to restrictions and limitations with regard to the application of invasive techniques especially in well-preserved or fully wrapped mummies (Wurst et al., 2020). Moreover, most of the work has focused on the identification of pathogens such as *M. tuberculosis* (Bos et al., 2014; Kay et al., 2015), hepatitis B and variola viruses (Kahila Bar-Gal et al., 2012; Duggan et al., 2016; Patterson Ross et al., 2018), as well as *H. pylori* (Maixner et al., 2016).

Nevertheless, there is growing evidence that some human DNA may survive in mummies from hot and dry climates, for example genomic DNA from a 4000-year-old Egyptian mummy head, and the reconstruction of mitochondrial genomes and genome-wide data of mummies from Middle Egypt dating from the late New

Kingdom to the Roman Period (Schuenemann et al., 2017; Loreille et al., 2018). Improvement in sampling techniques, DNA extraction methods and whole-genome sequencing technologies, including specific targeted-enrichment applications, will further improve the potential of obtaining full genomes from well-preserved individuals, including skeletal remains. In the last decade, a large number of ancient human genome sequencing projects have been performed, with data on more than 1100 ancient genomes (Marciniak & Perry, 2017) dating back to the period of Neanderthals and early hominins, from 35 000 to 430 000 years ago (Green et al., 2010; Krause et al., 2010; Meyer et al., 2016). In the future, *in-silico* analyses, using bioinformatics and computer simulation of such genomes should help us understand and estimate past prevalence of genetic risk factors associated with ASCVD, as well as provide insights into possible changes during major population events, such as the transition from Palaeolithic hunting and gathering to Neolithic farming. However, studies focusing on comparing the presence of calcified arteries with an individual's genotype are limited due to the lack of soft tissue preservation in skeletal remains, even where calcified vessels are recovered with skeletons from burial sites in exceptional cases (Binder & Roberts, 2014). However, improved awareness and excavation/retrieval techniques should increase their recovery (see Chapter 12). Radiological and ancient DNA investigations of ASCVDs in ancient human remains have clearly demonstrated that heart disease is not a phenomenon restricted to modern times, and its current prevalence is only partly linked to our current lifestyle. Instead, arterial calcifications indicating ASCVD have been found in mummies dating back more than 5000 years. Moreover, studies of the Iceman and a seventeenth-century Korean mummy provide strong evidence that genetic factors may have played a role in the development of ASCVD in ancient populations, as they do today. The presence and interaction of environmental and genetic risk factors in the development of CVD impacts our ability to make individual predictions about which risks were most important then and may help us to develop effective prevention and treatment strategies today. The study of ancient humans can provide new and unique insights into the genetic background of the pathophysiology of ASCVD and its interaction with lifestyle factors. This further supports current efforts focusing on understanding and combating the most common cause of death in the modern world.

References

Allam, A. H., Thompson, R. C., Wann, L.S., Miyamoto, M.I. and Thomas, G.S. (2009). Computed tomographic assessment of atherosclerosis in ancient Egyptian mummies. *Journal of the American Medical Association*, 302(19), 2091–4.

Allam, A. H., Thompson, R. C., Wann, L. S., et al. (2011). Atherosclerosis in ancient Egyptian mummies: The Horus study. *Journal of the American College of Cardiology Cardiovascular Imaging*, 4, 315–27.

Aufderheide, A. C., Salo, W., Madden, M., et al. (2004). A 9,000-year record of Chagas' disease. *Proceedings of the National Academy of Sciences USA*, 101(7), 2034–9.

Barfield, L. (1992). Modisches aus der Jungsteinzeit Werkzeuge und Kleidung. In E. Koller, A. Lippert and A. Payrleitner, eds., *Der Zeuge aus dem Gletscher: das Rätsel der frühen Alpen-Europäer*. Wien, Austria: Ueberreuter, pp. 180–7.

Binder, M. and Roberts, C. A. (2014). Calcified structures associated with human skeletal remains: Possible atherosclerosis affecting the population buried at Amara West, Sudan (1300–800BC). *International Journal of Paleopathology*, 6, 20–9.

Bos, K. I., Schuenemann, V. J., Golding, G. B., et al. (2011). A draft genome of *Yersinia pestis* from victims of the Black Death. *Nature*, 478, 506–10.

Bos, K. I., Harkins, K. M., Herbig, A., et al. (2014). Pre-Columbian mycobacterial genomes reveal seals as a source of New World human tuberculosis. *Nature*, 514(7523), 494–7.

Brandt, G., Haak, W., Adler, C. J., et al. (2013). Ancient DNA reveals key stages in the formation of central European mitochondrial genetic diversity. *Science*, 342, 257–61.

Brandt, G,, Szécsényi-Nagy, A., Roth, C., Alt, K. W. and Haak, W. (2015). Human paleogenetics of Europe: The known knowns and the known unknowns. *Journal of Human Evolution*, 79, 73–92.

Chen, S. N., Ballantyne, C. M., Gotto, A. M. Jr. and Marian, A. J. (2009). The 9p21 susceptibility locus for coronary artery disease and the severity of coronary atherosclerosis. *BMC Cardiovascular Disorders*, 9, 3.

Coia, V., Cipollini, G., Anagnostou, P., et al. (2016). Whole mitochondrial DNA sequencing in Alpine populations and the genetic history of the Neolithic Tyrolean Iceman. *Scientific Reports*, 6, 18932.

Collins, M. J., Nielsen-Marsh, C. M., Hiller, J., et al. (2002). The survival of organic matter in bone: A review. *Archaeometry*, 44, 383–94.

Cooper, A. and Poinar, H. N. (2000). Ancient DNA: Do it right or not at all. *Science*, 289, 1139.

Coronary Artery Disease (C4D) Genetics Consortium. (2011). A genome-wide association study in Europeans and South Asians identifies five new loci for coronary artery disease. *Nature Genetics*, 43, 339–44.

Cox, S. L., Ruff, C. B., Maier, R. M. and Mathieson, I. (2019). Genetic contributions to variation in human stature in prehistoric Europe. *Proceedings of the National Academy of Sciences USA*, 116(43), 21484–92.

Deloukas, P., Kanoni, S., Willenborg, C., et al. (2013). Large-scale association analysis identifies new risk loci for coronary artery disease. *Nature Genetics*, 45, 25–33.

Dickson, J. H., Oeggl, K., Holden, T. G., et al. (2000). The omnivorous Tyrolean Iceman: Colon contents (meat, cereals, pollen, moss and whipworm) and stable isotope analyses. *Philosophical Transactions of the Royal Society B, Biological Sciences*, 355, 1843–9.

Do, R., Stitziel, N. O., Won, H. H., et al. (2015). Exome sequencing identifies rare LDLR and APOA5 alleles conferring risk for myocardial infarction. *Nature*, 518, 102–6.

Duggan, A. T., Perdomo, M. F., Piombino-Mascali, D., et al. (2016). Seventeenth century variola virus reveals the recent history of smallpox. *Current Biology*, 26(24), 3407–12.

Erdmann, J., Grosshennig, A., Braund, P. S., et al. (2009). New susceptibility locus for coronary artery disease on chromosome 3q22.3. *Nature Genetics*, 41, 280–2.

Erdmann, J., Kessler, T., Munoz Venegas, L. and Schunkert, H. (2018). A decade of genome-wide association studies for coronary artery disease: The challenges ahead. *Cardiovascular Research*, 114(9), 1241–57.

Ermini, L., Olivieri, C., Rizzi, E., et al. (2008). Complete mitochondrial genome sequence of the Tyrolean Iceman. *Current Biology*, 18, 1687–93.

Fernandes, D. M., Mittnik, A., Olalde, I., et al. (2020). The spread of steppe and Iranian-related ancestry in the islands of the western Mediterranean. *Nature Ecology and Evolution*, 4, 334–45.

Francalacci, P., Morelli, L., Angius, A., et al. (2013). Low-pass DNA sequencing of 1200 Sardinians reconstructs European Y-chromosome phylogeny. *Science*, 341, 565–9.

Gaber, O. and Kunzel, K. H. (1998). Man from the Hauslabjoch. *Experimental Gerontology*, 33(7–8), 655–60.

Gaeta, R., Fornaciari, A., Izzetti, R., Caramella, D. and Giuffra, V. (2019). Severe atherosclerosis in the natural mummy of Girolamo Macchi (1648–1734), 'major writer' of Santa Maria della Scala Hospital in Siena (Italy). *Atherosclerosis*, 280, 66–74.

Gilbert, M. T., Barnes, I., Collins, M.J., et al. (2005). Long-term survival of ancient DNA in Egypt: Response to Zink and Nerlich (2003). *American Journal of Physical Anthropology*, 128(1), 110–14.

Gómez-Carballa, A., Catelli, L., Pardo-Seco, J., et al. (2015). The complete mitogenome of a 500-year-old Inca child mummy. *Scientific Reports*, 5, 16462.

Gostner, P. and Egarter Vigl, E. (2002). Report of radiological-forensic findings on the Iceman. *Journal of Archaeological Science,* 29, 323–6.

Gostner, P., Pernter, P., Bonatti, G., Graefen, A. and Zink, A. R. (2011). New radiological insights into the life and death of the Tyrolean Iceman. *Journal of Archaeological Science*, 38, 3425–31.

Green, R. E., Krause, J., Briggs, A.W., et al. (2010). A draft sequence of the Neandertal genome. *Science*, 328, 710–22.

Hajdinjak, M., Fu, Q., Hübner, A., et al. (2018). Reconstructing the genetic history of late Neanderthals. *Nature*, 555(7698), 652–6.

Handt, O., Richards, M., Trommsdorff, M., et al. (1994). Molecular genetic analyses of the Tyrolean Ice Man. *Science*, 264, 1775–8.

Harbeck, M., Seifert, L., Hänsch, S., et al. (2013). *Yersinia pestis* DNA from skeletal remains from the sixth century AD reveals insights into Justinianic Plague. *PLoS Pathogens*, 9(5), e1003349.

Hawass, Z., Gad, Y. Z., Ismail, S., et al. (2010). Ancestry and pathology in King Tutankhamun's family. *Journal of the American Medical Association*, 303, 638–47.

Higuchi, R., Bowman, B., Freiberger, M., Ryder, O. A. and Wilson, A. C. (1984). DNA sequences from the quagga, an extinct member of the horse family. *Nature*, 312, 282–4.

Hofreiter, M., Serre, D., Poinar, H. N., Kuch, M. and Pääbo, S. (2001). Ancient DNA. *Nature Reviews Genetics*, 2, 353–9.

Itan, Y., Powell, A., Beaumont, M. A., Burger, J. and Thomas, M. G. (2009). The origins of lactase persistence in Europe. *PLoS Computational Biology*, 5, e1000491.

Janko, M., Stark, R. W. and Zink, A. (2012). Preservation of 5300 year old red blood cells in the Iceman. *Journal of the Royal Society Interface*, 9, 2581–90.

Jannot, A. S., Ehret, G. and Perneger, T. (2015). P $<5 \times 10^{-8}$ has emerged as a standard of statistical significance for genome-wide association studies. *Journal of Clinical Epidemiology*, 68, 460–5.

Kahila Bar-Gal, G., Kim, M. J., Klein, A., et al. (2012). Tracing hepatitis B virus to the sixteenth century in a Korean mummy. *Hepatology*, 56, 1671–80.

Kay, G. L., Sergeant, M. J., Zhou, Z., et al. (2015). Eighteenth-century genomes show that mixed infections were common at time of peak tuberculosis in Europe. *Nature Communications*, 6, 6717.

Keller, A., Graefen, A., Ball, M., et al. (2012). New insights into the Tyrolean Iceman's origin and phenotype as inferred by whole-genome sequencing. *Nature Communications*, 3, 698.

Keller, M., Spyrou, M. A., Scheib, C.L., et al. (2019). Ancient *Yersinia pestis* genomes from across Western Europe reveal early diversification during the First Pandemic (541–750). *Proceedings of the National Academy of Sciences USA*, 116(25), 12363–72.

Kessler, T., Vilne, B. and Schunkert, H. (2016). The impact of genome-wide association studies on the pathophysiology and therapy of cardiovascular disease. *EMBO Molecular Medicine*, 8, 688–701.

Key, F. M., Posth, C., Krause, J., Herbig, A. and Bos, K. I. (2017). Mining metagenomic data sets for ancient DNA: Recommended protocols for authentication. *Trends in Genetics*, 33(8), 508–20.

Kim, M. J., Kim, Y. S., Oh, C. S., et al. (2015). Anatomical confirmation of computed tomography-based diagnosis of the atherosclerosis discovered in seventeenth century Korean mummy. *PLoS One*, 10(3), e0119474.

Kirsanow, K. and Burger, J. (2012). Ancient human DNA. *Annals of Anatomy*, 194, 121–32.

Krause, J., Fu, Q., Good, J. M., et al. (2010). The complete mitochondrial DNA genome of an unknown hominin from southern Siberia. *Nature*, 464(7290), 894–7.

Lindahl, T. (1993). Instability and decay of the primary structure of DNA. *Nature*, 362, 709–15.

Loh, P.-R., Danecek, P., Palamara, P. F., et al. (2016). Reference-based phasing using the Haplotype Reference Consortium panel. *Nature Genetics*, 48, 1443–8.

Loreille, O., Ratnayake, S., Bazinet, A. L., et al. (2018). Biological sexing of a 4000-year-old Egyptian mummy head to assess the potential of nuclear DNA recovery from the most damaged and limited forensic specimens. *Genes (Basel)*, 9(3), 135.

Luke, M. M. (2009). Polymorphisms associated with both noncardioembolic stroke and coronary heart disease: Vienna Stroke Registry. *Cerebrovascular Diseases*, 28, 499–504.

McPherson, R., Pertsemlidis, A., Kavaslar, N., et al. (2007). A common allele on chromosome 9 associated with coronary heart disease. *Science*, 316, 1488–91.

Maixner, F., Overath, T., Linke, D., et al. (2013). Paleoproteomic study of the Iceman's brain tissue. *Cellular and Molecular Life Sciences*, 70(19), 3709–22.

Maixner, F., Krause-Kyora, B., Turaev, D., et al. (2016). The 5300-year-old *Helicobacter pylori* genome of the Iceman. *Science*, 351, 162–5.

Maixner, F., Turaev, D., Cazenave-Gassiot, A., et al. (2018). The Iceman's last meal consisted of fat, wild meat, and cereals. *Current Biology*, 28(14), 2348–2355.e9.

Marciniak, S. and Perry, G. H. (2017). Harnessing ancient genomes to study the history of human adaptation. *Nature Reviews Genetics*, 18(11), 659–74.

Marenberg, M. E., Risch, N., Berkman, L. F., Floderus, B. and de Faire, U. (1994). Genetic susceptibility to death from coronary heart disease in a study of twins. *New England Journal of Medicine*, 330, 1041–6.

Marota, I., Basile, C., Ubaldi, M. and Rollo, F. (2002). DNA decay rate in papyri and human remains from Egyptian archaeological sites. *American Journal of Physical Anthropology*, 117(4), 310–18.

Marquet, P. A., Santoro, C. M., Latorre, C., et al. (2012). Emergence of social complexity among coastal hunter-gatherers in the Atacama Desert of northern Chile. *Proceedings of the National Academy of Sciences USA*, 109(37), 14754–60.

Mathieson, I., Alpaslan-Roodenberg, S., Posth, C., et al. (2018). The genomic history of southeastern Europe. *Nature*, 555, 197–203.

Meyer, M., Fu, Q., Aximu-Petri, A., et al. (2014). A mitochondrial genome sequence of a hominin from Sima de los Huesos. *Nature*, 505, 403–6.

Meyer, M., Arsuaga, J. L., de Filippo, C., et al. (2016). Nuclear DNA sequences from the Middle Pleistocene Sima de los Huesos hominins. *Nature*, 53, 504–7.

Molto, J. E., Loreille, O., Mallott, E. K., et al. (2017). Complete mitochondrial genome sequencing of a burial from a Romano-Christian cemetery in the Dakhleh Oasis, Egypt: Preliminary indications. *Genes (Basel)*, 8(10), 262.

Müller, W., Fricke, H., Halliday, A. N., McCulloch, M. T. and Wartho, J. A. (2003). Origin and migration of the Alpine Iceman. *Science*, 302, 862–6.

Murphy, W. A., zur Nedden, D., Gostner, P., et al. (2003). The Iceman: Discovery and imaging. *Radiology*, 226, 614–29.

Myers, R. H., Kiely, D. K., Cupples, L. A. and Kannel, W. B. (1990). Parental history is an independent risk factor for coronary artery disease: The Framingham Study. *American Heart Journal*, 120, 963–9.

Nerlich, A. G., Haas, C. J., Zink, A., Szeimies, U. and Hagedorn, H. G. (1997). Molecular evidence for tuberculosis in an ancient Egyptian mummy. *Lancet*, 350(9088), 1404.

Newton-Cheh, C. (2009). A common variant at 9p21 is associated with sudden and arrhythmic cardiac death. *Circulation*, 120, 2062–8.

Oeggl, K., Kofler, W., Schmidl, A., et al. (2007). The reconstruction of the last itinerary of 'Ötzi', the Neolithic Iceman, by pollen analyses from sequentially sampled gut extracts. *Quaternary Science Reviews*, 26, 853–61.

Orlando, L., Ginolhac, A., Zhang, G., et al. (2013). Recalibrating *Equus* evolution using the genome sequence of an early Middle Pleistocene horse. *Nature*, 499, 74–8.

Pääbo, S. (1984). Über den Nachweis von DNA in altägyptischen Mumien. *Das Altertum*, 30, 213–18.

Pääbo, S. (1985). Molecular cloning of ancient Egyptian mummy DNA. *Nature*, 314, 644–5.

Pääbo, S., Poinar, H., Serre, D., et al. (2004). Genetic analyses from ancient DNA. *Annual Review of Genetics*, 38, 645–79.

Patterson Ross, Z., Klunk, J., Fornaciari, G., et al. (2018). The paradox of HBV evolution as revealed from a 16th century mummy. *PLoS Pathogens*, 14, e1006750.

Pernter, P., Gostner, P., Egarter-Vigl, E. and Rühli, F. J. (2007). Radiologic proof for the Iceman's cause of death (ca 5300 BP). *Journal of Archaeological Science*, 34, 1784–6.

Pernter, P., Pedrinolla, B. and Gostner, P. (2018). Das Herz des Mannes aus dem Eis. Ein Paläoradiologischer Fall. *Rofo*, 190(1), 61–4.

Piombino-Mascali, D., Jankauskas, R., Tamošiūnas, A., et al. (2014). Atherosclerosis in mummified human remains from Vilnius, Lithuania (eighteenth–nineteenth centuries AD): A computed tomographic investigation. *American Journal of Human Biology*, 26(5), 676–81.

Prüfer, K., Racimo, F., Patterson, N., et al. (2014). The complete genome sequence of a Neanderthal from the Altai Mountains. *Nature*, 505, 43–9.

Rasmussen, M., Li, Y., Lindgreen, S., et al. (2010). Ancient human genome sequence of an extinct Palaeo-Eskimo. *Nature*, 463, 757–62.

Rollo, F., Ermini, L., Luciani, S., et al. (2006). Fine characterization of the Iceman's mtDNA haplogroup. *American Journal of Physical Anthropology*, 30, 557–64.

Ruff, C. B., Holt, B. M., Sládek, V., et al. (2006). Body size, body proportions, and mobility in the Tyrolean 'Iceman'. *Journal of Human Evolution*, 51(1), 91–101.

Ruffer, M. A. (1911). On arterial lesions found in Egyptian mummies (1580 BC–535 AD). *Journal of Pathology and Bacteriology*, 16, 453–62.

Salo, W. L., Aufderheide, A. C., Buikstra, J. and Holcomb, T. A. (1994). Identification of *Mycobacterium tuberculosis* DNA in a pre-Columbian Peruvian mummy. *Proceedings of the National Academy of Sciences USA*, 91(6), 2091–4.

Samadelli, M., Melis, M., Miccoli, M., Egarter-Vigl, E. and Zink, A. R. (2015). Complete mapping of the tattoos of the 5300-year-old Tyrolean Iceman. *Journal of Cultural Heritage*, 16(5), 753–8.

Samani, N. J., Erdmann, J., Hall, A. S., et al. (2007). Genome wide association analysis of coronary artery disease. *New England Journal of Medicine*, 357, 443–53.

Sankararaman, S., Mallick, S., Dannemann, M., et al. (2014). The genomic landscape of Neanderthal ancestry in present-day humans. *Nature*, 507, 354–7.

Schuenemann, V. J., Singh, P., Mendum, T. A., et al. (2013). Genome-wide comparison of medieval and modern *Mycobacterium leprae*. *Science*, 341, 179–83.

Schuenemann, V. J., Peltzer, A., Welte, B., et al. (2017). Ancient Egyptian mummy genomes suggest an increase of Sub-Saharan African ancestry in post-Roman periods. *Nature Communications*, 8, 15694.

Seiler, R., Spielman, A. I., Zink, A. and Rühli, F. J. (2013). Oral pathologies of the Neolithic Iceman, c.3,300 BC. European *Journal of Oral Science*, 21(3 Pt 1), 137–41.

Shen, G. Q., Li, L., Rao, S., et al. (2008). Four SNPs on chromosome 9p21 in a South Korean population implicate a genetic locus that confers high crossrace risk for development of coronary artery disease. *Arteriosclerosis Thrombosis and Vascular Biology*, 28, 360–5.

Shin, D. H., Oh, C. S., Hong, J. H., et al. (2017). Paleogenetic study on the seventeenth century Korean mummy with atherosclerotic cardiovascular disease. *PLoS One*, 12(8), e0183098.

Skoglund, P. Malmstrom, H., Raghavan, M., et al. (2012). Origins and genetic legacy of Neolithic farmers and hunter-gatherers in Europe. *Science*, 336, 466–9.

Smith, J. G., Melander, O., Lövkvist, H., et al. (2009). Common genetic variants on chromosome 9p21 confers risk of ischemic stroke: A large-scale genetic association study. *Circulation: Cardiovascular Genetics*, 2, 159–64.

Spindler, K. (2000). *Der Mann im Eis. Neue Sensationelle Erkenntnisse über die Mumie in den Ötztaler Alpen.* Munich: Goldmann.

Spindler, K. and Osers, E. (1995). *The Man in the Ice. The Preserved Body of a Neolithic Man Reveals the Secrets of the Stone Age.* London: Phoenix.

Stary, H. C., Chandler, A. B., Dinsmore, R. E., et al. (1995). A definition of advanced types of atherosclerotic lesions and a histological classification of atherosclerosis: A report from the Committee on Vascular Lesions of the Council on Arteriosclerosis, American Heart Association. *Circulation*, 92, 1355–74.

Sudlow, C., Gallacher, J., Allen, N., et al. (2015). UK biobank: An open access resource for identifying the causes of a wide range of complex diseases of middle and old age. *PLoS Medicine*, 12(3), e1001779.

Thompson, R. C., Allam, A. H., Lombardi, G. P., et al. (2013). Atherosclerosis across 4000 years of human history: The Horus study of four ancient populations. *Lancet*, 381(9873), 1211–22.

Thompson, R. C., Allam, A. H., Zink, A., et al. (2014). Computed tomographic evidence of atherosclerosis in the mummified remains of humans from around the world. *Global Heart*, 9(2), 187–96.

Wagner, D. M., Klunk, J., Harbeck, M., et al. (2014). *Yersinia pestis* and the Plague of Justinian 541–543 AD: A genomic analysis. *Lancet Infectious Diseases*, 14, 319–26.

Wann, L. S., Narula, J., Blankstein, R., et al. (2019). Atherosclerosis in sixteenth-century Greenlandic Inuit mummies. *Journal of the American Medical Association Network Open*, 2(12), e1918270.

Wurst, C., Paladin, A., Wann, L. S., et. al. (2020). Minimally invasive bone biopsies of fully wrapped mummies guided by computed tomography and fibre-optic endoscopy: Methods and suggested guidelines. *Journal of Archaeological Science: Reports*, 31, 102363.

Yujing, L., Wujisguleng, W. and Long, C. (2012). Food uses of ferns in China: A review. *Acta Societatis Botanicorum Poloniae*, 81, 263–70.

Zink, A. and Nerlich, A. G. (2003). Molecular analyses of the 'Pharaos:' Feasibility of molecular studies in ancient Egyptian material. *American Journal of Physical Anthropology*, 121(2), 109–11.

Zink, A. R., Sola, C., Reischl, U., et al. (2003). Characterization of *Mycobacterium tuberculosis* complex DNAs from Egyptian mummies by spoligotyping. *Journal of Clinical Microbiology*, 41, 359–67.

Zink, A., Grabner, W. and Nerlich, A. G. (2005). Molecular identification of human tuberculosis in recent and historic bone tissue samples: A study on the role of molecular techniques for the study of historic tuberculosis. *American Journal of Physical Anthropology*, 126, 32–47.

Zink, A., Wann, L. S., Thompson, R. C., et al. (2014). Genomic correlates of atherosclerosis in ancient humans. *Global Heart*, 9(2), 203–9.

Zink, A., Samadelli, M., Gostner, P. and Piombino-Mascali, D. (2019). Possible evidence for care and treatment in the Tyrolean Iceman. *International Journal of Paleopathology*, 25, 110–17.

6   Cardiovascular Disease in Nile Valley Mummies

Exploring the Need for a More Systematic Approach That Accounts for Vessel Prevalence, Links to Oral Health and the Impact of Dual-Energy CT Scanning

Daniel Antoine, Marie Vandenbeusch, Rebecca Whiting and Benjamin Moreno

6.1   Introduction

Computed tomography (CT) is transforming our understanding of mummification in ancient Egypt, revealing a complex evolution of the preparation of the body for its journey to the afterlife and the methods used to preserve it (Ikram & Dodson, 1998; Taylor, 2001, 2010; Aufderheide, 2003; Antoine & Vandenbeusch, 2021). For example, new analyses and large-scale reviews of the treatment of the brain and organs have highlighted previously unappreciated temporal and regional variations, as well as differences according to status (Wade et al., 2011; Wade & Nelson, 2013a, 2013b; Nelson & Wade, 2015; Antoine & Vandenbeusch, 2021). Increasingly, CT scans are also being used to gain a better understanding of the biological profile and lives of the individuals who were mummified (Taylor & Antoine, 2014), including large-scale studies that have investigated the past prevalence of cardiovascular diseases (CVDs) (Allam et al., 2009, 2011; see also Chapter 4). The mummies curated at the British Museum represent one of the largest collections of Nile valley mummies outside of Egypt and include naturally mummified individuals from medieval Sudan (see Antoine & Ambers, 2014; Taylor, 2014). Using the latest scientific methods, their ongoing analysis is providing new insights into past burial practices and beliefs, and the process of mummification. Information on the latter is rarely found in other sources of evidence, including written texts. By using dual-energy CT scanning and by applying methods developed in biological anthropology, and particularly within its subdisciplines of bioarchaeology and forensic anthropology, this research is also revealing new insights into human biology, diet and the state of health of individual people at the time of their deaths (Taylor & Antoine, 2014; Antoine & Vandenbeusch, 2016, 2021). Here we present three examples of atherosclerosis and broadly discuss the approaches currently used to record CVD in mummified remains, particularly the need for a more systematic approach that allows like-for-like comparisons across publications. Ideally, using standardised approaches should account for the arteries and organs that were removed by the embalmer during mummification as the extent of their removal often varies by individual, region and period. However, we should be cognisant that of those arteries and organs that remain, varying preservation and CT scanning resolution will impact our ability to observe and identify atherosclerosis.

Cardiovascular Disease in Nile Valley Mummies   99

Finally, because clinical research has revealed links between cardiovascular and oral diseases (Joshipura et al., 2009; Carrizales-Sepúlveda et al., 2018), these links are also examined, particularly as periapical lesions, tooth decay and periodontal disease are often observable in dental and skeletal remains, as well as on CT scans of mummified remains.

6.2   Mummification in the Nile Valley: Implications for the Survival of Internal Organs and the Detection of Atheromas

The desert environment found throughout most of Egypt and Sudan has allowed many mummified bodies to survive to this day in an excellent state of preservation. Most were deliberately mummified, while some were naturally preserved by the dry and arid conditions. In Egypt, the practice of mummifying the dead appears to have evolved over a period of around 3500 years. Influenced by geographical and socioeconomic factors, specific methods were developed by individual embalmers or embalming workshops, and these appear to have changed over time, and may have included elements of trial and error (Ikram & Dodson, 1998: 276–92; Aufderheide, 2003: 212–58; Antoine & Vandenbeusch, 2021). The preservation and proper treatment of the body would ensure a person's existence into the afterlife by maintaining a link between the body and consciousness (Taylor, 2001: 15–24). The process of mummification was also used to transform the physical remains of the deceased into a divine image, incorporating elements that would reflect the attributes and qualities of the gods (see Ikram & Dodson, 1998: 15–21; Taylor, 2001: 10–45).

Rare examples of naturally desiccated individuals have been recovered at Predynastic sites such as Gebelein (c. 3500–3300 BCE) (Antoine & Ambers, 2014; Taylor & Antoine, 2014: 22–43; Friedman et al., 2018). Buried in shallow pits in close contact with the hot desert sand, the chance discoveries of these natural mummies by ancient Egyptians may have guided their beliefs towards a need to preserve the body (Ikram & Dodson, 1998: 108; Taylor, 2001; Antoine & Ambers, 2014), and led to what appears to be early mummification attempts from the middle of the fourth millennium BCE (see Jones et al., 2014, 2018). Concurrently, the increasingly complex mortuary practices that emerged in the centuries prior to 3000 BCE (Ikram & Dodson, 1998: 21–60) would have prevented or limited natural mummification, encouraging the search for alternative methods of preservation. As artificial mummification developed, embalmers began to experiment with the removal of the most perishable internal organs in the belief that the procedure would stop decomposition. To further aid preservation and transform the physical remains into a divine image, the embalmers also started to dry, anoint and wrap bodies in linen. Approaches and embalming techniques (including the removal of specific organs, the use of packing materials and the placement of subcutaneous insertions) evolved and varied over time (Antoine & Vandenbeusch, 2021). Internal organs of the chest and abdomen (including their surrounding arteries) were often removed from the early Old Kingdom (c. 2600 BCE) onwards, usually via an incision in the left flank (see Wade & Nelson, 2013a, 2013b), and preserved by applying the same method used for the body (Ikram & Dodson, 1998: 276–92; Taylor, 2001: 64–76; Aufderheide, 2003: 257–9). To dry the body, embalmers used a natural salt compound called natron in powder form that was mostly composed of sodium carbonate decahydrate and sodium bicarbonate (Ikram & Dodson 1998: 112–13; Aufderheide 2003: 255–6; Taylor & Antoine 2014: 53–9). Not only was natron an efficient desiccating agent, it also broke down body fat (Taylor, 2001: 55–7). As atherosclerotic plaques initially develop as accumulations of cholesterol-rich lipids, it remains unclear if natron's proficiency to break down fat also affects the preservation of, and our ability to detect, arterial plaque in artificially desiccated Egyptian remains. This is most likely to have an impact on the early stages of atherosclerosis, prior to formation of calcified nodules or fibrocalcific plaque in blood vessels (for stages of plaque development, see Insull, 2009; Bentzon et al., 2014). Although dual-energy CT (see below) can improve the differentiation of plaque components, the early stages of atherosclerosis development are often not visible on most CT scanners (Saremi & Achenbach, 2015), possibly more so after desiccation via natron.

Once dried, the body would be 'rebuilt', which could often involve filling empty spaces (e.g. the chest and abdomen) with a range of materials including earth, sawdust, dried lichen or linen (Ikram & Dodson, 1998: 160–4; Aufderheide, 2003: 252–4; Łucejko et al., 2017). Molten resins (i.e. in their liquid state; often from pine, spruce, cedars, *Pistacia* resin or bitumen; see Clark et al., 2016; Łucejko et al., 2017) were usually applied to the surface of the body, as well as inside cavities such as the skull and chest. Any removed organs were also embalmed with oils and resins, wrapped, and placed into vessels known as canopic jars from about 2600 BCE (Aufderheide, 2003: 258). From the Third Intermediate Period (c. 1069–656 BCE) onwards, the separately dried organ packages were occasionally returned to the mummy, and were placed either inside the chest and abdomen or on top of the body. Although organs were traditionally placed into four bundles (usually enclosing the liver, lungs, stomach and intestines; see Antoine & Vandenbeusch, 2021), the number of organ packages varies over time (Taylor, 2001: 72). In some intentionally mummified individuals, no attempts were made to remove the organs. In one such example, a mummified young man who lived during the Roman period (c. second century CE), his remains – both inside and out – are remarkably preserved despite the in-situ internal organs being present (catalogued as British Museum EA 6713; Antoine & Vandenbeusch, 2016: 159–75; Antoine & Vandenbeusch, 2021). The brain was often removed, usually by accessing the cranium via the nasal aperture (see Aufderheide, 2011). The heart, significantly for the study of CVD, was often left in place by embalmers (Wade & Nelson, 2013b) and was viewed as the centre of intellect and memory by ancient Egyptians (Taylor, 2010: 54). Finally, wrapping of the body usually involved layers of linen that can vary in thickness and occasionally incorporate additional layers of resin, with early embalmers also making use of matting and animal skins (Ikram & Dodson, 1998: 153–92; Taylor, 2001: 57–64; Antoine & Vandenbeusch, 2021).

6.3 Analysing Mummified Remains for Signs of Cardiovascular Disease via CT Scans

6.3.1 CT Scanning, Volume Rendering and Identifying Atheromas in Mummified Remains

6.3.1.1 Advances in Volume Rendering

As outlined in Antoine and Vandenbeusch (2021), the latest generation of volume-rendering software and CT scanners offer many advantages, some of which are likely to significantly improve our ability to detect CVD in newly investigated and previously scanned mummified remains. Modern CT scanners can capture the image of an adult body in a few seconds, generating around 6000–10 000 slices (or tomograms), referred to as DICOMs (Digital Imaging and Communications in Medicine), with a slice thickness of around 0.3 mm (Ynnerman et al., 2016). At the British Museum, these X-ray slices are then combined by using VG Studio Max, a specialised volume-rendering software developed for the analysis and visualisation of CT scan data. Volume rendering produces accurate and very detailed three-dimensional images of the body inside the wrappings, known as visualisations. These take into account density, allowing tissues to be carefully identified and separated, a process called segmentation. Embalming materials and tissues can then be virtually peeled away, isolated and observed separately, providing a better understanding of the mummy's internal structures, as well as insightful three-dimensional cross-sections. As highlighted by Cox (2015), studying CT scans of mummified remains should nonetheless account for the impacts of both taphonomic changes and the process of mummification on what is visualised on a scan. Their analysis can often suffer from a lack of interpretative models, particularly as CT scanners were developed and calibrated for use with living humans, and not dehydrated remains (Gerald, 2015). A better understanding of the underlying physics, including overall limitations, is still required (Gerald, 2015).

The segmentation of different tissues or embalming materials should not be based solely on density, especially in areas where they are in close contact. This is particularly true when resin (often applied on top as well as within the body; see above) has permeated and combined the soft tissues and embalming materials (e.g. resin-soaked textiles applied on top of the skin or within the body cavity). In such cases, the anatomical structure and precise limits of individual organs and soft tissues can be hard to ascertain, rendering their accurate segmentation difficult if not impossible (e.g., the face of the mummy of Ameniryirt: Antoine & Vandenbeusch, 2021). When this occurs, tissues and organs need to be delineated on each of the thousands of two-dimensional X-ray slices using manual segmentation. By using this labour-intensive approach, the margins of each tissue or structure can often be accurately and correctly identified so that the limits of low-density elements (e.g. arteries) can be imaged on three-dimensional visualisations (and not solely studied on the DICOM slices). This can allow for a clearer understanding of the relationship between pathological areas and their surrounding tissues. Without such careful segmentation, the three-dimensional models run the risk of accidentally removing biological features of interest when the embalming materials are virtually removed. Once colours are added to the three-dimensional renderings, such errors can, regrettably, be easily missed. The time constraints of manual segmentation and the high costs of most volume-rendering packages often limit this approach. However, once delineated, tissues and embalming materials can be virtually removed one by one and studied in isolation. The mummies presented here were analysed using this approach with the help of VG Studio Max volume-rendering software. Most were also CT scanned using the latest generation of multidetector scanners, a dual-energy CT scanner.

6.3.1.2 The Advantages of Dual-Energy CT Scanning

Rather than using a single energy source and its detector, dual-energy CT scanners use two X-ray sources, as well as two sets of detectors within one scanner. Significantly for the analysis of low-density arteries and the detection of relatively small atheromas of a higher density, dual-energy CT scanners allow for a combination of low-energy spectra (80 or 100 kV) and high-energy spectra (120 or 140 kV). A combination of the lower settings (80 and 120 kV) is, for example, optimal when scanning lower-density mummies (e.g. thinly wrapped or unwrapped mummies and non-adults; see Antoine & Vandenbeusch, 2021). These dual-energy datasets improve tissue segmentation (Ynnerman et al., 2016) and, importantly for the study of calcium-rich atheromas, facilitate the isolation (or omission) of voxels that specifically contain calcium (Tozer Fink & Fink, 2018). Both detailed segmentation protocols and the isolation of specific tissues allow skeletal remains (and calcified tissues such as atheromas) and their surrounding soft tissues to be studied separately or in combination, offering a clearer understanding of their three-dimensional relationship (Taylor & Antoine, 2014: 103–4). Responses to the two energy spectra can help differentiate tissues (McCollough et al., 2015) and offer compositional information beyond that attainable from single-energy CT (Coursey et al., 2010). This has been successfully used in mummified animals to distinguish low-density bones from desiccated soft tissues (Bewes et al., 2016). In mummified human remains, dual-energy CT scanning has also been shown to improve semi-automated segmentation techniques and reduce manual segmentation times (Friedman et al., 2012). Finally, the streak-like artefacts produced around metal objects placed in or around the body by embalmers (e.g., metal amulets; see Taylor & Antoine, 2014: 68–91) when imaged by a CT scanner can be moderated by employing state-of-the-art reconstruction algorithms, modified scanning protocols and multi-energy CT scanning (see Ynnerman et al., 2016). Multi-energy CT scanners have been available since 2006 (McCollough et al., 2015). Although the advantages they offer are clear, they are not commonly found in hospitals and most studies on mummified remains are still carried out using scanners with a single energy source. However, a dual CT spectrum can also be generated with a single source CT by scanning the mummy twice at different wavelength settings. The datasets can be combined using the latest volume-rendering software as long as the mummified remains have not been moved between scans.

6.3.1.3 Identifying Atheromas in Mummified Remains

With few multi-energy scanners available at the time of their comprehensive study of atherosclerosis in Egyptian mummies, Allam et al. (2011) used a single source CT. Nonetheless, the authors discuss how the enhanced spatial resolution of newer machines, particularly multi-energy machines, should improve plaque characterisation in the blood vessels of mummified remains, with dual-energy CT likely to help distinguish the calcium hydroxyapatite present in atherosclerotic plaque from the natron employed in mummification (Allam et al., 2011: 325). The latter is mostly composed of sodium carbonate decahydrate and sodium bicarbonate (see Section 6.2) which, in some mummies, was not only placed inside the body (e.g. chest cavity) but would also have permeated into the soft tissues. The extent to which natron enters tissues as it dehydrates the body remains unclear. In some dual-energy CT scans, thousands of small high-density dots can be seen throughout the body's soft tissues. These are possibly the result of the natron treatment and may occur when large amounts are required to desiccate the body (e.g. the overweight mummy of a young man, catalogued as British Museum EA 6713; Antoine & Vandenbeusch, 2016: 160–87).

The amount and resolution of the data captured via multi-energy scanning not only improves segmentation, but can also be used to generate clear and detailed three-dimensional models that capture both the lower-density and higher-density elements (e.g. soft tissues and small calcifications versus larger calcified tissues) without compromising one over the other. This crucial aspect is particularly relevant when attempting to detect pathological changes that occur in lower-density arteries and involve higher-density atheromas of varying sizes. Indeed, tube voltage and tube current have been shown to impact image quality and the detectability of calcium-containing structures in *ex vivo* studies of coronary plaque deposits, with settings at 80, 120 and 140 kV affecting the CT density of all plaque types, particularly calcified plaques (see Saremi & Achenbach, 2015). A similar investigation at 80 and 140 kV showed that dual-energy CT improved the differentiation of calcified plaques from non-calcified plaques, with calcified lesions having a significantly higher attenuation (appearing denser or brighter on the scan) at 80 kV (Barreto et al., 2008; see also Saremi & Achenbach, 2015). This suggests that the inclusion of a lower-energy spectrum (80 or 100 kV) in a multi-energy scan of mummified remains will not only benefit the detection of the desiccated arteries, but will also improve the visibility of smaller or poorly calcified atheromas. The greater clarity of dual-energy spectra also allows a better understanding of which internal organs and arteries were removed as part of the embalming process and, of those that were not taken out, which have been successfully preserved. Higher-resolution data help identify the surviving organs and mummified tissues, something that is not always straightforward, with embalmers using a range of approaches to preserve the body (see Section 6.2). It also benefits the detection of any pathological changes, particularly as tissues shrink and become distorted as they dry.

6.3.2 Establishing Age at Death, Biological Sex and the Past Prevalence of Atheromas in Mummified Remains

6.3.2.1 Age at Death

Improvements in CT scanning and visualisation techniques are allowing researchers to scrutinise the bones of mummified individuals in previously unattainable detail without the need to unwrap them. Skeletal elements can be virtually scored for age using methods developed for the study of skeletal remains by biological anthropologists (bioarchaeologists and forensic anthropologists: Antoine & Vandenbeusch, 2021; see also Taylor & Antoine, 2014; Antoine & Vandenbeusch, 2016; Hawass & Saleem, 2016; Nystrom, 2019). Although some studies of atherosclerosis in mummified remains are now employing well-established scoring systems to estimate age at death and confirm the biological sex of the individuals analysed, many reports do not describe, reference or make use of the clearly defined and published methods. The use of systematic and repeatable methods/standards would allow for like-for-like comparisons across studies and clarify how the biological profile of each mummified individual was established (including those affected by CVD). Disentangling objective data (e.g. age scores) from their interpretation (e.g. approximate age at death) also allows published data to be reinterpreted using the latest scientific approaches, and small-scale studies to be integrated into larger analyses of the past prevalence of CVD.

Although risk factors for CVD can develop during childhood and adolescence, today it is mostly associated with adults and old age (Daniels et al., 2011). However, atherosclerosis has been shown to begin in children as young as nine years of age (see Friedemann et al., 2012) and future study cohorts may benefit from the inclusion of non-adult mummies. When analysing the mummies curated at the British Museum, the largely consistent and regular sequence of dental development (excluding the highly variable third molar) is primarily used to establish a developmental stage (see Ubelaker, 1989: 64) and estimate of the age at death of non-adults (see Hillson, 1996: 118–47; Hillson, 2014: 28–69). As the bones of the maturing body have different growth patterns and time scales of development, the times of appearance and fusion of epiphyses and the size and shape of growing bones are also employed (see Scheuer & Black, 2000). Both approaches are used to establish an overall approximate age at death and assign individuals to age cohorts: preterm (less than 37 weeks), full-term (37–42 weeks), infancy (0–1 years), early childhood (2–5 years), late childhood (6–10 years), puberty (11–15 years) and adolescent (16–19 years). These cohorts are based on the age ranges discussed in Scheuer and Black (2000: 368–9) and White et al. (2012: 381–5), as well as the recommendations outlined in Buikstra and Ubelaker (1994: 21-37). These subdivisions allow for comparison between age cohorts and other published data, and account for the difficulties in assigning a precise age at death.

In mummified adults, dental wear and the presence of osteoarthritis are sometimes employed to establish an age at death but both can be influenced by factors other than age (Hillson, 1996: 239–42; Waldron, 2019: 724–5). Age-related changes to the pubic symphysis (Brooks & Suchey, 1990; Buikstra & Ubelaker, 1994: 21–37) can provide a more reliable age-at-death, and its morphology can be assessed using CT datasets. The pubic joint was, for example, successfully imaged in 44 clinical CT scans from the Boston University Medical Center in patients aged 19–89 years, with age being estimated using the Suchey–Brooks method (Wink, 2014). In most (79.5 per cent), the Suchey–Brooks phase assigned to the patient matched their independently known age and the presence of clearly observable changes on the three-dimensional images (e.g. bony nodules and the extent of the pubic symphyseal rim), and offered good intra-observer reliability (Wink, 2014). Merritt's analysis of CT scans of 420 cadavers aged 20–79 years at death from Australia's Victorian Institute of Forensic Medicine also clearly identified billowing on the symphysis face in younger individuals, as well as changes to the appearance of the ventral rampart and the dorsal margin; over 70 per cent of the cohort were placed in the correct age group (Merritt, 2018a). A systematic review of CT age estimation from the pubic symphysis using the Suchey–Brooks method by Warrier et al. (2021) further supports this approach, with the majority of the individuals in published studies assigned to the correct age group, and scores showing good inter- and intra-observer reliability (see also Lottering et al., 2013; Hall et al., 2019; Hisham et al., 2019). CT visualisations of changes to the pubic symphysis are now being used to estimate the age at death of mummified individuals (Taylor & Antoine, 2014; Antoine & Vandenbeusch, 2016, 2021; Hawass & Saleem, 2016) but challenges remain. Establishing the presence of certain age-related changes (e.g. porosity) remains difficult (Merritt, 2018a) and appears to result in a slight tendency to under-age individuals in the Suchey–Brooks phases III and above (Wink, 2014). The broad age ranges of the scoring method also have a significant overlap (see Buikstra & Ubelaker, 1994: 21–37 and discussions in Wink, 2014; Warrier et al., 2021) that only allow for an approximate age at death to be established. Here, CT visualisation of the changes to the pubic symphysis were scored after Brooks and Suchey (1990) and, following Buikstra and Ubelaker (1994: 21–37), results were used to determine whether a mummified individual was *most likely* to have died as a young adult (20–34 years), middle-aged adult (35–49 years) or old adult (50 years or older).

Although not used in this study, cranial suture closure and degenerative changes at sternal ends of ribs (see Buikstra & Ubelaker, 1994: 21–37; White et al., 2012: 379–427) have also been used to determine the age at death of mummified adults (Hawass & Saleem, 2016). However, the reliability of both approaches has been the focus of much debate (Nikita, 2013; Muñoz et al., 2018; Ruengdit et al., 2020) and it remains unclear if such age-related changes can be correctly assessed via CT (Moskovitch et al., 2010; Merritt, 2018b). CT scans may offer a clearer evaluation of ectocranial suture closure (Ruengdit et al., 2020). When tested on an autopsy sample of 231 individuals aged between 19 and 89 years, Boyd et al. (2015) were able to distinguish younger ($<$40 years) from older ($>$60 years) individuals. As noted in Antoine and Vandenbeusch (2021), applying the sternal rib end method on well-preserved and articulated mummified remains may also help researchers identify the rib being scored (usually the first or fourth rib is required; Işcan et al., 1984). Further

CT testing of both methods should also help develop recording protocols adapted to mummified remains that account for scan resolution on the data observed (e.g. on assessing cranial suture closure) and the impact of embalming processes on the areas being assessed (e.g. damage to the sternal rib end; see Rühli & Böni, 2000).

6.3.2.2 Estimating or Confirming the Biological Sex

When soft tissues are poorly preserved, the biological sex of mummified adults can also be estimated or confirmed using the dimorphic traits of the skeleton. Knowing an individual's biological sex is also necessary for some age estimation methods (e.g. those focused on the public symphysis and rib ends; see previous section). Dimorphic traits can be assessed via three-dimensional visualisation by virtually removing the segmented soft tissues and embalming materials. However, cranial morphological traits may not be suitable due to the overall gracile nature of many Nile Valley populations. With cranial traits usually scored across a range from 1 (female) to 5 (male) (see Buikstra & Ubelaker, 1994: 16–19), ancient Egyptian male skulls often have an overall score of 2 or 3 (rather than the more robust 4 or 5 scores) and ancient Egyptian females appear to be slightly robust, with an average score of 2 (see Godde et al., 2018). The dimorphic traits of the pelvis should always be accorded greater weight when estimating the biological sex as the female pelvis is adapted to child-bearing and childbirth; the pelvis was used to confirm the biological sex of the adults in this study (see Buikstra & Ubelaker, 1994: 16–19; Bruzek, 2002; White & Folkens, 2005: 385–7).

6.3.2.3 Recording Arteries, Atheromas and Other Related Pathological Changes

Ancient Egyptian embalming practices evolved over time, with different regions and mummification workshops employing a range of approaches and treatments (see Section 6.2). This has resulted in varying levels of vessel preservation. Although naturally mummified individuals can be very well preserved, their overall preservation can also differ from one individual to the next (Friedman et al., 2018). To account for such variations, all detectable arteries and the presence of the heart should be systematically recorded and assessed for signs of CVD. Here, the approach used by Allam et al. (2011) was employed to record the presence of both the heart and any preserved vascular tissues that had not been removed by the embalmers. These were primarily identified using their density, morphology, homogeneity and expected anatomical position. In addition to their likely position, Allam et al. (2011: 317) also note that vascular tissues and the heart are best identified using their relationship with contiguous structures, particularly in three-dimensional visualisations. As per their recommendations, arterial vascular regions in this study were divided into the five distinct beds after Allison et al. (2014): carotid, coronary, aortic, iliac and peripheral vascular beds (femoral/popliteal/tibial arteries). As with Allam et al. (2009, 2011), clear calcifications in the vessel wall of an identifiable artery were interpreted as *diagnostic of atherosclerosis*. If there was no clear vessel wall, calcifications along or near an artery's expected course were interpreted as *probable atherosclerosis*. Any vessel displacements caused by the removal of internal organs or the insertion of internal or subcutaneous packing during embalming should also be accounted for (e.g. neck and throat packing may compress the carotid arteries), as should the insertion of high-density elements often found amongst the packing materials used by embalmers. These may easily be mistaken for calcifications (e.g. stones, faience amulets, natron).

As atherosclerosis is now considered a chronic inflammatory disease that includes an autoimmune element (Singh et al., 2002), and the accumulation of inflammatory cells in an artery's inner membrane enhances inflammatory processes that lead to the development of atherosclerotic lesions (Cichoń et al., 2017), other detectable pathological changes should also be recorded. However, with internal organs often removed or modified as part of the embalming process, evaluating the presence of pathological changes in mummified remains can be challenging (see Aufderheide, 2003: 418–99). The remaining organs and soft tissues, when successfully preserved, dry, shrink and become distorted. This can impede the detection of lesions, and changes affecting the skeleton are often easier to detect and interpret on the CT scan images. However, only a limited number of diseases usually result in changes to bones, with many taking several years to affect the skeleton (see examples in Roberts & Manchester, 2005; Waldron, 2009; Buikstra, 2019). As noted in Antoine and Vandenbeusch (2021), identifying and interpreting pathological changes in a desiccated, embalmed and, when organs have been removed, incomplete body can be difficult and, with such a partial picture, some pathological changes remain undetected or are hard to interpret, and cause of death is rarely established.

6.4 New CT Scans, New Stories: Towards a More Systematic Approach

The mummified remains curated at the British Museum are currently the focus of an extensive programme of research that makes use of the latest dual-energy CT scanning technology housed at Royal Brompton and Harefield NHS Trust, London (Taylor & Antoine, 2014; Antoine & Vandenbeusch, 2016, 2021; all scans were performed on days that did not impact on patient use). Without the need to unwrap them, their analysis is providing new information on past funerary beliefs and practices in the Nile Valley, as well as unique insights into the biology and state of health of these mummified individuals. Eight natural and artificially preserved mummified individuals were analysed to feature in the 2014–15 British Museum exhibition entitled *Ancient Lives, New Discoveries*. Spanning from about 3500 BCE to about 700 CE, each was carefully chosen to explore different Nile Valley cultures and periods, from probable villagers to members of high-ranking families (see Taylor & Antoine, 2014). The six adults in the exhibition once belonged to communities extending from the Fayum, in Upper Egypt to the Fourth Cataract region in Sudan, and they were analysed for signs of pathological change, including CVD. Two of these individuals had previously been analysed by Allam et al. (2011) as part of their study of atherosclerosis in ancient Egyptian mummies, with no atheromas detected.

Similarly, the mummy of Nesperennub, a priest who worked at the temple of Khonsu in Karnak, was the focus of the *Mummy: The Inside Story* exhibition held at the British Museum in 2004 (Taylor, 2004), and was toured internationally until 2013. Once again, no atheromas were detected in the CT scan taken almost two decades ago. As with the mummies in the *Ancient Lives, New Discoveries* exhibition, the mummy of Nesperennub was rescanned using the latest generation of dual-energy CT scanners, revealing entirely new insights into his mummification and state of health that challenge previously established findings. To contextualise these new discoveries, detectable pathological changes in all seven mummified individuals are reported. As some of these mummies featured in earlier studies, they offered an opportunity to investigate if new scanners (and three-dimensional visualisation software) improve the detection of atheromas in mummified remains.

6.4.1   Gebelein Man B (British Museum EA 32754)

One of seven Predynastic mummies curated at the British Museum, Gebelein Man B was buried in an oval or circular shallow grave in a tightly flexed position without a coffin. Close contact with the hot and arid Egyptian sands has naturally mummified his body. Discovered in the 1890s in a cemetery at the site of Gebelein in Upper Egypt, we know relatively little of his burial context or status (Budge, 1920; Dawson & Gray, 1968). However, all seven burials are characteristic of the Predynastic funerary tradition and, although Gebelein Man B did not yield sufficient collagen to be radiocarbon dated, hair and bone collagen samples from four of the other mummies produced dates ranging from 3932 to 3030 cal BCE (68.2 per cent probability) consistent with Egypt's Predynastic period (Friedman et al., 2018). His skin, hair and nails are all well preserved and he does not display any visible signs of deliberate embalming. As with the two other Gebelein mummies who had previously been scanned (Antoine & Ambers, 2014; Ynnerman et al., 2016), the CT data also reveal that most of his internal organs and arteries are remarkably preserved, and he shows no signs of invasive treatments (Taylor & Antoine, 2014; Antoine & Vandenbeusch, 2021). As with the other mummified individuals in this study, biological sex was estimated or confirmed using the dimorphic traits of the skeleton and any preserved soft tissues, respectively. In the case of Gebelein Man B, his very well preserved soft tissues clearly identify him as male. The three-dimensional visualisation of the CT scan shows that Gebelein Man B's pubic symphysis (Figure 6.1) exhibits no or little remodelling and he was most likely a young adult aged between 20 and 34 years when he died (Taylor & Antoine, 2014: 22–43; Antoine & Vandenbeusch, 2021). CT scanning also revealed that part of his digestive tract and what remains of his last meal are preserved on the inside of his pelvis (Taylor & Antoine, 2014: 31–5). Such well-preserved natural mummies offer a rare opportunity to study organs and vessels that were often removed by embalmers and seldom survived. However, in these particular remains, no pathological changes were detected.

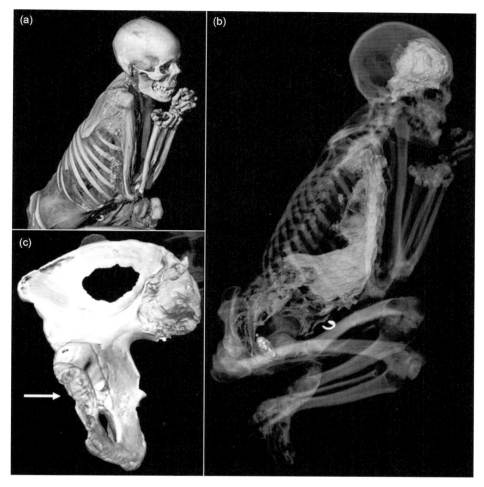

Figure 6.1 (a–c) CT scan visualisations of a naturally preserved Predynastic mummy from Gebelein, Upper Egypt (British Museum EA 32754). The transparency view (b) reveals the preservation of his internal organs. His pubic symphysis, clearly visible in the visualisation of the right pelvis (c), shows no or little remodelling (arrow). Source: courtesy of the Trustees of the British Museum. (A black and white version of this figure will appear in some formats. For the colour version, please refer to the plate section.)

6.4.2 Tamut (British Museum EA 22939)

The style of Tamut's cartonnage case indicates that she lived in the earlier part of the Twenty-second Dynasty (c. 900 BCE) (Taylor & Antoine, 2014: 68–91). With different versions of her name used on her outer casing, Tamut appears to be an abbreviation, with Tayesmutengebtiu likely to be the most correct version of her full name see Taylor & Antoine, 2014: 77). Inscriptions on her cartonnage reveal she was a married woman and priestess, or Chantress of Amun, most probably in the Great Temple of Amun in Karnak (Taylor & Antoine, 2014: 78). The presence of a metal amulet on top of her pubic symphysis affected the X-rays passing through that area, preventing a clear assessment of her age at death. Although a poor indicator of age, Tamut's teeth confirm that she was an adult and show signs of advanced dental attrition, with most of her tooth crowns worn to the roots. Despite the wear, only a single periapical lesion was detected at the end of the root of the upper-left first premolar. An incision on the left flank had been used to remove her internal organs and her body cavity was filled with packing materials, textiles and four bundles that most probably contain her separately desiccated organs. The insertion of the packing and bundles made it difficult to determine if her heart was left in place. As was typical of the period, and to give a lifelike appearance to her features post desiccation, packing materials and textile had been inserted in Tamut's mouth, nose and throat. Despite being compressed by this packing (Figure 6.2), both of her carotid arteries reveal the presence of atheromas. The arteries in Tamut's legs are also well preserved and calcified plaque deposits were detected in both of her femoral arteries (Figure 6.2).

6.4.3   Nesperennub (British Museum EA 30720)

The style of Nesperennub's coffin and his titles suggest that he lived and was buried in the Theban area of the Nile Valley during the Twenty-second Dynasty (c. 800 BCE). A priest from Thebes, he held several positions within the sacred complex of Karnak, where Amun was worshipped. Age-related changes to the pubic symphysis suggest he was a middle-aged adult of between 35 and 49 years old when he died. Packing materials were used to preserve the shape of Nesperennub's face. A substance similar to resin was placed in his mouth, while pieces of textile coated with resin appear to have been inserted into his neck. Nesperennub's internal organs, which had been removed and desiccated, were repositioned inside his chest. The presence of the heart is hard to ascertain, in part due to these packing materials and cloth bundles, and it may not have been successfully preserved. Nesperennub's teeth show signs of incredibly high dental wear and most of his tooth crowns are no longer visible. The lower resolution of previous X-rays and less sophisticated CT scans (Taylor, 2004) had not fully captured the extent of Nesperennub's poor state of oral health, revealing numerous lesions that had previously remained undetected. Until now, he was believed to have had only a single periapical lesion but the improved resolution of dual-energy scanners reveals that most of his remaining 29 teeth and root sockets showed signs of disease (Vandenbeusch & Antoine, 2021: 82–86). An incredible 15 have periapical lesions and tooth decay was detected on 11 teeth at the time of his death (Figure 6.3). With such high dental wear, tooth decay may have affected even more of Nesperennub's teeth. However, the same wear and decay has destroyed much of the evidence. Where present, areas of demineralisation caused by the decay can be seen between teeth (interproximal caries), on the root surfaces just below the crowns (cervical root caries) or within the pulp chambers (gross caries; see Hillson, 1996: 269–84). The CT scan cross-sections of several of the affected teeth reveal that the decay had breached the pulp chamber, resulting in chronic infection and the

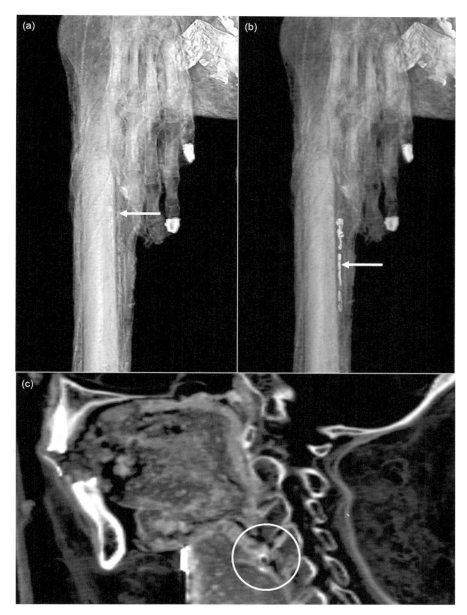

Figure 6.2 CT scan visualisations and DICOM image of the mummified remains of Tamut, a Twenty-second Dynasty priestess (British Museum EA 22939). The arteries in her legs are well preserved (a, arrow), with large atheromas detected in both of her femoral arteries. The one found within the right artery (b, arrow) has been segmented to allow for a clearer visualisation. The packing materials and textile inserted in Tamut's mouth and throat (c) can clearly be seen on the DICOM image (longitudinal section). Despite the insertion of these packing materials, atheromas can clearly be seen in both carotid arteries (atheroma within the left artery circled). Source: courtesy of the Trustees of the British Museum. (A black and white version of this figure will appear in some formats. For the colour version, please refer to the plate section.)

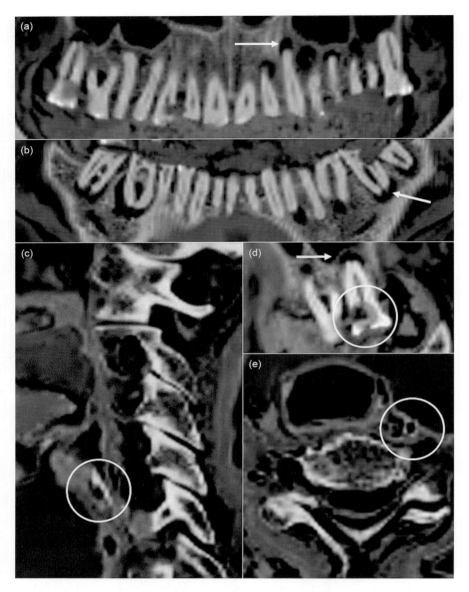

Figure 6.3 DICOM images of the mummified remains of Nesperennub, a Theban priest from the Twenty-second Dynasty who was probably aged 35–49 years when he died (British Museum EA 30720). Nesperennub's teeth in both upper and lower jaws (a, b) are highly worn, with barely any enamel remaining. At least 15 teeth have periapical lesions at the end of their roots (two examples are highlighted with arrows) and 11 teeth show signs of decay at the time of death. In one of the upper molars (d), the tooth decay has breached the pulp chamber and demineralised the surrounding dentine (circled), with the decay or an earlier breach from the high dental wear resulting in the formation of a periapical lesion (arrow). Although packing materials were inserted in Nesperennub's neck as part of the embalming process, atheromas were found on the inner surfaces of both carotid arteries (c, e, circled). Source: courtesy of the Trustees of the British Museum.

formation of at least one abscess and many other periapical lesions. Atheromas were found on the inner surfaces of his carotid arteries (Figure 6.3) and he would therefore have been at risk of CVD.

6.4.4 Padiamenet (British Museum EA 6682)

From the Twenty-fifth Dynasty (c. 700 BCE), Padiamenet's cartonnage case indicates he was the Chief Doorkeeper and Chief Barber of the Domain of Ra in the temple of Amun in Karnak (see Taylor & Antoine, 2014: 92–111). His pubic symphysis had begun to remodel and he was most probably 35–49 years old when he died. The CT scan also reveals that he had several large periapical lesions at the roots of his upper left canine, upper right first premolar and both lower first molars (Figure 6.4). They were most probably the result of the advanced dental wear visible on many of Padiamenet's teeth. Although he was mummified with care and is well preserved, his head appears to have detached itself between the third and fourth cervical vertebrae during the embalming, and was reattached using two wooden poles. The longer of the two (around 24 cm in length) was inserted into the throat via an opening in the neck, accidentally dislodging the sternum and upper ribs. With much heavy bandaging, resins and padding added to the neck area to hold the poles in position, the carotid arteries can no longer be identified. His internal organs were also carefully removed and the insertion of a pole into the chest makes it difficult to assess whether the heart (and surrounding arteries) was left in place. Nonetheless, the CT scan shows that one of Padiamenet's femoral arteries has a large atheroma (Figure 6.4).

6.4.5 Mummy of a Man (British Museum EA 22814)

Part of a group of mummies presented to the Prince of Wales (the future King Edward VII) in 1869, the mummification of this unnamed man is fairly consistent with the Twenty-sixth Dynasty (c. 600 BCE) and he appears to have originated from Thebes (Taylor & Antoine, 2014: 44–67). The CT scan and three-dimensional visualisation shows clear changes to the outline and surface of his pubic symphysis, with both suggesting he was most probably between 35 and 49 years old when he died. However, some of the changes are hard to visualise due to the low density of the pubic bones and he may actually have been older ($\geq$50 years). Most of the organs in his chest and abdomen were removed during embalming, and the cavity was filled with dense packing material. His heart appears to have been left in place and is preserved within granular material inserted by the embalmers. Most of his teeth are heavily worn and three of his anterior teeth (upper right central incisor, lower left and right central incisors) have periapical lesions at the ends of their roots. These may not have been abscesses at the time of death and may have instead been filled with a granuloma or a cyst (see Hillson, 1996: 284–7). Unfortunately, without being able to assess the walls of the lesions for signs of porosity, something that remains a challenge with current CT scans, it is not possible to distinguish an abscess from a

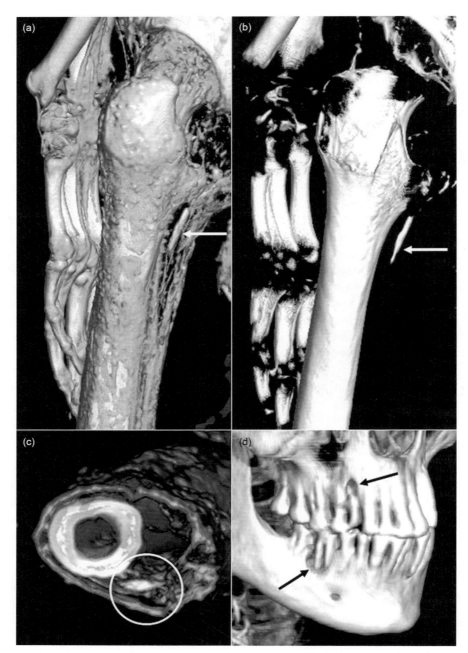

Figure 6.4 CT scan visualisations of the mummified remains of Padiamenet, Chief Doorkeeper and Chief Barber during the Twenty-fifth Dynasty (British Museum EA 6682). He was around 35–49 years old when he died and had four periapical lesions, two of which can be seen on the visualisation of his skull (d, arrows). CT scans of his left leg, shown with (a) and without (b) soft tissues, reveal a large atheroma within the femoral artery (arrows). The atheroma and vessel wall (c, circled), as well as the soft tissues surrounding the femur, are clearly visible in the cross-section. Source: courtesy of the Trustees of the British Museum. (A black and white version of this figure will appear in some formats. For the colour version, please refer to the plate section.)

granuloma or cyst. Here, advanced dental wear appears to have exposed the pulp chamber to the bacteria in the oral cavity, triggering the initial inflammatory processes. His upper right lateral incisor is also missing, and its root socket has fully remodelled. The tooth may have been lost from a prior periapical lesion. Finally, much of his upper-right first molar crown has been destroyed by tooth decay and large periapical lesions have developed at the ends of each of the molar's three roots. No atheromas were detected.

6.4.6   Mummy of a Man from Roman Egypt (British Museum EA 6704)

Dating to around the first to third centuries CE, this distinctively wrapped adult male mummy from the Roman period (see Taylor & Antoine, 2014: 134–49) had his internal organs removed and chest cavity filled with what appear to be organ bundles, resin and packing materials. Dense and solid packing was also pushed into the upper chest cavity and mouth. The heart is not visible and may have been dislodged when the packing was inserted. It was not possible to estimate his age at death due to the dense packing in the pelvic area. Five of his molar teeth are missing, possibly due to tooth decay, and the root sockets have remodelled (see Taylor & Antoine, 2014: 143–4). The lower right third molar has a large occlusal surface cavity and periapical lesions are clearly visible around the roots of a molar and four premolars. No atheromas were detected.

6.4.7   Natural Mummy from Medieval Sudan (British Museum EA 83133)

Recovered during the rescue campaign preceding the building of the Merowe dam, this naturally mummified body from the area of the Fourth Nile Cataract in Sudan is remarkably preserved. The remains of this woman belong to a group of 50 natural mummies dating to the Medieval Period (c. 600–1500 CE) donated by Sudan's National Corporation for Antiquities and Museums, and held at the British Museum where they are currently the focus of an extensive programme of research. Passively conserved to allow for the application of a broad range of analytical techniques (Wills & Antoine, 2015), this adult female was discovered at site 3-J-23, close to the modern village of et-Tereif and radiocarbon dated to around 655–775 CE (Antoine & Ambers, 2014; Taylor & Antoine, 2014: 170–5). With no detectable signs of deliberate embalming, her skin and internal organs are very well preserved. Her brain, lungs, liver, heart and other organs, as well as many arteries have survived and, although desiccated, they are recognisable. With few degenerative changes, her pubic symphysis suggests she was a young adult, most probably between 20 and 34 years old when she died. Apart from her lower canine teeth, which appear to have been deliberately removed as part of a cultural practice seen elsewhere in Sudanese archaeological sites from the Neolithic onwards, and the presence of a Christian tattoo on the upper part of her right thigh (see Vandenbeusch & Antoine, 2015; Antoine & Vandenbeusch, 2021), no other (pathological) changes were observed.

6.5 Investigating the Past Prevalence of Atheroma in Nile Valley Mummies

Overall findings are summarised in Table 6.1 following Allam et al. (2011) and include additional pathological changes.

Assessing the past prevalence of CVD in mummified remains can be challenging. As highlighted by this small study of seven adults, the removal of organs by embalmers can limit the available evidence, something that should be – but is not always – accounted for. Although more complete and well preserved, the naturally mummified individuals analysed here are both young adults (20–34 years) and neither showed signs of pathological changes in their arteries. Of the other five artificially embalmed individuals, three had detectable atheromas located in their femoral and/or carotid arteries. Two of the five embalmed mummies (EA 6682 and EA 22814) had previously been scanned using single-energy CT set at 130 kV by Allam et al. (2011; mummy list in supplementary materials). Although Allam and colleagues had rigorously assessed these individuals, Padiamenet's atheroma (EA 6682) was not detected. Similarly, the atheromas in Nesperennub's carotid arteries (EA 30720), as well as the presence of numerous periapical lesions and tooth decay, were not recorded when he was analysed as part of the *Mummy: The Inside Story* exhibition (see Taylor, 2004). However, CVD had not been the focus of the research. Once again, the data were obtained via single-energy CT set at 120 kV and did not benefit from the more sophisticated three-dimensional visualisation software available today; only a single periapical lesion was detected at the time (see Taylor, 2004: 18–21).

The present study appears to have benefited from the higher spatial resolution of dual energy, something that Allam et al. (2011: 325) had themselves suggested would improve atheroma detectability. The ability to combine a low-energy spectrum (100 kV) with a high-energy one (140 kV), as was used here, appears to aid the visualisation of both the preserved vessels and previously undetected atheromas. Indeed, most of the arteries not removed by the embalmer were observable and the pA category (probable atherosclerosis with calcifications along or near an artery's expected course; see Table 6.1) was not required. Tamut's (EA 22939) carotid arteries were also identified despite being compressed by the insertion of packing materials and textile in her throat and mouth, with both vessels revealing the presence of clear atheromas. The study, although limited in scope, also reveals that the embalmers' efficiency makes it more likely that pathological changes are found in the arteries that are not usually removed or impacted by packing materials (i.e. the carotid and peripheral vascular beds). Any attempt at calculating the true prevalence of atheromas based on mummified remains should account for the actual presence/absence of the vessels, particularly as overall preservation and embalming methods often differ between individuals, as well as by period and by region (e.g. the mummified young man from Roman Egypt with fully preserved and intact internal organs in Antoine & Vandenbeusch, 2021: figure 12). If a 'population'-based study is being conducted, it is important to know how many of the individuals had vessels preserved and how many were/were not affected. This should be combined with data that record exactly which vessels are preserved and how many of those were affected by CVD.

Table 6.1 Cardiovascular findings in mummified Nile Valley individuals.

Mummy	Name	Period	Date	Location	Occupation	Age (years)	Sex	Heart	Carotid	Coronary	Aortic	Iliac	Femoral Popliteal Tibial	Other pathological changes
EA 32754	Unknown	Predynastic	4000–3000 BCE	Gebelein	Unknown	20–34	M	0	0	0	0	0	0	
EA 22939	Tamut	22nd Dynasty	c. 900 BCE	Thebes	Chantress of Amun	Adult	F	NO	A	NO	NO	NO	A	Dental pathology
EA 30720	Nesperennub	22nd Dynasty	c. 800 BCE	Thebes	Priest	35–49	M	NO	A	NO	NO	NO	0	Dental pathology
EA 6682	Padiamenet	25th Dynasty	c. 700 BCE	Thebes	Chief Doorkeeper and Chief Barber	35–49	M	NO	NO	NO	NO	NO	A	Dental pathology
EA 22814	Unknown	26th Dynasty	c. 600 BCE	Thebes	Unknown	35–49/50+	M	0	NO	0	NO	NO	0	Dental pathology
EA 6704	Unknown	Roman	100–300 CE	Thebes?	Unknown	Adult	M	NO	0	NO	NO	NO	0	
EA 83133	Unknown	Medieval	655–775 CE	Fourth Cataract, Sudan	Unknown	20–34	F	0	0	0	0	0	0	
Atheroma prevalence									2/5 (40%)	0/3 (0%)	0/2 (0%)	0/2 (0%)	2/7 (29%)	

0, observable with no atheroma; NO, not observable; A, atherosclerosis with calcifications in the vessel wall; pA, probable atherosclerosis with calcifications along or near an artery's expected course (not required in this study). For additional pathological changes and mummification methods, see text. All mummies apart from EA 22814 were analysed using a dual-energy CT scanner combination of 100 kV and 140 kV, which appears optimal for adult mummies.

\The way the data are presented in this chapter should also allow for the results to be integrated into broader studies. Of the seven adult individuals analysed, 43 per cent ($n = 3$) had atheromas. However, this overall prevalence does not account for the missing arterial beds. Once missing vessels are accounted for, 29 per cent ($n = 2$ out of 7 observed) and 40 per cent ($n = 2$ out of 5 observed) of the individuals with peripheral and carotid arteries preserved, respectively, had atheromas (see Table 6.1). Of the two female mummies, only Tamut (50 per cent prevalence) had pathological changes in both her femoral and carotid arteries but her age at death could not be determined. The other female is a naturally mummified young adult from medieval Sudan with well-preserved vessels and no detectable atheromas. Two of the five male individuals also had atheromas (40 per cent prevalence) and both are estimated to have been between 35 and 49 years old when they died. From around 900 to 700 BCE, all three mummies with signs of CVD were part of the Theban priesthood and the ancient Egyptian elite. As such, Tamut, Nesperennub and Padiamenet most probably had access to a diet rich in animal fat (see David et al., 2010) and although atherosclerosis is influenced by the interaction of multiple genetic and environmental factors, it is usually associated with obesity and a diet rich in cholesterol (see Chapter 2). However, the picture is incomplete, with many missing vessels in all but the two younger naturally mummified individuals. Nonetheless, the advantages of dual-energy CT are apparent and allow a better understanding of what organs and vessels remain in mummies, as well as the identification of previously undetected atheromas. If this is truly the case, results from previous studies made using single-energy scanners should be regarded as a minimum presence/prevalence and any comparisons between published works should account for the use of different scanning and imaging techniques.

More recently, atherosclerosis has also been linked with poor oral health, particularly periodontal (gum) disease (Carrizales-Sepúlveda et al., 2018), with the periodontal pathogens triggering a chronic inflammatory state that promotes atheroma plaque development (see below). In view of Nesperennub's extremely poor oral health, he is likely to have had severe periodontal disease and, combined with the inflammatory responses caused by tooth decay and periapical lesions, dental disease may have directly or indirectly been the cause of his death (see Clarke, 1999; Joshipura et al., 2009; Kim et al., 2013; Carrizales-Sepúlveda et al., 2018; Bayetto et al., 2020). Tamut and Padiamenet also show signs of dental disease, with periapical lesions found in both, and are also likely to have had periodontal disease.

6.6 Oral Health and Cardiovascular Disease

Today, the World Health Organization (WHO) reports that CVD is the main cause of death across the world (World Health Organization, 2022), with periodontal disease the eleventh most prevalent disease globally (Global Burden of Disease, 2017 Janakiram et al., 2020). Recent clinical investigations have highlighted a link between periodontal disease and increased risk of CVD, including atherosclerosis (Carrizales-Sepúlveda et al., 2018 Zardawi et al., 2021), with periodontal disease an important independent causal risk factor for both atherosclerosis and ischaemic stroke (Joshipura et al., 2009). Periodontal disease and atherosclearosis appear to be linked to the same inflammatory pathways (Loos & Van Dyke, 2020).

6.6.1 Contributing Factors Linked to Periodontal Disease

The walls of arterial vessels are composed of four layers around the lumen, the space through which blood and circulatory elements flow. A thin layer of epithelial cells lines the lumen, under which is the intima followed by an internal elastic membrane known as the media, and the outmost adventitia (Ettinger, 2016: 129–60). Several factors can cause initial dysfunction or injury to the epithelial lining of arteries. This in turn leads to the movement of monocytes and lipids into the intima, initiating an atheroma (Ettinger, 2016: 129–60). These causal factors include hyperlipidaemia, hypertension, toxins, viruses, immune responses or systemic inflammation (Ettinger, 2016: 132), some of which have been linked to periodontal disease. Systemic inflammation is caused by an increase in inflammatory mediators in the circulatory system, such as C-reactive protein (CRP), fibrinogen and interleukin-6 (IL-6). These signalling proteins and cytokines have been shown to encourage epithelial dysfunction (Amar et al., 2003) and monocyte binding, a process that is uncommon in healthy epithelial cells (Ettinger, 2016: 137) and can lead to atherosclerosis. Periodontal disease has been clinically linked with increases of these inflammatory mediators in the bloodstream (Amar et al., 2003; Scannapieco et al., 2003; D'Aiuto et al., 2004; Leivadaros et al., 2005; Fedele et al., 2011). Noack et al. (2001) reported that patients with periodontal disease had significantly higher CRP levels, while D'Aiuto et al. (2004) found that both CRP and IL-6 levels dropped when periodontal disease was treated. However, although the clinical literature reveals a progressive and consistent reduction in systemic inflammation when periodontal therapy is applied (see D'Aiuto et al., 2013), others have highlighted a lack of standardisation when measuring periodontal disease, meaning that studies may not be comparing like with like (Scannapieco et al., 2003; Linden et al., 2013).

Thrombosis also usually involves an increase in inflammatory mediators in blood, with clotting factors such as fibrinogen and plasminogen activator inhibitor (PAI)-1 released from the liver (Schenkein & Loos, 2013). This leads to a prothrombotic state within the body, and the pressure exerted on the epithelial cells of the arterial walls can cause injury or cell dysfunction that may initiate the formation of an atheroma. Clinical studies have also shown that there may be increased PAI-1 levels in patients with periodontal disease (Bizzarro et al., 2007) and the extraction of affected teeth results in a reduction in both PAI-1 and fibrinogen (Taylor et al., 2006), reducing the risk of a thrombotic state. Antibodies produced by the response to periodontal bacteria (see Schenkein and Loos, 2013) can also promote systemic inflammation beyond the periodontal lesions. Studies have suggested that the periodontal bacteria themselves (Reyes et al., 2013), as well as bacterial components (Noack et al., 2001: 1225), can enter the bloodstream and directly infiltrate arterial epithelial cells, causing injury and dysfunction that leads to atherosclerosis. As noted by Aarabi et al. (2015), periodontal pathogens have been identified within atherosclerotic lesions and thrombi isolated from patients with myocardial infarction, and there is growing evidence for shared genetic susceptibility factors in both of these inflammatory diseases. However, further clinical evidence is required to clarify this particular pathway (Schenkein & Loos, 2013).

Lipids are also involved in the formation of atheromas via macrophage activity, or by the transformation of smooth muscle cells into foam cells (Huff & Pickering, 2015; Ettinger, 2016). This process requires a high concentration of lipids in the bloodstream (Ettinger, 2016) and elevated lipid concentrations have been observed in patients with periodontal disease. Lösche et al. (2000) found that patients affected by the latter also had higher levels of cholesterol and of low-density lipoprotein cholesterol and triglycerides. Similarly, Nibali et al. (2007) found that individuals with periodontal disease had significantly higher levels of low-density lipoprotein cholesterol in the bloodstream compared with those lacking the condition. Schenkein and Loos (2013) suggest that although the production and movement of cholesterol around the human body is a normal process, it may be influenced by inflammation or the presence of infection. In periodontal disease, lipopolysaccharides can be released into the bloodstream as bacterial surface components (Darveau et al., 1997; Cekici et al., 2014) and their systemic distribution may encourage increased synthesis of cholesterol in the liver (see Schenkein & Loos, 2013: 61). This results in a higher-than-normal concentration of lipids in the blood, termed dyslipidaemia. Once this state has been reached, the lipids are free to enter an atheroma in bulk and aid in the formation of foam cells.

6.6.2 Recording Periodontal Disease in Mummified Remains

In bioarchaeology, periodontal disease is recorded through the examination of the alveolar bone supporting the teeth. Originally, this was done by measuring the distance between the alveolar crest (AC) and the cemento-enamel junction (CEJ), a method used in clinical dentistry by probing the periodontal pocket to assess periodontal ligament attachment loss (Russell, 1956; Davies & Picton, 1969; Davies et al., 1969). However, as the teeth wear down on their occlusal surfaces, they are pushed further out into the mouth to maintain occlusion, a process called continuous eruption (Murphy, 1959; Newman & Levers, 1979; Levers & Darling, 1983; Whiting et al., 2019). This extends the AC/CEJ measurement but does not reflect periodontal attachment loss. Although some archaeological studies continue to employ this method (Alexandersen, 1967; Lukacs, 1989; Lavigne & Molto, 1995; Eshed et al., 2006; Meller et al., 2009; Masotti et al., 2013), assessing changes to the morphology of the alveolar crest (see Papapanou et al., 1988; Papapanou & Wennström, 1991; Persson et al., 1998) is also used clinically (Hausmann et al., 1991; Papapanou & Wennström, 1991; Persson et al., 1998; Rams et al., 2018). This approach, pioneered by Kerr (1988), is now favoured in bioarchaeological research and has been used to examine the past prevalence of periodontal disease in Britain (Kerr, 1986, 1991, 1998), to highlight the importance of age and sex on its prevalence (Wasterlain et al., 2011) and to understand the effect of urbanisation and changing diets on Nile Valley populations (Whiting et al., 2019).

In mummified remains, the drying process and shrinkage of the soft tissues does not allow periodontal disease to be assessed via the gingival soft tissue. Applying the scores devised by Kerr to CT data is complex. Studies show that bone demineralisation may only be detected radiographically once it has reached 30–50 per cent or more (Page & Eke, 2007; Research, Science and Therapy Committee, 2003). Subtle changes in bone morphology may be difficult to detect, particularly Kerr's score 2 as it equates to the increased vascularity and porosity seen in gingivitis. However, the recent use of subtraction imaging (improved visualisation of radiographic changes between pairs of radiographs by subtracting unchanged backgrounds) might compare well with Kerr's earlier stages, with demineralisations as low as 5 per cent being detected (Gröndahl & Gröndahl, 1983). This kind of imaging currently focuses on treatment, not diagnosis (Research, Science and Therapy Committee, 2003; Page & Eke, 2007; Corbet et al., 2009), and further research is needed to evaluate its use on archaeological skeletal and mummified human remains. The more destructive stages of periodontal disease (such as Kerr's scores 4 and 5) involve clear bone loss in the vertical plane. Such changes to the alveolar bone are often recorded in clinical research (Papapanou et al., 1988; Hausmann et al., 1991; Persson et al., 1998; Rams et al., 2018) and can be recognised as an area of oblique radiolucency in a radiograph that extends apically beside the tooth root, with signs of bone resorption. Nonetheless, scoring such changes on CT data, even dual-energy data, remains a challenge. The alveolar bone can be extremely thin and any vertical bone loss hard to detect. In view of Nesperennub's extremely poor dental health, he almost certainly had periodontal disease and some vertical bone loss is apparent. The findings in Tamut and Padiamenet are less clear. However, an increasing body of new research suggests that tooth decay (Aarabi et al., 2018; Kim et al., 2019) and periapical lesions (Garg & Chaman, 2016; Berlin-Broner et al., 2017; Conti et al., 2020; González-Navarro et al., 2020) are also linked to the development of atherosclerosis. This appears to be due to the chronic oral inflammation associated with some stages of these conditions. However, many risk factors are common to these diseases and may act as confounding factors that can bias the results (Jiménez-Sánchez et al., 2020) and larger longitudinal epidemiological studies are required.

6.7   Conclusion

As highlighted in this volume, CVDs are not a feature of the modern world. Although atheromas appear to have been frequent among the mummified inhabitants of the Nile Valley, the evidence is biased towards high-status individuals who could afford mummification. The 'simple' burial or less elaborate body preparation afforded to most ancient Egyptians was not conducive to soft tissue preservation and naturally mummified individuals are rare. As suggested in David et al. (2010), the greater wealth of high-status individuals may have exposed them to different risk factors linked to CVD when compared with poorer people, such as a diet with a higher proportion of animal fat and, perhaps, longer lives and a higher prevalence of obesity. Further work on the naturally mummified individuals from medieval Sudan curated at the British

Museum may offer a different perspective. Shifts in embalming practices over time and the limitations of single-energy CT are also likely to further skew the prevalence data. Because of the limited number of published studies, the complex and varied evolution of mummification in ancient Egypt is still relatively poorly understood. Overall temporal changes require further research and little is known of regional differences over time (Antoine & Vandenbeusch, 2021). In order to calculate true prevalence data, each mummified individual needs to be carefully assessed/reassessed in order to determine which organs and vessels were removed by the embalmer and base prevalence on those that have survived for analysis.

In this small study, atheromas were found in 29 per cent (n = 2 out of 7 observed) and 40 per cent (n = 2 out of 5 observed) of the individuals with preserved peripheral and carotid arteries, respectively. All three individuals with signs of CVD also had dental caries and/or periapical cavities, and most probably had periodontal disease in life. Clinical research reveals that poor oral health, particularly periodontal disease, can increase the risk of developing atherosclerosis via several pathways. However, the earlier stages of periodontal disease can be hard to assess via CT scanning. As scanning methods continue to improve, including the use of phase-contrast X-ray synchrotron microtomography to analyse smaller mummified remains in unprecedented detail (Porcier et al., 2019; Berruyer et al., 2020), it should be possible to score degenerative changes to the alveolar bone using the Kerr method. Future synchrotron beamlines currently in development should soon make it possible to scan whole bodies. These new scanning methods will enable a comprehensive survey of mummified blood vessels for signs of arterial plaque, including pre-calcification stages, and further explore links between CVD and oral health. Near infrared spectroscopy may also offer a method for detecting the early stages of atherosclerosis, prior to plaque calcification (see Nerlich et al., 2020). However, as atherosclerotic plaques initially develop as accumulations of cholesterol-rich lipids, it remains unclear if natron's proficiency in breaking down fat also affects our ability to detect early arterial plaque formation in artificially mummified ancient Egyptian remains. Until such methods are available, a combination of dual-energy CT scanning and advanced three-dimensional visualisation technology appears to offer the best options for analysing mummified remains in detail without the need to unwrap them. As highlighted here, dual-energy CT should allow a better understanding of what organs and vessels remain, as well as the identification of previously undetected atheromas and their relationship with surrounding soft tissues. Some atheromas are still likely to be missed and studies based on the CT scan analyses of mummified remains should only be regarded as providing data to calculate a minimum prevalence of *calcified* lesions, particularly when some of the organs and surrounding vessels have been removed by the embalmers. Possible discrepancies in the data obtained from single- and multi-energy scanners require further investigation but any data comparisons with already published studies ought to account for the use of differing scanning and imaging techniques. Although destructive, the use of genetic, chemical and histological analyses is also providing valuable new approaches that may support findings (see Chapters 3 and 5; Nerlich et al., 2020).

The benefits of both dual-energy CT on the visualisation of atheromas and a more systematic approach that accounts for the presence of preserved and detectable arteries (whether or not affected by atherosclerosis) should offer a clearer assessment of the past prevalence of CVD. The use of standardised and clearly defined methods to age and sex mummified individuals, as well as the type of scanner and its settings, should also enable like-for-like comparisons across publications and allow for the integration of smaller case studies into broader datasets. As noted in Nelson and Wade (2015: 942), different methods and recording systems, as well as a lack of comparable datasets, frequently limits the study of mummified remains to individual case studies. Evaluating the past prevalence of CVD would strongly benefit from large-scale comparative approaches that allow individual findings to be contextualised into larger studies. In view of their association with CVDs, both in clinical research and in the mummies examined here, the presence of tooth decay, periodontal disease and periapical lesions should also be recorded. Frequently found in ancient Egyptian mummified remains, dental and gum disease may partly explain why atheromas are often present in Nile Valley populations.

References

Aarabi, G., Eberhard, J., Reissmann, D. R., Heydecke, G. and Seedorf, U. (2015). Interaction between periodontal disease and atherosclerotic vascular disease: Fact or fiction? *Atherosclerosis*, 241(2), 555–60.

Aarabi, G., Heydecke, G. and Seedorf, U. (2018). Roles of oral infections in the pathomechanism of atherosclerosis. *International Journal of Molecular Sciences*, 19(7), 1978.

Alexandersen, V. (1967). The pathology of the jaws and the temporomandibular joint. In D. Brothwell and A. Sandison, eds., *Diseases in Antiquity*. Springfield, IL: Charles C. Thomas, pp. 551–98.

Allam, A. H., Thompson, R. C., Wann, L. S., Miyamoto, M. I. and Thomas, G. S. (2009). Computed tomographic assessment of atherosclerosis in ancient Egyptian mummies. *Journal of the American Medical Association*, 302(19), 2091–4.

Allam, A. H., Thompson, R. C., Wann, L. S., et al. (2011). Atherosclerosis in ancient Egyptian mummies: The Horus study. *Journal of the American College of Cardiology Cardiovascular Imaging*, 4(4), 315–27.

Allison, M. A., Criqui, M. H. and Wright, C. M. (2004). Patterns and risk factors for systemic calcified atherosclerosis. *Arteriosclerosis, Thrombosis and Vascular Biology*, 24, 331–6.

Amar, S., Gokce, N., Morgan, S., et al. (2003). Periodontal disease is associated with brachial artery endothelial dysfunction and systemic inflammation. *Arteriosclerosis, Thrombosis and Vascular Biology*, 23, 1245–9.

Antoine, D. and Ambers, J. (2014). The scientific analysis of human remains from the British Museum Collection: Research potential and examples from the Nile Valley. In A. Fletcher, D. Antoine and J. D. Hill, eds., *Regarding the Dead: Human Remains in the British Museum*. London: British Museum Press, pp. 20–30.

Antoine, D. and Vandenbeusch, M. (2016). *Egyptian Mummies. Exploring Ancient Lives*. Sydney: Museum of Applied Arts and Sciences.

Antoine, D. and Vandenbeusch, M. (2021). Human mummies from ancient Egypt and Nubia: An overview and new insights from the British Museum collection. In D. H. Shin and R. Bianucci, eds., *The Handbook of Mummy Studies*. Singapore: Springer, pp. 565–628.

Aufderheide, A. C. (2003). *The Scientific Study of Mummies*. Cambridge: Cambridge University Press.

Aufderheide, A. C. (2011). The enigma of ancient Egyptian excerebration. *Yearbook of Mummy Studies*, 1, 7–10.

Barreto, M., Schoenhagen, P., Nair, A., et al. (2008). Potential of dual-energy computed tomography to characterize atherosclerotic plaque: Ex vivo assessment of human coronary arteries in comparison to histology. *Journal of Cardiovascular Computed Tomography*, 2(4), 234–42.

Bayetto, K., Cheng, A. and Goss, A. (2020). Dental abscess: A potential cause of death and morbidity. *Australian Journal of General Practice*, 49, 563–7.

Bentzon, J. F., Otsuka, F., Virmani, R. and Falk, E. (2014). Mechanisms of plaque formation and rupture. *Circulation Research*, 114(12), 1852–66.

Berlin-Broner, Y., Febbraio, M. and Levin, L. (2016). Association between apical periodontitis and cardiovascular diseases: A systematic review of the literature. *International Endodontic Journal*, 50(9), 847–59.

Berruyer, C., Porcier, S. M. and Tafforeau, P. (2020). Synchrotron 'virtual archaeozoology' reveals how Ancient Egyptians prepared a decaying crocodile cadaver for mummification. *PLoS One*, 15(2), e0229140.

Bewes J. M., Morphett, A., Pate, F. D., et al. (2016). Imaging ancient and mummified specimens: dual-energy CT with effective atomic number imaging of two ancient Egyptian cat mummies. *Journal of Archaeological Science: Reports*, 8, 173–7.

Bizzarro, S., Van Der Velden, U., Ten Heggeler, J. M. A. G., et al. (2007). Periodontitis is characterized by elevated PAI-1 activity. *Journal of Clinical Periodontology*, 34, 574–80.

Boyd, K. L., Villa, C. and Lynnerup, N. (2015). The use of CT scans in estimating age at death by examining the extent of ectocranial suture closure. *Journal of Forensic Science*, 60, 363–9.

Brooks, S. and Suchey, J. (1990). Skeletal age determination based on the os pubis: A comparison of the Acsadi–Nemeskeri and Suchey–Brooks methods. *Human Evolution*, 5, 227–38.

Bruzek, J. (2002). A method for visual determination of sex using the human hip bone. *American Journal of Physical Anthropology*, 117, 157–68.

Budge, E. A. W. (1920). *By Nile and Tigris: A Narrative of Journeys in Egypt and Mesopotamia on Behalf of the British Museum Between the Years 1886 and 1913*. London: John Murray.

Buikstra, J. E. (ed.) (2019). *Ortner's Identification of Pathological Conditions in Human Skeletal Remains*, 3rd ed. London: Academic Press.

Buikstra, J. E. and Ubelaker, D. H. (eds.) (1994). *Standards for Data Collection from Human Skeletal Remains*. Arkansas Archaeological Survey Research Series No. 44. Fayetteville, AR: Arkansas Archaeological Survey.

Carrizales-Sepúlveda, E. F., Ordaz-Farías, A., Vera-Pineda, R. and Flores-Ramírez, R. (2018). Periodontal disease, systemic inflammation and the risk of cardiovascular disease. *Heart, Lung and Circulation*, 27 (11), 1327–34.

Cekici, A., Kantarci, A., Hasturk, H. and Van Dyke, T. E. (2014). Inflammatory and immune pathways in the pathogenesis of periodontal disease. *Periodontology 2000*, 64, 57–80.

Cichoń, N., Lach, D., Dziedzic, A., Bijak, M. and Saluk, J. (2017). Procesy zapalne w aterogenezie [The inflammatory processes in atherogenesis]. *Polski Merkuriusz Lekarski*, 42(249), 125–8.

Clark, K. A., Ikram, S. and Evershed, R. P. (2016). The significance of petroleum bitumen in ancient Egyptian mummies. *Philosophical Transactions of the Royal Society A, Mathematical, Physical and Engineering Sciences*, 374(2079), 20160229.

Clarke, J. H. (1999). Toothaches and death. *Journal of the History of Dentistry*, 47(1), 11–13.

Conti, L. C., Segura-Egea, J. J., Cardoso, C. B. M., et al. (2020). Relationship between apical periodontitis and atherosclerosis in rats: Lipid profile and histological study. *International Endodontic Journal*, 53, 1387–97.

Corbet, E. F., Ho, D. K. L. and Lai, S. M. L. (2009). Radiographs in periodontal disease diagnosis and management. *Australian Dental Journal*, 54(Suppl 1), S27–S43.

Coursey, C. A., Nelson, R. C., Boll, D. T., et al. (2010). Dual-energy multidetector CT: How does it work, what can it tell us, and when can we use it in abdominopelvic imaging? *Radiographics*, 30(4), 1037–55.

Cox, S. L. (2015). A critical look at mummy CT scanning. *Anatomical Record*, 298, 1099–110.

D'Aiuto, F., Parkar, M., Andreou, G., et al. (2004). Periodontitis and systemic inflammation: Control of the local infection is associated with a reduction in serum inflammatory markers. *Journal of Dental Research*, 83, 156–60.

D'Aiuto, F., Orlandi, M. and Gunsolley, J. C. (2013). Evidence that periodontal treatment improves biomarkers and CVD outcomes. *Journal of Clinical Periodontology*, 40(Suppl 14), S85–S105.

Daniels, S. R., Pratt, C. A. and Hayman, L. L. (2011). Reduction of risk for cardiovascular disease in children and adolescents. *Circulation*, 124(15), 1673–86.

Darveau, R. P., Tanner, A. and Page, R. C. (1997). The microbial challenge in periodontitis. *Periodontology 2000*, 14, 12–32.

David, A. R., Kershaw, A. and Heagerty, A. (2010). Atherosclerosis and diet in ancient Egypt. *Lancet*, 375 (9716), 718–19.

Davies, D. M. and Picton, D. C. A. (1969). A study of the periodontal state in two hundred and two skulls of primitive peoples. *Journal of Periodontal Research*, 4, 230–4.

Davies, D. M., Picton, D. C. A. and Alexander, A. G. (1969). An objective method of assessing the periodontal condition in human skulls. *Journal of Periodontal Research*, 4, 74–7.

Dawson, W. R. and Gray, P. H. K. (1968). *Catalogue of Egyptian Antiquities in the British Museum I: Mummies and Human Remains*. London: British Museum Press.

Eshed, V., Gopher, A. and Hershkovitz, I. (2006). Tooth wear and dental pathology at the advent of agriculture: New evidence from the Levant. *American Journal of Physical Anthropology*, 130, 145–59.

Ettinger, S. (2016). Atherosclerosis and arterial calcification. In: S. Ettinger, ed., *Nutritional Pathophysiology of Obesity and Its Comorbidities: A Case-study Approach*. London: Academic Press, pp. 129–60.

Fedele, S., Sabbah, W., Donos, N., Porter, S. and D'Aiuto, F. (2011). Common oral mucosal diseases, systemic inflammation, and cardiovascular diseases in a large cross-sectional US survey. *American Heart Journal*, 161, 344–50.

Friedemann, C., Heneghan, C., Mahtani, K., et al. (2012). Cardiovascular disease risk in healthy children and its association with body mass index: Systematic review and meta-analysis. *British Medical Journal*, 345, e4759.

Friedman, R., Antoine, D., Talamo, S., et al. (2018). Natural mummies from Predynastic Egypt reveal the world's earliest figural tattoos. *Journal of Archaeological Science*, 92, 116–25.

Friedman, S. N., Nguyen, N., Nelson, A. J., et al. (2012). Computed tomography (CT) bone segmentation of an ancient Egyptian mummy: A comparison of automated and semiautomated threshold and dual-energy techniques. *Journal of Computer Assisted Tomography*, 36(5), 616–22.

Garg, P. and Chaman, C. (2016). Apical periodontitis: Is it accountable for cardiovascular diseases? *Journal of Clinical and Diagnostic Research*, 10(8), ZE08–ZE12.

Gerald, C. (2015). Considered limitations and possible applications of computed tomography in mummy research. *Anatomical Record*, 298, 1088–98.

Global Burden of Disease (GBD) 2016 Disease and Injury Incidence and Prevalence Collaborators. (2017). Global, regional, and national incidence, prevalence, and years lived with disability for 328 diseases and injuries for 195 countries, 1990–2016: A systematic analysis for the Global Burden of Disease Study 2016. *Lancet*, 390, 1211–59.

Godde, K., Thompson, M. M. and Hens, S. M. (2018). Sex estimation from cranial morphological traits: Use of the methods across American Indians, modern North Americans, and ancient Egyptians. *Homo*, 69 (5), 237–47.

González-Navarro, B., Segura-Egea, J. J., Estrugo-Devesa, A., et al. (2020). Relationship between apical periodontitis and metabolic syndrome and cardiovascular events: A cross-sectional study. *Journal of Clinical Medicine*, 9(10), 3205.

Gröndahl, H. G. and Gröndahl, K. (1983). Subtraction radiography for the diagnosis of periodontal bone lesions. *Oral Surgery, Oral Medicine, Oral Pathology*, 55, 208–13.

Hall, F., Forbes, S., Rowbotham, S. and Blau, S. (2019). Using PMCT of individuals of known age to test the Suchey–Brooks method of aging in Victoria, Australia. *Journal of Forensic Sciences*, 64, 1782–7.

Hausmann, E., Allen, K. and Clerehugh, V. (1991). What alveolar crest level on a bite-wing radiograph represents bone loss? *Journal of Periodontology*, 62, 570–2.

Hawass, Z. and Saleem, S. N. (2016) *Scanning the Pharaohs: CT Imaging of the New Kingdom Royal Mummies*. Cairo: The American University in Cairo Press.

Hillson, S. (1996). *Dental Anthropology*. Cambridge: Cambridge University Press.

Hillson, S. (2014). *Tooth Development in Human Evolution and Bioarchaeology*. Cambridge: Cambridge University Press.

Hisham, S., Abdullah, N., Noor, M. H. M. and Franklin, D. (2019). Quantification of pubic symphysis metamorphosis based on the analysis of clinical MDCT scans in a contemporary Malaysian population. *Journal of Forensic Sciences*, 64(6), 1803–11.

Huff, M. W. and Pickering, J. G. (2015). Can a vascular smooth muscle-derived foam-cell really change its spots? *Arteriosclerosis, Thrombosis and Vascular Biology*, 35, 492–5.

Ikram, S. and Dodson, A. (1998). *The Mummy in Ancient Egypt: Equipping the Dead for Eternity*. London: Thames and Hudson.

Insull, W., Jr. (2009). The pathology of atherosclerosis: plaque development and plaque responses to medical treatment. *American Journal of Medicine*, 122(1 Suppl), S3–S14.

Işcan, M. Y., Loth, S. R. and Wright, R. K. (1984). Metamorphosis at the sternal rib end: a new method to estimate age at death in white males. *American Journal of Physical Anthropology*, 65, 147–56.

Janakiram C. and Dye, B. A. (2020). A public health approach for prevention of periodontal disease. *Periodontology 2000*, 84(1), 202–214.

Jiménez-Sánchez, M. C., Cabanillas-Balsera, D., Areal-Quecuty, V., et al. (2020). Cardiovascular diseases and apical periodontitis: association not always implies causality. *Medicina Oral, Patologia Oral y Cirugia Bucal*, 25(5), e652–e659.

Jones, J., Higham, T. F. G., Oldfield, R., O'Connor, T. P. and Buckley, S. A. (2014). Evidence for prehistoric origins of Egyptian mummification in Late Neolithic burials. *PLoS One*, 9(8), e103608.

Jones, J., Higham, T. F. G., Chivall, D., et al. (2018). A prehistoric Egyptian mummy: evidence for an 'embalming recipe' and the evolution of early formative funerary treatments. *Journal of Archaeological Science*, 100, 191–200.

Joshipura, K., Zevallos, J. C. and Ritchie, C. S. (2009). Strength of evidence relating periodontal disease and atherosclerotic disease. *Compendium of Continuing Education in Dentistry*, 30(7), 430–9.

Kerr, N. W. (1986). Dental examination of the Aberdeen Carmelite collection: late Medieval 1300-1600. In E. Cruwys and R. Foley, eds., *Teeth and Anthropology*. BAR International Series 291. Oxford: BAR Publishing, pp. 189–200.

Kerr, N. W. (1988). A method of assessing periodontal status in archaeologically derived skeletal material. *Journal of Paleopathology*, 2, 67–78.

Kerr, N. W. (1991). Prevalence and natural history of periodontal disease in Scotland: the mediaeval period (900-1600 AD). *Journal of Periodontal Research*, 26, 346–54.

Kerr, N. W. (1998). The prevalence and natural history of periodontal disease in Britain from prehistoric to modern times. *British Dental Journal*, 185, 527–35.

Kim, J. K., Baker, L. A., Davarian, S. and Crimmins, E. (2013). Oral health problems and mortality. *Journal of Dental Sciences*, 8(2), 115–20.

Kim, K., Choi, S., Chang, J., et al. (2019). Severity of dental caries and risk of coronary heart disease in middle-aged men and women: a population-based cohort study of Korean adults, 2002–2013. *Scientific Reports*, 9, 10491.

Lavigne, S. E. and Molto, J. E. (1995). System of measurement of the severity of periodontal disease in past populations. *International Journal of Osteoarchaeology*, 5, 265–73.

Leivadaros, E., Van Der Velden, U., Bizzarro, S., et al. (2005). A pilot study into measurements of markers of atherosclerosis in periodontitis. *Journal of Periodontology*, 76, 121–8.

Levers, B. G. H. and Darling, A. I. (1983). Continuous eruption of some adult teeth of ancient populations. *Archives of Oral Biology*, 25, 401–8.

Linden, G. J., Lyons, A. and Scannapieco, F. A. (2013). Periodontal systemic associations: review of the evidence. *Journal of Clinical Periodontology*, 40(Suppl 14), S8–S19.

Loos B. G. and Van Dyke, T. E. (2020). The role of inflammation and genetics in periodontal disease. *Periodontology 2000*, 83(1), 26–39.

Lösche, W., Karapetow, F., Pohl, A., Pohl, C. and Kocher, T. (2000). Plasma lipid and blood glucose levels in patients with destructive periodontal disease. *Journal of Clinical Periodontology*, 27, 537–41.

Lottering, N., MacGregor, D. M., Meredith, M., Alston, C. L. and Gregory, L. S. (2013). Evaluation of the Suchey–Brooks method of age estimation in an Australian subpopulation using computed tomography of the pubic symphyseal surface. *American Journal of Physical Anthropology*, 150, 386–99.

Łucejko, J., Connan, J., Orsini, S., Ribechini, E. and Modugno, F. (2017). Chemical analyses of Egyptian mummification balms and organic residues from storage jars dated from the Old Kingdom to the Copto-Byzantine period. *Journal of Archaeological Science*, 85, 1–12.

Lukacs, J. R. (1989). Dental paleopathology: Methods for reconstructing dietary patterns. In M. Iscan and K. Kennedy, eds., *Reconstruction of Life from the Skeleton*. New York: A. R. Liss, pp. 261–86.

McCollough, C. H., Leng, S., Yu, L. and Fletcher, J. G. (2015). Dual- and multi-energy CT: Principles, technical approaches, and clinical applications. *Radiology*, 276(3), 637–53.

Masotti, S., Onisto, N., Marzi, M. and Gualdi-Russo, E. (2013). Dento-alveolar features and diet in an Etruscan population (sixth–third c. BCE) from northeast Italy. *Archives of Oral Biology*, 58, 416–26.

Meller, C., Urzua, I., Moncada, G. and Von Ohle, C. (2009). Prevalence of oral pathologic findings in an ancient pre-Columbian archeologic site in the Atacama Desert. *Oral Diseases*, 15, 287–94.

Merritt, C. E. (2018a). Part II. Adult skeletal age estimation using CT scans of cadavers: revision of the pubic symphysis methods. *Journal of Forensic Radiology and Imaging*, 14, 50–7.

Merritt, C. E. (2018b). Part I. Adult skeletal age estimation using CT scans of cadavers: Revision of the fourth rib methods. *Journal of Forensic Radiology and Imaging*, 14, 39–49.

Moskovitch, G., Dedouit, F., Braga, J., et al. (2010). Multislice computed tomography of the first rib: A useful technique for bone age assessment. *Journal of Forensic Sciences*, 55(4), 865–70.

Muñoz, A., Maestro, N., Benito, M., et al. (2018). Sex and age at death estimation from the sternal end of the fourth rib. Does İşcan's method really work? *Legal Medicine*, 31, 24–9.

Murphy, T. (1959). Compensatory mechanisms in facial height adjustment to functional tooth attrition. *Australian Dental Journal*, 4, 312–23.

Nelson, A. J. and Wade, A. D. (2015). Impact: Development of a radiological mummy database. *Anatomical Record*, 298, 941–8.

Nerlich, A. G., Galassi, F. M. and Bianucci, R. (2020). The burden of arteriosclerotic cardiovascular disease in ancient populations. In D. Shin and R. Bianucci, eds., *The Handbook of Mummy Studies*. Singapore: Springer.

Newman, H. N. and Levers, B. G. (1979). Tooth eruption and function in an early Anglo-Saxon population. *Journal of the Royal Society of Medicine*, 72, 341–50.

Nibali, L., D'Aiuto, F., Griffiths, G., et al. (2007). Severe periodontitis is associated with systemic inflammation and a dysmetabolic status: A case–control study. *Journal of Clinical Periodontology*, 34, 931–7.

Nikita, E. (2013). Quantitative assessment of the sternal rib end morphology and implications for its application in aging human remains. *Journal of Forensic Sciences*, 58(2), 324–9.

Noack, B., Genco, R. J., Trevisan, M., et al. (2001). Periodontal infections contribute to elevated systemic C-reactive protein level. *Journal of Periodontology*, 72, 1221–7.

Nystrom, K. (2019). *The Bioarchaeology of Mummies*. New York: Routledge.

Page, R. C. and Eke, P. I. (2007). Case definitions for use in population-based surveillance of periodontitis. *Journal of Periodontology*, 78, 1387–99.

Papapanou, P. N. and Wennström, J. L. (1991). The angular bony defect as indicator of further alveolar bone loss. *Journal of Clinical Periodontology*, 18, 317–22.

Papapanou, P. N., Wennström, J. L. and Gröndahl, K. (1988). Periodontal status in relation to age and tooth type: A cross-sectional radiographic study. *Journal of Clinical Periodontology*, 15, 469–78.

Persson, R. E., Rollender, L. G., Laurell, L. and Persson, G. R. (1998). Horizontal alveolar bone loss and vertical bone defects in an adult patient population. *Journal of Periodontology*, 69, 348–56.

Porcier, S. M., Berruyer, C., Pasquali, S., et al. (2019). Wild crocodiles hunted to make mummies in Roman Egypt: Evidence from synchrotron imaging. *Journal of Archaeological Science*, 110, 105009.

Rams, T. E., Listgarten, M. A. and Slots, J. (2018). Radiographic alveolar bone morphology and progressive periodontitis. *Journal of Periodontology*, 89, 424–30.

Research, Science and Therapy Committee (2003). Position paper: Diagnosis of periodontal diseases. *Journal of Periodontology*, 74, 1237–47.

Reyes, L., Herrera, D., Kozarov, E., Roldán, S. and Progulske-Fox, A. (2013). Periodontal bacterial invasion and infection: Contribution to atherosclerotic pathology. *Journal of Clinical Periodontology*, 40(Suppl 14), S30–S50.

Roberts, C. and Manchester, K. (2005). *The Archaeology of Disease*, 3rd ed. Stroud: Sutton Publishing.

Ruengdit, S., Case, D. T. and Mahakkanukrauh, P. (2020). Cranial suture closure as an age indicator: A review. *Forensic Science International*, 307, 110111.

Rühli, F. J. and Böni, T. (2000). Radiological aspects and interpretation of post-mortem artefacts in ancient Egyptian mummies from Swiss collections. *International Journal of Osteoarchaeology*, 10(2), 153–7.

Russell, A. (1956). A system of classification and scoring for prevalence surveys of periodontal disease. *Journal of Dental Research*, 35, 350–9.

Saremi, F. and Achenbach, S. (2015). Coronary plaque characterization using CT. *American Journal of Roentgenology*, 204, W249–W260.

Scannapieco, F. A., Bush, R. B. and Paju, S. (2003). Associations between periodontal disease and risk for atherosclerosis, cardiovascular disease, and stroke: A systematic review. *Annals of Periodontology*, 8, 38–53.

Schenkein, H. A. and Loos, B. G. (2013). Inflammatory mechanisms linking periodontal diseases to cardiovascular diseases. *Journal of Clinical Periodontology*, 40(Suppl 14), S51–S69.

Scheuer, L. and Black, S. (2000). *Developmental Juvenile Osteology*. London: Academic Press.

Singh, R. B., Mengi, S. A., Xu, Y. J., Arneja, A. S. and Dhalla, N. S. (2002). Pathogenesis of atherosclerosis: A multifactorial process. *Experimental and Clinical Cardiology*, 7(1), 40–53.

Taylor, J. H. (2001). *Death and the Afterlife in Ancient Egypt*. London: British Museum Press.

Taylor, J. H. (2004). *Mummy: the Inside Story*. London: British Museum Press.

Taylor, J. H. (2010). *Egyptian Mummies*. London: British Museum Press.

Taylor, J. H. (2014). The collection of Egyptian mummies at the British Museum: Overview and potential for study. In A. Fletcher, D. Antoine and J. D. Hill, eds., *Regarding the Dead: Human Remains in the British Museum*. London: British Museum Press, pp. 103–14.

Taylor, J. H. and Antoine, D. (2014). *Ancient Lives, New Discoveries: Eight Mummies, Eight Stories*. London: British Museum Press.

Taylor, B. A., Tofler, G. H., Carey, H. M. R., et al. (2006). Full-mouth tooth extraction lowers systemic inflammatory and thrombotic markers of cardiovascular risk. *Journal of Dental Research*, 85, 74–8.

Tozer Fink, K. R. and Fink, J. R. (2018). Principles of modern neuroimaging. In R. G. Ellenbogen, L. N. Sekhar and N. Kitchen, eds., *Principles of Neurological Surgery*, 4th ed. Philadelphia: Elsevier, pp. 62–86.

Ubelaker, D. H. (1989). *Human Skeletal Remains*, 2nd ed. Washington, DC: Taraxacum Press.

Vandenbeusch, M. and Antoine, D. (2015). Under Saint Michael's protection: A tattoo from Christian Nubia. *Journal of the Canadian Centre for Epigraphic Documents*, 1, 15–19.

Vandenbeusch, M. and Antoine, D. (2021). *Mummies of ancient Egypt. Rediscovering ancient lives*. Tokyo: The British Museum and Asahi Shimbun.

Wade, A. D. and Nelson, A. J. (2013a). Evisceration and excerebration in the Egyptian mummification tradition. *Journal of Archaeological Science*, 40(12), 4198–206.

Wade, A. D. and Nelson, A. J. (2013b). Radiological evaluation of the evisceration tradition in ancient Egyptian mummies. *Homo*, 64, 1–28.

Wade, A. D., Nelson, A. J. and Garvin, G. J. (2011). A synthetic radiological study of brain treatment in ancient Egyptian mummies. *Homo*, 62, 248–69.

Waldron, T. (2009). *Palaeopathology*. Cambridge: Cambridge University Press.

Waldron, T. (2019). Joint disease. In J. E. Buikstra, ed., *Ortner's Identification of Pathological Conditions in Human Skeletal Remains*, 3rd ed. London: Academic Press.

Warrier, V., Kanchan, T., Shedge, R., Krishan, K. and Singh, S. (2021). Computed tomographic age estimation from the pubic symphysis using the Suchey–Brooks method: A systematic review and meta-analysis. *Forensic Science International*, 325, 110811.

Wasterlain, S. N., Cunha, E. and Hillson, S. (2011). Periodontal disease in a Portuguese identified skeletal sample from the late nineteenth and early twentieth centuries. *American Journal of Physical Anthropology*, 145, 30–42.

White, T. D. and Folkens, P. A. (2005). *The Human Bone Manual*. Burlington, MA: Elsevier Academic Press.

White, T. D., Black, M. T. and Folkens, P. A. (2012). *Human Osteology*. London: Academic Press.

Whiting, R., Antoine, D. and Hillson, S. (2019). Periodontal disease and 'oral health' in the past: new insights from ancient Sudan on a very modern problem. *Dental Anthropology*, 32, 30–50.

Wills, B. and Antoine, D. (2015). Developing a passive approach to the conservation of naturally mummified human remains from the Fourth Cataract region of the Nile Valley. *British Museum Technical Research Bulletin*, 9, 49–56.

Wink, A. E. (2014). Pubic symphyseal age estimation from three-dimensional reconstructions of pelvic CT scans of live individuals. *Journal of Forensic Science*, 59(3), 696–702.

World Health Organization. (2021). Cardiovascular Diseases Fact Sheet. www.who.int/news-room/fact-sheets/detail/cardiovascular-diseases-(cvds) (accessed 21 December 2022).

Ynnerman, A., Rydell, T., Antoine, D., et al. (2016). Interactive visualization of 3D scanned mummies at public venues. *Communications of the ACM*, 59(12), 72–81.

Zardawi, F., Gul, S., Abdulkareem, A., Sha, A., and Yates, J. (2021). Association between periodontal disease and atherosclerotic cardiovascular diseases: revisited. *Frontiers in Cardiovascular Medicine*, 7, 625579.

7 Atherosclerosis among the Elites

A Bioarchaeological Investigation of Seventeenth- to Nineteenth-Century Mummified Human Remains from Palermo, Sicily (Italy) and Vilnius (Lithuania)

Dario Piombino-Mascali, Rimantas Jankauskas, Albert Zink and Stephanie Panzer

7.1 Introduction

As early as the mid-nineteenth century, tangible evidence of cardiovascular disease (CVD) was found in Egyptian mummies, indicating that these people must have experienced atherosclerosis in the same way as modern humans do (Czermak, 1852; Ruffer, 1921). It has been suggested that the origin of the condition among the Egyptian elites was their diet, given that these people consumed food rich in saturated fat (David et al., 2010). However, we do not possess much data on the non-elite individuals from the Nile Valley, as they could not afford mummification. The frequency of such findings in ancient mummies has recently been the subject of important systematic studies assessing whether atherosclerosis was a condition primarily associated with the lifestyle and rich diet of Egyptian elites, or whether it was also prevalent among ancient populations inhabiting very different environments. These studies have shown that atherosclerosis was common in the mummified remains of people who lived in different geographic areas and had a wide range of diet and lifestyles, with non-traditional risk factors (e.g. inhalation of smoke from open fires and chronic infection and/or inflammation) possibly contributing to the development of CVD (Allam et al., 2009, 2011; Abdelfattah et al., 2013; Thompson et al., 2013). In further studies, atherosclerosis has been attested in other mummified remains, including the Neolithic Iceman and a pre-agricultural hunter-gatherer population (Aufderheide & Rodríguez Martín, 1998; Murphy et al., 2003; Thompson et al., 2013). This came as a surprise, since hunter-gatherers have long been considered to be physically fit and free from chronic CVD based on the assumed absence of traditional risk factors, such as being overweight, lack of physical activity and the consumption of processed food (O'Keefe & Cordain, 2004). A more recent study on the Tsimané, a forager-horticulturalist population of the Bolivian Amazon, has shown the lowest levels of coronary artery disease of any population recorded to date and which appears to be the result of their healthy lifestyle (Kaplan et al., 2017; see also Chapter 14). However, there is a growing body of evidence that genetic factors play a significant role in CVD (Roberts et al., 2012) and prehistoric populations may also have been subject to these genetic influences (Keller et al., 2012). Research also indicates that atherosclerosis is an inherent component of the ageing process and thus unrelated to any specific diet (Thompson et al., 2013; Rodgers et al., 2019).

In order to further investigate the prevalence of atherosclerosis in past human populations and to provide additional insights into potential risk factors, this study analysed computed tomography (CT) scans of a small number of naturally and anthropogenically mummified remains from Palermo, Italy and Vilnius, Lithuania, both dating from the seventeenth to nineteenth centuries CE. CT scanning was used to identify evidence of atherosclerotic plaques using the non-invasive approach employed in mummy research (O'Brien et al., 2009). In order to make the data comparable, evidence of advanced atherosclerotic lesions was assessed according to the standards employed by other scholars (Stary et al., 1995; Allison et al., 2004; Allam et al., 2011). An important part of the study was to use the contemporary historical data to hypothesise about the lived experiences of these people, and to understand whether these may have influenced the onset of atherosclerosis. Consequently, the aim of the project was to compare the biological data with information from contemporary sources in order to provide a plausible biocultural interpretation of any findings.

7.2 Materials and Methods

Within the framework of two different research projects, carried out in two different European countries, CT scanning was used to analyse selected mummies from both sites; 17 of 1949 inhumations curated in the Capuchin Catacombs of Palermo, Sicily, and 7 of 23 human mummies held in the crypt of the Dominican Church of the Holy Spirit of Vilnius, Lithuania, were chosen for study (Tables 7.1–7.3). The Capuchin Catacombs were opened in 1599 as a burial place for deceased brothers, but they were later used by the nobility and the middle classes who could afford such a treatment, including religious dignitaries (Piombino-Mascali, 2017, 2018). Over time, they became a well-known funerary complex described by voyagers, writers and intellectuals such as Alexandre Dumas, Fanny Lewald and Guy de Maupassant (Cardin, 2014; Piombino-Mascali, 2018). The bodies held in the Catacombs were both naturally and deliberately mummified, the former via a simple process of dehydration of the soft tissue in special preparation rooms, and the latter through evisceration and the use of chemical preservatives (Panzer et al., 2010). In contrast, the mummies found in the crypt of the Dominican Church of the Holy Spirit in Vilnius, also belonging to the nobility and the middle class, were all naturally mummified by environmental conditions conducive to the preservation of the bodies: a dry and cool environment, and protection from rainwater by the overlying structure (Cardin, 2014).

The selection of mummies for this study was based on their remarkable external preservation, with only partial tissue degradation evident when compared with the other mummies in the two crypts. Prior to scanning, the mummies were macroscopically assessed to roughly estimate age at death and sex. Information on the adopted protocols can be found in Piombino-Mascali et al. (2014) and Panzer et al. (2018). Assessment of atherosclerosis was conducted in accordance with the protocol described by Thompson et al. (2013), including identification of the heart and specific arteries, and the possible recognition of calcifications within arterial walls. Calcification in a detectable artery was considered pathognomonic for atherosclerosis,

132   Dario Piombino-Mascali et al.

while calcification along the expected course of an artery but without preserved remains of a blood vessel was considered to be probable atherosclerosis. The vascular regions of the body were divided into different groups comprising the carotid, coronary, aortic, iliac or femoral, popliteal or tibial arteries. Both studies were non-invasive in nature and did not involve autopsy of the remains, since this is no longer accepted by most research groups due to ethical concerns (Piombino-Mascali & Gill-Frerking, 2019).

7.3   Results

Although they were not selected for targeted research on CVDs, the mummies proved to be useful for such a study because of their near-complete preservation of the blood vessels, including those of the neck, torso and extremities.

Calcifications consistent with atherosclerosis were found in four Palermo mummies of the 17 studied (23.5 per cent) (Tables 7.1 and 7.2). Mummy P9, an artificially preserved mature adult, showed a small atheroma at the bifurcation of the left carotid artery. Mummy P18, a naturally mummified Capuchin brother, revealed atheromas in both internal carotid arteries over the intracranial course. Furthermore, P19, the natural mummy of an adult (male) priest, revealed distinct atheromas in his right and left common iliac arteries, slight calcifications in his left internal iliac artery, and in his right distal superficial femoral and popliteal arteries. Finally, mummy P27, belonging to another (male) priest, showed a slight atheroma at the bifurcation of his

Table 7.1 Eleven anthropogenically mummified adult mummies from Palermo showing presence/absence of atherosclerosis.

Mummy	P1	P2	P3	P4	P8	P9	P11	P12	P14	P21	P27
Sex	M	M	M	M	M	M	M	M	M	M	M
Age	A	A	A	A	A	A	A	A	14 years	A	A
Atherosclerosis											
Carotid	–	X	–	–	–	+	–	X	–	X	+
Coronary	–	X	X	–	–	X	–	X	X	X	+
Aortic	–	X	X	–	–	X	–	X	X	X	+
Iliac or femoral	–	X	–	–	–	–	–	X	X	X	+
Popliteal or tibial	–	X	–	–	–	–	–	X	–	X	–
Calcification											
Aortic valve leaflets	–	X	X	–	–	X	–	X	X	X	–
Mitral valve annulus	–	X	X	–	–	X	–	X	X	X	X
Mitral valve leaflets	–	X	X	–	–	X	–	X	X	X	X

M, male; F, female; A, adult; +, present; –, absent; X, not assessed due to chemical injection or heart being unpreserved.

Table 7.2 Six naturally mummified adults from Palermo showing presence/absence of atherosclerosis.

Mummy	P10	P13	P15	P18	P19	P25
Sex	M	M	M	M	M	M
Age	A	73 years	A	A	56 years	A
Atherosclerosis						
Carotid	–	–	–	+	–	–
Coronary	–	–	–	–	–	–
Aortic	–	–	–	–	–	–
Iliac or femoral	–	?	–	–	+	–
Popliteal or tibial	–	–	–	–	+	–
Calcifications						
Aortic valve leaflets	X	X	X	X	X	X
Mitral valve annulus	X	X	X	X	X	X
Mitral valve leaflets	X	X	X	X	X	X

M, male; F, female; A, adult; +, present; –, absent; X, not assessed due to chemical injection or heart being unpreserved.

Table 7.3 Three naturally mummified adults from Vilnius showing presence/absence of atherosclerosis.

Mummy	VD3	VD9	VD12
Sex	M	F	M
Age	A	A	A
Atherosclerosis			
Carotid	+	+	+
Coronary	+	+	+
Aortic	+	+	+
Iliac or femoral	+	+	+
Popliteal or tibial	–	+	+
Calcification			
Aortic valve leaflets	+	–	+
Mitral valve annulus	+	+	–
Mitral valve leaflets	–	–	–

M, male; F, female; A, adult; +, present; –, absent.

right carotid artery and in his aortic arch, as well as distinct atheromas in his coronary arteries, and semicircular calcifications in his distal abdominal aorta; atheromas in his right common iliac artery and a slight calcification in the right and left internal iliac arteries were also noted (Figure 7.1).

In the study of the seven Vilnius mummies, four of them had well-preserved hearts and six had preserved intracranial, cervical, thoracic, abdominal, pelvic and peripheral arteries. Such extensive preservation made these mummies ideal for the current study. In total, three of the four adult mummies examined (75 per cent) (Table 7.3) showed clear evidence of atherosclerosis. Specifically, mummy VD3, that of an obese

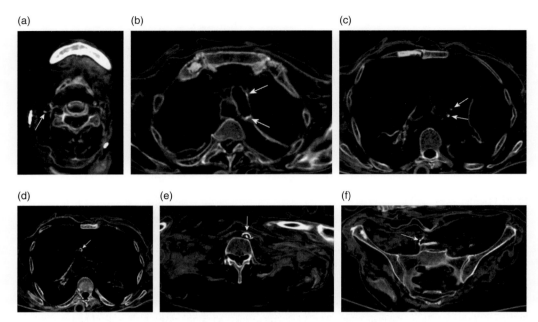

Figure 7.1 Mummy P27. (a) Axial CT reformatted image showing a slight calcification at the bifurcation of the right carotid artery (arrow). (b) Axial reformatted CT image illustrating small calcifications of the aortic arch (arrows). (c) Axial CT reformatted image demonstrating distinct calcifications of the coronary arteries, probably left anterior descending coronary artery (upper arrow) and left circumflex coronary artery (lower arrow). (d) Axial CT reformatted image demonstrating semicircular calcification of the right coronary artery (arrow). (e) Axial CT reformatted image showing distinct semicircular calcifications of the distal abdominal aorta (arrow). (f) Axal CT reformatted image illustrating calcifications of the right iliac artery (arrow).

adult male, has atheromas in his aortic valve leaflets/cusps and distinct calcification of his mitral annulus, but preserved leaflets without calcification. In addition, two adjacent semicircular sickle-shaped calcifications were seen at the level of his third and fourth lumbar vertebrae in the region of the abdominal aorta. A detectable calcification of the aortic bifurcation within the intervertebral disc space between his fourth and fifth lumbar vertebrae was also observed (Figure 7.2). The purported outcome of a trans-exudate that may have been caused by heart and/or renal failure, a haemorrhage, liquefaction necrosis or even adipocere formation, appearing in the form of dried fluid with different layers, was observed in a number of locations in this male body: inferior vena cava, dorsal thoracic cavity bilaterally, left atrium, left ventricle, upper and lower abdomen, deep pelvis, urinary bladder, urethra, distal trachea and proximal ends of the bronchi. Furthermore, mummy VD9, that of an obese adult female, showed distinct coronary atherosclerosis along with calcification of her mitral annulus (the anatomical junction between the ventricle and the left atrium) (Figure 7.3). Again, dried fluid displaying different layers, a detectable

Atherosclerosis among the Elites

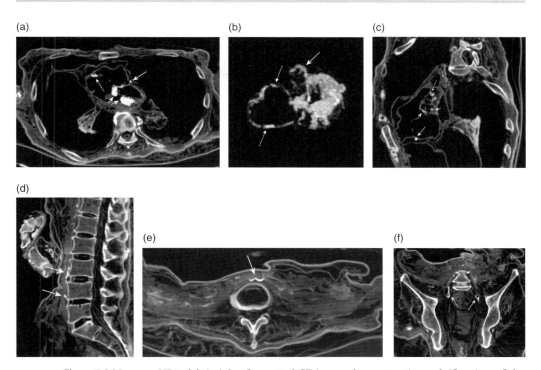

Figure 7.2 Mummy VD3. (a) Axial reformatted CT image demonstrating calcification of the left anterior descending coronary artery (arrow) and the right coronary artery (dotted arrow). Note distinct calcification of the mitral annulus (short arrows). (b) Three-dimensional CT reconstructions of the heart illustrating calcification of the mitral annulus, as well as atherosclerosis of the left anterior descending coronary artery (arrow) and the right coronary artery (dotted arrows). (c) CT reformatted image at the level of the aortic valve showing calcifications of the aortic valve leaflets (short arrows) and atherosclerosis of the left anterior descending artery (arrow) and the right coronary artery (dotted arrow). (d) Sagittal CT reformatted image demonstrating atherosclerosis of the distal abdominal aorta (arrows). (e) Axial CT reformatted image at the level of the third/fourth lumbar vertebrae showing two adjacent semicircular sickle-shaped calcifications (arrow). (f) Coronal CT reformatted image illustrating atherosclerosis of the iliac arteries on both sides (arrows).

sedimentation effect and internal fragmentation could be observed. This was localised in her distal trachea, inferior vena cava, on the left lung remnants, in the left ventricle and atrium, the right ventricle, and in the dorsal parts of the pericardial space. Intrathoracic fluid was also seen bilaterally and dorsally. Likewise, we observed it internally and ventrally on some intestinal loops, in the pelvic region, anterior of the sacrum, and inside the urinary bladder and vagina. As with the previous mummy, the interpretation of such findings is challenging. Finally, mummy VD12, that of an adult male, showed atheromas in his aortic valve leaflets, as well as in his arteries.

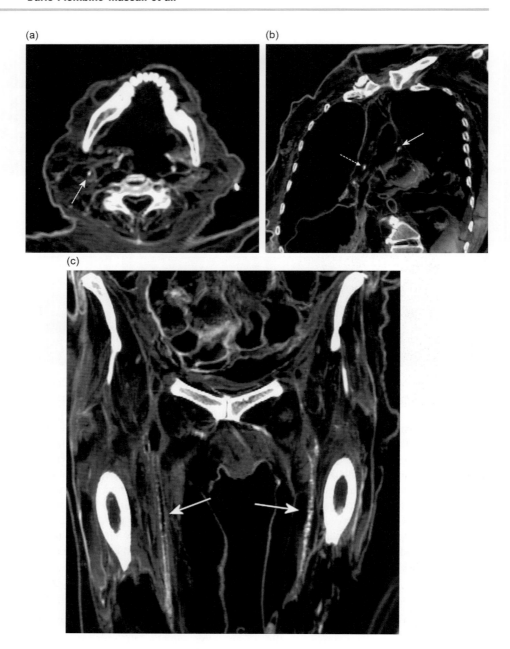

Figure 7.3 Mummy VD9. (a) Axial CT reformatted image showing a small calcification at the bifurcation of the right carotid artery (arrow). (b) Paracoronal CT reformatted image demonstrating coronary atherosclerosis of the left anterior descending coronary artery (arrow) and the right coronary artery (dotted arrow). (c) Coronal CT reformatted image illustrating distinct calcifications of the superficial femoral arteries on both sides (arrows). (d) Parasagittal CT reformatted image demonstrating distinct calcifications of the anterior tibial artery of the right lower leg (arrows).

(d)

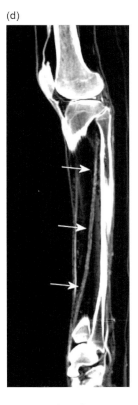

Figure 7.3 (*cont.*)

7.4 Discussion

Our study suggests that atherosclerosis was prevalent in people buried at both sites, and included the wealthy of both regions. This is because the investigated mummies represent a selected part of their communities. In these cases, the middle- and upper-class members of society were supporters of the Capuchin and Dominican orders and could afford a burial space in these crypts (Frick, 2013; Piombino-Mascali, 2018). Favourable environmental conditions such as low temperature, adequate ventilation and protection from groundwater or rainfall provided an environment that preserved these unique mummies. In some, the procedures and chemical preservatives used in embalming also contributed to their excellent state of preservation. Thus, the remarkably preserved vasculature enabled a detailed assessment of CVDs (Aufderheide, 2003).

In the case of the Palermo mummies, we could positively confirm identity for only three of the 17 mummies studied, including an adolescent (aged 14) and two older adults who died at the ages of 56 and 73 years. A confirmed precise identification was not possible for the other individuals, including those in the Vilnius sample, and an age at death could only be estimated from our anthropological and radiological data. These suggest that the majority of the investigated remains represented people who were likely to be over 30 years of age, based on bone fusion and dental abrasion (Martin, 1988; Cox, 2000). Our findings are consistent with clinical data on atherosclerosis, which demonstrate widespread involvement of all five arterial groups (carotid, coronary, aortic, iliac or femoral, popliteal or tibial) at some point before reaching the age of 50 years for both sexes (Allison et al., 2004). Furthermore, considering the higher socioeconomic status of those affected by atherosclerosis, as well as two overweight Lithuanian mummies (VD3 and VD9), a sedentary life with little exercise and a diet rich in carbohydrates and fat may have been contributing factors. Physical exercise, which can help to prevent development of coronary artery disease and reduce symptoms in patients with established CVD, may have not been practiced during their later life (Al-Mamari, 2009).

Within the Sicilian mummies (southern part of Europe), atherosclerosis appears to have been less prevalent when compared to those in Lithuania (northeastern Europe). Considering the geographical distance between the two samples, it could be speculated that these results may partly reflect their differing diets, cultures and environments. Many of the decedents buried in the Sicilian Catacombs may have had eating patterns comparable to what is nowadays called the 'Mediterranean diet', which is considered to be one of the best diets for preventing CVD. This appears to be due to the ideal synergy of various cardioprotective nutrients and food that characterises this diet, including fish, olive oil, fruit, vegetables, whole grains, nuts and legumes (Widmer et al., 2015). The rich and diverse resources available to Sicilians at the dawn of the Middle Ages would have included pasta, bread, vegetables, fruit and small game (Santoro, 2013). Furthermore, fifteenth-century documents related to the then Archbishop of Palermo inform us about the diet of local clergymen and included olive oil, legumes such as fava beans, lentils and chickpeas, as well as hulled wheat, almonds and pasta, most of which are still eaten today. In addition, we know that the archbishop also possessed a large quantity of red wine of different types (Santoro, 2013). Red wine contains some antioxidant substances present in the skin and seeds of grapes, including polyphenols. When drunk in moderate amounts, it is known to reduce cholesterol levels, prevent coagulation and thrombosis, and enable vasodilation (Avellone et al., 2006). Evidence of alcohol was found in the form of ethyl glucuronide in the hair of some of the mummies using liquid chromatography/gas spectrometry analysis, ethyl glucuronide being a water-soluble and stable metabolite of ethanol formed in the body after ingestion of alcohol (Musshoff et al., 2013). The lower rates of atherosclerosis seen in the Sicilian mummies may also be explained by the inclusion of fish in the diet. Because of Palermo's geographical location, fish would have been available fresh, dried and salted (Santoro, 2013). Eating fish regularly has also been found to be protective against coronary heart disease and has been linked to lower rates of atherosclerosis of the carotid artery due to the presence of high levels of polyunsaturated fatty acids (Buscemi et al., 2014). The consumption of fish became more common from the late Middle Ages onwards, possibly due to the church prohibiting the eating of meat on specific days of the year (Fornaciari, 2008). Therefore, it might be speculated that the individuals studied here may have had less atherosclerosis due, in part, to consumption of fresh fish from the Mediterranean.

In contrast to the data on the mummies from Sicily, the diet of Lithuanians during this era may have been particularly atherogenic, which is also supported by stable isotope analysis (see Reitsema et al., 2015). The writings of Georg Forster, a German professor of natural history who lived in Vilnius during the eighteenth century, also provide a valuable historical source (Forster, 1988). Through his letters, which represent an authoritative ethnographic source, we can deduce that meat consumption among the city's upper classes was common, and that game meat was served frequently. Vegetables, including leafy greens, and fruit were only occasionally available, with the exception of berries, partly as a consequence of the cold climate of the region. Additionally, Forster informs us that salted fish and meat were the main sources of nourishment, and flaxseed oil was regularly consumed especially during periods of fasting. A high-sodium diet can, of course, lead to hypertension, which is itself a risk factor for atherosclerosis. In addition, studies on animals indicate that a high salt intake increases the formation of vascular superoxide, considered a major risk factor in vascular pathophysiology and which promotes atherosclerosis (Ketonen et al., 2005). Interestingly, flaxseed is believed to suppress atherosclerosis, but not its oil (Prasad, 2009). Therefore, behaviour, especially dietary choice, may have promoted the onset of atherosclerosis at a young age. Forster notes that overfeeding was considered the correct way to nourish children, and we know that obesity is associated with atherosclerosis in both teenagers and adults today (Strong et al., 1999; McMahan et al., 2006). In addition to the above-mentioned cardiovascular risk factors, a diet rich in animal fat also seems likely for the individuals from Lithuania as three calcified gallstones were noted in the obese woman. Gallstones are associated with a high-fat diet and have also been observed in other mummies (Munizaga et al., 1978; Gostner et al., 2011). Finally, at least once a week men and women were reportedly very drunk, indicating significant alcohol consumption (Forster, 1988). As mentioned previously, light drinking can possibly afford some protection against atherosclerosis due to its antithrombotic effects and inhibition of the atherogenic process. However, heavy drinkers are considered to be at higher risk for both atherosclerosis and coronary heart disease (Kiechl et al., 1998; Murray et al., 2002). Another potential risk factor for the development of atherosclerosis is exposure to particulate matter in smoke. Tobacco was first introduced into Europe in the sixteenth century, and soon appeared on pharmacopoeias for its alleged medical properties. Indeed, some believed in its health benefits (Charlton, 2004). Therefore, its use by elite groups can be speculated. In addition, wood smoke emanating from open fires used for cooking, heating and industrial purposes may have played a role in the development of atherosclerosis (Campen et al., 2010). Living in a cold climate, many of the citizens of Vilnius were likely to have been exposed to poor air quality from fires, and heavy smoke inhalation seems to have been an inevitable consequence of living in the city (Sarti, 2003). Indeed, Forster maintained as many as six or seven fireplaces in his house (Forster, 1988). Additionally, we know that infection was one of the main causes of death in many pre-industrial societies, and city dwellers in particular were heavily exposed to pathogens through poor living conditions (Ridker, 2002).

Chronic infections can also cause inflammation, which appears to be associated with CVD (Marson et al., 2004; Finch, 2010). It is quite plausible that infection/inflammation represented an important cardiovascular risk factor for the individuals analysed here, and infectious diseases were common among the Vilnius inhabitants (Duggan et al., 2016; Giffin et al., 2020). Notably, the high-status people buried in the crypt showed evidence of pulmonary tuberculosis (Piombino-Mascali et al., 2015), indicating that the affluent were not and are not immune from contracting tuberculosis. Additionally, in two of the investigated mummies mitral valve annular calcifications were found (Boon et al., 1997; Gulati et al., 2011), a finding that was first described in a palaeopathological context by Allam et al. (2011). However, the mitral valve leaflets were unaffected. Epidemiological studies suggest a strong association between mitral valve annular calcification and atherosclerosis (Boon et al., 1997).

CVDs are highly prevalent in Lithuania today (Laucevičius et al., 2019). Clinical studies have shown that clinically diagnosed atherosclerosis is more frequent in Lithuania than in other countries such as Sweden (Kristenson et al., 2000). This increased frequency may arise not only from common traditional risk factors in Lithuania, but also from population-specific genetic risk factors (Pepalytė et al., 2012). Interestingly, a mutation of the *LDLR* gene that predisposes to familial hypercholesterolaemia – previously identified in Ashkenazi Jews (many of whom actually originated from Lithuania) and which may be common among present-day Lithuanians – was recently identified in the country for the first time (Badarienė et al., 2016). Although limited in data, the distinctive findings described here support those of other scholars who have described the presence of atherosclerosis in ancient preserved bodies with different lifestyles and diets, such as the ancient Egyptians and the Aleuts (Zimmerman, 1993; Allam et al., 2009, 2011). Nevertheless, as previously noted by others (Thompson et al., 2013; Charlier et al., 2014), imaging mummies does not provide pathoanatomical confirmation of lesions and it remains difficult to differentiate atherosclerotic calcifications from those caused by other conditions. However, histological investigations often require an autopsy, which irreparably compromises the integrity of mummies, potentially impacting future research (Gaeta et al., 2013, 2018). Furthermore, we acknowledge that taphonomic changes related to the mummification process may also affect interpretation (Rühli et al., 2004). However, in many of the mummies we investigated here, tissue preservation was surprisingly high, suggesting minor post-depositional changes, at least for the areas of the body investigated in this study.

7.5   Conclusions and Perspectives

As confirmed in three mummies from Vilnius and four mummies from Palermo, atherosclerosis was present in ancient populations, and this study adds to a large body of data from other mummified remains from different times and places. Bioarchaeological evidence provides new pathways for modern clinical research, including investigation for possible genetic risk factors for atherosclerosis over time. Genomic studies in contemporary humans have revealed a growing number of genetic risk factors that are associated with CVDs, and specifically single nucleotide polymorphisms (SNPs) that predispose individuals to development of CVD (McPherson, 2007; Roberts et al., 2012). In a bioarchaeological context, for instance, a detailed genetic analysis of the nuclear genome of the mummy of the 5300-year-old Tyrolean Iceman (known as Ötzi) uncovered a strong genetic predisposition for increased risk of coronary heart disease (Keller et al., 2012). This led to major calcifications in the carotid arteries, distal aorta and right iliac artery, as seen in the CT scans of his body (Murphy et al., 2003). It has also been demonstrated that this prehistoric man was homozygous for an SNP located in chromosomal region 9p21 that is currently regarded as one of the strongest genetic predictors of CVD and which has been confirmed in several studies as a major risk locus (McPherson, 2007).

However, while genetic factors may play a role in the premature development of the disease, historical and bioarchaeological evidence suggests that diet and the environment (as seen today) may also have been risk factors among the investigated individuals. European mummies from the mediaeval and modern periods provide valuable palaeopathological insights that can further our understanding of CVDs by combining ethnographic, documentary and biomedical data. A future genomic investigation of the mummies from Sicily and Lithuania could reveal further insights into the interaction between environmental and genetic aetiologies on the development of coronary heart disease, and may help explain the difference in prevalence between the two groups.

References

Abdelfattah, A., Allam, A. H., Wann, L. S., et al. (2013). Atherosclerotic cardiovascular disease in Egyptian women: 1570 BCE–2011 CE. *International Journal of Cardiology*, 167, 570–4.

Allam, A. H., Thompson, R. C., Wann, L. S., Miyamoto, M. I. and Thomas, G. S. (2009). Computed tomographic assessment of atherosclerosis in ancient Egyptian mummies. *Journal of the American Medical Association*, 302(19), 2091–4.

Allam, A. H., Thompson, R. C., Wann, L. S., et al. (2011). Atherosclerosis in ancient Egyptian mummies: The Horus study. *Journal of the American College of Cardiology Cardiovascular Imaging*, 4(4), 315–27.

Allison, M. A., Criqui, M. H. and Wright, C. M. (2004). Patterns and risk factors for systemic calcified atherosclerosis. *Arteriosclerosis, Thrombosis and Vascular Biology*, 24, 331–6.

Al-Mamari, A. (2009). Atherosclerosis and physical activity. *Oman Medical Journal*, 24(3), 173–8.

Aufderheide, A. C. (2003). *The Scientific Study of Mummies*. Cambridge: Cambridge University Press.

Aufderheide, A. C. and Rodríguez Martín, C. (1998). *The Cambridge Encyclopedia of Human Paleopathology*. Cambridge: Cambridge University Press.

Avellone, G., Di Garbo, V., Campisi, D., et al. (2006). Effects of moderate Sicilian red wine consumption on inflammatory biomarkers of atherosclerosis. *European Journal of Clinical Nutrition*, 60, 41–7.

Badarienė, J., Petrikonytė, D., Ryliškyte, L. and Šerpytis, P. (2016). 'Lithuanian' mutation finally found in Lithuania. *American Journal of Medicine*, 129(6), e13–14.

Boon, A., Cheriex, E., Lodder, J. and Kessels, F. (1997). Cardial valve calcification: Characteristics of patients with calcification of the mitral annulus or aortic valve. *Heart*, 78, 472–4.

Buscemi, S., Nicolucci, A., Lucisano, G., et al. (2014). Habitual fish intake and clinically silent carotid atherosclerosis. *Nutrition Journal*, 13, 2.

Campen, M. J., Lund, A. K., Doyle-Eisele, M. L., et al. (2010). A comparison of vascular effects from complex and individual air pollutants indicates a role for monoxide gases and volatile hydrocarbons. *Environmental Health Perspectives*, 118(7), 921–7.

Cardin, M. (2014). *Mummies Around the World: An Encyclopedia of Mummies in History, Religion, and Popular Culture.* Santa Barbara, CA: ABC Clio.

Charlier, P., Wils, P., Froment, A. and Huynh-Charlier, I. (2014). Arterial calcifications from mummified materials: Use of micro-CT scan for histological differential diagnosis. *Forensic Science, Medicine and Pathology*, 10, 461–5.

Charlton, A. (2004). Medical uses of tobacco in history. *Journal of the Royal Society of Medicine*, 92, 292–6.

Cox, M. (2000). Ageing adults from the skeleton. In M. Cox and S. Mays, eds., *Human Osteology in Archaeology and Forensic Science.* London: Greenwich Medical Media, pp. 61–82.

Czermak, J. N. (1852). Beschreibung und mikroskopische Untersuchung zweierägyptischer Mumien. *Sitzungsberichte der Akademie der Wissenschaften Mathematisch-Naturwissenschaftliche Klasse*, 9, 427–69.

David, A.R., Kershaw, A. and Heagerty, A. (2010). Atherosclerosis and diet in ancient Egypt. *Lancet*, 375, 718–19.

Duggan, A. T., Perdomo, M. F., Piombino-Mascali, D., et al. (2016). Seventeenth century variola virus reveals the recent history of smallpox. *Current Biology*, 26(24), 3407–12.

Finch, C. E. (2010). Evolution of the human lifespan and diseases of ageing: Roles of infection, inflammation, and nutrition. *Proceedings of the National Academy of Sciences USA*, 107(Suppl 1), 1718–24.

Fornaciari, G. (2008). Food and disease at the Renaissance courts of Naples and Florence: A paleonutritional study. *Appetite*, 51(1), 11–14.

Forster, G. (1988). *Laiškai iš Vilniaus.* Vilnius: Mokslas.

Frick, D. (2013). *Kith, Kin, and Neighbors: Communities and Confessions in Seventeenth-century Wilno.* Ithaca, NY: Cornell University Press.

Gaeta, R., Giuffra, V. and Fornaciari, G. (2013). Atherosclerosis in the Renaissance elite: Ferdinand I King of Naples (1431–1494). *Virchows Archiv*, 462, 593–5.

Gaeta, R., Ventura, L. and Fornaciari, G. (2018). Atherosclerosis in the Italian mummies (Fifteenth–twentieth century). *Pathologica*, 110(3), 159–60.

Giffin, K., Lankapalli, A. K., Sabin, S., et al. (2020). A treponemal genome from an historic plague victim supports a recent emergence of yaws and its presence in fifteenth century Europe. *Scientific Reports*, 10, 9499.

Gostner, P., Pernter, P., Bonatti, G., Graefen, A. and Zink, A. R. (2011). New radiological insights into the life and death of the Tyrolean Iceman. *Journal of Archaeological Sciences*, 38, 3425–31.

Gulati, A., Chan, C., Duncan, A., et al. (2011). Multimodality cardiac imaging in the evaluation of mitral annular caseous calcification. *Circulation*, 123, e1–2.

Kaplan, H., Thompson, R. C., Trumble, B. C., et al. (2017). Coronary atherosclerosis in indigenous South American Tsimane: A cross-sectional cohort study. *Lancet*, 389, 1730–9.

Keller, A., Graefen, A., Ball, M., et al. (2012). New insights into the Tyrolean Iceman's origin and phenotype as inferred by whole-genome sequencing. *Nature Communications*, 3, 698.

Ketonen, J., Merasto, S., Paakkari, I. and Mervaala, E. M. A. (2005). High sodium intake increases vascular superoxide formation and promotes atherosclerosis in apolipoprotein E-deficient mice. *Blood Pressure*, 14(6), 373–82.

Kiechl, S., Willeit, J., Rungger, G., et al. (1998). Alcohol consumption and atherosclerosis: What is the relation? Prospective results from the Brunek study. *Stroke*, 29, 900–7.

Kristenson, M., Lassvik, C., Bergdahl, B., et al. (2000). Ultrasound determined carotid and femoral atherosclerosis in Lithuanian and Swedish men: The LiVicordia study. *Atherosclerosis*, 151, 501–8.

Laucevičius, A., Rinkūnienė, E., Ryliškyte, L., et al. (2019). Primary prevention strategy for cardiovascular disease in Lithuania. *Seminars in Cardiovascular Medicine*, 25, 14–39.

McMahan, C. A., Gidding, S. S., Malcom, C. T., et al. (2006). Pathobiological determinants of atherosclerosis in youth risk scores are associated with early and advanced atherosclerosis. *Pediatrics*, 118(4), 1447–55.

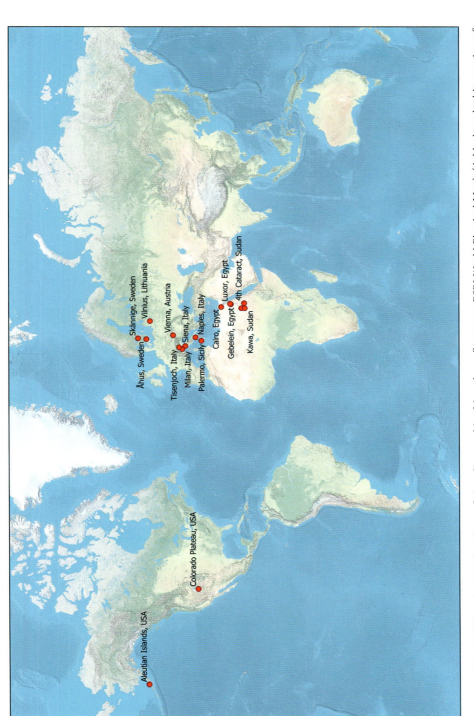

Figure 1.2 Map showing locations of sites discussed in this volume (basemap: ESRI World Physical Map). (A black and white version of this figure will appear in some formats.)

Figure 2.5 An obese man wooing a tall lean woman outside a mausoleum, representing dropsy and consumption. Coloured etching by T. Rowlandson, 1810. Source: Wellcome Collection. (A black and white version of this figure will appear in some formats.)

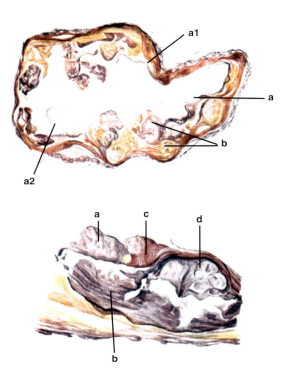

Figure 3.1 The upper figure shows a section through an almost completely calcified posterior peroneal artery (a, a1, a2, remnants of endothelium and fenestrated membrane; b, calcified patches). The lower figure displays a section of a calcified patch of an ulnar artery (a, d, calcified patches; b, partially calcified muscular coat; c, annular muscular fibre). Source: adapted from Ruffer (1911), figure 9-10, plate XLIV. (A black and white version of this figure will appear in some formats.)

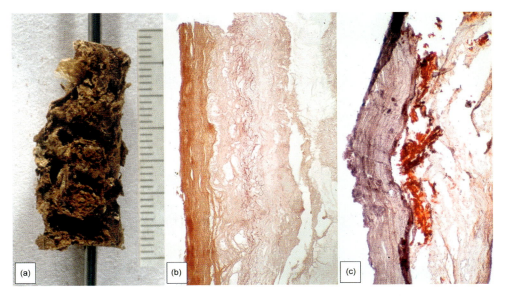

Figure 3.2 Atherosclerosis in the carotid artery of Ferrante I of Aragon. (a) Right common carotid artery: the wall is distorted but the lumen is open. (b) Histological section of the artery with foamy fatty material between the muscular layers (H&E, ×40). (c) Sub-intimal atheroma (Oil Red O, ×40). (A black and white version of this figure will appear in some formats.)

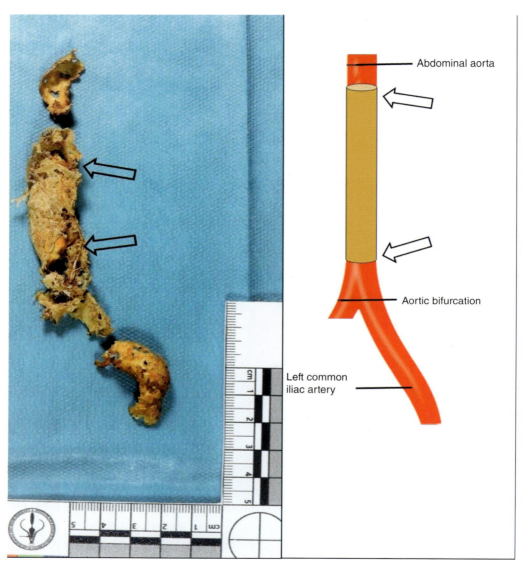

Figure 3.3 Atherosclerosis in the aorta of Girolamo Macchi. The abdominal aorta up to the bifurcation of the common iliac arteries (11 cm): The wall of this very well-preserved aorta is completely calcified, with the lumen partially obstructed by large plaques of about 2 cm in length (arrows). (A black and white version of this figure will appear in some formats.)

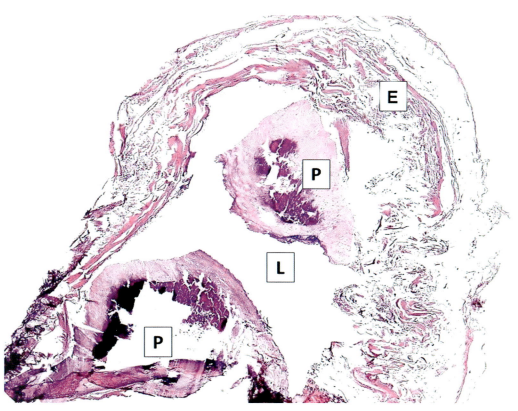

Figure 3.4 Histological section of the abdominal aorta of Girolamo Macchi: the elastic layers of the wall are partially preserved (E) along with the adipose tissue around the vessel; the lumen (L) appears partially stenotic, caused by two large calcified atherosclerotic plaques (P) with cholesterol crystals and necrotic material (H&E, ×25). (A black and white version of this figure will appear in some formats.)

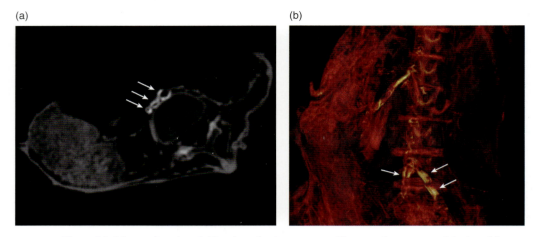

Figure 4.1 Atherosclerotic calcifications in the common iliac arteries on an axial view (a) and colorised three-dimensional volume coronal view (b) in the Egyptian mummy Ahmose-Meryet-Amon, a Princess who lived during the Second Intermediate Period (c. 1580–1550 BCE). (A black and white version of this figure will appear in some formats.)

Figure 4.2 (a) Calcific atherosclerotic lesions (arrows) in the leg arteries of the Egyptian mummy of Hataiy, a scribe from the Eighteenth Dynasty (c. 1550–1295 BCE), coronal view, thick slab, right leg bones digitally removed. (b) Heavy coronary artery calcifications in a female Unangan, Aleutian Island mummy, three-dimensional reconstruction, sagittal view. (A black and white version of this figure will appear in some formats.)

Figure 4.4 Photograph of the face of the mummy of Lady Rai, 1570–1530 BCE, Cairo Museum of Antiquity. (A black and white version of this figure will appear in some formats.)

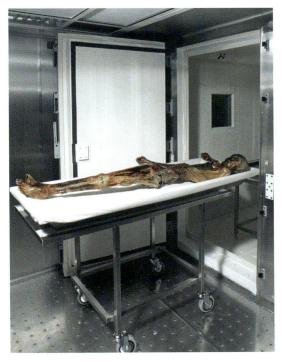

Figure 5.3 The Iceman is stored in a special cooling chamber at the South Tyrolean Museum of Archaeology. (A black and white version of this figure will appear in some formats.)

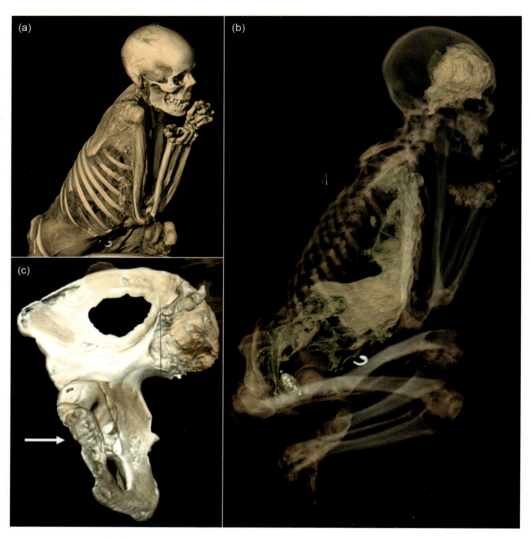

Figure 6.1 (a–c) CT scan visualisations of a naturally preserved Predynastic mummy from Gebelein, Upper Egypt (British Museum EA 32754). The transparency view (b) reveals the preservation of his internal organs. His pubic symphysis, clearly visible in the visualisation of the right pelvis (c), shows no or little remodelling (arrow). Source: courtesy of the Trustees of the British Museum. (A black and white version of this figure will appear in some formats.)

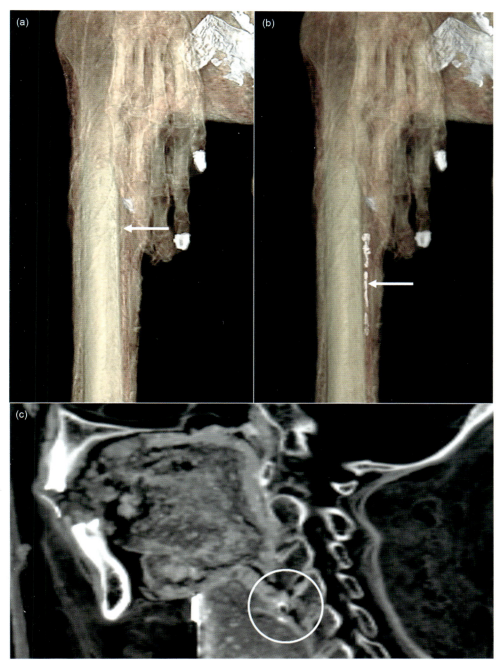

Figure 6.2 CT scan visualisations and DICOM image of the mummified remains of Tamut, a Twenty-second Dynasty priestess (British Museum EA 22939). The arteries in her legs are well preserved (a, arrow), with large atheromas detected in both of her femoral arteries. The one found within the right artery (b, arrow) has been segmented to allow for a clearer visualisation. The packing materials and textile inserted in Tamut's mouth and throat (c) can clearly be seen on the DICOM image (longitudinal section). Despite the insertion of these packing materials, atheromas can clearly be seen in both carotid arteries (atheroma within the left artery circled). Source: courtesy of the Trustees of the British Museum. (A black and white version of this figure will appear in some formats.)

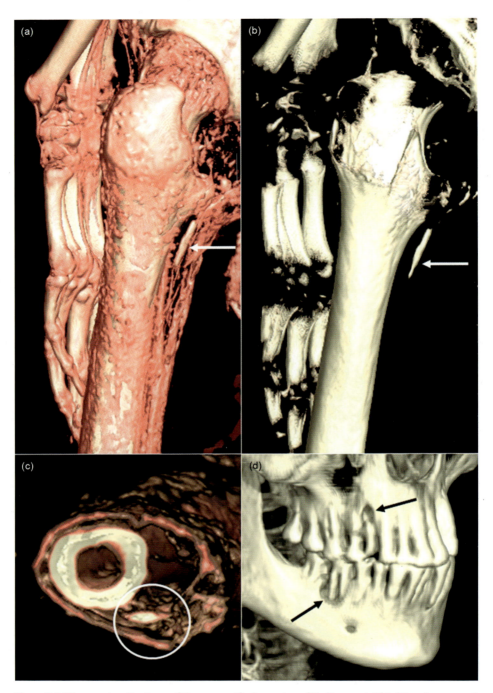

Figure 6.4 CT scan visualisations of the mummified remains of Padiamenet, Chief Doorkeeper and Chief Barber during the Twenty-fifth Dynasty (British Museum EA 6682). He was around 35–49 years old when he died and had four periapical lesions, two of which can be seen on the visualisation of his skull (d, arrows). CT scans of his left leg, shown with (a) and without (b) soft tissues, reveal a large atheroma within the femoral artery (arrows). The atheroma and vessel wall (c, circled), as well as the soft tissues surrounding the femur, are clearly visible in the cross-section. Source: courtesy of the Trustees of the British Museum. (A black and white version of this figure will appear in some formats.)

Figure 8.1 The ancient settlement of Amara West on the northern bank of the Nile. Source: Trustees of the British Museum. (A black and white version of this figure will appear in some formats.)

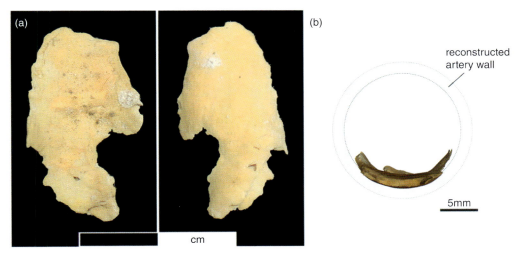

Figure 8.2 (a) Calcified plaque associated with Sk244-4; (b) three-dimensional scan of the plaque in cross-section. Source: Trustees of the British Museum. (A black and white version of this figure will appear in some formats.)

Figure 8.3 Calcified plaques associated with Sk244-6 in situ in the neck area and in detail (inset). Source: Trustees of the British Museum. (A black and white version of this figure will appear in some formats.)

Figure 8.4 Calcified plaques associated with Sk237 in situ along the lumbar spine and in detail (inset). Source: Trustees of the British Museum. (A black and white version of this figure will appear in some formats.)

Figure 8.5 Calcified plaques associated with Sk305-4 in situ and in detail (inset). Source: Trustees of the British Museum. (A black and white version of this figure will appear in some formats.)

Figure 9.1 Emptying skulls from the Monastery of Skänninge demonstrating large calcifications
Source: Staffan Hyll. (A black and white version of this figure will appear in some formats.)

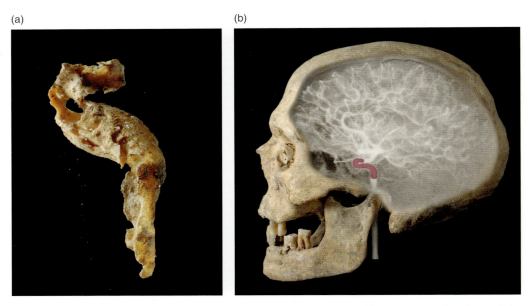

Figure 9.2 a) Photograph of the calcified internal carotid artery b) Reconstructed position of the calcification within the cranial vascular system. (A black and white version of this figure will appear in some formats.)

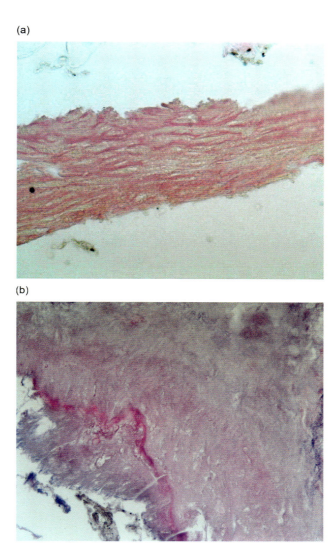

Figure 9.3 (a, b) Microphotographs of the carotid vessel wall after decalcification, sectioning and staining with elastin Van Gieson staining. Note the thickened vessel wall filled with fibrous tissue. (A black and white version of this figure will appear in some formats.)

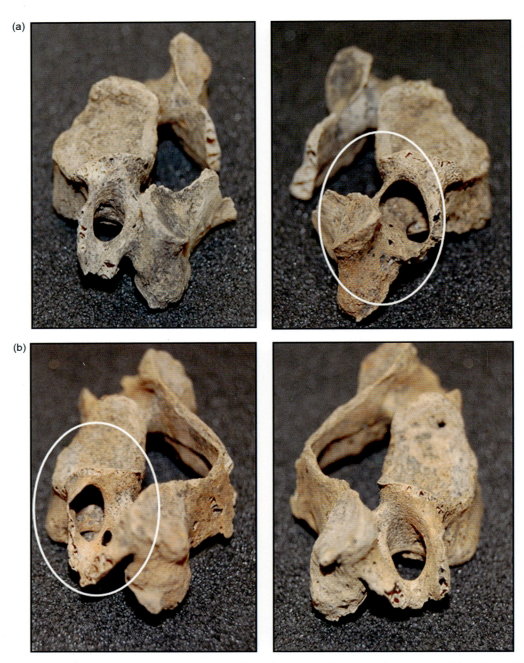

Figure 10.2 Superior lateral views of the C3 (a) and C5 (b) from skeleton 561-25. The sides with smooth-walled depressions are circled, with each defect 2–4 mm in depth. Source: courtesy of the Trustees of the British Museum. (A black and white version of this figure will appear in some formats.)

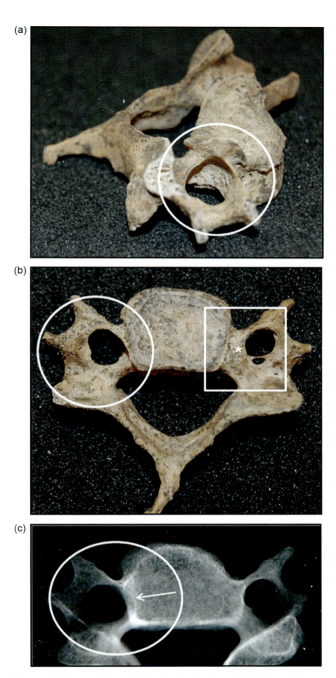

Figure 10.3 Lateral (a) and inferior (b, c) views of C3 from skeleton 1083-11, with the side affected by the pressure defect circled on all three. The remodelling is best seen from the inferior view (b), which reveals a clear enlargement of the transverse foramen and the loss of bone between the transverse foramen and the vertebral body. On the non-affected side (square), the bone bridge between the transverse foramen and the body of the vertebra (*) is present. The pressure defect has also encroached onto the vertebral body and created a sclerotic margin (arrow) that is visible radiographically (c). The presence of an accessory transverse foramen on the left side has not affected the course of the vertebral artery. Source: courtesy of the Trustees of the British Museum. (A black and white version of this figure will appear in some formats.)

(a)

(b)

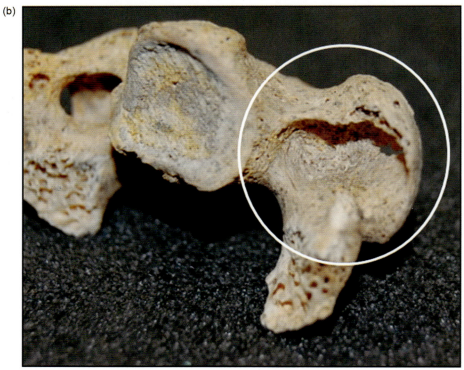

Figure 10.4 Inferior view of C2 from skeleton 1075-11. Despite post-mortem damage to the left transverse process, a pressure defect (circle) can clearly be seen encroaching into the vertebral body and the superior articular surface. Source: courtesy of the Trustees of the British Museum. (A black and white version of this figure will appear in some formats.)

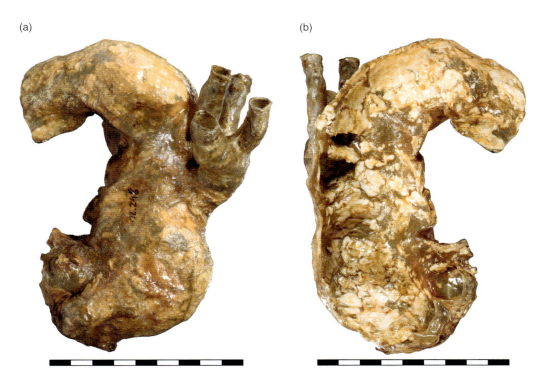

Figure 11.1 Ascending (bottom) and descending (top) arch of the aorta with arteriosclerotic calcifications, visible as white irregular structures of different sizes: (a) anterior exterior view; (b) posterior interior view of the vessel which has been cut in half (MN 12.248). Source: NHM Vienna, Reichmann. (A black and white version of this figure will appear in some formats.)

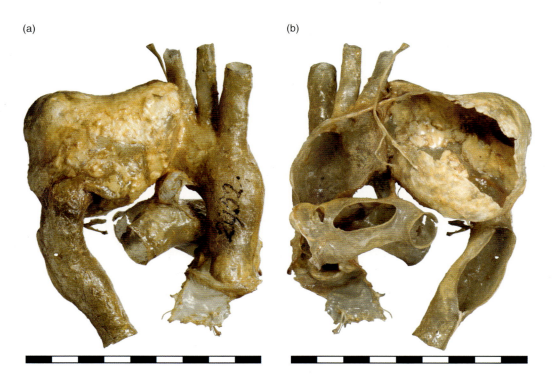

Figure 11.2 Aortic aneurysm with calcifications in the aortic arch, visible as white structures. (a) Posterior view with the widening of the aortic aneurysm and the white solid structure of the calcification particularly clear on the portion of the vessel towards the left side of the image. (b) Anterior view with the vessels opened for better visibility; note the white concretions on the interior surface of the vessel on the right side of the image (MN 2952). Source: NHM Vienna, Reichmann. (A black and white version of this figure will appear in some formats.)

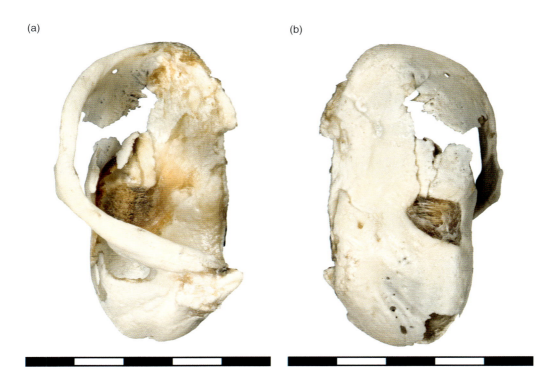

Figure 11.3 Calcified portion of the heart sac (pericardium). (a) Anterior view, with superior aspect at the top of the image. (b) Posterior view, with superior aspect at the top of the image; note that only the calcified portion of the lowest part (apex) of the heart sac is preserved (MN 17.747/1546). Source: NHM Vienna, Reichmann. (A black and white version of this figure will appear in some formats.)

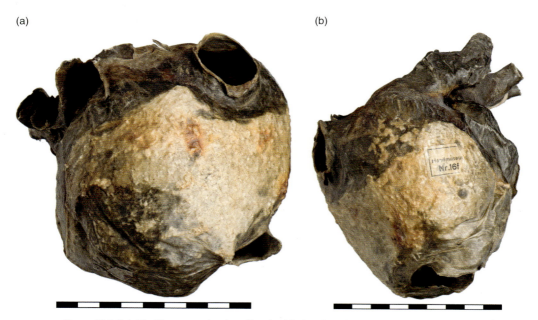

Figure 11.4 Calcified heart sac (pericardium) with dried cardiac soft tissue. (a) Anterior view with the aorta at the top of the image and towards the right side. (b) Inferior view of the posterior aspect of the pericardium showing the extensive yellowish calcified structure; the aorta is directed towards the left side of the image at the top (MN 3036). Source: NHM Vienna, Reichmann. (A black and white version of this figure will appear in some formats.)

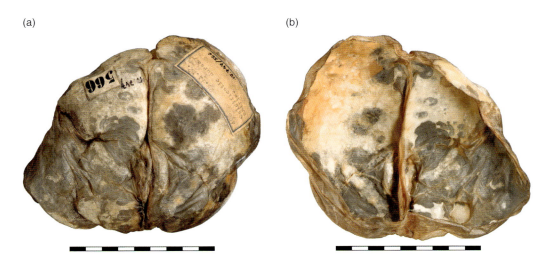

Figure 11.5 Calcified tissue within the meninges (membranous covering of the brain). (a) External/superior view of the dura mater (outermost layer of the three meninges). (b) Internal/inferior view: the white structure visible is calcified tissue within the dried soft tissue of the meninges (MN 17.747/566). Source: NHM Vienna, Reichmann. (A black and white version of this figure will appear in some formats.)

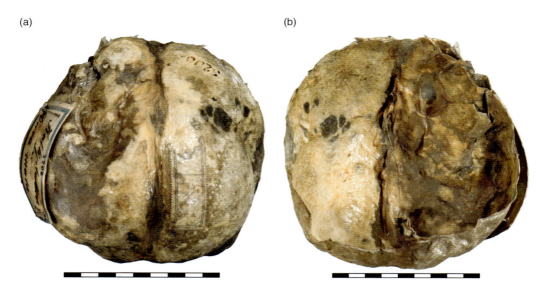

Figure 11.6 Calcified tissue within the meninges. (a) External/superior view of the meningeal tissue: note the cream to yellowish deposits of calcified tissue. (b) Internal/inferior view: the cream to yellowish widespread solid structure within the dried meningeal tissue is the calcified structure (MN 3206). Source: NHM Vienna, Reichmann. (A black and white version of this figure will appear in some formats.)

Figure 12.3 Calcified tibial artery in situ in a medieval burial from Austria. (A black and white version of this figure will appear in some formats.)

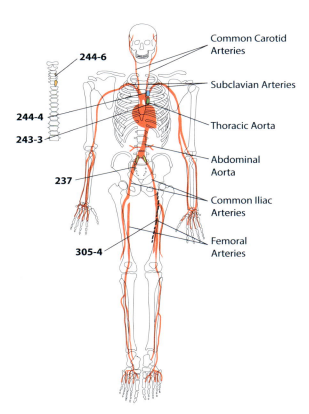

Figure 12.4 Major arteries in the human body and sites most likely to develop arterial calcification. Source: Binder and Roberts (2014). (A black and white version of this figure will appear in some formats.)

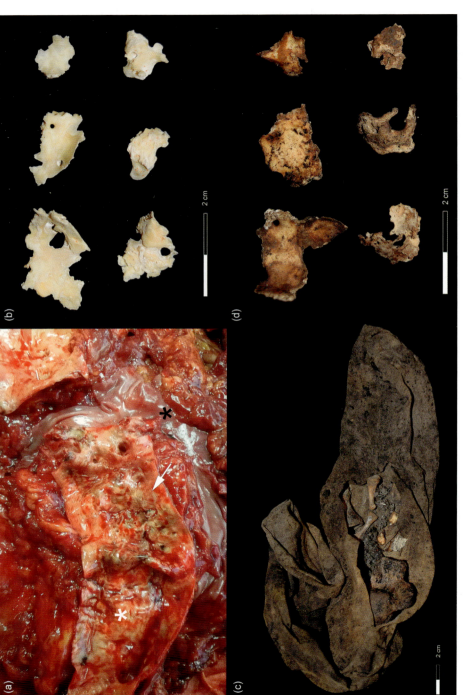

Figure 13.1 Atherosclerotic plaques found in situ. (a) A calcifying atheroma (white arrow) in the open aorta (white asterisk) in a well-preserved cadaver taken during an autopsy at the Medico-Legal Institute of Milan (black asterisk shows the diaphragm). (b) Details of atherosclerotic calcifications following maceration of an atheroma and complete separation of the soft tissue. (c) Atherosclerotic calcifications found in the sock of an individual from the CAL Milano Cemetery Skeletal Collection under study at the LABANOF (University of Milan), exhumed after 15 years of burial in a cemetery of Milan. (d) Details of atherosclerotic calcifications recovered with skeletal remains. (A black and white version of this figure will appear in some formats.)

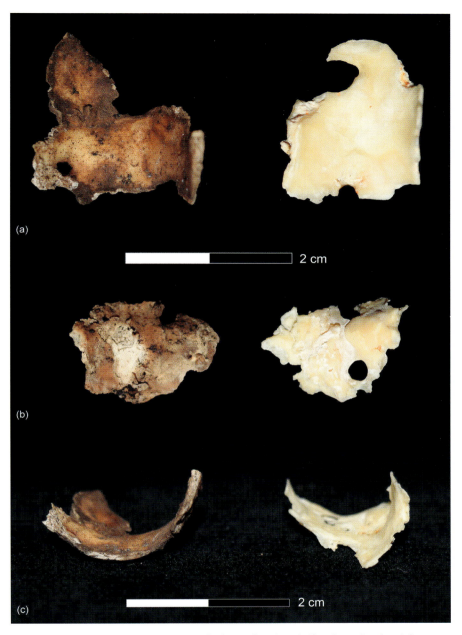

Figure 13.2 Morphological appearance of atherosclerotic calcifications. On the right are atherosclerotic calcifications after extraction from well-preserved cadavers during autopsies at the Medico-Legal Institute of Milan and after maceration for several weeks (until the soft tissue was completely separated); note the pale-yellow coloration of the plaques. On the left are atherosclerotic calcifications collected with skeletal remains of an individual from the identified CAL Milano Cemetery Skeletal Collection (under study at the LABANOF, University of Milan); note the coloration of the plaques, which ranges from yellow to brown. (a) View from the interior of the artery: Note the smooth and even concave surface of the plaque. (b) View from the exterior of the arterial wall: Note the multilayered convex surface of the plaque. (c) Cross-sectional view: Note the convex–concave or half-cylindrical shape of the calcifications. (A black and white version of this figure will appear in some formats.)

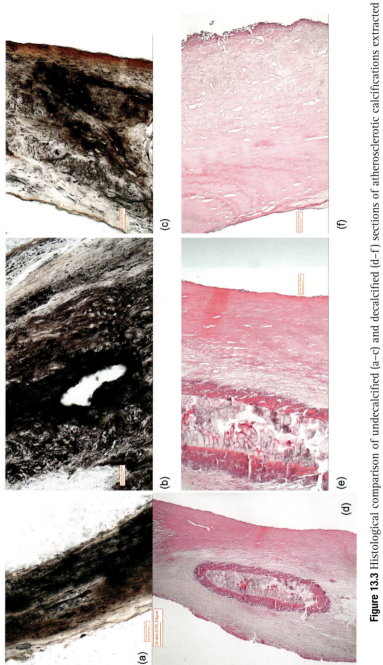

Figure 13.3 Histological comparison of undecalcified (a–c) and decalcified (d–f) sections of atherosclerotic calcifications extracted from well-preserved cadavers. Undecalcified sections illustrate the stratified structure of atherosclerotic plaques; original magnification ×2.5 (a), ×10 (b), ×10 (c). Decalcified sections from the same autopsy plaque, semi-thin sample stained with H&E showing 'ghosts' of macrophages (foam) cells and a calcified core (d and e, dark purple); original magnification ×2.5 (d), ×10 (e), ×10 (f). (A black and white version of this figure will appear in some formats.)

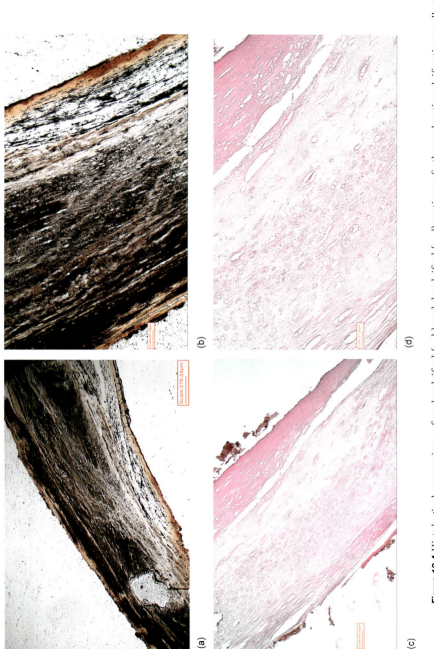

Figure 13.4 Histological comparison of undecalcified (a, b) and decalcified (c, d) sections of atherosclerotic calcifications collected with skeletal remains of an individual from the CAL Milano Cemetery Skeletal Collection (Milan, Italy). Undecalcified sections: original magnification ×2.5 (a), ×10 (b). Decalcified sections of the same calcification stained with H&E, with post-mortem contamination (c, brown staining) and 'ghosts' of macrophages (foam) cells; original magnification ×10 (c), ×20 (d). (A black and white version of this figure will appear in some formats.)

Figure 14.1 Images of Tsimane lifestyle: (a) Tsimane individual crossing the Maniqui River at sunrise; (b) Tsimane dwellings; (c) inside a Tsimane dwelling; (d) woman crushing dried corn; (e) Tsimane woman retrieving water from a nearby stream; (f) two Tsimane hunters in the forest. Sources: (a) Ben Trumble; (b–d) Jonathan Stieglitz; (e, f) Michael Gurven. (A black and white version of this figure will appear in some formats.)

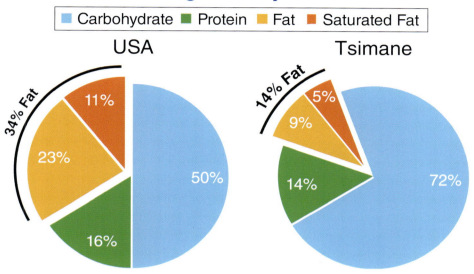

Figure 14.2 Comparison of major dietary components of US and Tsimane populations. (A black and white version of this figure will appear in some formats.)

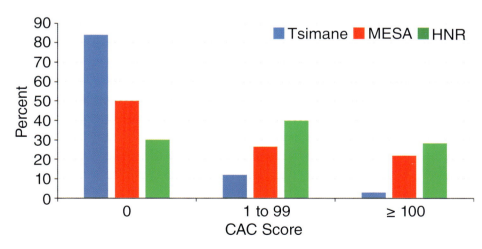

Figure 14.3 Percentage of Tsimane CAC scores in three risk categories compared with the general cross-sectional population-based participants from the MESA study (Budoff et al., 2013) and the Heinz Nixdorf Recall (HNR) study (Schmermund et al., 2002). (A black and white version of this figure will appear in some formats.)

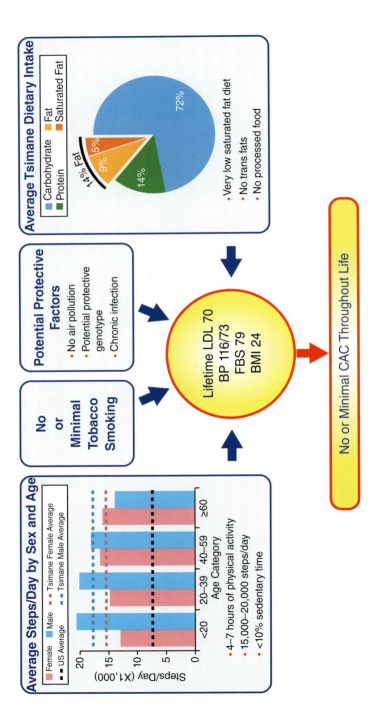

Figure 14.5 Concepts of how multiple factors contribute to the remarkably low rates of coronary arterial calcification in the Tsimane. (A black and white version of this figure will appear in some formats.)

McPherson, R. (2007). A common allele on chromosome 9 associated with coronary heart disease. *Science*, 316, 1488–91.

Marson, P., Zanchin, G. and Stefanutti, C. (2004). Some historical considerations on the inflammatory theory of atherosclerosis. *Reumatismo*, 56(3), 215–19.

Martin, R. (1988). *Anthropologie: Handbuch der Vergleichenden Biologie des Menschen.* Stuttgart: Gustav Fisher Verlag, Band I, pp. 421–43.

Munizaga, J., Allison, M. J. and Paredes, C. (1978). Cholelithiasis and cholecystitis in pre-Columbian Chileans. *American Journal of Physical Anthropology*, 48(2), 209–12.

Murphy, W. A., Jr, zur Nedden, D., Gostner, P., et al. (2003). The Iceman: Discovery and imaging. *Radiology*, 226, 614–29.

Murray, R. P., Connett, J. E., Tyas, S. L., et al. (2002). Alcohol volume, drinking pattern, and cardiovascular disease morbidity and mortality: Is there a U-shaped function? *American Journal of Epidemiology*, 155, 242–8.

Musshoff, F., Brockmann, C., Madea, B., Rosendahl, W. and Piombino-Mascali, D. (2013). Ethyl glucuronide findings in hair samples of the Capuchin Catacombs of Palermo. *Forensic Science International*, 232, 213–17.

O'Brien, J. J., Battista, J. J., Romagnoli, C. and Chhem, R. K. (2009) CT imaging of human mummies: A critical review of the literature (1979–2005). *International Journal of Osteoarchaeology*, 19, 90–8.

O'Keefe, J. H. Jr and Cordain, L. (2004). Cardiovascular disease resulting from a diet and lifestyle at odds with our Paleolithic genome: How to become a twenty-first century hunter-gatherer. *Mayo Clinic Proceedings*, 79, 101–8.

Panzer, S., Zink, A. R. and Piombino-Mascali, D. (2010). Radiologic evidence of anthropogenic mummification in the Capuchin Catacombs of Palermo, Sicily. *Radiographics*, 30(4), 1123–32.

Panzer, S., Augat, P., Zink, A. R. and Piombino-Mascali, D. (2018). CT checklist and scoring system for the assessment of soft tissue preservation in human mummies: application to catacomb mummies from Palermo, Sicily. *International Journal of Paleopathology*, 20, 50–9.

Pepalytė, I., Kučinskienė, Z. A., Grigalionenė, K., et al. (2012). Genetic variants that participate in oxidation processes and/or oxidative stress and are associated with atherosclerosis. *European Medicine, Health and Pharmacology Journal*, 3, 13–16.

Piombino-Mascali, D. (2017). The lovely bones: Capuchin catacombs of Palermo. In C. Rodríguez-Maffiotte Martín, ed., *Athanatos. Inmortal. Muerte e inmortalidad en poblaciones del pasado.* Tenerife: Cabildo de Tenerife, pp. 127–31.

Piombino-Mascali, D. (2018). *Le Catacombe dei Cappuccini: Guida storico-scientifica.* Palermo: Kalós.

Piombino-Mascali, D. and Gill-Frerking, H. (2019). The mummy autopsy: Some ethical considerations. In K. Squires, D. Errikson and N. Márquez-Grant, eds., *Ethical Approaches to Human Remains.* Cham, Switzerland: Springer, pp. 605–25.

Piombino-Mascali, D., Jankauskas, R., Tamošiūnas, A., et al. (2014). Atherosclerosis in mummified human remains from Vilnius, Lithuania (eighteenth–nineteenth centuries AD): A computed tomographic investigation. *American Journal of Human Biology*, 26(5), 676–81.

Piombino-Mascali, D., Jankauskas, R., Tamošiūnas, A., et al. (2015). Evidence of probable tuberculosis in Lithuanian mummies. *Homo*, 66(5), 420–31.

Prasad, K. (2009). Flaxseed and cardiovascular health. *Journal of Cardiovascular Pharmacology*, 54(5), 369–77.

Reitsema, L. J., Kozłowski, T., Jankauskas, R., Drążkowska, A. and Krajewska, M. (2015). Dieta przedstawicieli elit społecznych Rzeczypospolitej na podstawie analizy stabilnych izotopów węgla i azotu w szczątkach szkieletowych. In A. Drążkowska, ed., *Kultura funeralna elit Rzeczpospolitej od XVI do XVIII wieku na terenie Korony i Wielkiego Księstwa Litewskiego. Próba analizy interdyscyplinarnej.* Toruń: Wydawnictwo Naukowe Uniwersytetu Mikołaja Kopernika, pp. 230–45.

Ridker, P. M. (2002). On evolutionary biology, inflammation, infection, and the causes of atherosclerosis. *Circulation*, 105, 2–4.

Roberts, R., Marian, A. J., Dandona, S. and Stewart, A. F. T. (2012). Genomics in cardiovascular disease. *Journal of the American College of Cardiology*, 64, 2029–37.

Rodgers, J. L., Jones, J., Bolleddu, S. I., et al. (2019). Cardiovascular risks associated with gender and aging. *Journal of Cardiovascular Development and Disease*, 6(2), 19.

Ruffer, M. A. (1921). *Studies in the Palaeopathology of Egypt*. Chicago: University of Chicago Press.

Rühli, F. J., Chhem, R. K. and Böni, T. (2004). Diagnostic paleoradiology of mummified tissue: interpretation and pitfalls. *Canadian Association of Radiologists Journal*, 55(4), 218–27.

Santoro, D. (2013). Salute dei re, salute del popolo: Mangiare e curarsi nella Sicilia tardomedievale. *Anuario de Estudios Medievales*, 43(1), 259–89.

Sarti, R. (2003). *Vita di casa: Abitare, mangiare, vestire nell'Europa moderna*. Roma-Bari: Laterza.

Stary, H. C., Chandler, A. B., Dinsmore, R. E., et al. (1995). A definition of advanced types of atherosclerotic lesions and a histological classification of atherosclerosis: A report from the Committee on Vascular Lesions of the Council on Atherosclerosis, American Heart Association. *Arteriosclerosis, Thrombosis and Vascular Biology*, 92, 1355–74.

Strong, J. P., Malcom, G. T., McMahan, C. A., et al. (1999). Prevalence and extent of atherosclerosis in adolescents and young adults: Implications for prevention from the pathobiological determinants of atherosclerosis in Youth Study. *Journal of the American Medical Association*, 281, 727–35.

Thompson, R. C., Allam, A. H., Lombardi, G. P., et al. (2013). Atherosclerosis across 4000 years of human history: The Horus study of four ancient populations. *Lancet*, 381, 1211–22.

Widmer, R. J., Flammer, A. J., Lerman, L. O. and Lerman, A. (2015). The Mediterranean diet, its components, and cardiovascular disease. *American Journal of Medicine*, 128(3), 229–38.

Zimmerman, M. R. (1993). The paleopathology of the cardiovascular system. *Texas Heart Institute Journal*, 20, 252–7.

Part II

Cardiovascular Diseases Associated with Human Skeletal Remains

8 Calcified Structures as Potential Evidence of Atherosclerosis Associated with Human Skeletal Remains from Amara West, Nubia (1300–800 BCE)

Michaela Binder and Charlotte A. Roberts

8.1 Introduction

The Papyrus Ebers, written in ancient Egypt in *c.* 1550 BCE, provides the earliest known historic medical description of cardiovascular diseases (CVDs), likely attesting to the widespread occurrence of these conditions (Nunn, 1996: 85–7). However, evidence to prove that they were indeed a frequent health problem in antiquity remains scarce and confined to mummified remains despite the multitude of human remains discovered and analysed since the beginning of archaeological exploration of the Nile Valley (Davies & Walker, 1993; Binder 2019). This chapter presents six skeletonised individuals with associated calcified structures, most likely representing arterial calcifications, from the Egyptian colonial settlement of Amara West in Nubia (1300–800 BCE). By thorough examination of the archaeological, environmental and cultural context, we aim to illustrate the wide range of risk factors for CVDs that would have been present at this ancient settlement as well as in past human populations in general. In addition, the study highlights the benefits of careful excavation to recover evidence of CVD in the archaeological record.

8.2 Amara West: An Egyptian Settlement in Ancient Nubia

After the ancient Egyptian empire finally conquered its southern neighbour, the empire of Kerma in Nubia (modern Sudan), during the New Kingdom period (1500–1070 BCE), a series of temple-towns were built along the banks of the Nile in order to fulfil administrative and logistic functions within Egypt's complex colonial strategies. One of those settlements, Amara West, located on the northern bank of the Nile in modern Sudan (Figure 8.1), has been the focus of an extensive archaeological research project carried out in the town, the surrounding cemeteries and the wider landscape since 2008 under the auspices of the British Museum (Spencer, 2009). The project aims to gain a comprehensive understanding of life and living conditions in a colonial settlement in occupied Nubia, its development and integration within the cultural sphere of the local Nubian populations, and the impact of the changing climate on the settlement (Spencer et al., 2012; Spencer, 2014, 2017). Amara West was founded during the reign of King Seti I (1290–79 BCE) to become the new administrative capital of Upper Nubia, the southernmost province of the Egyptian empire during the later phase of the New Kingdom

Figure 8.1 The ancient settlement of Amara West on the northern bank of the Nile. Source: Trustees of the British Museum. (A black and white version of this figure will appear in some formats. For the colour version, please refer to the plate section.)

(1300–1070 BCE). Originally situated on an island surrounded by the main branch of the Nile to the south and a perennial side-channel to the north, the town was built according to contemporary Egyptian architectural patterns featuring a walled town with a square plan, a sandstone temple, administrative buildings, storage areas and residential quarters both within and outside the town wall. Based on the size of the densely packed mud-brick houses, the relatively small settlement would have housed a population of 100–200 people Based on historic records as well as archaeological evidence, it can be assumed that Amara West would have housed administrative elite and military personnel serving the Egyptian empire as part of a growing community consisting of local Nubians and a small number of Egyptians relocated to Nubia (Buzon, 2006). Archaeobotanical, archaeozoological and bioarchaeological research suggest a mainly agriculturally based community with a reliance on livestock (sheep/goat, cattle and pig) and plant cultivation (emmer wheat, barley; Ryan et al., 2012). Despite the formal end of Egyptian control over Nubia, the settlement continued to exist for at least another three centuries even though evidence for this later period of occupation is still confined to graves in the cemeteries. Geoarchaeological research indicates increasing aridification of the area over time, ultimately leading to the abandonment of Amara West around 800 BCE (Woodward et al., 2017).

8.3 Health and Living Conditions at Amara West

Associated with the settlement are two separate cemetery areas, one on a low escarpment overlooking the town to the north-west and reserved for the elite

(Cemetery D), with the other in a wadi to the north-east used by the non-elite population living at Amara West (Cemetery C) (Binder, 2011, 2017; Binder et al. 2011). Between 2009 and 2016, 52 graves were documented and excavated from Cemetery C and 23 from Cemetery D. The earliest graves in both cemeteries date to the time of foundation of the town during the Nineteenth Dynasty. Both areas continued to be used throughout the New Kingdom and well into the post-New Kingdom period, with burials as late as the eighth century BCE. Funerary rituals at Amara West were remarkably varied and included both Egyptian and Nubian elements combined into a highly complex hybrid culture. Grave architecture ranged from large-scale pyramid tombs with multiple underground burial chambers, built according to contemporary practices of the Egyptian elite, to Nubian burial mounds atop underground niches. While some individuals chose to be displayed as Egyptians in death through aspects of mummification, painted wooden coffins and adornment with amulets of Egyptian gods, others were buried in Nubian-style wooden funerary beds, sometimes in a crouched position. Almost nowhere in the cemetery is the division clear-cut and almost all graves combine elements of both cultures. However, similar to trends in the settlement, after initially being predominantly Egyptian in character, the Nubian elements became markedly more prominent during the later phases of use.

The assemblage of articulated skeletal human remains studied comprised 50 New Kingdom and 155 post-New Kingdom individuals; 35.9 per cent of all adult individuals were men and 46.1 per cent women, while non-adult individuals accounted for 27.5 per cent of the total population. Analysis of the skeletal human remains focused on pathological changes in order to shed light on life and living conditions at Amara West, and whether ongoing climatic and cultural changes during the time of occupation of the settlement had any influence on the occurrence of disease. The most significant results include a low mean stature and growth delays in children, indicating nutritional deficiencies during childhood, high frequencies of chronic respiratory disease, evidence of malnutrition (scurvy), and high levels of osteoarthritis, trauma and poor oral health (Binder, 2014; Binder & Spencer, 2014). In diachronic comparison of the results, the earlier New Kingdom group had already experienced considerable environmental stress and a further deterioration in health then occurred during the post-New Kingdom period. This was most likely related to climatic changes affecting the area in the early first millennium BCE (Woodward et al., 2017). These appear to have led to decreased agricultural productivity of the area and poor access to water, an increasing influx of aeolian sand and ultimate abandonment of the settlement by 800 BCE.

8.4   Methods of Recovery and Analysis

Excavation of the human skeletal remains was carried out by trained bioarchaeologists. All calcified structures were recognisable and recorded in situ to establish anatomical location in relation to the bones of the body. They were wrapped in acid-free tissue paper and stored separately in small cardboard or plastic containers. Analysis of the skeletal remains was carried out at the Institute for Bioarchaeology Laboratory of the British Museum using standard bioarchaeological methods, as recommended by Buikstra and Ubelaker (1994) and the British Association for Biological Anthropology and Osteoarchaeology (BABAO) (Brickley & McKinley, 2004). Sex was estimated based on morphological features of the pelvis and skull (Buikstra & Ubelaker, 1994; Bruzek, 2002). Age estimation was based on degeneration of the pubic symphysis (Brooks & Suchey, 1990) and auricular surface (Lovejoy et al., 1985). Pathological conditions were assessed macroscopically and with the use of a hand lens ($\times 10$ magnification) as per Ortner (2003: 46). Bone formation and bone destruction can't be observed on teeth. Their distribution pattern was then observed and differential diagnoses considered. Evidence of remodelling of destructive lesions was also recorded, as was the presence or absence of woven or lamellar bone formation.

The calcified structures were assigned separate skeleton sample numbers (SS) and photographed. SS68 and SS69b were further analysed using scanning electron microscopy (SEM; Hitachi S-3700N variable pressure) in order to characterise their surfaces. Chemical component analysis was carried out as part of SEM using energy-dispersive X-ray spectroscopy (EDS). In addition, all structures were subject to plain film radiography (Portable GE Medical MPX X-ray unit) and processed digitally using a Kodak Point-of-Care CR120 system. Three-dimensional images of SS68 and SS69b were produced using a surface scanner (NextEngine 3D Laser Scanner). Histological analyses were not carried out on the structures due to their destructive nature as well as the uncertainties related to reaching a conclusive diagnosis through the process (see below).

8.5 The Individuals with Calcified Structures

8.5.1 New Kingdom Burials (1300–1070 BCE)

The skeleton Sk244-4 was that of a middle-aged adult male (35–50 years) buried in the non-elite Cemetery C, even though the architecture of the grave, featuring a large Nubian-style tumulus on top of an extensive Egyptian-style five-chambered subterranean burial structure, suggests an elevated social status. Strontium isotope analysis carried out on one of this man's teeth suggests he grew up locally but in death was represented with attributes of both Egyptian and Nubian culture.

The skeleton was intact and moderately well preserved; despite the good preservation of the bone surfaces, structurally the bones were brittle and fragmented. Bioarchaeological examination of the skeleton revealed remodelled new bone formation on the visceral surfaces of five right ribs, indicating that the man had suffered from chronic lung disease that had caused inflammation of the lower respiratory tract at some point during his life. The exact cause of the disease could not be established due to the non-specific nature of the changes and the absence of any further differential diagnostic options beyond 'lung disease'. Changes in the alveolar

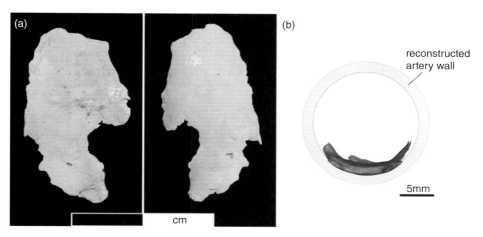

Figure 8.2 (a) Calcified plaque associated with Sk244-4; (b) three-dimensional scan of the plaque in cross-section. Source: Trustees of the British Museum. (A black and white version of this figure will appear in some formats. For the colour version, please refer to the plate section.)

bone attest to moderate periodontal disease (based on the recording system by Brothwell, 1981). Healed compression fractures were observed in the vertebral bodies of the tenth thoracic and fourth lumbar vertebrae.

One large calcified plaque was recovered from the heavily fragmented chest cavity of Sk244-4. The plaque is of very hard consistency, yellow coloured and irregular, and oval in shape (length 23.0 mm, thickness 0.9 mm). In cross-section, the plaque has a semicircular outline (Figure 8.2).

On SEM the surface of the plaque presented as very dense and homogeneous. EDS was carried out in order to shed light on the chemical composition of the material, and confirmed its calcified nature. Digital microscopic imaging ($\times 30$ magnification) further showed a smooth surface texture, and radiographic examination revealed a dense internal structure.

A middle-aged adult male (Sk244-6) was buried alongside Sk244-4 in the central western burial chamber of grave 244. If, and if so in what way, the two men were related remains unclear since neither funerary records nor genetic data are available. However, burial within the same tomb may indicate familial ties as was common in the Egyptian cultural sphere (Richards, 2005). The skeleton was intact with bone preservation similar to that of Sk244-4. The palaeopathological profile of Sk244-6 also includes evidence of chronic lung disease with remodelled new bone formation visible on the visceral surfaces of the shafts of three right and four left ribs. In addition, the man had chronic inflammatory disease affecting the maxillary and frontal sinuses (upper respiratory tract) as well as the walls of the outer ear channel and mastoid process. New bone formation and vessel impressions in the roof of both orbital cavities have been linked to an inflammatory process of the eye (Wapler et al., 2004). Furthermore, this man's dentition was affected by a number of dental diseases, including dental calculus, periodontal disease and several periapical cavities.

Figure 8.3 Calcified plaques associated with Sk244-6 in situ in the neck area and in detail (inset). Source: Trustees of the British Museum. (A black and white version of this figure will appear in some formats. For the colour version, please refer to the plate section.)

Five calcified plaques were recovered from the area of the neck alongside the spine between the sixth cervical and second thoracic vertebrae (Figure 8.3) and within the thoracic cavity. Looting of the bodies had caused some post-depositional disarticulation in the upper body, even though the skeletal elements were still largely in an anatomically correct position. Nevertheless, minor displacement of the calcifications cannot be excluded. The calcified structures are of a hard texture and also yellowish in colour. The largest plaque (SS69a; Figure 8.3, inset) is irregularly elongated, with a length of 17.4 mm, width 10 mm and thickness 1.3 mm. The surface structure is homogeneous with smooth edges under high magnification (×35). The smaller calcifications recovered from the region along the cervical and upper thoracic spine range in size from 9.0 × 12 mm (SS69b–e; Figure 8.3, inset) to 4.4 × 5.0 mm, with an average thickness of 0.6 mm. The cross-sections of all structures are again semicircular.

8.5.2 Post-New Kingdom Burials (1070–800 BCE)

Skeleton Sk243-3 represents a middle-aged adult female (35–50 years) from a post-New Kingdom non-elite tomb in Cemetery C. She was buried in a large subterranean burial chamber together with 16 other individuals. Remnants of textile found alongside her body suggest that the woman was likely wrapped in a shroud before she was placed in a supine position inside the chamber. The skeleton was reasonably well preserved and fully articulated even though slight dislocation of the anatomical connections of the upper body suggests minor post-depositional interference with her body. A range of pathological changes indicate that the woman experienced repeated episodes of ill health, including poor dental health and chronic diseases of the upper and lower respiratory tract.

Only one small calcified structure with a semicircular cross-section (SS67, 14.6 × 8.9 mm, 1.1 mm in thickness) was present in the upper thoracic area along the right side of the spine. However, the calcification may have been slightly displaced during post-depositional disturbance of the burial.

Another middle-aged adult female (Sk237) with multiple calcified structures was also found in the non-elite Cemetery C in a small east–west orientated burial niche on the bottom of a vertical shaft. This new type of funerary structure first appears at Amara West during the ninth to tenth centuries BCE and potentially indicates significant cultural changes taking place in the region during this time. The woman was buried in a supine position on a wooden funerary bed typical of Nubian funerary ritual. Preservation of the skeleton was good with no signs of post-depositional disturbance of the burial. Pathological changes in the bones again attest to heavy physical labour, chronic respiratory diseases and poor oral health. In addition, the woman had sustained some major trauma; this included a compound fracture of the sternum, which had not fully healed at the time of her death and may have been directly connected to her (early) death through associated soft tissue injuries to the chest.

Eight round to oval-shaped calcified structures of varying sizes and of a hard yellow texture were documented in the abdominal area over the lumbar vertebrae and orientated parallel to the body's axis (Figure 8.4). The two largest examples are elongated and oval-shaped (SS37a, 18.7 × 7.3 mm, thickness 1.2 mm; SS37b, 15.5 × 5.9 mm, thickness 1.0 mm) and their cross-sections were curved. The smaller fragments were more irregularly shaped, ranging in size from 8.6 × 7.7 mm to 6.0 × 5.0 mm.

Sk305-4 was a middle-aged adult female who was buried in an Egyptian-style double-chambered tomb in the elite cemetery of Amara West alongside three other adult individuals. Wooden fragments in the tomb suggest that she was placed on a wooden funerary bed in a supine body position. Her well-preserved skeleton was fully articulated with no signs of any significant post-depositional interference of the body. Remodelled new bone formation on the shafts of three right and three left middle ribs was also observed. She had extensive dental disease, with the majority of teeth being lost ante-mortem. Her health problems included evidence of osteoarthritis in the bones of the arms, legs and spine, a healed fracture of a thoracic vertebra, and healed chronic new bone formation on the endocranial surface of her skull, the long bones of the legs and the ribs (lower respiratory tract), likely due to inflammation of the meninges, periosteum of the long bones and the pleura attached to the ribs.

The calcified structures found associated with Sk305-4 were markedly different to those observed with the other individuals. At excavation they presented as a line of whitish coloured tubular calcifications of up to 14 mm in length running along the medial side of the right femur from the area of the femoral neck inferiorly over a

Figure 8.4 Calcified plaques associated with Sk237 in situ along the lumbar spine and in detail (inset). Source: Trustees of the British Museum. (A black and white version of this figure will appear in some formats. For the colour version, please refer to the plate section.)

length of 25 cm (Figure 8.5). In contrast to the other calcifications, they were tubular in shape with their full circumference preserved intact through most of the length of the structure, with a diameter of 4–5 mm (SS5). The walls of the calcification reach a thickness of up to 0.4–0.5 mm.

Discovered in 2014, the niche burial of a middle-aged adult male (Sk249) had largely been disturbed and thus inferences about body position and the association of specific funerary containers or other grave goods could not be made with any certainty. Only the ribs, spine, right forearm and hand were preserved in full articulation at the bottom of the niche. He had experienced a wide array of health challenges, including complete ante-mortem loss of all his teeth, a chronic lung condition, extensive osteoarthrosis of a range of joints, and fractures to the left clavicle and the spinous process of a cervical vertebra. Both sacroiliac joints were completely fused and due to the lack of further differential diagnostic features, the cause remains unclear.

Lodged among the articulated ribs were the remains of several fragments of thin, tubular, calcified structures aligned in a row about 5 cm long. The largest preserved fragments measured up to 4 mm in length with a reconstructed diameter of 4–5 mm.

8.6 Identification of the Calcified Structures

Identification of the calcified structures as calcified atheromas was based on the following considerations: morphological appearance, their anatomical position within

Figure 8.5 Calcified plaques associated with Sk305-4 in situ and in detail (inset). Source: Trustees of the British Museum. (A black and white version of this figure will appear in some formats. For the colour version, please refer to the plate section.)

the body, as represented by the skeleton, as well as comparison with published clinical studies and analysis of intact mummies (Towler, 2008; Allam et al., 2009; Thompson et al., 2013; see also Chapters 4 and 5).

Calcified structures were recovered from the upper chest and neck area of individuals Sk244-4, Sk244-6 and Sk243-3. The structures SS69a (Sk244-6, Figure 8.3), SS68 (Sk244-4, Figure 8.2) and SS67 (Sk243-3) were all very similar, with a rounded shape and semi-cylindrical cross-section, suggesting they originated from a cylindrical structure with an estimated diameter of 2–2.5 cm. This conforms to the average diameter of the aorta descendens or aorta abdominalis suprarenalis (Kahraman et al., 2006). The curvature of the second calcification recovered with Sk244-6 (SS69b) is consistent with a diameter of 0.8–0.9 cm. Based on the location of SS69b and some smaller calcified plaques found between the sixth cervical and second thoracic vertebrae, as well as their width that is consistent with published values in living people (Engelhorn et al., 2006), an origin in the subclavian artery appears most likely. Calcifications in these vessels have also been reported in Egyptian mummies (Sandison, 1962).

The anatomical position of the calcified arteries in the lumbar area of Sk237 (Figure 8.4) suggests an origin in the iliac artery. The curvature observed in the larger calcifications is consistent with a cylindrically shaped structure of 0.5–0.7 cm in diameter, which also falls well within the standard range reported for the common iliac artery in clinical studies (Malnar et al., 2010). Strong parallels were further found in atheromatous plaques diagnosed on computed tomography (CT) scans of mummified human remains (Allam et al., 2009). The location of the calcifications associated with Sk305-4 is consistent with the position of the common femoral artery. The observed diameter of the intact calcified structures (0.4–0.5 cm) further supports this assumption as it falls within average clinical values of intact femoral arteries (Sandgren et al., 1999). Identification of the anatomical site from which the calcifications found with Sk249 were associated is more difficult due to the fragmentary nature of the structures and the disturbance of the body, even though they can most likely be considered as in situ. However, their diameters and positions would be most consistent with the location of the renal arteries.

The calcifications observed in the individuals from Amara West do not conform to the appearance known for any other condition. Their semi-cylindrical shape and their relative anatomical positions with skeletons Sk244-4, Sk244-6, Sk237 and Sk243-3 argues for an identification of calcified arterial plaques as atheromas and that they were suffering from atherosclerosis. In contrast, calcification of the circumferences distinguishes the structures associated with Sk305-4 (Figure 8.5) and Sk249 from those observed in the other individuals and suggests a different pathophysiological pathway. In combination with the absence of narrowing of the arterial lumen, circumferential calcification is a common feature of medial arterial calcification in contrast to atherosclerotic calcification (Lehto et al., 1996; Towler, 2008). Medial calcification typically occurs in the arteries associated with the upper and lower limbs but also in the medium-sized visceral and kidney arteries, and they are particularly common in the uterine, femoral and tibial arteries (Sinha et al., 2008). Thus they also represent the most likely cause for the calcifications observed in Sk305-4 and Sk249.

8.7 Atherosclerosis at Amara West: Exploring Potential Risk Factors Leading to CVDs in Ancient Nubia

Atherosclerosis, together with other less common forms of CVD, are the leading cause of death worldwide today. Generally assumed to be a disease of modern lifestyle-related risk factors (smoking, obesity, hypertension), its history and epidemiology in the past is virtually unknown. However, on closer examination, many of the factors assumed to cause atherosclerosis would have affected people in the past as well. Considering contextual evidence, including archaeological, environmental and palaeopathological data, a number of reasons can be identified that help explain why, contrary to modern assumptions, people at ancient Amara West would have equally suffered from atherosclerosis.

8.7.1 Indoor Air Pollution and Chronic Respiratory Diseases

Exceeded only by nutritional factors, the second most important cause of atherosclerosis today is smoking tobacco (Lusis, 2000). The pathophysiological mechanisms by which smoking triggers cardiovascular events include atherosclerotic changes with narrowing of the vascular lumen, as well as the induction of a hypercoagulable state that leads to an increased risk of acute thrombosis (Centers for Disease Control, 2010). Smoking tobacco would of course not have been practiced at Amara West. However, an elevated risk for CVDs due to tobacco smoke has recently been found to be very similar to another mechanism, the habitual inhalation of smoke from organic biomass open fires (Danielsen et al., 2011; Unosson et al., 2013; Shan et al., 2014; Fatmi & Coggon, 2016).

The significant negative influence of open fires on the health of the inhabitants of Amara West is amply evidenced by two factors: secondary skeletal markers of chronic respiratory diseases and contextual archaeological evidence. Damage to the respiratory tissues due to environmental pollution can cause chronic pulmonary diseases that in the skeleton lead to new bone formation on the inner, visceral side of the ribs (Eyler et al., 1996; Lambert, 2002; Davies-Barrett et al., 2019). However, there is a wide range of other conditions that can cause these bone changes, including tuberculosis, lung cancer, chronic bronchitis and pneumonia (Roberts et al., 1994; Roberts, 1999; Lambert, 2002; Santos & Roberts, 2006). The changes occurring on the ribs are not pathognomonic for any one condition, and thus in the absence of further differential diagnostic features, such as bone changes or pathogen ancient DNA (Nicklisch et al., 2012; Müller et al., 2014), they cannot be attributed to any of those options.

At Amara West, new bone formation on the ribs affected 60.0 per cent (15/25) of New Kingdom and 54.2 per cent (39/72) of post-New Kingdom individuals with preserved ribs. This also included all six individuals with associated calcified atheromatous plaques. Further differential diagnostic features allowing for a more precise identification of the underlying causes were not observed at Amara West and, based on the environmental, historical and archaeological context of the individuals, every one of them is well within reason. However, archaeological evidence suggests that indoor air pollution would have very likely been a major health issue in this ancient settlement. Hearths and cylindrical clay-lined ovens for cooking, fuelled by wood, charcoal and dung, but also kilns used for manufacturing ceramics or metalwork were frequently uncovered within houses, courtyards and small roofed spaces, all of which likely had little ventilation (Spencer, 2017). These findings indicate that likely everyone living at Amara West would have habitually inhaled smoke arising within and from those structures and would consequently have been exposed to risk factors causing CVDs that were equally comparable to the risks of frequent tobacco smoking in today's world.

A second common cause of new bone formation on the ribs, bacterial pneumonia, has also been linked to atherosclerosis (Rosenfeld & Campbell, 2011). Pneumonia is an infectious disease that may have already been widespread since early on in human history, its symptoms first being described by the Greek physician Hippocrates (Feigin, 2004). Thus, the disease would have likely affected people at Amara West as well and represents another potential risk factor leading to atherosclerosis in the inhabitants of the ancient settlement (Kelley & Micozzi, 1984, Santos & Roberts, 2006).

8.7.2 Dental Disease

The relationship between dental diseases, in particular periodontal disease and an increased risk of atherosclerosis, has been recognised in medical research since the late 1980s (Beck & Offenbacher, 2001; Haynes & Stanford, 2003; see also Chapter 2). However, the exact mechanisms remain under debate and may likely include several different options (reviewed by Bartova et al., 2014). Poor oral health with high rates of caries, periapical lesion formation and ante-mortem tooth loss was exceedingly prevalent amongst the Amara West population. Periodontal disease affected 84.6 per cent (11 of 13 individuals) of the New Kingdom and 85.1 per cent (40 of 43 individuals) of the post-New Kingdom group. The main causes would have been a highly cariogenic diet in combination with high levels of dental wear due to abrasive materials like grit or sand in the diet. Of the individuals showing evidence for arterial calcification, all had also suffered from moderate or severe periodontal disease. As a consequence, dental diseases, particularly periodontal disease, are another common risk factor that would have contributed to the occurrence of atherosclerosis at Amara West.

8.7.3 Infectious Burden

Over the past decade, the contribution of bacterial and/or viral infections to the pathogenesis of atherosclerosis, either through infection of blood vessel cells directly or via the indirect effects of cytokines or acute-phase proteins induced by infection at non-vascular sites (Rosenfeld & Campbell 2011; Sessa et al., 2014), has also received increasing attention in clinical research. Even though the diagnosis of infectious diseases in palaeopathology remains challenging (see chapters 10–13 in Buikstra, 2019), a high prevalence is evident at Amara West. Evidence of inflammatory conditions potentially of infectious origin was widespread (Binder, 2014), affecting almost all of the inhabitants of the ancient settlement. While identification of the exact causes of these lesions is not possible, the palaeopathological evidence in combination with the mortality profile, environmental context, housing patterns and settlement density suggest the presence of diseases such as malaria, tuberculosis and pneumonia as well as a potential host of other viral, bacterial and parasitic diseases. Consequently, if indeed infectious diseases contribute to atherosclerosis, the burden of infectious diseases affecting the population at Amara West would have likely represented another major contributory factor to the occurrence of the disease.

8.7.4 Genetic Effects

Alongside environmental factors such as a person's diet or habitual smoking, genetic factors have long been recognised as important determinants for susceptibility to atherosclerosis (Lusis, 2000). Recent research has revealed a wide range of mono-genetic diseases, candidate genes, genetic polymorphisms and susceptibility loci associated with atherosclerotic diseases that potentially open new pathways for prevention and treatment of these diseases (Kovacic & Bakran, 2012; Lusis, 2012). In palaeopathology, recent findings in mummies have also led researchers to argue for an inherited genetic predisposition as a main reason for the development of atherosclerosis in ancient populations (Thompson et al., 2013). In particular, this has been suggested for ancient Egyptians, as seen in the high prevalence of advanced atherosclerosis in Egyptian mummies (Zink et al., 2011). However, direct biomolecular evidence for a genetic predisposition in past human populations is so far limited to Ötzi, the Iceman who lived in the Central European Alps about 5000 years ago (Keller et al., 2012).

In addition, research has shown that certain genetic factors increase the risk of atherosclerosis being inherited within families (Pandey et al., 2013). At Amara West, individuals Sk244-4 and Sk244-6 both had preserved calcified plaques and were buried next to each other within the same grave. Even though it is currently impossible to prove familial ties with any certainty, it nevertheless remains a strong possibility given the historically documented practice of using burial chambers for family groups (Richards, 2005). Consequently, while a genetic predisposition to atherosclerosis in Nile Valley populations is certainly within reason and would explain the higher prevalence of associated bioarchaeological evidence found in archaeological records of the region (Zink et al., 2011; see also Chapter 3), compared with the rest of the world, research into its genetics or epidemiology in African countries is still too scarce to argue for or against this claim (World Health Organization, 2018).

8.7.5 Diabetes

The calcified structures associated with Sk305-4 differ in appearance to those observed with the other individuals at Amara West. With the entire circumference being calcified, they rather fit the criteria of medial arterial calcification. The main reasons for this type of calcification are diabetes and end-stage chronic kidney disease, as well as old age (Towler, 2008). In addition, extensive 'railroad track-like' calcifications in the peripheral arteries of the lower limbs like those seen in individual Sk305-4 commonly occur as a secondary sign in diabetes mellitus (Lehto et al., 1996; Towler, 2008). Even though there are literary sources from Egyptian medical papyri that have tentatively been interpreted as evidence for diabetes (Loriaux, 2006), the antiquity and paleoepidemiology of this disease in the study of archaeological skeletons are unknown, due to the fact that this disease does not cause any recognisable skeletal changes (Aufderheide & Rodríguez-Martín, 1998: 343). To date, only one piece of evidence of bone damage potentially secondary to diabetes has been described from ancient Egypt (Dupras et al., 2010), alongside soft tissue changes ascribed to the disease in an Egyptian mummy (Marx & D'Auria, 1986). Even though the skeleton of Sk305-4 does not feature any other unusual pathological changes, providing further evidence that the woman may have indeed suffered from diabetes, the possibility is nevertheless not without reason.

8.8 Conclusions

The six individuals from Amara West, Sudan with calcified arteries or arterial plaques provide evidence that CVDs were already a health hazard in ancient times. Despite the apparent absence from the bioarchaeological record, the example of Amara West showcases that improved excavation methods, including awareness by excavators and better knowledge of the morphological appearance of arterial calcifications, could in future lead to an increase in the dataset of evidence of CVDs. This study further highlights the importance of integrating palaeopathological data into the broader archaeological, environmental and sociocultural context of the population under study in order to elucidate potential risk factors leading to atherosclerosis in the past.

Acknowledgements

This research was made possible through the support of the National Corporation of Antiquities and Museums of Sudan, in particular Abdel Rahman Ali and inspectors Shadia Abdu Rabo and Mohamed Saad Mohamed. Thanks are due to the director of the Amara West Research Project, Neal Spencer (Department of Ancient Egypt and Sudan, British Museum). Curator of human remains at the British Museum, Daniel Antoine, provided valuable support. Financial support for the bioarchaeological examination of the human remains from Amara West was granted by the British Academy, Fondation Michela Schiff-Giorgini, The Leverhulme Trust and the Institute for Bioarchaeology.

References

Allam, A. H., Thompson, R. C., Wann, L. S., Miyamoto, M. I. and Thomas, G. S. (2009). Computed tomographic assessment of atherosclerosis in ancient Egyptian mummies. *Journal of the American Medical Association*, 302(19), 2091–4.

Aufderheide, A. C. and Rodríguez-Martín, C. (1998). *The Cambridge Encyclopaedia of Human Paleopathology*. Cambridge: Cambridge University Press.

Bartova, J., Sommerova, P., Lyuya-Mi, et al. (2014). Periodontitis as a risk factor of atherosclerosis. *Journal of Immunology Research*, 2014, 636893.

Beck, J. D. and Offenbacher, S. (2001). The association between periodontal diseases and cardiovascular diseases: A state-of-the-science review. *Annals of Periodontology*, 6(1), 9–15.

Binder, M. (2011). The tenth–nineth century BC: New evidence from Cemetery C of Amara West. *Sudan and Nubia*, 15, 39–53.

Binder, M. (2014). *Health and diet in Upper Nubia through climate and political change: A bioarchaeological investigation of health and living conditions at ancient Amara West between 1300 and 800BC*. Unpublished PhD thesis, Durham University.

Binder, M. (2017). The New Kingdom cemeteries at Amara West. In N. Spencer, A. Stevens and M. Binder, eds., *Nubia in the New Kingdom: Lived Experience, Pharaonic Control and Indigenous Traditions. Proceedings of the Annual Egyptological Colloquium, British Museum 11–12 July 2013*. Leuven: Peeters, pp. 589–612.

Binder, M. (2019). The role of physical anthropology in Nubian archaeology. In D. Raue, ed., *The Handbook of Nubian Archaeology*. Berlin: DeGruyter, pp. 103–28.

Calcifications as Evidence of Atherosclerosis at Amara   161

Binder, M. and Spencer, N. (2014). The bioarchaeology of Amara West in Nubia: Investigating the impacts of political, cultural and environmental change on health and diet. In A. Fletcher, D. Antoine and J. D. Hill, eds., *Regarding the Dead*. London: British Museum Press, pp. 125–39.

Binder, M., Spencer, N. and Millet, M. (2011). Cemetery D at Amara West: The Ramesside Period and its aftermath. *British Museum Studies in Ancient Egypt and Sudan*, 16, 47–99.

Brickley, M. and McKinley, J. I. (eds.) (2004). *Guidelines to the Standards for Recording Human Remains*. Reading: Institute of Field Archaeologists.

Brooks, S. and Suchey, J. M. (1990). Skeletal age determination based on the os pubis: A comparison of the Acsádi–Nemeskéri and Suchey–Brooks methods. *Human Evolution*, 5(3), 227–38.

Brothwell, D. R. (1981). *Digging Up Bones*. Ithaca, NY: Cornell University Press.

Bruzek, J. (2002). A method for visual determination of sex, using the human hip bone. *American Journal of Physical Anthropology*, 117(2), 157–68.

Buikstra, J. E. (ed.) (2019). *Ortner's Identification of Pathological Conditions in Human Skeletal Remains*, 3rd ed. New York: Academic Press.

Buikstra, J. E. and Ubelaker, D. H. (1994). *Standards for Data Collection from Human Remains*. Lafayetteville, AK: Arkansas Archaeological Survey.

Buzon, M. R. (2006). Health of the non-elites at Tombos: Nutritional and disease stress in New Kingdom Nubia. *American Journal of Physical Anthropology*, 130(1), 26–37.

Centers for Disease Control. (2010). Cardiovascular diseases. In *How Tobacco Smoke Causes Disease: The Biology and Behavioral Basis for Smoking-Attributable Disease. A Report of the Surgeon General*. Atlanta, GA: Centers for Disease Control and Prevention. Available at www.ncbi.nlm.nih.gov/books/NBK53012/

Davies, W. V. and Walker, R. (eds.) (1993). *Biological Anthropology and the Study of Ancient Egypt*. London: British Museum Press.

Davies-Barrett, A., Antoine, D. and Roberts, C. A. (2019). Inflammatory periosteal reaction on ribs associated with lower respiratory tract disease: A method for recording prevalence from sites with differing preservation. *American Journal of Physical Anthropology*, 15(3), 530–42.

Danielsen, P. H., Moller, P., Jensen, K. A., et al. (2011). Oxidative stress, DNA damage, and inflammation induced by ambient air and wood smoke particulate matter in human A549 and THP-1 cell lines. *Chemical Research in Toxicology*, 24, 168–84.

Dupras, T. L., Williams, L. J., Willems, H. and Peeters, C. (2010). Pathological skeletal remains from ancient Egypt: The earliest case of diabetes mellitus? *Practical Diabetes International*, 27, 358–63.

Engelhorn, C. A., Engelhorn, A. L., Cassou, M. F., et al. (2006). Intima–media thickness in the origin of the right subclavian artery as an early marker of cardiovascular risk. *Arquivos Brasileros de Cardiologia*, 87 (5), 609–14.

Eyler, W. R., Monsein, L. H., Beute, G. H., et al. (1996). Rib enlargement in patients with chronic pleural disease. *American Journal of Roentgenology*, 167, 921–6.

Fatmi, Z. and Coggon, D. (2016). Coronary heart disease and household air pollution from use of solid fuel: A systematic review. *British Medical Bulletin*, 118(1), 91–109.

Feigin, R. (2004). *Textbook of Pediatric Infectious Diseases*, 5th ed. Philadelphia: W. B. Saunders, p. 299.

Haynes, W. G. and Stanford, C. (2003). Periodontal disease and atherosclerosis: From dental to arterial plaque. *Arteriosclerosis, Thrombosis and Vascular Biology*, 23, 1309–11.

Kahraman, H., Ozaydin, M., Varol, E., et al. (2006). The diameters of the aorta and its major branches in patients with isolated coronary artery ectasia. *Texas Heart Institute Journal*, 33(4), 463–8.

Keller, A., Graefen, A., Ball, M., et al. (2012). New insights into the Tyrolean Iceman's origin and phenotype as inferred by whole-genome sequencing. *Nature Communications*, 3, 698.

Kelley, M. A. and Micozzi, M. (1984). Rib lesions in chronic pulmonary tuberculosis. *American Journal of Physical Anthropology*, 65, 381–6.

Kovacic, S. and Bakran, M. (2012). Genetic susceptibility to atherosclerosis. *Stroke Research and Treatment*, 2012, 5.

Lambert, P. M. (2002). Rib lesions in a prehistoric Puebloan sample from southwestern Colorado. *American Journal of Physical Anthropology*, 117, 281–92.

Lehto, S., Niskanen, L., Suhonen, M., Rönnemaa, T. and Laakso, M. (1996). Medial artery calcification: A neglected harbinger of cardiovascular complications in non-insulin-dependent diabetes mellitus. *Arteriosclerosis, Thrombosis and Vascular Biology*, 16(8), 978–83.

Loriaux, D. L. (2006). Diabetes and the Ebers Papyrus: 1552 B.C. *The Endocrinologist*, 16(2), 55–6.

Lovejoy, C. O., Meindl, R. S., Pryzbeck, T. R. and Mensforth, R. P. (1985). Chronological metamorphosis of the auricular surface of the ilium: A new method for the determination of adult skeletal age at death. *American Journal of Physical Anthropology*, 68, 15–28.

Lusis, A. J. (2012). Genetics of atherosclerosis. *Trends in Genetics*, 28(6), 267–75.

Lusis, A. J. (2000). Atherosclerosis. *Nature*, 407(6801), 233–41.

Malnar, D., Klasan, G. S., Miletic, D., et al. (2010). Properties of the celiac trunk: anatomical study. *Collegium Antropologicum*, 34(3), 917–21.

Marx, M. and D'Auria, S. H. (1986). CT examination of eleven Egyptian mummies. *Radiographics*, 6(2), 321–30.

Müller, R., Roberts, C. A. and Brown, T. A. (2014). Biomolecular identification of ancient *Mycobacterium tuberculosis* complex DNA in human remains from Britain and continental Europe. *American Journal of Physical Anthropology*, 153(2), 178–89.

Nicklisch, N., Maixner, F., Ganslmeier, R., et al. (2012). Rib lesions in skeletons from early Neolithic sites in Central Germany: On the trail of tuberculosis at the onset of agriculture. *American Journal of Physical Anthropology*, 149(3), 391–404.

Nunn, J. F. (1996). *Ancient Egyptian Medicine*. London: British Museum Press.

Ortner, D. J. (2003). *Identification of Pathological Conditions in Human Skeletal Remains*. London: Academic Press.

Pandey, A. K., Blaha, M. J., Sharma, K., et al. (2013). Family history of coronary heart disease and the incidence and progression of coronary artery calcification: Multi-Ethnic Study of Atherosclerosis (MESA). *Atherosclerosis*, 232(2), 369–76.

Richards, J. E. (2005). *Society and Death in Ancient Egypt: Mortuary Landscapes of the Middle Kingdom*. Cambridge: Cambridge University Press.

Roberts, C. A. (1999). Rib lesions and tuberculosis: the current stage of play. In G. Pálfi, O. Dutour, J. Deák, and I. Hutás, eds., *Tuberculosis: Past and Present*. Budapest/Szeged: Golder Book Publishers and Tuberculosis Foundation, pp. 311–16.

Roberts, C. A., Lucy, D. and Manchester, K. (1994). Inflammatory lesions of ribs: An analysis of the Terry Collection. *American Journal of Physical Anthropology*, 95(2), 169–82.

Rosenfeld, M. E. and Campbell, L. A. (2011). Pathogens and atherosclerosis: update on the potential contribution of multiple infectious organisms to the pathogenesis of atherosclerosis. *Thrombosis and Haemostasis*, 106(5), 858–67.

Ryan, P., Cartwright, C. and Spencer, N. (2012). Archaeobotanical research in a pharaonic town in ancient Nubia. *British Museum Technical Research Bulletin*, 6, 97–107.

Sandgren, T, Sonesson, B., Ahlgren, A. and Länne, T. (1999). The diameter of the common femoral artery in healthy human: Influence of sex, age, and body size. *Journal of Vascular Surgery*, 29(3), 503–10.

Sandison, A. T. (1962). Degenerative vascular disease in the Egyptian mummy. *Medical History*, 6(1), 77–81.

Santos, A. L. and Roberts, C. A. (2006). Anatomy of a serial killer: Differential diagnosis of tuberculosis based on rib lesions of adult individuals from the Coimbra Identified Skeletal Collection, Portugal. *American Journal of Physical Anthropology*, 130(1), 38–49.

Sessa, R., Pietro, M. D., Filardo, S. and Turriziani, O. (2014). Infectious burden and atherosclerosis: A clinical issue. *World Journal of Clinical Cases*, 2(7), 240–9.

Shan, M., Yang, X., Ezzati, M., et al. (2014). A feasibility study of the association of exposure to biomass smoke with vascular function, inflammation, and cellular aging. *Environmental Research*, 135, 165–72.

Sinha, S., Eddington, H. and Kalra, P. A. (2008). Vascular calcification: Mechanisms and management. *British Journal of Cardiology*, 15(6), 316–21.

Spencer, N. (2009). Cemeteries and a late Ramesside suburb at Amara West. *Sudan and Nubia*, 13, 47–61.

Spencer, N. (2014). Amara West: Considerations on urban life in occupied Kush. In D. Welsby and J. R. Anderson, eds., *The Fourth Cataract and Beyond: Proceedings of the 12th International Conference for Nubian Studies*. Leuven: Peeters, pp. 457–85.

Spencer, N. (2017). Building on new ground: The foundation of a colonial town at Amara West. In N. Spencer, A. Stevens and M. Binder, eds., *Nubia in the New Kingdom: Lived Experience, Pharaonic Control and Indigenous Traditions. Proceedings of the Annual Egyptological Colloquium, British Museum 11–12 July 2013*. Leuven: Peeters, pp. 323–97.

Spencer, N., Macklin, M. G. and Woodward, J. C. (2012). Reassessing the abandonment of Amara West: The impact of a changing Nile? *Sudan and Nubia*, 16, 37–43.

Thompson, R. C., Allam, A. H., Lombardi, G. P., et al. (2013). Atherosclerosis across 4000 years of human history: The Horus study of four ancient populations. *Lancet*, 381(9873), 1211–22.

Towler, D. A. (2008). Vascular calcification: A perspective on an imminent disease epidemic. *IBMS BoneKEy*, 5(2), 41–58.

Unosson, J., Blomberg, A., Sandström, T., et al. (2013). Exposure to wood smoke increases arterial stiffness and decreases heart rate variability in humans. *Particle and Fibre Toxicology*, 10, 20.

Wapler, U., Crubézy, E. and Schultz, M. (2004). Is cribra orbitalia synonymous with anemia? Analysis and interpretation of cranial pathology in Sudan. *American Journal of Physical Anthropology*, 123, 333–9.

Woodward, J., Macklin, M., Spencer, N., et al. (2017). Living with a changing river and desert landscape at Amara West. In N. Spencer, A. Stevens and M. Binder, eds., *Nubia in the New Kingdom: Lived Experience, Pharaonic Control and Indigenous Traditions. Proceedings of the Annual Egyptological Colloquium, British Museum 11–12 July 2013*. Leuven: Peeters, pp. 225–52.

World Health Organization. (2018). *Noncommunicable Diseases: Country Profiles 2018*. Geneva: WHO. Available at https://apps.who.int/iris/handle/10665/274512 (accessed 15 July 2019).

Zink, A. R., Gostner, P., Selim, A., Pusch, C. M. and Hawass, Z. (2011). Epidemiology and prevalence of atherosclerosis in royal Egyptian mummies. Paper presented at the 38th Annual Meeting of the Paleopathology Association, Minneapolis, Minnesota, 11–13 April 2011. Abstract available at https://paleopathology-association.wildapricot.org/resources/Documents/PPA%20Progs%20and%20Abstracts/38th%20Annual%20Meeting%202011%20Program%20_%20Abstracts.pdf

9 Intracranial Atherosclerosis in Medieval Scandinavia

Caroline Arcini and Elisabet Englund

9.1 Introduction

In past human populations, atherosclerosis has been identified in mummies from different regions of the world, and from a range of chronological periods (for extensive reviews see Chapters 3 and 4). This current study from Sweden aims to contribute to the limited evidence for atherosclerosis associated with human skeletal remains by presenting examples of atherosclerosis in another part of the body. We describe two well-preserved cemeteries in Åhus and Skänninge (1237–1536 CE) in present-day Sweden where several individuals with atherosclerosis of the internal carotid artery were discovered. The cemeteries belonged to the monastic order of the Blackfriars and were used as a burial place for brothers from the convent as well as wealthy individuals in the community who could afford to pay to be buried there. Written sources in the Swedish Diplomatarium, a collection of documents from the Medieval Period in the National Archives of Sweden, indicate that it was the aristocracy (e.g. councillors, lawmakers and knights) who paid for burial at the monastery (Menander, 2018).

9.2 Material and Methods

The findings from the skeletal remains reported here derive from a larger study of 290 skeletons from two archaeological sites in Sweden: Åhus in the province of Scania, and Skänninge in the province of Östergötland, both dated to the Medieval Period (1237–1536 CE). Both cemeteries belonged to Blackfriars friaries and because archaeological excavations have shown that women and children were also buried in their churchyards, it was concluded that they were not only used by the Blackfriars themselves but also by people who lived outside the friaries (Odelman & Melefors, 2008; Menander & Arcini, 2013). During the Medieval Period, burial sites in towns were used very intensively and older graves were often disturbed and damaged as new burials took place; this can affect the completeness of the skeletons recovered from these sites. Therefore, some of the individuals presented here are represented only by part of a skull without a maxilla or mandible. The age and sex of all the individuals were estimated using accepted standards for data collection from human skeletal remains described in Buikstra and Ubelaker (1994). Table 9.1 summarises the overall demographic data for both collections, and the number and frequency of individuals affected.

Table 9.1 The age and sex of individuals showing evidence of atherosclerosis from Blackfriars monasteries in Åhus and Skänninge in Medieval Sweden.

Age group	Sex	No. of individuals for each age group	No. of affected individuals for each age group	Frequency of affected individuals (%) for each age group
Åhus				
20–39 years	F	67	0	0
40–59 years	F	32	4	12.5
60+ years	F	17	5	29.4
Total	F	116	9	7.7
Skänninge				
20–39 years	M	86	0	0
40–59 years	M	65	7	10.8
60+ years	M	23	9	39.1
Total	M	174	16	9.1

The cemeteries were investigated as part of an assignment for the National Heritage Board in Sweden between 1996 and 2002–11 (Arcini, 2003, 2015a, 2015b), and there was no specific focus on finding the type of pathological evidence described in this chapter from the skulls studied. However, the archaeologist received instructions to leave the cleaning of the skulls to the osteologist. The first incidental finding of evidence later identified as calcified arteries led to a continued search. This resulted in a systematic investigation of soil from the skulls and further instructions for other archaeologists to continue this detailed work. The special conditions of the soil, mainly comprising sand, allowed good preservation of the skeletons and made emptying of the skulls possible and straightforward.

During analysis of the skeletons, small and large (1–3 cm long), fragile, curved, calcified cylinder-shaped fragments measuring 5 mm in diameter were recovered when emptying soil from the interior of several crania (Åhus, 9/116; Skänninge, 16/174) (Figures 9.1 and 9.2). The calcifications were collected by the osteologist. Once the first calcification had been identified as from one of the blood vessels of the brain, based on the shape and diameter of the cylinder, a systematic examination was carried out for similar calcifications with the same dimensions and size. Because the pieces of calcified vessels were fragile, they were stored in small glass jars. One of the 25 calcified vessels was selected for histological preparation and examination. The vessel was gently soaked in formalin, decalcified and embedded in paraffin. Following this, 5-μm thick sections were stained with haematoxylin and eosin (H&E) and elastin Van Gieson (EVG) in order to visualise the components of, and cellular structures within, the vessel wall, including elastin, smooth muscle cells and fibrous tissue.

Figure 9.1 Emptying skulls from the Monastery of Skänninge demonstrating large calcifications Source: Staffan Hyll. (A black and white version of this figure will appear in some formats. For the colour version, please refer to the plate section.)

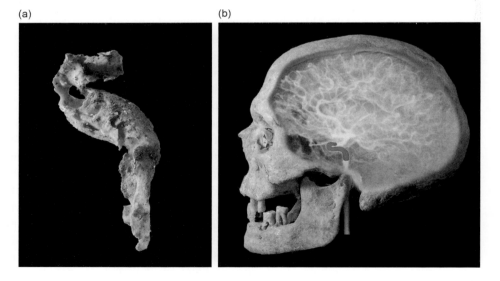

Figure 9.2 a) Photograph of the calcified internal carotid artery b) Reconstructed position of the calcification within the cranial vascular system. (A black and white version of this figure will appear in some formats. For the colour version, please refer to the plate section.)

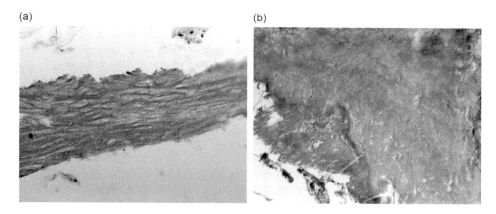

Figure 9.3 (a, b) Microphotographs of the carotid vessel wall after decalcification, sectioning and staining with elastin Van Gieson staining. Note the thickened vessel wall filled with fibrous tissue. (A black and white version of this figure will appear in some formats. For the colour version, please refer to the plate section.)

9.3 Results

The fragments of all the calcifications found at Åhus and Skänninge were identified as parts of blood vessels representing the carotid siphon, a particularly curved intracranial part of the internal carotid artery. The vessel selected for histological analysis was processed and analysed at the Department of Pathology, Lund University. The sections exhibited the expected microscopic structure of an artery affected by atherosclerosis (Figure 9.3): increased wall thickness with the internal elastic lamina located deep within the wall.

Once analysis had confirmed that the intial sample represented calcification, further examination of the skeletons in the two separate cemeteries revealed that pieces of calcified blood vessels representing the internal carotid artery were present in 8.6 per cent (25 of 290) of the adult individuals. Of the 25 individuals affected, 9.1 per cent (16 of 174) of the men and 7.7 per cent (9 of 116) of the women were affected (see Table 9.1). In addition, calcified arteries were found in both women and men buried in different parts of the friary: the cloister, the church and the cemetery areas. Estimation of the age of the affected individuals showed that they were all most likely to be over 40 years of age, and some were estimated to be over 60 years according to the methodology proposed by Milner et al. (2021) (see Tables 9.1 and 9.2).

It was also noted that among those affected by atherosclerosis, nine had severe osteoarthritis with eburnation on one or several of the bones of the large joints (shoulder, elbow, hip or knee). One individual was diagnosed with bladder stones, one with gout, and four displayed indications of osteoporosis such as vertebral compression fractures and reduced bone density. Dental diseases such as caries, as well as periodontal disease, were generally common among the adults in these cemeteries.

Table 9.2 Age, sex, stature and evidence of disease in the skeletons with cranial calcification.

Grave number	Sex, age at death	Stature (cm)	Teeth present	Caries	Periapical lesions	Teeth lost ante-mortem	Fracture/ weapon wound	Osteoarthritis (OA)	Osteochondrosis	Gout	Other
Skänninge											
Intact graves											
70479	M, 50+	–	12	1	0	14	X	0	0	0	0
70945	M, 60+	177	11	0	0	23	X	X	0	X	0
14490	M, 60+	168	22	2	0	6	X	X	0	0	0
25189	F, 60+	166	23	3	0	9	0	X	0	0	0
25283	M, 50+	–	19	1	0	10	X	X	X	0	0
21383	M?, 50+	155	7	1	0	0	X	0	X	0	0
70548	M, 60+	169	24	2	0	6	0	X	X	0	Osteomyelitis
70525	M, 40+	–	31	0	2	0	0	0	0	0	0
70562	M, 60+	–	30	0	0	0	X	X	X	0	0
Disturbed graves (only the skull present)											
70515	F, 50+	–	–	–	–	–	–	–	–	–	–
70538	F, 40+	–	–	–	–	–	–	–	–	–	–
70729	F, 50+	–	–	–	–	–	–	–	–	–	–
2000223	F, 60+	–	–	–	–	–	–	–	–	–	–
70399	M, 50+	–	–	–	–	–	–	–	–	–	–
70456	M, 50+	–	–	–	–	–	–	–	–	–	–
Åhus											
21	M, 50–60	163	17	0	0	11	X	X	0	0	Calculus formation covering the occlusal surface of the teeth, but only on the right side of the jaw
29	M, 45–60	170	30	0	2	0	X	0	X	0	0
156	M, 40–60	173	27	0	0	2	X	0	0	0	0
157	F, 50+	166	28	0	0	1	0	X	0	0	0
165	M, 60+	170	25	4	1	4	0	X	X	0	0
174	F, 50+	163	32	0	0	0	0	X	0	0	0
225	F, 40+	160	18	4	0	8	X	0	0	0	X
252	M, 40+	171	27	2	0	4	0	0	0	0	0

X, change is present; 0, studied but no change.

Among the individuals affected by atherosclerosis who had their dentition preserved 19 per cent (3 of 17 individuals) showed chronic periapical lesions and 52 per cent (9 of 17 individuals) had dental caries. Antemortem tooth loss was the most common dental problem of those who had atherosclerosis (70 per cent, 12 of 17 individuals). Two of the affected individuals had heavy deposits of calculus on their teeth but only on the right side of their mouths, suggesting that they had not actively been utilising that side for eating for several months/years prior to death. Infectious diseases were seen in the entire group, including septic arthritis, osteomyelitis, periostitis and specific infections such as leprosy, tuberculosis and syphilis; however, among the individuals with atherosclerosis only one had evidence of an infection (osteomyelitis of the tibia and fibula).

9.4 Discussion

The carotid arteries are major blood vessels in the neck that supply blood to the brain, neck and face. The reason why evidence for atherosclerosis was found in skeletons from these sites is because the skeletal remains were excavated carefully to prevent teeth with one root falling out and, in order to do that, the skulls were not emptied on site but in the laboratory. In other words, this find is due to a combination of the excavation method used (i.e. the crania were examined following excavation) and the preservation conditions. The calcifications associated with atherosclerosis were found inside the skull, where they had been protected from taphonomic damage and potential oversight during excavation.

What could have been the cause or causes of atherosclerosis in these two cemetery populations in medieval Scandinavia, particularly with regard to potential risk factors for this condition? It is unlikely that people with type 1 diabetes would have survived in the Medieval Period, but those affected by type 2 diabetes may have lived for an average lifespan but might possibly have been at risk for complications like cardiovascular disease (CVD). In addition, hypertension may have been a complicating factor for individuals who experienced a relatively longer survival. Although tobacco was not available in the Medieval Period (Loewe, 1993), people were exposed to smoke to various degrees in their indoor and outdoor environments, primarily from fireplaces, but also in some of their workplaces where poor air quality was experienced. Prolonged exposure to air pollution has repeatedly been reported as a cause of CVDs (Hoek et al., 2013). In addition, lifelong exposure to recurrent infections may have been a contributory factor because such disorders, including dental diseases such as caries, periapical lesions (e.g. abscesses) and periodontal disease, were frequent during the Medieval Period in Scandinavia (Arcini, 1999). However, very few of the individuals with atherosclerosis displayed periapical lesions and inflammation, although more than half showed signs of periodontal disease and had lost teeth ante-mortem. Nevertheless, it is interesting to note that several skeletons were very osteoporotic, in addition to displaying signs of severe osteoarthritis, indicating that they had most probably reached old age. This is notwithstanding that both these conditions can also occur at younger ages (Driban et al., 2020).

In relation to the link between diet and CVD, the quality and quantity of food consumed by the general population in Medieval society varied depending on social class (Menander & Arcini, 2013). A comparison of animal bones found in rubbish pits at the Blackfriars monastery in Skänninge with those found at lay people's settlements in the town reveals that people living at the monastery had access to more or less the same type of foodstuffs (Menander & Arcini, 2013). According to the archaeozoological analysis of the animal bones from the site in Skänninge, meat was derived mainly from sheep and pigs, but occasionally from cattle (Vretemark, 2009). The analysis also showed that the population's diet also contained eggs and meat from domesticated chickens and geese. Remains of fish bones from the site in Skänninge further reveal that mainly marine fish, such as cod and herring, were consumed (Cardell, 2009). Botanical analysis of the plant remains at Skänninge indicated that the vegetable component of people's diets consisted of cabbage, peas, beans, onions and root vegetables and that foodstuffs were spiced with dill, borage, marjoram, mustard and thyme (Heimdahl, 2009).

Further detailed information about the diets in monasteries has been described by Bond (2001: 54–87). The monastic diet was strictly regulated by rules, and excessive eating was not allowed. However, the initially poor lifestyle experienced around 1200 CE, where only one meal per day was served, changed in the thirteenth century (Bond, 2001). Sometimes there were notable exceptions to prevailing rules, with bishops who visited the monasteries reporting cases of gluttony (Black, 1992: 54). Written sources also indicate that the Blackfriars in the Nordic countries who survived through begging during their journeys around the country would often stay at manor houses where they could have large and delicious meals. Furthermore, in preserved letters to the Pope, the Blackfriars from Denmark asked for permission to deviate from their dietary rules, for example consuming bread made from wheat flour instead of the usual rye bread (Jakobsen, 2008). Descriptions of eating habits further reveal that even among those who followed so-called strict rules, diets could contain a high proportion of saturated fats, which were ingested along with large amounts of beer and small quantities of vegetables (Bond, 2001).

Another valuable resource elucidating the lives of the Medieval clergy, the *Diarium Vadstenense*, a written source from Sweden, is a diary of the nuns and monks who lived in the monastery of the Bridgettine order in the town of Vadstena. It covers the period between 1336 and 1545 and contains accounts of the monks, nuns and others who were buried in the monastery cemetery. The document describes the nuns as being overweight to such an extent that it was believed to have contributed to their deaths, for example 'she fell backwards and since she was a fat woman, her intestines burst' (Gejrot, 1988: 281).

Although atherosclerosis was found in burial contexts serving the Blackfriars in the current study, the majority of those buried were not monks from the friary but mainly wealthy non-monastic people with a diet more varied and richer in meat than that of the 'commoners' within the community. The conclusion that it was not just the monks themselves who were buried at the friary is partly based on the fact that the graves excavated contained both men, women and children, graves that, according to written sources, mainly contained wealthy people who gave gifts to the friary. Based on this evidence, the atherosclerosis identified in these skeletons could have been the result of a combination of these people eating a diet high in saturated fats, along with being exposed to air pollution.

Another major factor potentially accounting for the occurrence of atherosclerosis in Medieval Sweden is age. In this study, all 25 individuals affected by atherosclerosis were estimated to be older than 40 years of age and several of them were probably older than 60 (see Table 9.1). The earliest church books in Sweden that mention age at death come from 1645; none are from the Medieval Period. However, the *Diarium Vadstenense* (covering the years 1336–1545) is an important source that describes people's ages. We know that, with few exceptions, women had to be 18 and men 25 before they could enter the monastery. For example, Brother Johannes Torstani, who died 48 years after inauguration to the monastery, must have been at least 73 years old (Gejrot, 1988: 431). According to these data, it becomes possible to calculate a minimum age at death for 37 per cent (182 of 497) of the nuns, monks, lay brothers, knights or wives; of these, 45 per cent reached an age of at least 60 years (Gejrot, 1988). Of those who were estimated to be at least 60 years of age, 17 per cent (14 of 81) reached 80 years of age or more. This indicates that, just like today, older age could have been a contributory risk factor for atherosclerosis for these Medieval individuals, but more widely in the Medieval Period.

The *Diarium Vadstenense* also shows interesting data concerning signs of the presence of vascular disease. There are, for example, several descriptions of men affected by a disease that resulted in both paralysis and loss of the ability to speak, some of whom died immediately while others survived 'lame and dumb' for up to 10 years (Gejrot, 1988: 93, 181–5, 429). The text includes descriptions of symptoms consistent with vascular disease resulting in a 'stroke' (or cerebrovascular accident) and/or a heart attack (acute myocardial infarction). Concerning lay brother Jesper, for example, it is written that 'he had been in bed for two years as a result of a stroke (*apoplexia percussus*)' (Gejrot, 1988: 346). Another example, from 1413, is Brother Tideke who, according to his brother in the neighbouring cell, 'woke up without feeling any pain [...] but upon leaving his cell suddenly felt pain and could thereupon go to the cabinet of the confessor only with help from another brother'. There he confessed his sins, was transported to the infirmary and died there just after he had received the sacrament. In the *Diarium Vadstenense*, a total 14 cases of sudden death are also mentioned, as are descriptions of men and women who had become paralysed and/or had lost the ability to speak (Gejrot, 1988). However, regarding the findings in this study, it cannot be proven that the atherosclerotic calcifications identified had caused a stroke or heart attack in specific people. Nevertheless, two individuals had extensive dental calculus formation on one side of their jaws, something that might have been caused by hemiplegia due to a stroke (could not chew on one side), but other causes for hemiplegia, such as Bell's palsy, must be considered (Zandian et al., 2014).

9.5 Conclusions

The identification of arterial calcification of the carotid siphon in 25 skulls from Medieval graves in Sweden suggests that intracranial atherosclerotic vascular disease was a health problem affecting Medieval Scandinavian society. Both men and women were affected, some individuals were quite old when they died and there were other old-age-related diseases among the skeletal remains. This study also demonstrates that the contemporary written literature documented that people were affected by atherosclerosis-related diseases such as strokes. At the same time, there are examples where written sources testify to overeating, and obesity as a result, for example in monasteries. This corresponds to the lives of people that today are similar and associated with CVD.

This study further shows that it is possible to find evidence for atherosclerosis not only in mummies but also in association with human skeletal remains. This is a discovery that opens up new possibilities for studying the frequency of CVDs among different social groups and populations worldwide in the past, which further contributes to our understanding of health and disease. It also provides further evidence that CVDs are not just a phenomenon of recent times. In future excavations it would be beneficial if more archaeologists were aware of the possibility of these types of finds with skeletons, not only carotid artery-related atheromas that may be found within the skull, but also calcified plaques related to other blood vessels such as the aorta.

References

Arcini, C. (1999). *Health and disease in early Lund: Osteo-pathologic studies of 3,305 individuals buried in the first cemetery area of Lund 990–1536*. Dissertation, Lund University.

Arcini, C. (2003). *Åderförkalkning och portvinstår: Välfärdssjukdomar i medeltidens Åhus*. Stockholm: Riksantikvarieämbetets förlag.

Arcini, C. (2015a). Hidden killer: A modern disease in a Medieval monastery. *Current World Archaeology*, 73, 36–8.

Arcini, C. (2015b). Living conditions in time of plague. In P. Lagerås, ed., *Environment, Society and the Black Death: An Interdisciplinary Approach to the Late-Medieval Crisis in Sweden*. Oxford: Oxbow Books, pp. 104–40.

Black, M. (1992). *The Medieval Cook Book*. London: British Museum Press.

Bond, J. (2001). Production and consumption of food and drink in the Medieval monastery. In G. Keevill, M. Aston and T. Hala, eds., *Monastic Archaeology: Papers on the Study of Medieval Monasteries*. Oxford: Oxbow Books, pp. 54–87.

Buikstra, J. E. and Ubelaker, D. H. (1994). *Standards for Data Collection from Human Remains*. Fayetteville, AK: Arkansas Archaeological Survey.

Cardell, A. (2009). Osteologisk analys av fiskbensmaterialet. Havsfisk – Munkarnas preferens. In A. Konsmar and H. Menander, eds., *S:t Olofs Konvent. Arkeologisk Undersökning – Skänninge Projektet*. Riksantikvariämbetet, UV Öst Rapport 2009:5.

Driban, J. B., Harkey, M. S., Liu, S. H., et al. (2020) Osteoarthritis and aging: Young adults with osteoarthritis. *Current Epidemiology Reports*, 7, 9–15.

Gejrot, C. (1988). *Diarium Vadstenense: The Memorial Book of Vadstena Abbey*. Stockholm: Almqvist & Wiksell.

Heimdahl, J. (2009). Makroskopisk analys av jordprover från S:t Olofs konvent, Skänninge. In A. Konsmar and H. Menander, eds., *S:t Olofs Konvent. Arkeologisk Undersökning - Skänningeprojektet.* Riksantikvariämbetet, UV Öst Rapport 2009:5.

Hoek, G., Krishnan, R. M., Beelen, R., et al. (2013). Long-term air pollution exposure and cardio-respiratory mortality: A review. *Environmental Health*, 12(1), 43.

Jakobsen, J. J. G. (2008). *Prædikebrødrenes Samfundsrolle I Middelalderens Danmark.* PhD dissertation, Afhandling Institut for Historie, Kultur og Samfundsbeskrivelse, Syddansk Universitet, Odense, Denmark.

Loewe, W. (1993). *Tobaksspinnarna och tobaksfabrikanterna i 1600-talets Stockholm.* Stockholm: Komm. för Stockholmsforskning.

Menander, H. (2018). *Den Goda Döden: Arkeologiska Studier Av Gravar och Begravningspraxis I S:t Olofkonventet I Skänninge.* Dissertation, Uppsala University, Uppsala.

Menander, H. and Arcini, C. (2013). Dominikankonventet S:t Olof. In R. Hedvall, K. Lindeblad and H. Menander, eds., *Borgare, Bröder Och Bönder. Arkeologiska Perspektiv På Skänninges äldre Historia.* Stockholm: Riksantikvarieämbetet, pp. 191–227.

Milner, G. R., Ousley, S. D. and Boldsen, J. L. (2021). Adult Age Estimated From New Skeletal Traits and Enhanced Computer-Based Transition Analysis. US Department of Justice Document No. 300659. Available at https://nij.ojp.gov/library/publications/adult-age-estimated-new-skeletal-traits-and-enhanced-computer-based-transition

Odelman, E. and Melefors, E. (2008). *Visbyfranciskanernas Bok.* Handskriften B 99 I Kungliga Biblioteket. Latinsk Text Utgiven Med översättning, Inledning Och Register. Arkiv På Gotland 5. Visby: Skriftserie för Landsarkivet i Visby och Gotlands Kommunarkiv.

Vretemark, M. (2009). Osteologis rapport: Animalosteologisk analys. In A. Konsmar and H. Menander, eds., *S:t Olofs Konvent. Arkeologisk Undersökning – Skänningeprojektet.* Riksantikvariämbetet, UV Öst Rapport 2009:5.

Zandian, A., Osiro, S., Hudson, R., et al. (2014). The neurologist's dilemma: a comprehensive clinical review of Bell's palsy, with emphasis on current management trends. *Medical Science Monitor*, 20, 83–90.

10 Abnormalities of the Vertebral Artery

Are Cervical Pressure Defects Being Overlooked in Palaeopathology?

Daniel Antoine and Tony Waldron

10.1 Introduction

The vascular system, as it passes through grooves and foramina along the surfaces of bones, can leave impressions on the skeleton. The areas where bones and vessels come into close contact can allow palaeopathologists to investigate vascular variations and pathological changes long after the loss of any soft tissues. For example, abdominal (Diekerhof et al., 2002; Ando et al., 2003) and thoracic (Sheeran & Sclafani, 2000; Takahashi et al., 2007) aneurysms can lead to lesions on the vertebrae. There have also been reports of arterial pressure defects found in archaeological and skeletal collections (see Kelley, 1979; Walker, 1983; Wakely & Smith, 1998; Ortner, 2003: 356–7). Most lesions are aortic in origin but the vertebral artery, as it courses through the transverse processes of the cervical vertebrae, provides an additional location that is seldom investigated. Because of its close proximity to bone, two abnormalities of the vertebral arteries – tortuosities and aneurysms – have been shown to produce pressure defects on the bodies of the cervical vertebrae (Waldron & Antoine, 2002). During its course through the transverse foramina, part of the vertebral artery can become looped or coiled and the abnormal (or tortuous) segment can cause pressure defects in the adjacent vertebral bodies. In addition to these tortuosities, the localised dilation caused by the weakening of the arterial wall in an aneurysm can also produce similar lesions (Waldron & Antoine, 2002). In both abnormalities, the resulting pressure defects usually have a smooth-walled appearance, with a sclerotic margin that is visible on a radiograph, and involve the body of the cervical vertebrae as well as the transverse or intervertebral foramina (Waldron & Antoine, 2002). Clinically, cervical lesions have been linked to multiple aetiologies, including atheroma (Hadley, 1958), osteophytosis (Harzer & Töndbury, 1966; Oga et al., 1996), disc degeneration (Nourbakhsh et al., 2010), neurofibromatosis type 1 (Peyre et al., 2007), connective tissue disorders such as Ehlers–Danlos syndrome (Edwards, 1969; Broadribb, 1970), Marfan syndrome and pseudoxanthoma elasticum (Giuffré & Sherkat, 1999), and trauma (Adeloye et al., 1970; Alves & Black, 1972; Rifkinson-Mann et al., 1986). The skeletal changes associated with these lesions are relatively discreet and few archaeological examples have been reported in the literature. To date, these include one adult from the Nubian C Group Cemetery at Hierakonpolis, Egypt, *c.* 2055–1700 BCE (Antoine, 2010), one adult from a Coffin Period site in Japan dating to *c.* 1600 years BP (Waldron & Antoine, 2002), two adults from medieval cemeteries in France (Billard & Fantino, 2011; Darton, 2014) and two adults from a fifteenth-century medieval cemetery site in Britain

(Viswani & Waldron, 1997; Waldron & Antoine, 2002). Without careful examination of the cervical vertebrae, evidence for such abnormalities is likely to be missed. This chapter provides a background to the anatomy of the vertebral arteries, describes the pathological changes that can affect these arteries, including their pathogenesis and aetiology, and proposes an operational definition for the identification of cervical vertebrae pressure defects[1] in skeletal remains. It also presents several new examples of individuals with cervical pressure defects, as well as, for the first time, past prevalence data in a population dating to the Meroitic period (first or second century CE) from the site of Kawa, Sudan.

10.2   Anatomy and Development of the Vertebral Arteries

The vertebral arteries are major arteries of the neck that usually originate from the postero-superior aspect of the first portion (central) of the subclavian artery (Hong et al., 2008). Coursing along each side of the cervical vertebrae, usually through (but not always) their transverse foramina, the vertebral arteries emerge within the skull to form the basilar artery. Part of the vertebrobasilar vascular system, the vertebral arteries supply blood to the muscles of the neck, upper spinal cord, cerebellum, brainstem (medulla oblongata) and the posterior part of the brain. The vertebral arteries have both extracranial and intracranial portions, with the extracranial portion usually divided into three segments (Figure 10.1) (see Hong et al., 2008). V1 denotes the segment from its origin to its entrance into the transverse foramina of the cervical vertebrae, V2 the segment through the transverse foramina and V3 the segment between its exit from the transverse foramina – typically those of the atlas – and its entrance into the skull through the foramen magnum. V4 refers to the intracranial segment. The anatomy of the vertebral arteries can be highly variable, with various malformations caused by its highly complex development and the haemodynamics of the arteries that supply the brainstem and spinal cord (Lasjaunias et al., 1985; Guiffrè & Sherkat, 1999).

In the preforaminal V1 segment, the vertebral arteries vary in how they originate from the subclavian artery in around 5 per cent of cases, affecting the left or the right side, or both (George & Laurian, 1987; Gluncie et al., 1999; Yuan, 2016). The origin can be double (Sukuki et al., 1978; Cavdar & Arisan, 1989; Takasato et al., 1992; Yuan, 2016), from the opposite side (Lemke et al., 1999; Yuan, 2016) or, infrequently, one side may be underdeveloped, incomplete or absent (George & Laurian, 1987; Yuan, 2016). The V1 segment frequently exhibits some tortuosity, with the tortuous segment looping or coiling itself into a range of forms and orientations (see Matula et al., 1997). The foraminal V2 segment begins when the vertebral arteries enter the transverse foramen. In 89.8–94.9 per cent of cases, this occurs at the level of C6

---

[1] The lesions have been variably described as erosions (Palmer & Sequiera, 1980), resorptions (Darton, 2014), invaginations (Curylo et al., 2000) and pressure defects (Waldron & Antoine, 2002). Though used by many authors, the term 'erosion' may not be the most appropriate as this is not a destructive process but a remodelling due to arterial pressure, and the term 'cervical pressure defect' is favoured here.

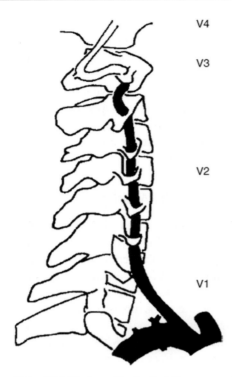

Figure 10.1 Diagram illustrating the course of the right vertebral artery (highlighted in black). V1 denotes the segment from its origin in the subclavian artery to its entrance into the transverse foramina of the cervical vertebrae, V2 the segment through the transverse foramina, V3 the segment between its emergence from the atlas and its entrance into the skull, and V4 the intracranial segment. Source: after Waldron and Antoine (2002).

(sixth cervical vertebra; see Adachi, 1928; Argenon et al., 1980; Bruneau et al., 2006; Hong et al., 2008; Nourbakhsh et al., 2010). However, the arteries also enter at C5 in 4.5–6.3 per cent, at C7 in 1.2–3 per cent and at C4 in 0.7–0.9 per cent of cases (Adachi, 1928 and Argenon et al., 1980, respectively). Nourbakhsh et al. (2010) report similar figures, with 5 per cent entering at C5, 1 per cent at C4, 0.8 per cent at C7 and only 0.2 per cent at C3 (see also Eskander et al., 2010). Argenon et al. (1980) also found that they occasionally entered at C3 (0.1 per cent of cases) and, in some rare instances, the vertebral arteries course through the neck without passing through any transverse processes (Wackenheim & Babin, 1969). In individuals where the origin of the vertebral artery is doubled, the lateral leg usually originates from the subclavian artery and typically enters lower (usually at C6) than the medial leg, which originates directly from the aorta (at C5 or, in fewer cases, C4) (see Koniyama et al., 1999; Rameshbabu et al., 2014). As the two vertebral arteries emerge from the atlas (C1), they pass posteriorly and medially (the extradural V3 segment) to enter the foramen magnum (V4 segment) and merge to form the basilar artery. However, in less than

1 per cent of cases, the vertebral arteries pass between the axis (C2) and C1, missing the latter's transverse foramen (Sato et al., 1994). Their path around C1 and C2 can also vary considerably (Iyer, 1927; see also Waldron & Antoine, 2002) and, in some cases, the location of the origin of the posterior inferior cerebellar artery (on the vertebral artery) occurs between these two vertebrae (Matula et al., 1997).

The left and right vertebral arteries can differ in size, with the left consistently being the more dominant and larger of the two at all levels (Eskander et al., 2010). As the embryological formation of transverse foramina is influenced by the vertebral arteries (Bruneau et al., 2006; Hong et al., 2008; Darton, 2014), the difference in vessel size is echoed in the sizes of the transverse foramina, and the side with the larger foramina is likely to reflect the dominant side. The relative size of the foramina can also be used to infer the level of entry of the vertebral arteries on both sides of the cervical vertebrae. Beneath the level of entry, foramina have been found to be significantly smaller than ones through which the vertebral arteries pass ($p < 0.0001$; Bruneau et al., 2006). As the left and right vertebral arteries do not necessarily enter at the same level and as each artery can have a doubled origin (Rameshbabu et al. 2014), the change in foramina size on each side may occur at a different cervical level within a spine. In addition to being smaller, pre-entry level foramina may also be crossed and divided into two by a thin bar of bone often described as accessory transverse foramina (recorded as a non-metric trait in bioarchaeology). Divided foramina can be relatively common and a study of 129 medieval Polish skeletons found that 30 per cent of all transverse foramina ($n = 196$) were double, with two additional examples (<1 per cent) of triple foramina (Kwiatkowska et al., 2014). During its course through the transverse foramina, tortuosities and aneurysms of the vertebral artery can produce detectable lesions on the cervical vertebrae. These pressure defects require the arteries to be in close proximity to the bone and are unlikely to occur prior to the arteries entering the foramina. When possible, differences in the artery's left and right level of entry should be taken into account when assessing pathological changes.

10.3 Tortuosity of the Vertebral Artery

10.3.1 Pathogenesis and Aetiology

First reported by Hadley in 1958, a tortuosity refers to a segment of the vertebral artery which has become coiled or looped. The tortuous (hence the term 'tortuosity') or abnormal section (also known as a dolichoarterial loop) can cause pressure defects in the neighbouring vertebra as it courses through the transverse foramina. Hadley (1958) believed them to be linked to abnormal accumulations of material in the inner layer of the vertebral artery wall (i.e. atheroma). Palmer and Sequeira's (1980) study found no such association, favouring instead a congenital aetiology (see also Babin & Haller, 1974), with an incidence in part affected by acquired factors (Palmer & Sequeira, 1980). In terms of aetiology, a localised deflection of the vertebral artery caused by bony outgrowths (osteophytosis) on the cervical vertebrae (Harzer &

Töndbury, 1966; Oga et al., 1996) has also been proposed. In addition, a significant correlation between tortuosities and age-related disc degeneration has been reported (Nourbakhsh et al., 2010). Normally fixed to the nerve root by a fibroligamentous band behind the anterior rim of the transverse process, the intertransverse portion of the artery (not fixed by the fibroligamentous band) appears to become more tortuous when the disc space height is reduced due to degeneration (Nourbakhsh et al., 2010). However, this study also noted that tortuosities can occur without any disc degeneration, suggesting a multiple aetiology. Variants of the vertebral artery's typical origin on the posterosuperior aspect of the subclavian arteries and abnormalities to the surrounding vessels may also have an impact. For example, Danziger and Bloch (1975) describe a patient with multiple cervical lesions caused by increased pressure to the left vertebral artery due to its atypical origin on the aortic arch, proximal to an aortic coarctation (i.e. congenital narrowing of the aorta). A vertebral artery tortuosity prevalence of 90 per cent has also been observed in patients with Loeys–Dietz syndrome (a connective tissue disorder similar to Marfan syndrome) due to a mutation of the genes encoding the transforming growth factor beta receptor (Kono et al., 2010).

10.3.2 Prevalence and Cervical Level Affected

Several studies have provided valuable insights into the prevalence of tortuosities and their impact on the cervical vertebrae. Based on 21 post-mortem examinations, Hadley (1958) reported a relatively high tortuosity prevalence of 19.1 per cent ($n = 4$). Palmer and Sequeira's larger retrospective analysis of 400 consecutive angiographic examinations found one or more cervical lesions in 7.8 per cent ($n = 31$) of patients from the Prince Henry Hospital, Sydney, Australia. With a similar distribution across the sexes (males, $n = 16$; females, $n = 15$), most of the lesions (93.5 per cent) were found in individuals over the age of 40 (Palmer & Sequeira, 1980). Patients spanning the fourth to eighth decades were examined and results revealed a rise in prevalence with age. Only 6.5 per cent of the lesions were found in patients in their fourth decade, with a prevalence of 0.5 per cent in that age group. Most of the lesions were recorded in patients in their fifth, sixth and seventh decades (20, 33.5 and 36.5 per cent of lesions, respectively), affecting 1.5, 2.5 and 2.75 per cent of patients in each of those decades. Only 3.5 per cent of the lesions were found in patients in their eighth decade which, due to the smaller cohort size, represents a prevalence of 10 per cent in that age group (Palmer & Sequeira, 1980). Lesions were also more frequently found on the left ($n = 31$) than the right ($n = 13$), the former being the side of the more dominant and larger of the two arteries (see above). These figures include seven patients with lesions on two cervical vertebrae, as well as five with bilateral lesions, with a total of 44 lesions observed in 31 patients (Palmer & Sequeira, 1980). Bilateral lesions, on both the same and separate vertebrae, have also been reported in other studies (Babin & Haller, 1974; Hyyppä et al., 1974; Salvador et al., 1981; Holden et al., 1996; Darton, 2014). Most of the lesions in Palmer and Sequeira's study were found on C4 ($n = 17$; 38.6 per cent) and C5 ($n = 13$; 29.6 per cent), followed by C6 ($n = 10$; 22.7 per cent), with fewer found on C2 and C3 ($n = 2$ for both; 4.5 per cent each). As stated above, most occurred on the left side (with 13 on the left and 4 on the right in C4) apart from C2 and C6, where the left and right were affected equally (Palmer & Sequeira, 1980).

The 7.8 per cent overall prevalence reported by Palmer and Sequeira's (1980) compares well with Tulsi and Perrett's (1975) earlier anatomical and radiological study of native Australian skeletal remains that were, at the time, available for research at the South Australian Museum and the Department of Anatomy. In their research, 10 out of 113 (8.9 per cent) vertebral columns were found to have cervical lesions suggestive of tortuosity. The distribution of the lesions appears to differ from that reported in Palmer and Sequeira (1980), with similar numbers recorded on the left (n = 6) and the right (n = 4). However, Tulsi and Perrett's (1975) dataset is smaller, with 113 individuals compared with Palmer and Sequeria's 400 patients. Once converted to percentages, their 60 per cent on the left and 40 per cent on the right compares more favourably with Palmer and Sequeira's 70 to 30 per cent distribution, highlighting the greater likelihood of the left artery being affected. However, the lesions discussed in Tulsi and Perrett (1975) were more evenly spread along the spine, with three found on C3 (30 per cent), two each on C4, C5 and C6 (20 per cent each) and one on C2 (10 per cent). While fewer individuals were examined, both studies suggest that lesions on C2 are less common, with some variation as to the involvement of C3. However, other researchers have also reported C2 lesions (Cooper, 1980; Roy-Camille et al., 1982), indicating that tortuous loops can affect most cervical vertebrae. A further study based on skeletal remains by Curylo et al. (2000) reported a comparatively lower prevalence of cervical lesions. Out of 222 spines from individuals curated in the early twentieth-century Hamann–Todd skeletal collection, curated at the Cleveland Museum of Natural History, only six (2.7 per cent) were found to have one or more cervical lesions (Curylo et al., 2000). However, only C3, C4, C5 and C6 were examined and the unexplained omission of C2 may have affected the overall prevalence data, preventing like-for-like comparisons with other publications. Though less frequent, some C2 lesions have been reported elsewhere (see above). Of the 400 patients examined by Palmer and Sequeira (1980), two out of 44 lesions were on C2 (4.5 per cent) and, out of 113 vertebral columns, Tulsi and Perrett (1975) reported only one C2 lesion (10 per cent of the recorded lesions). In their data on C3 to C6, Curylo et al. (2000) recorded a total of seven lesions on six individuals. All were unilateral, with three located on C3, a further three on C4, and one on C6. In one individual, lesions were present on both C3 and C6, with no evidence of pathological change on their fourth and fifth cervical vertebrae. As with Palmer and Sequeira (1980), lesions were more frequently found on the left (n = 5; 71.4 per cent) than the right side (n = 2; 28.6 per cent). Described as marked invaginations of the vertebral body, they were most probably the result of tortuosities but, as with Tulsi and Perrett (1975), it is unclear whether aneurysms were considered as part of a differential diagnosis.

A further study of 250 MRI scans of the vertebral artery from patients of the University of Massachusetts Medical School by Eskander et al. (2010) also concluded that C3 and C4 were the most commonly affected levels and that the majority (75 per cent) involved the left side. Based on patients ranging between 9 and 88 years old (mean age of 49 years), they also observed that the left artery was consistently larger than the right at all cervical levels. Research on 64 formalin-fixed cadavers from the USA with a mean age at death of 77 years (34 males; 30 females) by Nourbakhsh et al. (2010) found tortuosities in 13.4 per cent of all intertransverse spaces, further highlighting how common the abnormality can be in older individuals. They also noted a significant correlation between disc degeneration (defined as decreased disc space and osteophyte formation) and tortuosity (χ^2 = 40.2, p <0.001). Once again, most tortuosities were found in the fourth (20 per cent) and fifth (23 per cent) intertransverse spaces, which were also the areas with the highest rate of disc degeneration, followed by the sixth (15 per cent), third (12 per cent) and second (2 per cent) intertransverse spaces (Nourbakhsh et al., 2010). The primary focus of that research was to help identify the V2 segment of the vertebral artery during anterior approaches to the cervical spine for arterial repairs and, unfortunately, they did not systematically report the impact of the tortuosities on the cervical vertebrae. In only three cases (5 per cent of cadavers) was the artery described as having, as they put it, 'penetrated' into the vertebral body despite the large number of tortuosities observed (Nourbakhsh et al., 2010). It is likely that additional pressure defects, not easily seen in a dissection, would have been reported with the use of radiography. However, the clinical literature is also unclear as to how often tortuosities generate pressure defects on the vertebral bodies once a tortuous loop forms, nor do we know how rapidly bone remodelling occurs after the tortuous segment starts impacting the surrounding bone. As noted by Palmer and Sequeira (1980: 22), the transverse foramen's proximity to the body and its shape are likely to play a part in the formation of a defect:

When local arterial ectasia of any cause occurs, it seems logical that bone erosion would occur earlier when the foramen transversarium is small and would involve the vertebral body when the body to foramen distance is small. This offers a ready explanation as to why some patients with localised arterial tortuosity have erosions and others do not.

Overall, the studies reviewed here indicate that tortuous loops usually affect C3 to C6 and favour the left side, with lesions most often found on C3 and C4. The marked tendency to affect the left vertebral artery remains to be fully explained, and appears to be due to the dominance of the left artery (Eskander et al., 2010). Zimmerman and Farrell (1970) suggested that this may be the result of greater pressure in the dominant left side, but this was discounted by Obayashi et al. (1986). Despite one example noted in a six-year-old child (Tulsi & Perrett, 1975), prevalence appears to increase with age and most lesions occur over the age of 40 years (Palmer & Sequeira, 1980; see also Eskander et al., 2010). The association with advancing years may partly be due to an age-related loss of arterial elasticity (Palmer & Sequeira, 1980) and disc space height (Nourbakhsh et al., 2010).

10.3.3 Impact on the Cervical Vertebrae

The pressure exerted by the abnormally coiled or tortuous loop of the vertebral artery creates a defect or invagination in the body of the adjacent cervical vertebra (Slover

Abnormalities of the Vertebral Artery   181

& Kiley, 1965; Zimmerman & Farrell, 1970; Cooper, 1980; Dory, 1985; Curylo et al., 2000; Waldron & Antoine, 2002). The defect usually affects the bone between the transverse foramen and the body of the vertebra, creating a smooth-walled lesion of compact bone that has a sclerotic margin on a radiograph (Tulsi & Perrett, 1975; Holden et al., 1996; Waldron & Antoine, 2002). It can also involve the inferior margin (Anderson & Shealy, 1970; Zimmerman & Farrell, 1970; Sganzerla et al., 1987) or anterior surface of the pedicle (Waldron & Antoine, 2002).

The intervertebral foramen is also frequently widened (Barrett, 1974; Schimmel et al., 1976; Gatti et al., 1983; Glover et al., 1990; Schima et al., 1993; Vanrietvelde et al., 1999) and tends to assume, in both tortuosities and aneurysms (see below) of the vertebral artery, a more oblong shape (Lindsey et al., 1985). Widening of the intervertebral foramen may also be due to the congenital absence of the pedicle (Oh & Eun, 2008) or, in most cases, the presence of a benign nerve-sheath tumour of the peripheral nervous system known as a neurofibroma (Danziger & Bloch, 1975; Waldron & Antoine, 2002). However, in both of these conditions, the widened foramen tends to have a round or ovoid shape (Lindsey et al., 1985). The congenital absence of the pedicle should be easily identifiable (Oh & Eun, 2008) when the long arches of the cervical vertebrae are not damaged (something that is not always the case in archaeological assemblages). Neurofibromas may also erode the uncinate process of the vertebra on the affected side (see Wackenheim, 1977). These hook-shaped processes on the body's superior posterolateral borders (Wackenheim's sign) do not appear to be affected when the intervertebral foramen widening is the result of a tortuosity; Wackenheim's sign may be used to distinguish the two (Waldron & Antoine, 2002).

In fewer cases, tortuosities can also lead to enlargement of the transverse foramen (Lindsey et al., 1985; Freilich et al., 1986; Taitz & Arensburg, 1991; Brahee & Guebert, 2000; Waldron & Antoine, 2002) resulting in a tubular-shaped defect visible on transverse CT scans (Yünten et al., 1998). However, change to the size of the transverse foramen should account for variations between the left and right vertebral arteries, with the left usually being the more dominant and larger of the two (Bruneau et al., 2006; Eskander et al., 2010). Differences between the left and right foramina may therefore be expected and similarities between the two may indicate that the less dominant right side is enlarged or that both arteries are of a similar size. In addition, and as discussed above, the foramina can also be relatively smaller prior to the entry of the artery. Hence, the size of the transverse foramen of an affected vertebra should be compared with the foramina of adjacent cervical vertebrae and take into account possible differences between the left and right artery, as well as variations in size up and down the cervical spine that reflect the vertebral artery's point of entry. Unfortunately, comparisons may not always be possible in poorly preserved archaeological remains (see examples below).

10.3.4   Clinical Symptoms

In the majority of patients, tortuous loops do not appear to cause clinical symptoms and may explain why they are rarely observed in medical practice (Darton, 2014).

However, in some patients, the compression of the cervical nerve roots can trigger neurological symptoms (Anderson & Shealy, 1970; Obayashi et al., 1986; Glover et al., 1990; Kim et al., 2010). Central nervous system symptoms have also been observed in a 53-year-old male (Burnett & Staple, 1981). Occasionally, patients have reported pain in the neck area that can be alleviated by removing some of the bone around the neural foramen (i.e. an intervertebral foraminotomy) (Kricun et al., 1992).

10.4 Aneurysm of the Vertebral Artery

10.4.1 Pathogenesis and Aetiology

Localised aneurysms of the vertebral arteries may take three distinct forms, saccular, fusiform and dissecting, with all having a propensity to rupture (Andoh et al., 1992). In the saccular form (the most common), the dilation of the vessel is a localised side bulge rounded in shape. With a fusiform aneurysm, the vessel expands in all directions, while in the dissecting form there is a longitudinal rip in the arterial wall. Aneurysms can form on any part of the vertebral artery (see Pritz et al., 1981) but will only leave a detectable lesion on the skeleton when the arteries are passing through the transverse processes and are in close proximity to the cervical vertebrae. Cases that affect the cervical portion of the vertebral arteries have been described in two young children (Randall et al., 1994) and a 14-year-old girl with no apparent history of head or neck injury (Kikuchi & Kowada, 1983). Other examples affecting young adults have found an association with sport-related blunt trauma (Hadley et al., 1985), as well as an unusual case of 'head-banging' while playing in a rock band (Egnor et al., 1991). In older adults, cervical aneurysms are most commonly found in patients with neurofibromatosis type 1 (von Recklinghausen's disease), a genetic condition that causes (usually) non-cancerous tumours to grow along the nerves, resulting in a range of symptoms (Schubiger & Yasargil, 1978; Negoro et al., 1990; Schievink & Piepgras, 1991; Koenigsberg et al., 1997; Peyre et al., 2007). Cases have also been noted in patients with inherited connective tissue disorders such as Ehlers–Danlos syndrome (Edwards, 1969; Broadribb, 1970), Marfan syndrome and pseudoxanthoma elasticum (Giuffré & Sherkat, 1999). The latter, also known as Grönblad–Strandberg syndrome, can lead to a premature form of atherosclerosis (Chassaing et al., 2005), which has been reported by others as a possible cause of vertebral artery aneurysms (Thompson et al., 1979; Rifkinson-Mann et al., 1986).

Other reports are often associated with some form of trauma to the neck that results in a pseudoaneurysm. Also known as false aneurysms, they occur when an injury to a blood vessel wall leads to blood filling the space between the layers of the vessel wall in a manner that resembles a true aneurysm. Published examples that have resulted in a pseudoaneurysm of the vertebral artery include those due to stabbings and lacerations, gunshot wounds and road traffic accidents (Heifetz, 1945; Elkin & Harris, 1946; Kister & Rankow, 1966; Husni & Storer, 1967; Deutsch, 1969; Adeloye et al., 1970; Alves & Black, 1972; O'Connel et al., 1975; George &

Laurian, 1980; Rifkinson-Mann et al., 1986). Pseudoaneurysms of the vertebral artery have also been reported post surgery (Sumimura et al., 1988) and in cases of blunt force trauma (Hadley et al., 1985; Fakhry et al., 1988), as well as after chiropractic neck manipulation (Davidson et al., 1975). Though rare, non-traumatic aneurysms of the vertebral artery are also well reported (Jewell, 1977; Laurian et al., 1980; Pritz et al., 1981; Ekeström et al., 1983; Kikuchi & Kowada, 1983; Habozit & Battistelli, 1990; Youll et al., 1990; Catala et al.,1993; Buerger et al., 1999, 2000), including one associated with a congenital spinal malformation at the second cervical vertebra (Habozit & Battistelli, 1990).

10.4.2 Prevalence and Cervical Level Affected

Aneurysms of the vertebral artery are very rare (Kister & Rankow, 1966; Deutsch, 1969; Thompson et al., 1979; Buerger et al., 1999, 2000; Santos-Franco et al., 2008) and considerably less common than tortuosities. The annual incidence in the USA and France is about 1 in 100 000 and 1.5 in 100 000, respectively, with an age of onset in the fourth decade of life (Santos-Franco et al., 2008). They represent around 28 per cent of posterior circulation aneurysms and, when they do occur, most involve the V1 and V3 segments due to their greater mobility (Santos-Franco et al., 2008). The survey of clinical cases reviewed here shows that they also differ from tortuosities in the vertebral level affected, with aneurysms more frequently found in the upper part of the cervical spine, particularly C2. Unlike tortuosities, where the distribution across the sexes appears to be similar, aneurysms of the vertebral artery are also more commonly reported in males than females (see above; Kurata et al., 2012). Both abnormalities, however, seem to favour the left side and although some bilateral aneurysms have been described (Jewel, 1977), the majority appear to be unilateral.

10.4.3 Impact on the Cervical Vertebrae

Most clinical reports focus on angiographic findings and skeletal changes are seldom described in any detail. Nonetheless, aneurysms that occur in the foraminal V2 segment, when the vertebral arteries pass through the transverse foramen, result in pressure defects in the body of the vertebrae that are similar to those found in tortuosities. The lesions also have sclerotic margins (Schubiger & Yasargil, 1978; Kikuchi & Kowada, 1983) and both the intervertebral foramen (Schubiger & Yasargil, 1978; Thompson et al., 1979) and the transverse foramen (Laurian et al., 1980; Kikuchi & Kowada, 1983; Habozit & Battistelli, 1990) can be enlarged. However, when some form of trauma is involved, pressure defects only occur if patients survive sufficiently long enough for a pseudoaneurysm to form (Darton, 2014), which may not always be the case. The size of pseudoaneurysms and post-traumatic arteriovenous fistulas (abnormal communication between arteries and veins due to a traumatic vessel injury) appear to range from just a few millimetres to 5 cm or more (Schittek, 1999; Darton, 2014). They can affect any part of the transverse and

184   Daniel Antoine and Tony Waldron

intervertebral foramina (Waldron & Antoine, 2002) and are considered to be more irregular in shape (Waldron & Antoine, 2002; Darton, 2014).

10.4.4 Clinical Symptoms

As noted by Darton (2014), an increase in the use of CT and MRI scans to examine the neck of patients, particularly following road traffic accidents, is likely to lead to further incidental findings and provide a better understanding of the prevalence of both abnormalities, as well as their impact on the cervical vertebra. Dissecting aneurysms of the vertebrobasilar system have a high morbidity and mortality (Santos-Franco et al., 2008). As with tortuosity, compression of the cervical nerve roots is likely to cause neurological symptoms (Waldron & Antoine, 2002). In their extensive review of 75 published studies involving 1972 patients from around the world, Gottesman et al. (2012) found that the most common symptoms of vertebral artery dissecting aneurysms were dizziness/vertigo (58 per cent), headache (51 per cent) and neck pain (46 per cent). They also noted that strokes were one of the most commonly reported cerebrovascular complications (63 per cent). This was particularly true of extracranial dissections, making it one of the most common identifiable causes of stroke in adults aged 18–45 years, with an annual incidence of 1–1.5 per 100 000 (Gottesman et al., 2012). While transient ischaemic attack (14 per cent) and subarachnoid haemorrhage (10 per cent) were uncommon, the latter was only seen with intracranial dissections (Gottesman et al., 2012). Interestingly, less than half of the cases had obvious signs of trauma and only 7.9 per cent had a recognised connective tissue disease (Gottesman et al., 2012). Significantly, as stokes are one of the most commonly reported complications, bioarchaeologists should also look out for changes that may occur in chronic sufferers of the condition (e.g. asymmetrical muscular and bone atrophy; Talla et al., 2011), particularly when the cervical pressure defect is believed to be the result of an aneurysm (see criteria below).

10.5   Cervical Pressure Defects in Bioarchaeology

Cervical pressure defects are rarely reported in the bioarchaeological literature. In 1997, Vaswani and Waldron described an example found in a fifteenth-century male skeleton aged at least 45 years at the time of death and buried in the medieval cemetery at Southgate Street, Gloucester, UK. Located on the left side of C4's vertebral body, the oval-shaped lesion was approximately 15 × 9 mm, with its long axis at about 45 degrees to the horizontal, and around 6 mm at its greatest depth. Radiographically, the lesion had a dense sclerotic margin and the vertebra's left transverse foramen, despite some damage to its anterior wall, appeared to be slightly enlarged when compared with the one on the right. This was not the case in the top three cervical vertebrae, where no pathological changes were observed and the transverse foramina did not show any enlargement. This suggests that the enlargement noted on C4 was pathological and not due to the dominance of the left vertebral artery (see discussion above). Unfortunately, the cervical vertebra below the fourth was not present, preventing an assessment of the transverse foramina further down the cervical spine and the detection of any additional pathological changes. At the time of the publication, the lesion was presented as the earliest known example of an extracranial aneurysm of the vertebral artery. However, tortuosity had not been considered in the differential diagnosis and as part of the work on another cervical pressure defect from the same cemetery, Waldron and Antoine (2002) revised Vaswani and Waldron's (1997) original interpretation. Based on the lesion's location and appearance, they proposed that the pathological changes are more in keeping with tortuosity than an aneurysm.

Waldron and Antoine (2002) also presented two further archaeological examples of cervical pressure defects. The first, from the same fifteenth-century Southgate Street medieval cemetery as Vaswani and Waldron (1997), was a smooth pressure defect on the left side of the body of C6 from a female aged between 40 and 50 years at the time of death. All her cervical vertebrae bar the third were present, with some damage to the anterior parts and the loss of most transverse foramina (with the exception of the left one on the fifth cervical vertebra). The pressure defect was almost 6 mm in depth and measured 11×6 mm, with the long axis orientated anteriorly at a 45-degree angle. Extending laterally onto the anterior surface of the pedicle, the lesion had a dense sclerotic margin radiographically, and the interverte-bral foramen did not show any enlargement. Despite extensive damage to the transverse foramina, C6's left foramen (immediately next to the lesion) appeared to be larger than the one on the right side. With only one intact transverse foramen (left C5), it is unclear if this partly reflects the dominance of the left vertebral artery (as discussed above). Other pathological changes unconnected to the lesion were noted further down the spine, including fusion of the 8th to 10th thoracic vertebrae on the right side, as well as osteophytes on the lumbar and first sacral vertebrae. These additional changes are consistent with diffuse idiopathic skeletal hyperostosis (DISH) or Forestier's disease. Osteoarthritic changes were also present on the fourth lumbar vertebra and the atlanto-occipital joint. Waldron and Antoine (2002) considered tortuosity to be the most likely cause of the cervical defect and proposed that this arterial abnormality may not have resulted in any symptoms, let alone been the cause of death. They also suggested that, due to the discovery of two examples from a single burial site with less than 100 adult skeletons, many such abnormalities are being missed in palaeopathology, most probably due to the relatively discreet changes associated with these lesions.

Waldron and Antoine's (2002) second example was found in a male skeleton aged between 25 and 35 years, probably dating to the Coffin Period in Japan (c. 1600 years BP). Most of his skeleton was fragmentary and six of the seven surviving cervical vertebrae were in a poor state of preservation. C6 had an enlargement of the left transverse foramen, roughly in the shape of a figure-of-eight, and a shallow defect adjacent to the foramen on the anterior surface of the lamina that encroached onto the inferior facet joint. The left transverse foramen of the fifth cervical vertebra also showed signs of enlargement but poor preservation did not allow an assessment of the intervertebral foramen. No other pathological changes were observed on the spine. When compared with the defects described above, the shallowness of the defect, its location on the anterior surface of the lamina and the enlargement of two transverse foramina, including that of the vertebra above the defect, were all interpreted as being more in keeping with pressure from a larger abnormality, most probably the posterior surface of an aneurysmal sac that had extended upwards. No evidence of trauma was noted and the cause of the aneurysm, and whether it played a part in the cause of death, could not be determined. However, its size and location suggest it may have compressed the C6 nerve root, resulting in neurological symptoms in the left hand.

The earliest published example to date (Antoine, 2010) was identified on the spine of a young adult aged 20–34 years and buried in Tomb 6 at the Nubian C Group Cemetery at Hierakonpolis, Egypt (site HK27C; 2055–1700 BCE). Located on the left side of C3's vertebral body, the large smooth-walled pressure defect had extended laterally onto the anterior surface of the pedicle. The left transverse foramina of both C3 and C4 were enlarged but it is unclear if this represents the full extent of the pathological changes as the skeleton was incomplete, with no C5 and C6 preserved. Based on the appearance and location of the pressure defect on C3, tortuosity was regarded as the most likely cause. A further archaeological example of cervical lesions was also published by Billard and Fantino in 2011. Multiple pressure defects were observed on the cervical vertebrae of a 60-year-old-female excavated from an early medieval (fifth to sixth century) necropolis at Lathuile in Haute Savoie, France. The left side of the bodies of C3, C4 and C5 had concave and smooth-walled lesions with sharp edges. In C3 and C5, the lesions had spread to their left pedicles. The lower left articular facet of C3 also had evidence of osteoarthritis. As noted by Billard and Fantino (2011), the location and appearance of the lesions, as well as the involvement of multiple cervical levels that include the left side of C3 and C4 (see Sections 10.3.2 and 10.3.3), all strongly point towards a tortuosity of the vertebral artery. In 2014, Darton published another example of multilevel lesions found on C3 and C4 in a poorly preserved adult male dating to the Early Medieval Period. Excavated from a Merovingian cemetery located in eastern France, C3 and C4 were the only surviving cervical vertebrae, and Darton was not able to ascertain if the lesions represented the full extent of the pathological changes. The vertebrae had fused at their right articular processes, with the vertebral bodies joined at the uncinate processes and posterior rims. The left articular processes and the posterior arches were, unfortunately, not preserved. The lesion on the left side of the vertebral body of C4 was 7 mm deep and measured 13×8 mm. Oblong in shape, with the long axis orientated anteriorly at a 45-degree angle, the lesion extended beyond the side of the body into the now-damaged anterior surface of the pedicle. A second shallow defect measuring 9×7 mm was also found below the left uncinate process of C3. Both defects were smooth-walled and had visible sclerotic margins radiographically (Darton, 2014). The right pedicle of C4 also had two shallow smooth-walled defects. The larger of the two, below the uncinate process, measured 9×6 mm, with the second lower and more lateral lesion measuring 8×4 mm. As Darton (2014) argues, the concave and oblong lesions observed on the left of the spine, with their

Table 10.1 Cervical lesions in archaeological assemblages: The level (C1–C7), side affected (L, left; R, right) and most likely cause (T, tortuosity; A, aneurysm).

	Vaswani and Waldron (1997)	Waldron and Antoine (2002)	Waldron and Antoine (2002)	Antoine (2010)	Billard and Fantino (2011)	Darton (2014)
Age	≥45 years	40–50 years	25–35 years	20–34 years	60 years	Adult
Sex	Male	Female	Male	Unknown	Female	Male
Period and country	15th century, UK	15th century, UK	1600 years BP, Japan	2055–1700 BCE, Egypt	5th–6th century, France	5th–8th century, France
C1						
C2						
C3				L (T)	L (T)	L (T)
C4	L (T)				L (T)	L (T) R (A)
C5					L (T)	
C6		L (T)	L (A)			
C7						

smooth bases and sharp edges, compare well with the examples believed to be the result of tortuosities published in Vaswani and Waldron (1997), Waldron and Antoine (2002; case one) and Billard and Fantino (2011). Despite the absence of most cervical vertebrae, the location of the observable lesions, on C3 and C4, as well as the multilevel nature of the pathological changes, are also more in keeping with a tortuosity than an aneurysm (Darton, 2014). However, the shallowness of the changes on C4's right side is more in keeping with pressure from a larger abnormality such as an aneurysmal sac. As noted by Darton (2014), these lesions do not match the appearance of a tortuosity defect and, in view of the fusion of the two vertebrae, may be the result of a traumatic pseudoaneurysm caused by a secondary fracture of the right transverse process. Damage to the posterior arches and the absence of neighbouring vertebrae limits any further interpretation.

Overall, the paucity of cervical lesions in skeletal remains from archaeological sites contrasts with the prevalence reported in the clinical literature, particularly that of tortuosities, suggesting that abnormalities of the vertebral artery are being overlooked in bioarchaeology. The five archaeological cases of tortuosity summarised in Table 10.1 mirror the findings of clinical studies reviewed here, with tortuous loops affecting C3 to C6 and favouring the left side (100 per cent of cases), and lesions most often found on C3 and/or C4 (80 per cent of cases). Two of the reported individuals also involved multiple levels (Billard & Fantino, 2011; Darton, 2014). When age-at-death data were available, individuals with evidence of tortuosity were all over 40 years old bar one (Antoine, 2010). As we do not know at what age the lesions were initiated, this does not support an association with advancing years observed in clinical studies.

In two examples (Billard & Fantino, 2011; Darton, 2014), some form of joint disease or trauma may also have been an aetiological factor. In contrast, the evidence for two individuals possibly having cervical aneurysms was recorded on C4 and C6

(Waldron & Antoine, 2002; Darton, 2014). This differs from clinical studies where they are more frequently found in the upper part of the cervical spine, particularly C2. As with tortuosities, aneurysms of the vertebral artery tend to favour the left side but the example in Darton (2014) is on the right, where trauma may have played a role in its occurrence. Unlike tortuosities, aneurysms of the vertebral artery are more commonly reported in males, as was the case in both of the archaeological examples, and can occur in younger individuals, as in Waldron and Antoine (2002). With few cervical pressure defects reported in archaeological populations to date, these findings are hard to contextualise, particularly as none of the publications (ours included) provide prevalence data. In the future, recording methods that account for the presence and preservation of the cervical vertebrae (particularly the area of bone surrounding the transverse foramen) should allow for comparisons with clinical studies and provide insights into the past prevalence of abnormalities of the vertebral artery.

10.6 Recording and Interpreting Cervical Pressure Defects in Bioarchaeology: A Case Study from the Site of Kawa, Sudan

Most probably founded by the pharaoh Akhenaten in the fourteenth century BCE, the town of Kawa appears to have been abandoned in the fourth century CE. The associated cemetery is located several hundred metres to the east of the town and most of the graves appear to date from the later part of the Meroitic Period (first or second century CE; Welsby & Antoine, 2014). The human remains recovered were donated by Sudan's National Corporation of Antiquities and Museums to the Sudan Archaeological Research Society, who in turn donated them to the British Museum where their detailed analyses are ongoing.

10.6.1 Results

Of the 32 adults with cervical vertebrae analysed to date, most ($n = 29$) had at least four cervical vertebrae preserved: 21 had all seven, eight had at least four, one had three and two only had one. Smooth-walled depressions on the bodies of the cervical vertebrae identical to those published in the clinical and bioarchaeological literature were identified in four adults (12.5 per cent), two of whom had defects in two locations (Table 10.2). The age at death of the individuals with cervical lesions was established using age-related changes to joints of the pelvis (pubic symphysis and auricular surface; see Brooks & Suchey, 1990; Buikstra & Ubelaker, 1994: 21–32). The morphology of the pelvis was also used to determine their biological sex (Buikstra & Ubelaker, 1994: 16–19; Bruzek, 2002). Two are males aged 35–49 years (skeletons 207-193 and 561-25; Figure 10.2) and two are females, one aged 20–34 years (skeleton 1083-11; Figure 10.3) and the other aged 35–49 years (skeleton 1075-11; Figure 10.4). Only one of the males (207-193) had additional pathological changes in the cervical spine, with osteoarthritis affecting C2 and C6, and osteophytes and intervertebral disc disease observed on C6 (after Waldron,

Table 10.2 Observable cervical vertebrae, number with pressure defects and their locations.

	Vertebrae		Individual and side affected			
	Observed	Pressure defect	Skeleton 207-193 (male, 35–49 years)	Skeleton 561-25 (male, 35–49 years)	Skeleton 1075-11 (female, 35–49 years)	Skeleton 1083-11 (female, 20–34 years)
C1	29	0				
C2	28	2 (7.1%)	Right		Left	
C3	29	2 (6.9%)		Right		Right
C4	27	0				
C5	27	1 (3.7%)		Left		
C6	28	1 (3.6%)	Left			
C7	24	0				
Total	192	6	2	2	1	1

2009: 42–3). At Kawa, both the left and right vertebral arteries were equally affected, with three cervical pressure defects found on each side. In all four individuals, at least one of the lesions was located on either C2 or C3 (three on the right, one on the left; Table 10.2). In the two male individuals, these were part of a set of bilateral lesions, with the additional pressure defect located on C5 and C6 (both on the left).

10.6.2 Discussion

Although cervical defects are most likely to be the result of tortuosities or aneurysms of the vertebral artery, other conditions can produce similar changes in the vertebrae. These include solitary or aneurysmal bone cysts, chondroblastoma, fibrous dysplasia, giant cell tumour or interosseous lipoma (Waldron & Antoine, 2002). Often extending into the vertebral body, aneurysmal bone cysts mostly affect the posterior elements of the vertebrae (Danziger & Bloch, 1975; Cory et al., 1989). As noted above, neurofibromas usually erode the uncinate process of the vertebra (Wackenheim, 1977), something that does not appear to be the case when the intervertebral foramen widening is the result of a tortuosity (Wackenheim's sign in Waldron & Antoine, 2002). The location of metastasised bone tumours is also likely to be more random (Darton, 2014). However, none of these conditions is likely to result in defined smooth-walled lesions on the vertebral body and should be discounted from the differential diagnosis on morphological grounds (Waldron & Antoine, 2002). Nevertheless, distinguishing between a tortuosity and an aneurysm remains a challenge. Clinical findings suggest that most are likely to be the result of a tortuosity as aneurysms of the vertebral artery are relatively rare in populations today. The cervical level affected has previously been proposed as a way of distinguishing the aetiology of the defect (Waldron & Antoine, 2002; Darton, 2014). Although aneurysms tend to occur at a higher cervical level, the clinical literature suggests there is

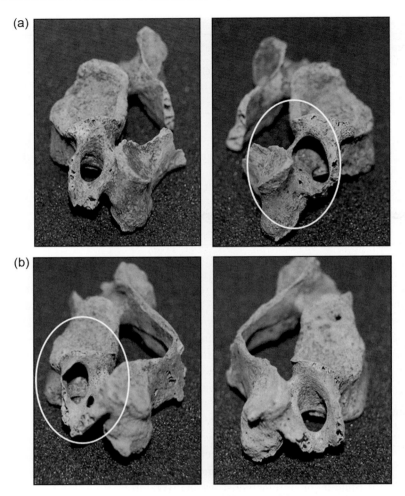

Figure 10.2 Superior lateral views of the C3 (a) and C5 (b) from skeleton 561-25. The sides with smooth-walled depressions are circled, with each defect 2–4 mm in depth. Source: courtesy of the Trustees of the British Museum. (A black and white version of this figure will appear in some formats. For the colour version, please refer to the plate section.)

sufficient variation in the level affected for this not to be a reliable criterion (Waldron & Antoine, 2002). The side affected should also not be relied upon, although both vertebral abnormalities tend to favour the left side. Most of the archaeological examples listed in Table 10.1 were attributed to tortuosities and, unlike defects interpreted as evidence of aneurysms, those linked to a tortuosity are clearly ovoid or oblong in shape. Although they range in size (from 7×9 mm to 9×15 mm), all have sharp and clearly delineated margins, and a noticeable depth (6–7 mm). In the two cases believed to be the result of pressure from an expanding aneurysmal sac, the defects were shallower and consequently not as clearly defined (see Waldron & Antoine, 2002; Darton, 2014). In Waldron and Antoine's (2002) example, the defect

Abnormalities of the Vertebral Artery

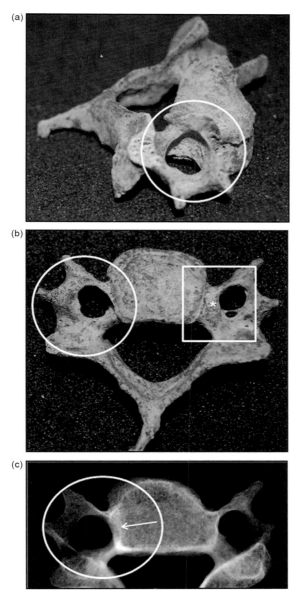

Figure 10.3 Lateral (a) and inferior (b, c) views of C3 from skeleton 1083-11, with the side affected by the pressure defect circled on all three. The remodelling is best seen from the inferior view (b), which reveals a clear enlargement of the transverse foramen and the loss of bone between the transverse foramen and the vertebral body. On the non-affected side (square), the bone bridge between the transverse foramen and the body of the vertebra (*) is present. The pressure defect has also encroached onto the vertebral body and created a sclerotic margin (arrow) that is visible radiographically (c). The presence of an accessory transverse foramen on the left side has not affected the course of the vertebral artery. Source: courtesy of the Trustees of the British Museum. (A black and white version of this figure will appear in some formats. For the colour version, please refer to the plate section.)

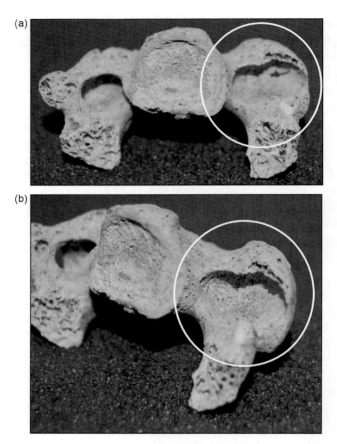

Figure 10.4 Inferior view of C2 from skeleton 1075-11. Despite post-mortem damage to the left transverse process, a pressure defect (circle) can clearly be seen encroaching into the vertebral body and the superior articular surface. Source: courtesy of the Trustees of the British Museum. (A black and white version of this figure will appear in some formats. For the colour version, please refer to the plate section.)

had also extended backwards, affecting the anterior surface of the lamina and enlarging the transverse foramen immediately above, as well as below, the lesion. The cervical pressure defects observed in the adults from Kawa were all ovoid or oblong in shape, with sharp and/or clearly delineated margins, suggesting they are all the result of tortuosities. Their size and depth also fall within range of lesions previously interpreted as the result of tortuosity (see Section 10.5 and Table 10.1). As with other published examples (Tulsi & Perrett, 1975; Holden et al., 1996; Waldron & Antoine, 2002), the defects had remodelled the bone between the transverse foramen and the body of the vertebra, creating smooth-walled lesions that had sclerotic margins radiographically (Figure 10.3). They also impinged into the body of the vertebrae, as well as the anterior surface of the pedicle (Figures 10.2 and 10.3), and in one example, the right transverse foramen was clearly enlarged (Figure 10.3; see also Lindsey et al., 1985; Freilich et al., 1986; Taitz & Arensburg, 1991; Yünten et al.,

1998; Brahee & Guebert, 2000; Waldron & Antoine, 2002). With tortuosities the most likely cause of the observed lesions, all four Kawa individuals may have experienced some neurological symptoms or neck pain (see Section 10.3.4).

Previous studies have shown that tortuous loops usually affect C3 to C6 and favour the left side, with lesions most often found on C3 and C4 (see Section 10.3.2). Unlike any of the previously published archaeological examples (see Table 10.1), two of the six lesions found at Kawa were on C2 (33 per cent) and three (50 per cent) were on the right side. Although often involving larger cohorts, lesions on C2 are also seldom reported in clinical studies (see Section 10.3.2). Out of 400 angiographic examinations, Palmer and Sequeira (1980) found that only two of the reported 44 cervical lesions were on C2 (4.5 per cent). The Hamann–Todd study (Curylo et al., 2000) did not include C2 but other examples have also been reported (see Cooper, 1980; Roy-Camille et al., 1982), including a single C2 lesion in a sample of 113 vertebral columns (Tulsi & Perrett, 1975). While lesions on C2 appear to be infrequent, their presence on C3–C6 is more variable, with C3 ranging from 4.5 to 30 per cent of the observed lesions (see Section 10.3.2). Once again, Kawa stands out with two of the six lesions found at the site located on C3 (33 per cent). The involvement of the right artery is also often reported but results from clinical and archaeological studies show that tortuosities consistently favour the left. This was not the case at Kawa, with both sides equally affected. However, this pilot study was limited to 32 adults and a full analysis of the site is required to further contextualise these unusual findings.

The lesions found lower down the spine, on C5 and C6, were both on the left side (Table 10.2). The influence of the vertebral artery's dominant left side on the formation of tortuous loops is still poorly understood. It remains unclear, for example, if a difference in arterial size and pressure affects all cervical levels in the same way. Arterial pressure, particularly on the left side, is likely to be greater lower down the vertebral artery, the end closest to its origin in the subclavian artery, possibly leading to a higher risk of tortuosities in the artery's left V1 and lower V2 segments. Should this be the case, lower cervical vertebrae may be more prone to developing tortuous loops on the left side, where the pressure is greatest, with the risk to both sides levelling out higher up the cervical spine. For example, an increased arterial pressure on the left vertebral artery, due to an atypical origin on the aortic arch, has been shown to result in multiple cervical lesions on the left side (see Danziger & Bloch, 1975). However, some larger studies have found the left and right sides to be equally affected at C2 and C6 (Palmer & Sequeira, 1980) and further research is needed to clarify the impact of the dominant left artery on the prevalence of lesions at different cervical levels.

As with other published studies, the number of individuals with lesions was similar across the sexes (Table 10.2). Three of the four skeletons were also 35–49 years old, with only one, a young adult female, aged 20–34 years (Figure 10.3). Apart from Antoine (2010; also 20–34 years), all the other skeletons with signs of a tortuosity that have been aged represented individuals over 40 years old. Although some lesions have been reported in a six-year-old child (Tulsi & Perrett, 1975) and patients as young as 34 years, the clinical literature also reveals an increase in prevalence with age, with most lesions occurring over the ages of 40 or 55 (Palmer & Sequeira, 1980 and Eskander et al., 2010, respectively). However, many reports are based on incidental findings and studies often deliberately focus on older age groups. Further research on archaeological remains may help clarify the prevalence of cervical pressure defects in younger age groups. A loss of disc space height with age may be a contributing factor (Nourbakhsh et al., 2010) but evidence of additional pathological changes in the cervical vertebrae were only observed on the spine of skeleton 207-193, aged 35–49 years old, with osteoarthritis, osteophytes and intervertebral disc disease on one of the two vertebrae with a lesion (C6). Multiple or bilateral lesions, as with the two males from Kawa, have also been reported in other studies (Babin & Haller, 1974; Hyypä et al., 1974; Salvador et al., 1981; Holden et al., 1996; Darton, 2014) and can occur on the same or separate vertebrae, affecting one or both sides. Out of a cohort of 400, Palmer and Sequeira (1980) found seven patients with two separate lesions on the same side, as well as five with bilateral lesions. Although some bilateral aneurysms have also been described in patients (Jewel, 1977), most are unilateral and the great majority of reported bilateral cases appear to be the result of tortuosities.

Based on a relatively small number of individuals, the prevalence of individuals from Kawa with one or more cervical pressure defects is 12.5 per cent (n = 4 out of 32; 95 per cent confidence interval (CI) 3.5–28.9). To date, this represents the first prevalence data from an archaeological population. The prevalence is lower than Hadley's (1958) original research (19.1 per cent; n = 4 out of 21; 95% CI 5.5–41.9) but higher than Palmer and Sequeira's (1980) large angiographic analysis (7.8 per cent; n = 31 out of 400; 95% CI 5.3–10.8), Tulsi and Perrett's (1975) anatomical and radiological study (8.9 per cent; n = 10 out of 113; 95% CI 4.3–15.7) and Curylo et al.'s (2000) analysis of the Hamann–Todd collection (2.7 per cent; n = 6 out of 222; 95% CI 1.0–5.8). However, the latter had not included C2. Since all the confidence intervals overlap, none of these differences is significant. Nevertheless, the Kawa results are based on a small group of a larger population and further work is needed to contextualise these initial findings, including an atypical percentage of defects on C2 and C3, and the equal distribution of lesions on the left and right sides. It also remains unclear if and when other pathological changes, including the presence of an accessory transverse foramen (see Figures 10.2 and 10.3), can affect the vertebral artery and lead to the formation of a cervical pressure defect.

10.7 Conclusion: Towards a Systematic Approach

Aneurysms of the vertebral artery appear to be rare and tortuosities usually lack symptoms, with both abnormalities seldom reported in the clinical literature. Cases are often limited to chance findings or autopsies, and their prevalence is likely to be underrepresented. Large-scale studies are also few and far between. The analysis of skeletal remains recovered from archaeological sites can make a significant contribution to our understanding of these abnormalities by moving away from individual case studies and, instead, should provide prevalence data that account for the preservation of the cervical vertebrae. The relatively discreet skeletal changes associated with such abnormalities explain why few examples have been reported in the bioarchaeological literature. Without the careful examination of the cervical vertebrae, evidence for such pressure defects is likely to be missed, overlooked or reported as being of no particular consequence. Clinical and bioarchaeological studies indicate that tortuosities and aneurysms of the vertebral artery are the most likely cause of pressure defects on the body of cervical vertebrae. In both cases, defects often (1) involve the pedicle and may cause the widening of the transverse foramen and intervertebral foramen. In most instances, (2) the defects also appear to be smooth-walled, with a sclerotic margin visible radiographically. As noted by Curylo et al. (2000) and Darton (2014), the formation of cervical pressure defects usually involves (3) the remodelling and loss of the bone between the medial margin of the uncovertebral joint (also known as Luschka's joint) and the medial border of the transverse foramen. As shown in Figure 10.3, this is best appreciated when viewed from the inferior surface of the vertebra and represents the clearest way of identifying a pressure defect. The loss of the small bone bridge between the foramen and the body (highlighted in Figure 10.3) often leads to a distinct enlargement of the transverse foramen and, most noticeably, the side of the vertebral body becomes the medial border of the transverse foramen. In most non-pathological cervical vertebrae, the medial border of the transverse foramen should not *anchor* itself directly onto the vertebral body Changes (1) (2) and (3) above should be used to identify cervical pressure defects in skeletal remains.

Distinguishing between the causes of a cervical pressure defect remains a challenge. Pressure from expanding aneurysmal sacs is most likely to create diffuse and poorly defined shallow lesions that can extend backwards, affecting the anterior surface of the lamina, and these can enlarge the transverse foramen above and below the lesion (see Waldron & Antoine, 2002; Darton 2014). Lesions associated with tortuosities are usually ovoid or oblong in shape and although they range in size, all have sharp and clearly delineated margins and a noticeable depth. Understanding past prevalence of both abnormalities across differing populations can provide new insights into their aetiologies, with tortuosities believed to be influenced by congenital (Babin & Haller, 1974) and acquired (Palmer & Sequeira, 1980) factors. Possible links with other cardiovascular diseases should also be investigated and although tortuosities do not appear to be linked with atheromas (see above; Palmer & Sequeira, 1980), strokes are one of the most commonly reported complications of extracranial dissecting aneurysms (Gottesman et al., 2012).

Based on a relatively small number of individuals, six lesions were observed at Kawa. The relatively high 12.5 per cent prevalence, the atypical location of lesions on C2 and C3, and the non-dominance of the left side, with an equal number of defects on the right side, all warrant further research. Forthcoming analyses from other Sudanese assemblages, including recently excavated adults and non-adults from Kawa, should help contextualise these findings and provide a clearer understanding of the past prevalence of cervical pressure defects in the Nile Valley. Ideally, future studies will not only account for the preservation of the cervical vertebrae, including the area of bone surrounding transverse foramen, they will attempt to systematically record the level of entry of the artery (when identifiable), the size of the bone bridge between the transverse foramen and cervical bodies, the size and shape of the transverse and intervertebral foramen, and the shape, size and depth of the actual defects. This should allow a clearer identification of the changes associated with cervical pressure defects and, notwithstanding other causes, help distinguish between tortuosities and aneurysms.

Acknowledgements

Sudan's National Corporation of Antiquities and Museums, the Sudan Archaeological Research Society and the Institute for Bioarchaeology are gratefully acknowledged. Images are courtesy of the Trustees of the British Museum. To Tony, thank you for your wonderful insights, academic rigour, teachings and friendship. You are sorely missed.

References

Adachi, B. (1928). *Das Arteriensystem der Japaner*. Kyoto: KenkyuSha.

Adeloye, A., Anomah, N. V. and Latunde, O. E. (1970). Traumatic aneurysm of the first portion of the right vertebral artery. *British Journal of Surgery*, 57, 312–14.

Alves, A. M. and Black, C. (1972). Post-traumatic extracranial aneurysm of the vertebral artery. *International Surgery*, 57, 422–6.

Anderson, R. E. and Shealy, C. N. (1970). Cervical pedicle erosion and rootlet compression caused by a tortuous vertebral artery. *Radiology*, 96, 537–8.

Ando, M., Igari, T., Yokohama, H. and Satokawa, H. (2003). CT features of chronic contained rupture of an abdominal aortic aneurysm. *Annals of Thoracic and Cardiovascular Surgery*, 9, 274–8.

Andoh, T., Shirakami, S., Nakashima, T., et al. (1992). Clinical analysis of a series of vertebral aneurysm cases. *Neurosurgery*, 31, 987–93.

Antoine, D. (2010). Pain in the neck? An abnormality from HK27C. *Nekhen News*, 22, 23.

Argenon, C., Francke, J. P., Sylla, S., et al. (1980). The vertebral arteries (segments V1 and V2). *Anatomia Clinica*, 2, 29–41.

Babin, E. and Haller, M. (1974). Correlation between bony radiological signs and dolichoarterial loops of the cervical vertebral artery. *Neuroradiology*, 7, 15–17.

Barrett, J. G. (1974). Enlargement of cervical intervertebral foramina by coiling of the vertebral artery. *Australasian Radiology*, 18, 171–4.

Billard, M. and Fantino, O. (2011). Erosions osseuses du rachis cervical par l'artère vertébrale: Aspects anatomiques à propos d'une observation ostéoarchéologique. *Paleobios*, 16, 58–62.

Brahee, D. D. and Guebert, G. M. (2000). Tortuosity of the vertebral artery resulting in vertebral erosion. *Journal of Manipulative and Physiological Therapy*, 23, 48–51.

Broadribb, A. J. (1970). Vertebral artery aneurysm in a case of Ehlers–Danlos syndrome. *British Journal of Surgery*, 57, 148–51.

Brooks, S. and Suchey, J. (1990). Skeletal age determination based on the os pubis: A comparison of the Acsadi–Nemeskeri and Suchey–Brooks methods. *Human Evolution*, 5, 227–38.

Bruneau, M., Cornelius, J. F., Marneffe, V., Triffaux, M. and George, B. (2006). Anatomical variations of the V2 segment of the vertebral artery. *Neurosurgery*, 59(1 Suppl 1), ONS20–4.

Bruzek, J. (2002). A method for visual determination of sex using the human hip bone. *American Journal of Physical Anthropology*, 117, 157–68.

Buerger, T., Lippert, H., Meyer, F. and Halloul, Z. (1999). Aneurysm of the vertebral artery near the atlas arch. *Journal of Cardiovascular Surgery (Torino)*, 40, 387–9.

Buerger, T., Meyer, F. and Halloul, Z. (2000). Non-traumatic aneurysm of the extracranial vertebral artery. *European Journal of Surgery*, 166, 180–2.

Buikstra, J. E. and Ubelaker, D. H. (1994). *Standards for Data Collection from Human Skeletal Remains*. Arkansas Archaeological Survey Research Series No. 44. Fayetteville, AK: Arkansas Archaeological Survey.

Burnett, K. R. and Staple, T. W. (1981). Case report 132. *Skeletal Radiology*, 6, 51–3.

Catala, M., Rancurel, G., Koskas, F., Martindelassalle, E. and Keiffer, E. (1993). Ischemic stroke due to spontaneous extracranial vertebral giant aneurysm. *Cerebrovascular Disease*, 3, 322–6.

Cavdar, S. and Arisan, E. (1989). Variations in the extracranial origin of the human vertebral artery. *Acta Anatomica*, 135, 236–8.

Chassaing, N., Martin, L., Calvas, P., Le Bert, M. and Hovnanian, A. (2005). Pseudoxanthoma elasticum: A clinical, pathophysiological and genetic update including 11 novel ABCC6 mutations. *Journal of Medical Genetics*, 42, 881–92.

Cooper, D. F. (1980). Bone erosion of the cervical vertebrae secondary to tortuosity of the vertebral artery. *Journal of Neurosurgery*, 53, 106–8.

Cory, D. A., Fritsch, S. A., Cohen, M. D., et al. (1989). Aneurysmal bone cysts: Imaging findings and embolotherapy. *American Journal of Roentgenology*, 153, 369–73.

Curylo, L. J., Mason, H. C., Bohlman, H. H. and Yoo, J. U. (2000). Tortuous course of the vertebral artery and anterior cervical decompression: A cadaveric and clinical case study. *Spine*, 25(22), 2860–4.

Danziger, J. and Bloch, S. (1975). The widened cervical intervertebral foramen. *Radiology*, 116, 671–4.

Darton, Y. (2014). Cervical vertebral erosion caused by bilateral vertebral artery tortuosity, predisposing to spinal, sprain: A medieval case study. *International Journal of Paleopathology*, 4, 47–52.

Davidson, K. C., Weiford, E. C. and Dixon, G. D. (1975). Traumatic vertebral artery pseudoaneurysm following chiropractic manipulation. *Radiology*, 115, 651–2.

Deutsch, H. J. (1969). Aneurysm of the vertebral artery: Medicine in Vietnam. *Laryngoscope*, 79, 134–40.

Diekerhof, C. H., Reedt Dortland, R. W. H., Oner, F. C. and Verbout, A. J. (2002). Severe erosion of lumbar vertebral body because of abdominal aortic false aneurysm. *Spine*, 27(16), 382–4.

Dory, M. A. (1985). CT demonstration of cervical vertebral erosion by tortuous vertebral artery. *American Journal of Neuroradiology*, 6, 641–2.

Edwards, A. (1969). Ehlers–Danlos syndrome with vertebral artery aneurysm. *Proceedings of the Royal Society of Medicine*, 62, 14–16.

Egnor, M. R., Page, L. K. and David, C. (1991). Vertebral artery aneurysm: A unique hazard of head banging by heavy metal rockers. *Pediatric Neurosurgery*, 17, 135–8.

Ekeström, S., Bergdahl, L. and Huttunen, H. (1983). Extracranial carotid and vertebral artery aneurysms. *Scandinavian Journal of Thoracic and Cardiovascular Surgery*, 17, 135–9.

Elkin, D. C. and Harris, M. H. (1946). Arteriovenous aneurysm of the vertebral vessels. *Annals of Surgery*, 124, 934–9.

Eskander, M. S., Drew, J. M., Aubin, M. E., et al. (2010). Vertebral artery anatomy: A review of two hundred fifty magnetic resonance imaging scans. *Spine*, 35(23), 2035–40.

Fakhry, S. M., Jacques, P. F. and Prater, H. J. (1988). Cervical vessel injury after blunt trauma. *Journal of Vascular Surgery*, 8, 501–8.

Freilich, M., Virapongse, C., Kier, E. L., Sarwar, M. and Bhimani, S. (1986). Foramen transversarium enlargement due to tortuosity of the vertebral artery. *Spine*, 11, 95–8.

Gatti, J.-M., Juan, L. H., Bironne, Ph. and Glowinski, J. (1983). Elargissement d'un trou de conjugaison cervical par une mégadolichoartère vertébrale. *La Presse Médicale*, 24, 2056.

George, B. and Laurian, C. (1980). Surgical approaches to the whole length of the vertebral artery with special reference to the third portion. *Acta Neurochirurgica*, 51, 259–72.

George, B. and Laurian, C. (1987). *The Vertebral Artery: Pathology and Surgery*. Wien: Springer-Verlag.

Glover, J. R., Kennedy, C. and Coral, A. (1990). Case report: Tortuous vertebral artery: Onset of symptoms during pregnancy. *Clinical Radiology*, 41, 66–8.

Gluncie, V., Ivkic, G., Marin, D. and Percac, S. (1999). Anomalous origin of both vertebral arteries. *Clinical Anatomy*, 12, 281–4.

Gottesman, R. F., Sharma, P., Robinson, K. A., et al. (2012). Clinical characteristics of symptomatic vertebral artery dissection: A systematic review. *Neurologist*, 18(5), 245–54.

Guiffré, R. and Sherkat, S. (1999). The vertebral artery: Developmental pathology. *Journal of Neurosurgical Sciences*, 43, 175–89.

Habozit, B. and Battistelli, J.-M. (1990). Spontaneous aneurysm of the extracranial vertebral artery associated with spinal osseous anomaly. *Annals of Vascular Surgery*, 4, 600–3.

Hadley, M. (1958). Tortuosity and deflection of the vertebral artery. *American Journal of Roentgenology*, 80, 306–12.

Hadley, M. N., Spetzler, R. F., Masferrer, R., Martin, N. A. and Carter, L. P. (1985). Occipital artery to vertebral artery bypass procedure. *Journal of Neurosurgery*, 63, 622–5.

Harzer, K. and Töndbury, G. (1966). Zum Verhalten der Arteria vertebralis in der alternden Halswirbelsäule. *Röntgenfortschritte*, 104, 696–7.

Heifetz, G. J. (1945). Traumatic aneurysm of the first portion of the left vertebral artery. *Annals of Surgery*, 122, 102–10.

Holden, A., Adler, B. and Song, S. (1996). Bilateral vertebral artery tortuosity with concomitant vertebral erosion: CT and MRA findings. *Australasian Radiology*, 40, 65–7.

Hong, J. T., Park, D. K., Lee, M. J., Kim, S. W. and An, H. S. (2008). Anatomical variations of the vertebral artery segment in the lower cervical spine. Analysis by three-dimensional computed tomography angiography. *Spine*, 33(22), 2422–6.

Husni, E. A. and Storer, J. (1967). The syndrome of mechanical occlusion of the vertebral artery: further observations. *Angiology*, 18, 106–16.

Hyyppä, S. E., Laasonen, E. M. and Halonen, V. (1974). Erosion of cervical vertebrae caused by elongaged and tortuous vertebral artery. *Neuroradiology*, 7, 49–51.

Iyer, A. A. (1927). Some anomalies of the origin of the vertebral artery. *Journal of Anatomy*, 62, 121–2.

Jewell, K. L. (1977). Bilateral extracranial vertebral artery aneurysms. *American Journal of Roentgenology*, 128, 324–5.

Kelley, M. A. (1979). Skeletal changes produced by aortic aneurysms. *American Journal of Physical Anthropology*, 51, 35–8.

Kikuchi, K. and Kowada, M. (1983). Nontraumatic extracranial aneurysm of the vertebral artery. *Surgical Neurology*, 19, 425–7.

Kim, H. S., Lee, J. H., Cheh, G. and Lee, S. H. (2010). Cervical radiculopathy caused by vertebral artery loop formation: a case report and review of the literature. *Journal of Korean Neurosurgical Society*, 48(5), 465–8.

Kister, S. J and Rankow, R. M. (1966). Traumatic aneurysm of the first portion of the left vertebral artery: a case report. *Plastic and Reconstructive Surgery*, 37, 546–51.

Koenigsberg, R. A., Aletich, V., DeBrun, G., Camras, L. R. and Ausman, J. L. (1997). Cervical vertebral arteriovenous fistula balloon embolization in a patient with neurofibromatosis type 1. *Surgical Neurology*, 47, 265–73.

Koniyama, M., Nakajima, H., Yamanaka, K. and Iwai, Y. (1999). Dual origin of the vertebral artery: Case report. *Neurologica Medica Chirurgica (Tokyo)*, 39, 932–7.

Kono, A. K., Higashi, M., Morisaki, H., et al. (2010). High prevalence of vertebral artery tortuosity of Loeys-Dietz syndrome in comparison with Marfan syndrome. *Japanese Journal of Radiology*, 28, 273–7.

Kricun, R., Levitt, L. P. and Winn, H. R. (1992). Tortuous vertebral artery shown by MR and CT. *American Journal of Roentgenology*, 159, 613–15.

Kurata, A., Suzuki, S., Iwamoto, K., et al. (2012). Altered hemodynamics associated with pathogenesis of the vertebral artery dissecting aneurysms. *Stroke Research and Treatment*, 2012, 716919.

Kwiatkowska, B., Szczurowski, J. and Nowakowski, D. (2014). Variation in foramina transversaria of human cervical vertebrae in the medieval population from Sypniewo (Poland). *Anthropological Review*, 77(2), 175–88.

Lasjaunias, P., Vallee, B., Person, H., Brugge, K. T. and Chu, M. (1985). The lateral spinal artery of the upper cervical spinal cord: Anatomy, normal variations, and angiographic aspects. *Journal of Neurosurgery*, 63, 235–41.

Laurian, C., George, B., Richard, T., Derome, D. and Guilmet, D. (1980). Intérét de l'abord chirurgical de l'artère vertébrale dans son segment extracranien à propos d'un anévrysme de l'artère vertébrale en C3. *Journal des Maladies Vasculaires (Paris)*, 5, 149–50.

Lemke, A.-J., Benndorf, G., Liebig, T. and Felix, R. (1999). Anomalous origin of the right vertebral artery: Review of the literature and case report of right vertebral artery origin distal to the left subclavian artery. *American Journal of Neuroradiology*, 20, 1318–21.

Lindsey, R. W., Piepmeier, J. and Burkus, K. (1985). Tortuosity of the vertebral artery: An adventitious finding after cervical trauma. *Journal of Bone and Joint Surgery*, 67A, 806–8.

Matula, C., Trattnig, S., Tschabitscher, M., Day, J. D. and Koos, W. Th. (1997). The course of the prevertebral segment of the vertebral artery: anatomy and clinical significance. *Surgical Neurology*, 48, 125–31.

Negoro, M., Nakaya, T., Terashima, K. and Sugita, K. (1990). Extracranial vertebral artery aneurysm with neurofibromatosis: endovascular treatment by detachable balloon. *Neuroradiology*, 31, 533–6.

Nourbakhsh, A., Yang, J., Gallagher, S., et al. (2010). A safe approach to explore/identify the V2 segment of the vertebral artery during anterior approaches to cervical spine and/or arterial repairs: Anatomical study. *Journal of Neurosurgery: Spine*, 12(1), 25–32.

Obayashi, T., Furuse, M., Tanaka, O. and Aihara, T. (1986). Tortuous vertebral artery simulating extradural spinal tumour. *Neurochirurgia*, 29, 96–8.

O'Connell, J., Sutton, D. and Kendal, D. (1975). Traumatic vertebral artery aneurysm. *British Journal of Radiology*, 48, 670–3.

Oga, M., Yuge, I., Terada, K., Shimizu, A. and Sugioka, Y. (1996). Tortuosity of the vertebral artery in patients with cervical spondylotic myelopathy. *Spine*, 21, 1085–9.

Oh, Y. M. and Eun, J. P. (2008). Congenital absence of a cervical spine pedicle: Report of two cases and review of the literature. *Journal of Korean Neurosurgical Society*, 44(6), 389–91.

Ortner, D. J. (2003). *Identification of Pathological Conditions in Human Skeletal Remains*, 2nd ed. San Diego, CA: Academic Press.

Palmer, F. J. and Sequiera, M. (1980). Cervical vertebral erosion and vertebral tortuosity: An angiographic study. *Australasian Radiology*, 24, 20–3.

Peyre, M., Ozanne, A., Bhangoo, R., et al. (2007). Pseudotumoral presentation of a cervical extracranial vertebral artery aneurysm in neurofibromatosis type 1: Case report. *Neurosurgery*, 61(3), E658.

Pritz, M. B., Chandler, W. F. and Kindt, G. W. (1981). Vertebral artery disease: Radiological evaluation, medical management, and microsurgical treatment. *Neurosurgery*, 9, 524–30.

Rameshbabu, C., Gupta, O. P., Gupta, K. K. and Qasim, M. (2014). Bilateral asymmetrical duplicated origin of vertebral arteries: Multidetector row CT angiographic study. *Indian Journal of Radiology and Imaging*, 24(1), 61–5.

Randall, J. M., Griffiths, P. D., Gardner-Medwin, D. and Gholkar, A. (1994). Thalamic infarction in childhood due to extracranial vertebral artery abnormalities. *Neuropediatrics*, 25, 262–4.

Rifkinson-Mann, S., Laub, J. and Haimov, M. (1986). A traumatic extracranial vertebral artery aneurysm: Case report and review of the literature. *Journal of Vascular Surgery*, 4, 288–93.

Roy-Camille, R., Thibierge, M. and Metzger, J. (1982). Exploration d'une lacune de l'axis chez une patiente cervicalgique. *La Nouvelle Presse Médicale*, 11, 453–4.

Salvador, M. R., Solé-Llenas, J. and Salvá, M. A. Q. (1981). Bilateral bone erosion of the cervical vertebrae caused by tortuosity of the vertebral arteries. *Neurochirurgia*, 24(6), 212–13.

Santos-Franco, J. A., Zenteno, M. and Lee, A. (2008). Dissecting aneurysms of the vertebrobasilar system: A comprehensive review on natural history and treatment options. *Neurosurgical Review*, 31(2), 131–40.

Sato, K., Watanabe, T., Yoshimoto, T. and Kameyama, M. (1994). Magnetic resonance imaging of C2 segmental type of vertebral artery. *Surgical Neurology*, 41, 45–51.

Schievink, W. I. and Piepgras, D. G. (1991). Cervical vertebral aneurysms and arteriovenous fistulae in neurofibromatosis type 1: Case reports. *Neurosurgery*, 29, 760–5.

Schima, W., Stigbauer, R., Trattnig, S., et al. (1993). Case report: Cervical intervertebral foramen widening caused by vertebral artery tortuosity: Diagnosis with MR and color-coded Doppler sonography. *British Journal of Radiology*, 66, 165–7.

Schimmel, D. H., Newton, T. H. and Mani, J. (1976). Widening of the cervical intervertebral foramen. *Neuroradiology*, 12, 3–10.

Schittek, A. (1999). Pseudoaneurysm of the vertebral artery. *Texas Heart Institute Journal*, 26, 90–5.

Schubiger, O. and Yasargil, M. G. (1978). Extracranial vertebral artery aneurysm with neurofibromatosis. *Neuroradiology*, 15, 171–3.

Sganzerla, E. P., Grimoldi, N., Vaccri, U., Rampini, P. M. and Gaini, S. M. (1987). Cervical vertebral erosion due to tortuous vertebral artery. *Surgical Neurology*, 28, 385–9.

Sheeran, S. R. and Sclafani, S. J. A. (2000). Syphilitic aneurysm of descending thoracic aorta causing vertebral body erosion and spastic paraparesis. *Emergency Radiology*, 7, 245–7.

Slover, W. P. and Kiley, R. F. (1965). Cervical vertebral erosion caused by tortuous vertebral artery. *Radiology*, 84, 112–14.

Sukuki, S., Kuwubara, K., Hatano, R. and Iwai, T. (1978). Duplicate origin of the left vertebral artery. *Neuroradiology*, 29, 27–9.

Sumimura, J., Nakao, K., Miyata, M., et al. (1988). Vertebral aneurysm of the neck. *Journal of Cardiovascular Surgery (Torino)*, 29, 63–5.

Taitz, C. and Arensburg, B. (1991). Vertebral artery tortuosity with concomitant erosion of the foramen of the transverse process of the axis: Possible clinical implications. *Acta Anatomica*, 141, 104–8.

Takahashi, Y., Sasaki, Y., Toshihiko, S. and Suehiro, S. (2007). Descending thoracic aortic aneurysm complicated with severe vertebral erosion. *European Journal of Cardiothoracic Surgery*, 31, 941–3.

Takasato, Y., Hayashi, H., Kobayashi, T. and Hashimoto, Y. (1992). Duplicated origin of the right vertebral artery with rudimentary and accessory left vertebral arteries. *Neuroradiology*, 34, 287–9.

Talla, R., Galea, M., Lythgo, N., Angeli, T. and Eser, P. (2011) Contralateral comparison of bone geometry, BMD and muscle function in the lower leg and forearm after stroke. *Journal of Musculoskeletal and Neuronal Interactions*, 11(4), 306–13.

Thompson, J. E., Eilber, F. and Baker, J. D. (1979). Vertebral artery aneurysm: case report and review of the literature. *Surgery*, 85, 583–5.

Tulsi, R. S. and Perrett, L. V. (1975). The anatomy and radiology of the cervical vertebrae and the tortuous vertebral artery. *Australasian Radiology*, 19, 258–64.

Vanrietvelde, F., Lemmerling, M., deRooy, J., et al. (1999). Non-invasive diagnostic assessment of extensive vertebral artery tortuosity with enlargement of the intervertebral foramen. *European Journal of Radiology*, 32, 149–52.

Viswani, M. and Waldron, H. A. (1997). The earliest case of extracranial aneurysm of the vertebral artery. *British Journal of Neurosurgery*, 11, 164–5.

Wackenheim, A. (1977). Eléments de séméiologie radiologique de l'artère vertébrale. In P. Kehr and A. Jung, eds., *Pathologie et chirurgie de l'artère vertébrale*. Paris: Expansion Scientifique Francaise, pp. 31–41.

Wackenheim, A. and Babin, E. (1969). Excursion extratransversaire de l'artére vertébrale. *La Presse Medicale*, 77, 1213–14.

Wakely, J. and Smith, A. (1998). A possible eighteenth to nineteenth century example of a popliteal aneurysm from Leicester. *International Journal of Osteoarchaeology*, 8, 56–60.

Waldron, T. (2009). *Palaeopathology*. Cambridge: Cambridge University Press.

Waldron, T. and Antoine, D. (2002). Tortuosity or aneurysm? The palaeopathology of some abnormalities of the vertebral artery. *International Journal of Osteoarchaeology*, 12, 79–88.

Walker, E. G. (1983). Evidence for prehistoric cardiovascular disease of syphilitic origin on the Northern Plains. *American Journal of Physical Anthropology*, 60, 499–503.

Welsby, D. A. and Antoine, D. (2014). *Kawa, the Pharaonic and Kushite Town of Gematon: History and Archaeology of the Site*. London: Sudan Archaeological Research Society.

Youll, B. D., Coutellier, A., Dubois, B., Leger, J. M. and Bousser, M. G. (1990). Three cases of spontaneous extracranial vertebral artery dissection. *Stroke*, 21, 618–25.

Yuan, S. M. (2016). Aberrant origin of vertebral artery and its clinical implications. *Brazilian Journal of Cardiovascular Surgery*, 31(1), 52–9.

Yünten, N., Alper, H., Calli, C., Selcuki, D. and Ustün, E.-E. (1998). Cervical osseous changes associated with vertebral artery tortuosity. *Journal of Neuroradiology*, 25, 136–9.

Zimmerman, H. B. and Farrell, W. J. (1970). Cervical vertebral erosion caused by vertebral artery tortuosity. *American Journal of Roentgenology*, 108, 767–70.

11 A Heart of Stone

A Review of Constrictive Pericarditis and Other Calcified Tissues from the Pathologic–Anatomical Collection at the Narrenturm in Vienna, Austria

Karin Wiltschke-Schrotta, Eduard Winter and Michelle Gamble

11.1 Introduction

The Pathologic–Anatomical Collection in Vienna, Austria, now housed in the Narrenturm ('Lunatic Tower', a mental health asylum built in the eighteenth century), offers a valuable reference collection for identifying calcified human tissue from archaeological contexts. This can be achieved through comparison of potential calcifications with documented pathological body parts that were collected from hospital patients for a teaching collection, mainly from the end of the eighteenth century until the mid-twentieth century.[1] Today, the collection continues to increase, primarily through donations from patients or from acquisition of neglected collections from hospitals in Austria.

Founded in 1796 by Johann Peter Frank, a physician and the Director of the General Hospital of Vienna at that time, the Pathologic–Anatomical Collection has since been used for teaching and scientific research. The initial collection of approximately 40 body parts quickly grew, reaching around 4500 when Carl von Rokitansky became head of the Department for Pathology at the Medical Faculty of the University of Vienna in 1833. From 1811, an Imperial decree had regulated dissections and the preparation of specimens for the collection. Unusual and rare examples had to be documented and prepared for future generations of medical students and doctors. However, it was not only the most spectacular examples of diseases that were preserved; examples from common diseases, such as syphilis or tuberculosis, were also collected for teaching purposes. Every professor had their own speciality, ranging from bone pathology to cardiovascular diseases. In 1971, the collection was transferred from the Department of Pathology to empty rooms in the nearby disused Narrenturm, for organisational reasons, and in 1974 it was declared an independent national museum. Finally, the collection was incorporated into the Department of Anthropology of the Natural History Museum of Vienna (NHMW) in 2012. After extensive renovation of the building and reorganisation of

---

[1] The Pathologic–Anatomical Collection at the Narrenturm was originally part of the medical teaching collection of the University of Vienna and is now a national archive within the Natural History Museum, Vienna (NHMW). There are no issues with surviving ancestral populations, and there are no ethical issues with using the collection for scientific research. All research projects are approved by a medical ethics commission appointed by the Department of Anthropology at the NHMW. For information regarding research proposals, contact the custodian of the collection at pas@nhm-wien.ac.at.

the collection, a new permanent exhibition on diseases of the human body opened to the public in 2021. This presents only a small portion of the whole collection. Now incorporating over 50 000 preserved body parts, moulds, tools, microscopes, pictures and other related items, the collection is one of the largest of its kind worldwide. From bones showing the effects of syphilis to rare genetic malformations preserved in wax moulds, the collection contains examples of a wide range of pathological changes caused by different diseases for scientists to explore. Selected examples from the Narrenturm have previously also been used by palaeopathologists and physicians such as Don Ortner and Walter Putschar to illustrate their textbook on the range of pathological conditions found in human skeletal remains (Ortner & Putschar, 1981; Ortner, 2003; Teschler-Nicola & Winter, 2013; Schamall et al., 2016; Buikstra, 2019).

Besides the exemplary physical examples of bodies and body parts afflicted by disease, the documentation of the collection is at the heart of its incredible value. A systematic catalogue was started in 1817 by Lorenz Biermayer and is still in use today. It offers detailed information, including the date of death, sex and age at death, as well as the cause of death, of the patient whose body part is stored in the collection. All the body parts within the collection came from patients who died in Vienna's General Hospital, and who were normally dissected within 24 hours of their death. Important pathological changes found during these autopsies were preserved and catalogued. The original autopsy records are also stored with the collection, but are only accessible for scientific research, thus anonymising the preserved body part unless necessary, for example if the personal information had implications for the diagnosis.

The aim of this study was to find suitable atherosclerotic examples within this collection for comparison with possible archaeological finds of atherosclerotic plaques, and to then describe and discuss the different possible forms of calcifications that can occur in the cardiovascular system. It is intended that this will provide a preliminary starting point or guide for bioarchaeological research that can potentially be used to aid in detecting similar human biological structures during excavation, and to inform palaeopathological analyses.

11.2 Selection of Cardiovascular Calcifications

For this study we searched for well-documented examples of potential cardiovascular calcifications from within the prepared Pathologic–Anatomical Collection. About 90 per cent of the prepared collection is searchable in a digital database for internal use. The terms, 'calcification', 'ossification' and 'cardiovascular' were entered into a keyword search. This highlighted 269 recorded cardiovascular calcifications within the collection. About 80 per cent of the examples were wet preparations, soft tissues and calcifications preserved and conserved in formaldehyde; nearly 15 per cent were dry preparations of the soft tissue and calcified tissue conserved by dehydration and smoking, and the rest were macerations resulting in only the calcified tissues.

Of the 269 examples of cardiovascular calcifications, we eliminated the wet preparations from consideration as our aim is to raise awareness of the nature of unusual calcifications that may potentially be identifiable in archaeological contexts (i.e. with skeletons). Since wet preparations are completely preserved body parts and it was not possible to see the dimensions of the calcified tissue and because such examples are unlikely to be found during archaeological excavation, they were considered inappropriate for this study. This resulted in a selection of dry and macerated examples to choose from. We selected six that we thought were somewhat visually and physically representative of the three general groups we wanted to explore: calcified blood vessels, calcified pericardia and calcified meninges.

Following this, further information about the patients and their various diseases was investigated in different collection catalogues and autopsy records. While there were no specific criteria to meet with regard to the examples we selected, we excluded those for which there were no records. The main purpose of this study is not a synthetic discussion of the nature of cardiovascular calcification, but rather a presentation of examples of cardiovascular calcifications that act as a preliminary reference source for the identification of irregular calcified objects from archaeological contexts.

11.3 Examples of Cardiovascular Calcifications

Six examples of cardiovascular calcification were selected as representative of conditions which could appear in the archaeological record, based on their physical properties (i.e. non-bone calcification). These are subdivided into three different categories: calcified blood vessels (Figures 11.1 and 11.2), calcification of the pericardium (Figures 11.3 and 11.4) and calcification of the meninges (Figures 11.5 and 11.6).

11.3.1 Calcified Blood Vessels

11.3.1.1 Arteriosclerosis of the Aorta

Calcifications within an aorta are very well represented by MN 12.248. This is a dry specimen that has been preserved and treated with resin (length 148 mm, height 70 mm, width 115 mm; Figure 11.1). The thickening and hardening of the superior arch of the aorta is visible in the form of a yellow plaque. These calcifications vary in thickness from about 1 to 2 mm, and are irregularly shaped and sized. They range from millimetre-wide sub-circular patches to solid plates several centimetres in length with a sub-rectangular or sub-square morphology (particularly clear on the interior surface of the specimen) and extend along the inner surface of the vessel, causing the surface of the calcifications to become rough and uneven. The plaque accumulation has thus hardened the artery. No autopsy record was available.

This historic example of an aorta with arteriosclerosis was prepared in about 1850 by the famous pathologist and Director of the University of Vienna, Carl

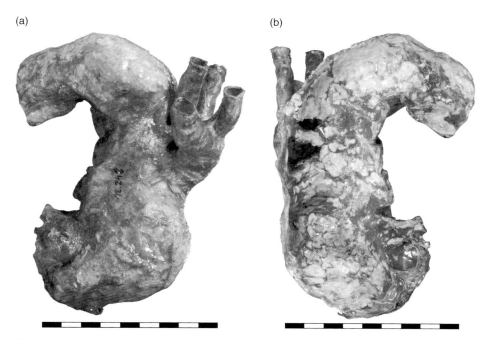

Figure 11.1 Ascending (bottom) and descending (top) arch of the aorta with arteriosclerotic calcifications, visible as white irregular structures of different sizes: (a) anterior exterior view; (b) posterior interior view of the vessel which has been cut in half (MN 12.248). Source: NHM Vienna, Reichmann. (A black and white version of this figure will appear in some formats. For the colour version, please refer to the plate section.)

von Rokitansky (1804–78). He collected pathological examples for teaching purposes for medical students. For that reason, he reorganised the Pathologic–Anatomical Collection of the General Hospital in Vienna and systematically added new examples.

11.3.1.2 Aortic Aneurysm

This example of a dried aortic arch (MN 2952; length 125 mm, height 58 mm, width 100 mm; Figure 11.2) shows a large swelling directly after the junction with the left subclavian artery. This dilatation (aneurysm = weakened vessel wall) is extensively covered by yellowish calcified tissue that has already fused as a coherent plate onto the intima of the artery. It is curved to follow the shape of the vessel, and has a consistent thickness of roughly 2–4 mm. The accumulation of this calcified tissue was responsible for the loss of elasticity of this blood vessel. Eventually this caused rupture of the aneurysm and led to the death of this young man.

The description of this 35-year-old male in the autopsy record notes that he was a large, healthy-looking, pale person (AKH, 18 October 1864, 48162/52). During dissection the cause of death was determined to be due to a heart attack ('cardiovascular accident') and the aneurysm in the aorta was a subsequent finding.

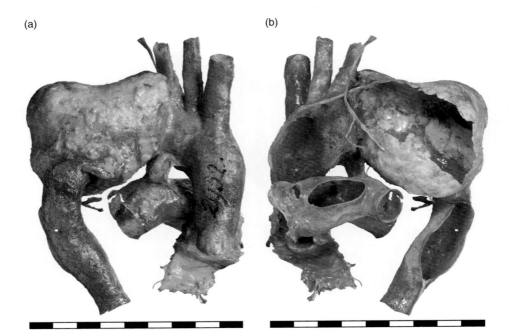

Figure 11.2 Aortic aneurysm with calcifications in the aortic arch, visible as white structures. (a) Posterior view with the widening of the aortic aneurysm and the white solid structure of the calcification particularly clear on the portion of the vessel towards the left side of the image. (b) Anterior view with the vessels opened for better visibility; note the white concretions on the interior surface of the vessel on the right side of the image (MN 2952). Source: NHM Vienna, Reichmann. (A black and white version of this figure will appear in some formats. For the colour version, please refer to the plate section.)

11.3.2 Calcifications of the Pericardium (Fibrous Sac Surrounding the Heart Muscle)

11.3.2.1 Calcified Pericardium: First Example

Pericarditis is inflammation of the pericardium and can be attributed to several aetiological factors, including viral, bacterial, fungal and other infections (Cameron et al., 1987; Pandian et al., 1989). Other possible causes of pericarditis include heart attack or as a complication of heart surgery, other medical conditions, injuries and specific medications (American Heart Association 2016; Cameron et al., 1987; Maisch, 1994).

This macerated example of a portion of a calcified pericardium (MN 17.747/1546; Figure 11.3) (Brandenburg & McGoon, 1987) was prepared by the Wieden Hospital in Vienna in 1934. It is solid and ivory in colour, with a length of 65 mm, width of 40 mm and depth of 45 mm. Inside there is a hollow space with a thickness of only a few millimetres. It most likely enveloped the apex of the heart. The exterior and interior surfaces are smooth, but the pericardium is irregular in shape, with several open spaces. Calcification of the pericardium is relatively rare and often has an

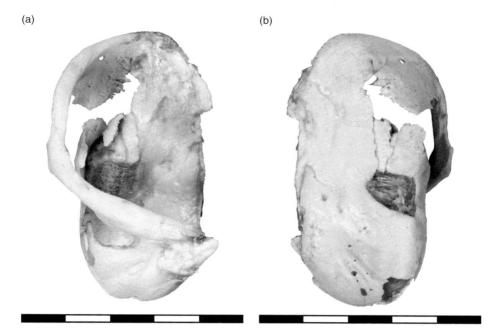

Figure 11.3 Calcified portion of the heart sac (pericardium). (a) Anterior view, with superior aspect at the top of the image. (b) Posterior view, with superior aspect at the top of the image; note that only the calcified portion of the lowest part (apex) of the heart sac is preserved (MN 17.747/1546). Source: NHM Vienna, Reichmann. (A black and white version of this figure will appear in some formats. For the colour version, please refer to the plate section.)

uncertain aetiology, mostly as a result of recurring inflammation, and is frequently associated with constrictive pericarditis (Bergmann et al., 2006; Schwefer et al., 2009; Khalid et al., 2019; Ferguson & Berkowitz, 2010 present a review of its identification, with reference to the causes of cardiac and pericardial calcifications).

On its own, pericarditis is asymptomatic and is neither necessary nor sufficient for a diagnosis of pericardial constriction. Its presence may suggest diffuse pericardial scarring and consequently it has some pathological involvement in pericardial constriction (Nguyen et al., 2014). The autopsy record states that the 46-year-old man from whom this calcified pericardium derives (Wieden 1934-628) did not die from this calcification; a cerebral abscess in the brain was diagnosed as the cause of death by the pathologist conducting the autopsy. Furthermore, pleural oedema was also identified in his lungs, which is often associated with heart problems (Mayo Clinic, 2018).

11.3.2.2 Calcified Pericardium: Second Example

This dried pericardium (which dates to c. 1867; width 140 mm, height 140 mm, depth 110 mm) with attached vessels shows calcification all around the heart sac caused by long-lasting inflammation of the pericardium (pericarditis) (MN 3036; Figure 11.4).

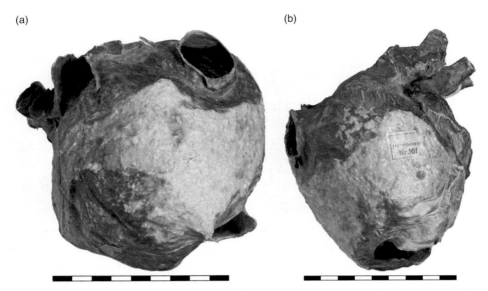

Figure 11.4 Calcified heart sac (pericardium) with dried cardiac soft tissue. (a) Anterior view with the aorta at the top of the image and towards the right side. (b) Inferior view of the posterior aspect of the pericardium showing the extensive yellowish calcified structure; the aorta is directed towards the left side of the image at the top (MN 3036). Source: NHM Vienna, Reichmann. (A black and white version of this figure will appear in some formats. For the colour version, please refer to the plate section.)

The majority of the external surface of the pericardium is encased in a solid 1-mm thick plate of calcified tissue (length 280 mm, maximum height 65 mm). The calcified tissue is yellowish in colour and uneven in texture, with small raised peaks that are irregularly scattered across its surface. The inner surface of the pericardium is relatively smooth and hollow where the heart muscle (myocardium) would have been. The calcification surrounding the heart muscle forms a very thin sub-spherical structure. The autopsy record notes that the male patient was 53 years old at death and his profession is listed as a carter; chronic hepatic cirrhosis and chronic pericarditis were identified as the causes of death (AKH, 1867-51650/851). The body of this man was described as large and bloated.

Carl von Rokitansky prepared this pericardium for teaching. From the 1880s to the 1970s it was part of the hands-on teaching collection of the Institute of Pathology at the Medical University in Vienna.

11.3.3 Calcifications of the Meninges Due to Cardiovascular Disease

11.3.3.1 Calcified Meninges in Connection with Cardiovascular Disease: First Example

This example of the dura mater shows calcifications in the form of widespread white patches covering large parts of its inner side (MN 17.747/566; prepared by Wieden

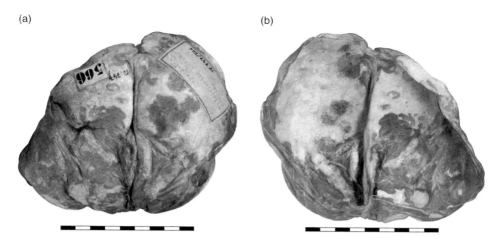

Figure 11.5 Calcified tissue within the meninges (membranous covering of the brain). (a) External/superior view of the dura mater (outermost layer of the three meninges). (b) Internal/inferior view: the white structure visible is calcified tissue within the dried soft tissue of the meninges (MN 17.747/566). Source: NHM Vienna, Reichmann. (A black and white version of this figure will appear in some formats. For the colour version, please refer to the plate section.)

Hospital in 1922; Figure 11.5). This calcified tissue (anteroposterior 140 mm, mediolateral 160 mm, height 45 mm) looks like 'liquid poured into a bowl'. It is visible in both hemispheres but is not symmetrical. The outer surface comprises the dura mater tissue, with calcifications attached only to its inner surface. This calcified structure is smooth and varies in thickness from less than 1 mm to 1.5 mm, with small round mounds extending inwards. As it follows the shape of the brain and skull, the calcification is curved.

The cause of death of this 50-year-old male was recorded in his autopsy record as inflammation of the heart (endocarditis) causing an ulcer of the aortic valve (autopsy record, Hospital Wieden, 15. 9. 1922, page 496). Thus, the calcifications present in the dura mater seemingly had no bearing on the death of the individual. Normal calcifications of the dura increase in frequency with age and are typically of no clinical significance. They are particularly common among the elderly and are rare in children (McKinney, 2017).

11.3.3.2 Calcified Meninges in Connection with Cardiovascular Disease: Second Example

This dried piece of dura mater was prepared by the General Hospital in Vienna in 1871. It was treated with resin and described as *Pseudemembrana ad facie mint. Durae matris* (which means 'pseudo-membrane in the dura mater, according to the latest interpretation'). This example (dimensions: anteroposterior 235 mm, mediolateral 245 mm, height 59 mm) shows extensive calcifications covering the inner side of the tissue of the dura mater (MN 3206; Figure 11.6). The two halves reveal differences in the characteristics of the ossified tissue. One hemisphere has a cream

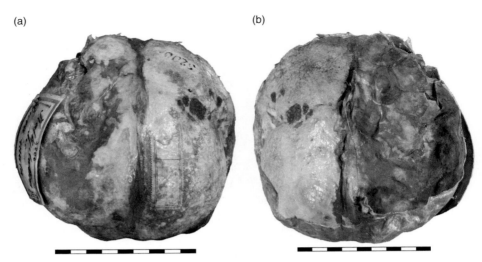

Figure 11.6 Calcified tissue within the meninges. (a) External/superior view of the meningeal tissue: note the cream to yellowish deposits of calcified tissue. (b) Internal/inferior view: the cream to yellowish widespread solid structure within the dried meningeal tissue is the calcified structure (MN 3206). Source: NHM Vienna, Reichmann. (A black and white version of this figure will appear in some formats. For the colour version, please refer to the plate section.)

to yellowish-coloured solid plate covering almost all of its interior surface. The other hemisphere shows irregular patches of calcification of differing thicknesses and sizes, from 1 to 5 mm. All the calcifications are held together by the dried soft tissue of the meninges, and they have a shiny appearance because of the application of resin.

The autopsy record notes that this 48-year-old man was a day labourer who suffered from several health issues prior to death (AKH, 1871-58448/297). The pathologist conducting the autopsy recorded that his pericardium was filled with liquid, the liver was adipohepatic (i.e. fatty degeneration of the liver), the spleen was enlarged and there was bleeding on the brain. The man was described as middle-sized, emaciated and pale. He died of cerebral oedema, according to his autopsy record. As with the example in Section 11.3.3.1, calcifications of the dura mater are common with increasing age and typically asymptomatic. Yet, in both cases, the men also had inflammation of the heart tissue resulting from cardiovascular disease, which suggests that, while clinically asymptomatic, extensive calcifications of the dura mater can be connected to underlying inflammation (McKinney, 2017).

11.4 Conclusions

Calcifications of the cardiovascular system are frequently diagnosed in clinical medicine and surgery (Cinar et al., 2006; Ferguson & Berkowitz, 2010; Ghavidel et al., 2012). The scarcity of cardiovascular calcifications from archaeological contexts can be considered an underrepresentation of their true frequency in the past (Aufderheide & Rodríguez-Martin, 1998; Binder & Roberts, 2014; Biehler-Gomez et al., 2018). A number of factors may explain this underrepresentation, but a good starting point for improving recovery is the ability to identify this type of calcified tissue during the excavation process and when soils are being sieved from grave contexts.

Six examples of cardiovascular calcification from the Pathologic–Anatomical Collection at the Narrenturm were selected for this chapter, representing specific, well-documented and specially prepared examples intended to aid in the future identification of calcified atherosclerotic tissue in archaeological contexts. We have focused our descriptions on these calcifications with the aim of raising awareness of the range of appearance of unusual cardiovascular disease-related calcifications that can occur in the human body. While we have endeavoured to provide detailed descriptions of these calcifications, this study is of course limited by the nature of the preparations (predominantly dried specimens). This study is further biased in that they are exclusively from European males who died between 1850 and 1934, and thus may represent a specific response to cardiovascular disease that could differ in other population demographics. However, the purpose of this chapter is to facilitate and encourage archaeologists in the field, and bioarchaeologists in the laboratory, to recognise and be aware of the diversity of calcifications associated with cardiovascular diseases. Moreover, it is intended to serve as a preliminary reference source for researchers and further encourages very cautious excavation of archaeological burials, including associated grave material such as soil, and the use of pathologic–anatomical collections as reference sources.

As a result of this study, we offer some key points to help with identification in the field.

1. Calcifications tend to be white or cream in colour and quite thin, but may vary in colour according to the soil in the grave.
2. Both their location in relation to the bones of the skeleton and their position in the grave can be used to help identify the nature of the calcification, for example which blood vessel was affected.
3. They tend to be irregular in shape and size, but when colour and location in relation to the skeleton are taken into account, plus their irregular shape, it may be possible to establish a clearer identification and thus possible diagnosis.

Cardiovascular calcifications may vary dramatically in size and shape, from ossified patches in the walls of blood vessels to ossification of the pericardium or the meninges and, given their frequency in populations today (World Health Organization, 2021), they are likely to occur in archaeological contexts as well. We believe that with careful excavation and the use of pathologic–anatomical collections like that in Vienna, in the future further examples of cardiovascular calcifications will be recognised in the field, identified during post-excavation processing and specifically diagnosed in relation to the actual body structures affected.

References

American Heart Association. (2016). What is pericarditis? www.heart.org/en/health-topics/pericarditis/what-is-pericarditis (accessed 18 March 2019).

Aufderheide, A. C. and Rodríguez-Martín C. (1998). *The Cambridge Encyclopedia of Human Paleopathology*. Cambridge: Cambridge University Press.

Bergmann, M., Vitrai, J. and Salman, H. (2006). Constrictive pericarditis: A reminder of a not so rare disease. *European Journal of Internal Medicine*, 17(7), 457–64.

Biehler-Gomez, L., Cappella, A., Castoldi, E., Martrille, L. and Cattaneo, C. (2018). Survival of atherosclerotic calcifications in skeletonized material: Forensic and pathological implications. *Journal of Forensic Sciences*, 63, 386–94.

Binder, M. and Roberts, C. A. (2014). Calcified structures associated with human skeletal remains: Possible atherosclerosis affecting the population buried at Amara West, Sudan (1300–800 BC). *International Journal of Paleopathology*, 6, 20–9.

Brandenburg, R. O. and McGoon, D. C. (1987). The pericardium. In R.O. Brandenburg, V. Fuster, E. R. Giuliani, D. C. McGoon, eds., *Cardiology: Fundamentals and Practice*. Chicago: Year Book Medical, pp. 1654–70.

Buikstra, J. E. (ed.) (2019). *Ortner's Identification of Pathological Conditions in Human Skeletal Remains*, 3rd ed. London: Academic Press.

Cameron, J., Oesterle, S. N., Baldwin, J. C. and Hancock, E. W. (1987). The etiologic spectrum of constrictive pericarditis. *American Heart Journal*, 113(2.1), 354–60.

Cinar, B., Enç, Y., Göksel, O., et al. (2006). Chronic constrictive tuberculous pericarditis: Risk factors and outcome of pericardiectomy. *International Journal of Tuberculosis and Lung Disease*, 10(6), 701–6.

Ferguson, E. C. and Berkowitz, E. A. (2010). Cardiac and pericardial calcifications on chest radiographs. *Clinical Radiology*, 65(9), 685–94.

Ghavidel, A. A., Gholampour, M., Kyavar, M., Mirmesdagh, Y. and Tabatabaie, M. B. (2012). Constrictive pericarditis treated by surgery. *Texas Heart Institute Journal*, 39(2), 199–205.

Khalid, N., Ahmad, S. A. and Shlofmitz, E. (2019). Pericardial calcification. In *StatPearls*. Treasure Island, FL: StatPearls Publishing. Available at www.ncbi.nlm.nih.gov/books/NBK538342/ (accessed 31 October 2022).

McKinney, A. M. (2017). Dural calcifications: Normal locations and appearances. In A. M. McKinney, ed., *Atlas of Normal Imaging Variations of the Brain, Skull, and Craniocervical Vasculature*. Cham, Switzerland: Springer, pp. 391–411.

Maisch, B. (1994). Pericardial diseases, with a focus on etiology, pathogenesis, pathophysiology, new diagnostic imaging methods, and treatment. *Current Opinion in Cardiology*, 9(3), 379–88.

Mayo Clinic. (2018). Pulmonary edema. www.mayoclinic.org/diseases-conditions/pulmonary-edema/symptoms-causes/syc-20377009#:~:text=Pulmonaryedemaisacondition,heartproblemscausepulmonar yedema (accessed 31 October 2022).

Nguyen, T., Phillips, C. and Movahed, A. (2014). Incidental findings of pericardial calcification. *World Journal of Clinical Cases*, 2(9), 455–8.

Ortner, D. J. (2003). *Identification of Pathological Conditions in Human Skeletal Remains*, 2nd ed. London: Academic Press.

Ortner, D. J. and Putschar, W. (1981). *Identification of Pathological Conditions in Human Skeletal Remains*. Washington, DC: Smithsonian Institution Press.

Pandian, N. G., Vignola, P., Johnson, R. A. and Scannell, J. G. (1989). Pericardial diseases. In K. A. Eagle, E. Haber, R. W. DeSanctis and W. G. Austen, eds., *The Practice of Cardiology*. Boston: Little, Brown, pp. 977–1011.

Schamall, D., Haring, E., Nebot, E., et al. (2016). Actinomycosis versus tuberculosis in ancient human bone: A pilot study. Poster presentation at 21st Congress of the European Paleopathology Association.

Schwefer, M., Aschenbach, R., Heidemann, J., Mey, C. and Lapp, H. (2009). Constrictive pericarditis, still a diagnostic challenge: Comprehensive review of clinical management. *European Journal of Cardiothoracic Surgery,* 36(3), 502–10.

Teschler-Nicola, M. and Winter, E. (2013). Meaningful stones: examples from the body stone collection of the Pathological–Anatomical Collection in the 'Fools Tower' Museum for Natural History Vienna (PASiN-NHM). *Archäologie Österreichs,* 24, 43–8.

World Health Organization. (2021). Cardiovascular diseases (CVDs). www.who.int/en/news-room/fact-sheets/detail/cardiovascular-diseases-(cvds) (accessed 31 October 2022).

12 'Absence of Evidence Is Not Evidence of Absence'

Why Is There a Lack of Evidence for Cardiovascular Disease in the Bioarchaeological Record?

Michaela Binder and Charlotte A. Roberts

12.1 Introduction

Over the past few years, bioarchaeological research in combination with genetic as well as contextual evidence has been challenging the misconception that cardiovascular diseases (CVDs) are a problem of modern life and living conditions (Thompson et al., 2013; Binder & Roberts, 2014; and chapters in this volume). However, the evidence for CVDs in the past has so far been largely confined to mummified human remains. The preservation of their soft tissues maintains the pathological evidence linked to CVD, including calcifications, in its original location within the blood vessels in which they developed. This allows for easy recognition of the lesions because the same diagnostic criteria used in clinical practice apply. However, mummified human remains only account for a fraction of the bioarchaeological record of humans in the past, and their preservation only occurs under very specialised environmental conditions or in certain cultural settings. Even if mummies are found, their study is often limited by religious, ethical or indeed financial restrictions, since the scientific analysis of mummified bodies requires specialised equipment such as computed tomography (CT) scanning (Gill-Frerking, 2021). In addition, mummification is often connected to a higher social status and, as a consequence, many insights into health and disease in the past gained from the study of mummified remains is heavily biased towards the elite. The vast majority of bioarchaeological studies focuses on human skeletal remains (Roberts, 2018: 159). In contrast to mummified remains, evidence commonly associated with the advanced stages of CVDs are very rarely documented with skeletal human remains. Consequently, our perception of wider morbidity and mortality patterns in past human populations lacks information about a population's experiences of a broader range of health problems in the past and potential causes of death. However, beyond bioarchaeology, there are other disciplines that can inform us about the history of disease. For example, medical history seen through documentary evidence can hint at what bioarchaeologists might be missing. As an example, the London Bills of Mortality (mid-seventeenth to nineteenth centuries), which list the number of deaths according to cause of death in all 130 parishes of London (Boyce, 2020), includes several causes of death that could be related to CVDs: apoplexy, diabetes, dropsy, French Pox, venereal and even 'suddenly'. Dobson (2008: 234–5), in her chapter on heart disease, further documents relevant historical evidence for CVD, such as the artist Leonardo da Vinci's fifteenth-century observations of atherosclerosis in the blood vessels of the elderly.

In this chapter, potential reasons for the lack of CVD evidence associated with human skeletal remains are explored, including those affecting the survival and identification of CVD calcifications in the archaeological record.

12.2 The Biochemistry of Arterial Calcifications

Calcification or mineralisation of, or within, blood vessels is defined as the pathological deposition of calcium in the vascular tissue, and it commonly occurs in the advanced stages of a wide range of CVDs (Wu, 2013). By far the most common cause of arterial calcification is atherosclerosis, with the resulting accumulation known as atheroma (Demer & Tintut, 2008). While originally assumed to be passive and degenerative, recent clinical research has shown that calcium deposition in the vascular system is an active process and physiologically similar to embryonic new bone formation (Abedin et al., 2004; Demer & Tintut, 2008). Despite pathophysiological differences in the complex pathways of calcification among different forms of vascular calcification (atherosclerosis, medial artery calcification, calcific aortic valve disease, calcific uraemic arteriolopathy and the vascular calcification of chronic inflammation; Table 12.1), they ultimately result in the osteogenic differentiation of vascular cells into ones responsible for the formation of bone tissue (Abedin et al., 2004). Histomorphologically, as well as biochemically, this resulting tissue is indistinguishable from bone, comprising bioapatite embedded in a cellular matrix (Doherty et al., 2003).

12.3 The Taphonomy of Human Bone

The term 'taphonomy' was first coined in 1940 by the Russian palaeontologist Ivan A. Efremov as 'the study of the transition (in all its details) of animal remains from the biosphere into the lithosphere' (Efremov, 1940, cited by Lyman, 2010). In bioarchaeology,

Table 12.1 Types of vascular calcification.

Type of calcification	Location	Associated conditions
Atherosclerotic calcification	Intima	Atherosclerosis, hyperlipidaemia, hypertension, inflammation
Medial vascular calcification	Tunica media	Type 2 diabetes mellitus, end-stage renal disease, advanced age
Aortic valve calcification	Aortic face of the leaflets	Hyperlipidaemia, congenital bicuspid valve, rheumatic heart disease
Vascular calciphylaxis (calcific uraemic arteriolopathy)	Microvessels	Type 2 diabetes, hyperthyroidism, end-stage renal disease

Sources: Abedin et al. (2004); Demer and Tintut (2008).

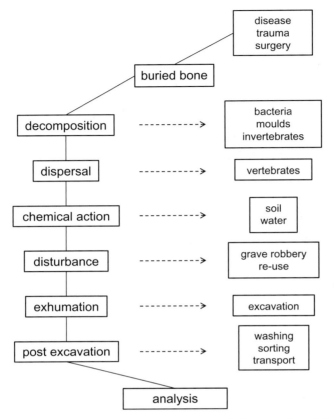

Figure 12.1 Factors influencing bone survival. Source: adapted from Waldron (1987: 56).

this term is usually applied to the processes that alter the physical characteristics of a body as well as its completeness from the time of death until the time of its analysis (White et al., 2011: 49; Martin et al., 2013: 106). In order to understand the composition and nature of any assemblage of human skeletal remains and to draw any valid conclusions when interpreting information gathered from their study, a knowledge and understanding of the many potential mechanisms influencing bone survival is vital (White et al., 2011: 49; Waldron, 1987: 56; Figure 12.1). Consequently, any attempt to try to evaluate the relative absence of evidence of CVDs in the past needs to include a consideration of human bone taphonomy.

The factors influencing the deterioration of human bone after death can broadly be classified into three basic categories (Nawrocki, 1995).

1. *Environmental or extrinsic factors* relate to the environment during deposition and can be further divided into abiotic (e.g. temperature, humidity, water exposure and chemical composition of the soil) and biotic (e.g. plants, carnivores, rodents and insects).

2. *Individual factors* are intrinsic characteristics of the deceased and include body weight, the presence of disease, age at death and biological sex.
3. *Cultural or behavioural actions* are those that act upon a deceased body such as the method of burial, or pre-burial preparatory processes such as embalming.

While a detailed discussion of the ways each of the wide range of taphonomic parameters influence the preservation of the human skeleton after death is beyond the scope of this chapter (for detailed discussions see, for example, Nawrocki, 1995, 2016; Martin et al., 2013: 105ff; Schotsmans et al., 2017), some of the most important factors are briefly highlighted in order to explore the potential of survival and excavation of markers of CVDs in the archaeological human skeletal record.

12.3.1 Environmental (Extrinsic) Factors

Amongst the multitude of factors at play in the taphonomy of human skeletal remains in archaeological contexts, the nature of the soil in which a body is buried has been identified as one of the most influential determinants affecting the survival of bone (Mays, 1998: 17). This includes relative soil acidity, the presence of water and microorganisms, as well as relative temperature. An acidic burial environment can lead to the dissolution of bone mineral (mostly hydroxyapatite) and thus the chance for bone survival decreases with a low soil pH (Lindsay, 1979: 181–2). Water also influences bone survival on both the macro and micro levels (Nawrocki, 2016). At the chemical level, water destroys bone by dissolving ions from the mineral fraction, thereby enhancing chemical degradation (Mays, 1998: 21). Accordingly, as the water permeability of soils increases, bone survival declines. In addition, water is necessary for the survival of microorganisms that contribute to the decay of bone (Mays, 1998: 19). These soil-dwelling organisms include algae, fungi and bacteria, which invade bone and break down bone collagen. This process releases acidic by-products that again dissolve bone mineral. On the other hand, too little water inhibits bacterial growth and in its most extreme form leads to the mummification of the body (Nawrocki, 2016). At a macroscopic level, periodic inundation, as well as freezing and thawing, lead to the fracturing of bone as it expands and contracts upon drying (Nawrocki, 2016). The third contributing factor is temperature, with higher temperatures increasing microbial activity and fostering chemical exchange between water and bone, both of which negatively affect skeletal preservation (Mays, 1998: 21).

Despite this multitude of influences on the survival of human bone in an archaeological setting, human skeletons have been recovered from most environmental contexts worldwide. (For overviews see, for example, Fibiger & Marquez-Grant, 2013 (worldwide); Steckel & Rose, 2002 (USA); Steckel et al., 2019 (Europe); Oxenham & Buckley, 2015 (Southeast Asia and Pacific region); and Edwards, 2013 (Africa).) In theory, if environmental conditions allow for the survival of human bone, then they should also enable the evidence for some CVDs to survive in the form of atheromatous calcifications. Nevertheless, they are largely missing from the archaeological record.

In order to shed light on what environmental conditions may be favourable to preservation of secondary calcified structures in an archaeological context, a meta-study was carried out using pathologically induced calcifications published in the standard palaeopathological literature as a proxy for atheromas. In addition to CVDs, calcification of soft tissue can occur due to a wide range of different pathological processes, including as a result of trauma (myositis ossificans), lung infections including tuberculosis (calcified pleura, nodules; Roberts et al., 1998), diffuse idiopathic skeletal hyperostosis, parasitic infections (e.g. calcified cysts; see Weiss & Møller-Christensen, 1971) and metabolic disorders such as hypervitaminosis A (Steinbock, 1989; Baud & Kramar, 1991). Biochemically, they have been shown to be almost indistinguishable from bone and are the result of similar pathophysiological pathways to calcification in CVDs (Baud & Kramar, 1991). Occasionally, they are also reported in the archaeological record even though, similar to evidence of CVDs, their number seems largely underrepresented when compared with clinical or medical historical records (Binder et al., 2016). Out of only 13 calcifications reported in our review of the literature of archaeological skeletal human remains, seven (53.8 per cent) were recovered from burials in cold and humid environments (Donoghue et al., 1998; Komar & Buikstra, 2003; Quintelier, 2009; Kristjánsdottír & Collins, 2011; Waters-Rist et al., 2014; Binder et al., 2016) and six (46.2 per cent) from burials in hot and dry environments (Strouhal & Jungwirth, 1977; Steinbock, 1989; Perry et al., 2008). No published calcifications came from hot and humid or cold and dry environments. This sample, admittedly very small, shows that the survival of calcified soft tissue is possible in a wide range of differing environmental conditions. The underrepresentation of examples from hot and humid, and cold and dry environments may also not be representative. Consequently, given physiological similarities between bone, pathologically calcified soft tissue in general and arterial calcifications, one can assume that the environmental variables that cause differential preservation are unlikely to account for the absence of calcification-linked CVDs in the archaeological record.

12.3.2 Intrinsic Factors

Individual characteristics of bones such as size, shape and density have also been shown to have a significant influence on the overall preservation of bone (Roberts, 2018: 59). While denser, heavier bones tend to survive better, more porous bones are much more prone to chemical exchange with the environment and thus more likely to deteriorate (Waldron, 1987). Based on this underlying principle, parameters such as biological sex, age at death and disease can also greatly impact the chance of survival of skeletal human remains (Roberts, 2018: 60). The bones of non-adults and older individuals suffering from general bone loss (osteoporosis) are generally less dense than those of adults and therefore also more prone to deterioration in the ground. Moreover, while it is still forming, non-adult bone also contains less bone mineral, which equally affects bone survival. Nevertheless, if conditions are favourable, which is generally more often than not, archaeologists also commonly find non-adult skeletons in cemeteries (Lewis, 2007; Roberts, 2018: 61).

With regard to the intrinsic, physiological characteristics of arterial calcifications, the clinical literature provides some information that may hold clues to the likelihood of preservation in the archaeological record. In the process of CT scanning, radio-density is measured in Houndsfield units (HU), a scale that reflects tissue density (Bibb et al., 2015). Bone density in living patients has been shown to range between +700 HU (cancellous bone) and +3000 HU (cortical bone). However, research on mummified human remains has shown that clinical HU values do not match those of ancient bone and HU values can differ considerably according to preservation conditions (Villa & Lynnerup, 2012). The latter may be partly due to the calibration of CT scanners as they are designed for living patients, which prevents direct comparisons with desiccated bodies (including dry bone). In this study, archaeo-logical dry bone from Scandinavia showed a mean HU value of 1248 for compact/cortical bone. On the other hand, arterial calcifications/plaques in the clinical record have been shown to reach a density of up to 1400 HU (Toussaint et al., 2007). A study analysing CT images of 141 calcified plaques in the extracranial carotid artery revealed values between 644.3 and 1137.7 HU (Saba & Mallarin, 2009). Based on these clinical studies, the density of calcified evidence of CVDs can safely be assumed to rest within the same range as bone. Despite decreasing density due to taphonomic decay of bone, these values suggest that, at least in theory, density cannot be a reason as to why evidence of CVDs rarely survives in the archaeological record, and arterial calcifications should be preserved.

12.3.3 Cultural/Behavioural Factors

The third category of taphonomic factors comprises cultural and behavioural factors related to the treatment of a body after death (Nawrocki, 1995). In the archaeological record this includes procedures for preparing the body for burial and the actual burial practices on the one hand, and all factors pertaining to discovery and excavation, as well as the recovery, handling and storage of the human remains once excavated on the other. While burial practice likely does not have an influence on the survival of calcified evidence of CVDs (the CVDs are contained within the body buried), preparation methods such as embalming and mummification have been shown to significantly impact their survival rate in a positive sense. This is because, to date, the majority of findings of calcified plaques have been made in mummies (see Chapters 3, 4, 5, 6 and 7). However, the removal of organs and surrounding vessels as part of ancient Egyptian mummification can also lead to the loss of several major arteries and this needs to be accounted for (see discussion in Chapter 6). It also remains questionable as to whether mummification allows for better preservation of calcifica-tions due to the biochemical processes used, or that it is simply the protective properties of the surrounding tissue that preserve the calcifications in situ and therefore prevents their loss post burial. This assumption leads us to think about what is perhaps the single most important influence on the preservation of evidence of CVDs: the processes occurring during archaeological excavation and post-excavation work. As these often have the greatest influence on the condition of the individual bones as well as the overall completeness of the skeleton, they warrant a more detailed discussion.

12.4 Excavation and Recovery of Skeletal Human Remains

In addition to all the taphonomic factors related to the burial environment and intrinsic bone characteristics, the excavation strategy represents the single most important factor in the overall preservation and completeness of human skeletal remains in the archaeological record. In an ideal setting, every skeleton is carefully exposed using appropriate tools to avoid any damage (McKinley & Roberts, 1993; Roberts, 2018: 77). Several studies and experiments, as well as the 15 years of personal experience of one of the authors (M. B.) as an excavator, have shown that when bones are only recovered by hand, smaller elements such as finger and hand bones, teeth or non-adult bones are often overlooked (Figure 12.2) (Mays, 1998: 15; see also Mays et al., 2012). In contrast, if all soil surrounding the skeleton or remaining in the grave after the skeleton is lifted is sifted through a fine mesh (<5 mm), the percentage of small bones and bone fragments preserved can be greatly improved. In advanced calcified atherosclerosis or medial vascular calcification, these bone-like structures can reach dimensions of up to several centimetres in

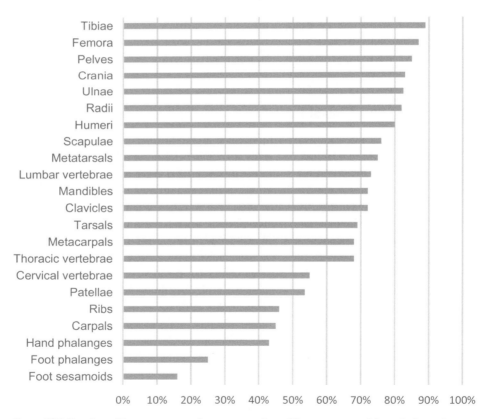

Figure 12.2 Number of bones recovered versus number of bones expected in a skeleton in an excavation where sieving was not carried out. Source: based on the numbers in Mays (1998: 15).

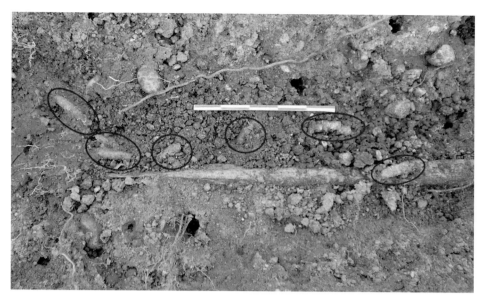

Figure 12.3 Calcified tibial artery in situ in a medieval burial from Austria. (A black and white version of this figure will appear in some formats. For the colour version, please refer to the plate section.)

length and a thickness of several millimetres (Figure 12.3). They therefore exceed the size of many of the skeletal elements in fetal or neonatal skeletons, or of ear or sesamoid bones of adult skeletons. Consequently, careful excavation together with sieving would certainly increase the discovery of calcified evidence of CVDs. Nevertheless, it is acknowledged that in commercial archaeological projects, where most skeletons are excavated, time and money can be limited and sieving of soil may not be an option. This is why bioarchaeologists should work closely with commercial company senior managers to explain the benefits of sieving, especially if those managers are not bioarchaeologists.

With regard to calcifications related to CVDs, sufficient care during recovery and sifting of the soil alone will not always suffice. The morphology of calcified plaques is largely non-specific and only varies marginally in size according to the blood vessel in which it originated. Consequently, in order to allow for further identification and for a diagnosis of the potential underlying causes of such calcifications, as well as providing interpretations within the context of the health of the individuals being studied, knowledge of the calcification's anatomical position (particularly in relation to the bones of the skeleton) is just as important as its mere presence (Figure 12.4). Crucially, identifying calcified plaques in situ, including how they relate to the past position of blood vessels, should be done immediately upon excavation, rather than simply recovering the calcified atheromas from the sieve afterwards.

However, recovery in situ presupposes knowledge on the part of the excavator about the morphology of what there is to find (Table 12.2), and where it might be found. For example, while most excavators will know what small finger and toe bones look like and can therefore find them, if care during excavation permits, in

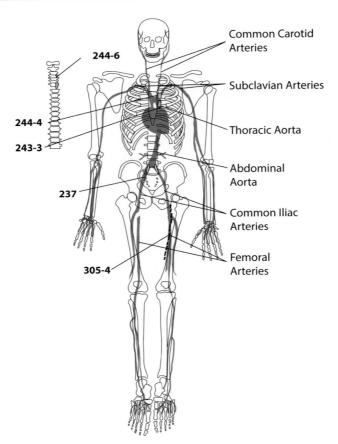

Figure 12.4 Major arteries in the human body and sites most likely to develop arterial calcification. Source: Binder and Roberts (2014). (A black and white version of this figure will appear in some formats. For the colour version, please refer to the plate section.)

both authors' experience human fetal bones have been mistaken for rodent bones and thus recovered together with other animal bones. Only after being correctly identified in the laboratory by the archaeozoologist were they then made available for further analysis to the bioarchaeologist. While this may be less problematic in a cemetery setting, in more unusual burial contexts such as within a house, the context is lost if the burial is not recognised as such, thus preventing any potentially very interesting insights into life in the past.

Returning to the question of calcified evidence of CVDs, the vast majority of excavators, with or without bioarchaeological experience, are not familiar with their morphology, nor do they always appreciate their potential preservation. It may be significant that in both instances reported in this volume (see Chapter 8) where calcifications have been found in situ in archaeological contexts, the discoveries were made by experienced bioarchaeologists with a strong background in human anatomy and palaeopathology. In addition, they were made within the setting of a

Table 12.2 Morphological features of calcified evidence of CVDs in contrast to bone.

	Atheromatous plaque	Medial arterial calcification	Bone
Colour	Yellow	Whitish-brown	Variable, most commonly shades of reddish-brown
Shape	Elongated concave plaques with smooth edges	Hollow regular tubes, smooth edges	Variable, if fragmented irregular edges
Texture/surface	Smooth, even surface with distinctive layering towards the edges	Coarse surface texture	Smooth, dense surfaces in compact bone, spongy appearance in spongious bone
Friability	Very hard	Friable	Variable, depending on bone type, size and state of preservation
Average size	<2–3 cm	<2–3 cm	Variable

Note: data are drawn from the authors' personal observations.

research-led excavation. In these cases, recovery can usually be carried out with fewer time constraints and more care applied during excavation work.

Consequently, we believe that the key to improving the palaeopathological record of evidence of CVDs in the past is to increase knowledge amongst those responsible for excavating human remains of the morphology of CVD-related calcifications. This should accompany the development of refined and careful excavation strategies. In addition, excavators should be better trained in basic human skeletal and vessel anatomy. This would aid in identifying areas of the burial context and skeleton where vessels once may have been so as to have an awareness of where calcified structures are most likely to be preserved (bearing in mind that soils, bones and calcified structures can 'move' during the burial time period). It would also better enable excavators to detect them, and differentiate between bone and calcified structures, and make excavators aware of where calcified structures related to CVD might occur in the grave and next to which bones (Figure 12.4). Atherosclerotic calcifications are most commonly observed in the aortic arch and carotid, subclavian, iliac, renal and femoral arteries. In contrast, medial vascular calcification affects the peripheral arteries of the legs and to a lesser degree the arms.

This volume includes the most comprehensive collection of published archaeological evidence of CVDs found with skeletal human remains. The images provided with each chapter illustrate the wide range of appearance of calcifications and is intended to educate and encourage those who are excavating and analysing human skeletal remains.

12.5 Conclusions and Recommendations

Careful consideration of the main taphonomic factors affecting skeletal preservation has shown that soil conditions, humidity and temperature, as well as size and/or density of bones, are not likely to account for the absence of evidence of CVDs in the archaeological record. Since both tissues (bones and calcified arteries) are biochemically similar, there is no reason why larger calcifications due to CVDs should not be preserved if bone survives too. The main challenge is most likely the lack of recognition and recovery of calcifications and/or lack of attention paid to the careful processing of skeletal remains following recovery.

Consequently, if the number of arterial calcifications recovered in association with human skeletal remains is to increase, thus extending our knowledge about CVD in past human populations, two main changes are needed.

1. Refined recovery strategies.
2. Increased awareness in excavators and in processors and analysers of human skeletal remains about the morphological appearance and anatomical location of these calcifications, and where they are likely to develop and present themselves in relation to the bones of the skeleton in a burial context.

Refined recovery strategies include careful exposure and excavation of the skeleton, paying particular attention to areas where these calcifications may occur and, when appropriate and possible, screening of all sediment removed from the grave context using a fine sieve. The latter should guarantee the detection of even the smallest calcifications. In addition, care also needs to be taken during the cleaning of skeletal remains; this is because the calcified structures often occur in close proximity to the bones of the skeleton and may therefore be found within sediment adhering to the bones.

Equally important is a general awareness of where these calcified structures are most likely to occur. Even though, in theory, arterial calcification can affect all vessels of the cardiovascular system, certain areas have proven to be particularly prone to CVDs, leading to the development of calcifications. Better training of excavators in basic human skeletal anatomy would equally be highly desirable, as this would not only aid in identifying areas of the skeleton where calcified structures might occur, but also better enable excavators to detect, record in situ and differentiate between bone, calcified structure and surrounding matrix.

References

Abedin, M., Tintut, Y. and Demer, L. L. (2004). Vascular calcification: Mechanisms and clinical ramifications. *Arteriosclerosis, Thrombosis and Vascular Biology*, 24, 1161–70.

Baud, C.-A. and Kramar, C. (1991). Soft tissue calcifications in paleopathology. In D. J. Ortner and A. C. Aufderheide, eds., *Human Paleopathology: Current Syntheses and Future Options*. Washington, DC: Smithsonian Institution Press, pp. 87–9.

Bibb, R., Eggbeer, D. and Paterson, A. (2015). *Medical Modelling*. Oxford: Elsevier.

Binder, M. and Roberts, C. (2014). Calcified structures associated with human skeletal remains: Possible atherosclerosis affecting the population buried at Amara West, Sudan (1300–800 BC). *International Journal of Paleopathology*, 6, 20–9.

Binder, M., Berner, M., Krause, H., Kucera, M. and Patzak, B. (2016). Scientific analysis of a calcified object from a post-medieval burial in Vienna, Austria. *International Journal of Paleopathology*, 14, 24–30.

Boyce, N. (2020). Bills of Mortality: Tracking disease in early modern London. *Lancet*, 395, 1186–7.

Demer, L. L. and Tintut, Y. (2008). Vascular calcification: Pathobiology of a multifaceted disease. *Circulation*, 117, 2938–48.

Dobson, M. (2008). *Disease: The Extraordinary Stories Behind History's Deadliest Killers*. London: Quercus.

Doherty, T. M., Asotra, K., Fitzpatrick, L. A., et al. (2003). Calcification in atherosclerosis: Bone biology and chronic inflammation at the arterial crossroads. *Proceedings of the National Academy of Sciences USA*, 100, 11201–6.

Donoghue, H. D., Spigelman, M., Zias, J., Gernaey-Child, A. M. and Minnikin, D. E. (1998). *Mycobacterium tuberculosis* complex DNA in calcified pleura from remains 1400 years old. *Letters in Applied Microbiology*, 27, 265–9.

Edwards, D. N. (2013). African perspectives on death, burial, and mortuary archaeology. In S. Tarlow and L. Nilsson Stutz, eds., *The Oxford Handbook of the Archaeology of Death and Burial*. Oxford: Oxford University Press, pp. 209–26.

Efremov, I. A. (1940). Taphonomy: new branch of paleontology. *Pan-American Geologist*, 74, 81–93.

Fibiger, L. and Marquez-Grant, N. (eds.) (2013). *The Routledge Handbook of Archaeological Human Remains and Legislation: An International Guide to Laws and Practice in the Excavation and Treatment of Archaeological Human Remains*. London: Routledge.

Gill-Frerking, H. (2021). Showing respect to the dead: The ethics of studying, displaying, and repatriating mummified human remains. In D. H. Shin and R. Bianucci, eds., *The Handbook of Mummy Studies*. Singapore: Springer, pp. 59–88.

Komar, D. and Buikstra, J. E. (2003). Differential diagnosis of a prehistoric biological object from the Koster (Illinois) Site. *International Journal of Osteoarchaeology*, 13, 157–64.

Kristjánsdóttir, S. and Collins, C. (2011). Cases of hydatid disease in medieval Iceland. *International Journal of Osteoarchaeology*, 21, 479–86.

Lewis, M. E. (2007). *The Bioarchaeology of Children: Perspectives from Biological and Forensic Anthropology*. Cambridge: Cambridge University Press.

Lindsay, W. L. (1979). *Chemical Equlibria in Soil*. New York: Wiley.

Lyman, R. (2010). What taphonomy is, what it isn't, and why taphonomists should care about the difference. *Journal of Taphonomy*, 8, 1–16.

McKinley, J. I. and Roberts, C. A. (1993). *Excavation and post-excavation treatment of cremated and inhumed remains*. Technical Paper Number 13. Birmingham: Institute of Field Archaeologists.

Martin, D. L., Harrod, R. P. and Pérez, V. R. (2013). *Bioarchaeology: An Integrated Approach to Working with Human Remains*. New York: Springer Science and Business Media.

Mays, S. (1998). *The Archaeology of Human Bones*. London: Routledge.

Mays, S., Vincent, S. and Campbell, G. (2012). The value of sieving of grave soil in the recovery of human remains: an experimental study of poorly preserved archaeological inhumations. *Journal of Archaeological Science*, 39, 248–54.

Nawrocki, S. P. (1995). Taphonomic processes in historic cemeteries. In A. Grauer, ed., *Bodies of Evidence: Reconstructing History Through Skeletal Analysis*. New York: Wiley-Liss, pp. 49–66.

Nawrocki, S. P. (2016). Forensic taphonomy. In S. Blau and D. Ubelaker, eds., *Handbook of Forensic Anthropology and Archaeology*. London: Routledge, pp. 284–94.

Oxenham, M. and Buckley, H. R. (2015). *The Routledge Handbook of Bioarchaeology in Southeast Asia and the Pacific Islands*. London: Taylor & Francis.

Perry, M., Newnam, J. and Gilliland, M. (2008). Differential diagnosis of a calcified object from a fourth to fifth century AD burial in Aqaba, Jordan. *International Journal of Osteoarchaeology*, 18, 507–22.

Quintelier, K. (2009). Calcified uterine leiomyomata from a post-medieval nunnery in Brussels, Belgium. *International Journal of Osteoarchaeology*, 19, 436–42.

Roberts, C. A. (2018). *Human Remains in Archaeology: A Handbook*, 2nd ed. York: Council for British Archaeology.

Roberts, C. A., Boylston, A., Buckley, L., Chamberlain, A. and Murphy, E. (1998). Rib lesions and tuberculosis: The palaeopathological evidence. *Tubercle and Lung Disease*, 79(1), 55–60.

Saba, L. and Mallarin, G. (2009). Window settings for the study of calcified carotid plaques with multi-detector CT angiography. *American Journal of Neuroradiology*, 30(7), 1445–50.

Schotsmans, E., Marquez-Grant, N. and Forbes, S. (eds.) (2017). *Taphonomy of Human Remains: Forensic Analysis of the Dead and the Depositional Environment*. New York: Wiley.

Steckel, R. H. and Rose, J. C. (eds.) (2002). *The Backbone of History: Health and Nutrition in the Western Hemisphere*. Cambridge: Cambridge University Press.

Steckel, R. H., Larsen, C. S., Roberts, C. A. and Baten, J. (eds.) (2019). *The Backbone of Europe: Health, Diet, Work and Violence Over Two Millennia*. Cambridge: Cambridge University Press.

Steinbock, R. T. (1989). Studies in ancient calcified soft tissues and organic concretions. I: A review of structures, diseases, and conditions. *Journal of Paleopathology*, 3, 35–8.

Strouhal, E. and Jungwirth, J. (1977). Ein verkalktes Myoma uteri aus der späten Römerzeit in Aegyptisch-Nubien. *Mitteilungen der anthropologischen Gesellschaft in Wien*, 107, 215–21.

Thompson, R. C., Allam, A. H., Lombardi, G. P., et al. (2013). Atherosclerosis across 4000 years of human history: The Horus study of four ancient populations. *Lancet,* 381, 1211–22.

Toussaint, N. D., Lau, K. K., Polkinghorne, K. R. and Kerr, P. G. (2007). Measurement of vascular calcification using CT fistulograms. *Nephrolology Dialysis and Transplantation*, 22, 484–90.

Villa, C. and Lynnerup, N. (2012). Hounsfield units ranges in CT-scans of bog bodies and mummies. *Anthropologischer Anzeiger*, 69, 127–45.

Waldron, T. (1987). The relative survival of the human skeleton: implications for palaeopathology. In A. Boddington, A. N. Garland and R. C. Janaway, eds., *Death, Decay and Reconstruction: Approaches to Archaeology and Forensic Science*. Manchester: Manchester University Press, pp. 55–64.

Waters-Rist, A. L., Faccia, K., Lieverse, A., et al. (2014). Multicomponent analyses of a hydatid cyst from an Early Neolithic hunter–fisher–gatherer from Lake Baikal, Siberia. *Journal of Archaeological Sciences*, 50, 51–62.

Weiss, D. L. and Møller-Christensen, V. (1971). Leprosy, echinococcosis and amulets: A study of a medieval Danish inhumation. *Medical History*, 15, 260–7.

White, T. D., Black, M. T. and Folkens, P. A. (2011). *Human Osteology*, 3rd ed. Cambridge, MA: Academic Press.

Wu, M., Rementer, C. and Giachelli, C. M. (2013). Vascular calcification: An update on mechanisms and challenges in treatment. *Calcified Tissue International*, 93, 365–73.

Part III

Contemporary Perspectives

13 The Challenging Diagnosis of Cardiovascular Disease in Skeletal Remains

Identifying Atherosclerotic Calcifications from Modern Documented Individuals

Lucie Biehler-Gomez, Emanuela Maderna and Cristina Cattaneo

13.1 Introduction

The very high prevalence of cardiovascular diseases in populations today makes their study unavoidable, necessary and of paramount importance in forensic sciences. Knowledge about pathological conditions affecting a skeletonised individual is crucial information for reconstructing the biological profile of a victim of crime and may be used in the individualisation and identification of an unknown deceased person (Cunha, 2006). In addition, a correct diagnosis of atherosclerosis in skeletal remains may provide information on the cause of death of the individual. For example, atherosclerosis causes stenosis of a blood vessel, which is not a fatal condition per se, but a ruptured plaque can cause a thrombosis and life-threatening complications, including myocardial infarction and stroke (Shah, 2003; Falk, 2006; Libby et al., 2011).

Atherosclerosis is a chronic, progressive, proinflammatory and fibroproliferative condition that creates plaques in the intima layer of the walls of large and medium-sized arteries (Lusis, 2000; Falk, 2006). Atherogenesis is a complicated multistep process that is still not fully understood. The initiation of the lesions is characterised by the accumulation and oxidation of low-density lipoprotein (LDL) particles in a haemodynamic site of preference in the intimal arterial wall. These LDLs, trapped in the subendothelial matrix, release proinflammatory molecules that will recruit monocytes and lymphocytes to the arterial wall, inducing a proinflammatory loop. Monocytes differentiate into macrophages and ingest the oxidised LDL, resulting in 'foam cell' formation or 'fatty streak', a hallmark of early atherosclerotic lesions. Macrophages undertake apoptosis and necrosis, creating a lipid-rich core within the plaque. Smooth muscle cells, which usually heal and repair the arterial wall after an injury, are recruited and migrate from the tunica media into the tunica intima of the artery and accumulate around the necrotic core. They form a fibrous cap, the intermediate lesion of atherosclerosis. Over the years, the lesion progresses in an outward direction, opposite to the lumen of the artery. A silent inflammatory process persists and may lead to plaque rupture, creating advanced lesions and setting the stage for thrombosis (Lusis, 2000; Glass & Witztum, 2001; Libby, 2003; Falk, 2006).

Over time, these plaques calcify. This ectopic and dystrophic calcification mechanism is an active, organised and regulated process akin to bone formation and performed by cells phenotypically similar to chondrocytes, osteoblasts and osteoclasts (Wexler et al., 1996; Doherty et al., 2003). Given that these calcified plaques are the direct product of the disease, they can act as surrogate markers for atherosclerosis (Doherty et al., 2003). As calcified material, they are able to survive decompositional processes and can therefore be found in skeletonised remains (Biehler-Gomez et al., 2018a).

The recovery of atherosclerotic calcifications among the skeletal remains of a given individual warrants the diagnosis of cardiovascular disease. This seems like a rather straightforward process; why then has atherosclerosis not been more commonly diagnosed in the context of skeletal remains? The answer is twofold: first, a careful and meticulous analysis of the skeleton and the associated soil is absolutely pivotal in the recovery of atherosclerotic calcifications in an archaeological excavation as much as in a forensic context (Subirana-Domènech et al., 2012; Biehler-Gomez et al., 2018a; see also Chapter 12); second, to diagnose the cardiovascular disease, one first needs to be able to recognise and identify its surrogate markers. Indeed, anthropologists cannot find what they are not trained to recognise.

In order to test the degree of awareness of atherosclerotic calcifications amongst students and professionals, we created a scenario where atherosclerotic calcifications (10–15 calcifications from modern and documented cases; Biehler-Gomez et al., 2018a) were placed together and close to the bones of a complete skeleton (from the CAL Milano Cemetery Skeletal Collection) aged over 60 (Cattaneo et al., 2018). This scenario was presented to undergraduate and graduate students in anthropology during practical classes as well as to experts attending international forensic conferences and workshops, in particular the 2017 Forensic Anthropology Society of Europe (FASE) meeting in Milan and the 2018 International Committee of the Red Cross (ICRC) Workshop on Forensic Human Identification of the Dead from Armed Conflicts and Catastrophes, also in Milan. In both student and professional settings, a lecture on skeletal pathological changes was held prior to the practical exercise, in which atherosclerotic calcifications were presented and discussed. However, not one person recognised the atherosclerotic calcifications in the practical scenario. Despite the lecture given beforehand and the ideal scenario where a pile of intact and clean calcifications, separated from associated soil, was placed in a single location (very unlikely in a real case), no trained student, forensic anthropologist, archaeologist, physical anthropologist, medical practitioner or forensic pathologist recognised the markers of disease. After they were told the true nature of these structures, they explained that while they saw them, they assumed that they were part of the soil or that they were unidentifiable bone fragments and instantly discarded them from further consideration. This experiment demonstrates the importance of training for the identification of atherosclerotic calcifications, even for experts in the field (see also Chapter 12).

The aim of this chapter is therefore to provide documentation on the characteristics of atherosclerotic calcifications from modern documented cases so that archaeologists

13.2 Materials and Methods

A total of 373 atherosclerotic calcifications from 72 modern and documented individuals were examined in this study (Table 13.1).

Of these, 200 were extracted from 60 well-preserved cadavers during autopsies performed at the Medico-Legal Institute of Milan (Italy), in accordance with Article 41 of the Italian National Police Mortuary Regulation (10 September 1990, no. 285); 21 individuals were female and 39 were male. While sex information was available for all individuals, age at death was only available for seven individuals in the sample. This gives a mean age of 74, ranging from 58 to 89 years. The causes of death included myocardial infarction and violent death (e.g. car accidents), but their medical histories were not known. The recognition of the calcifications was facilitated by their in-situ position, within the wall of the arteries, and thus constitute a gold standard for a diagnosis of atherosclerosis (Figure 13.1a). The soft-tissue samples extracted during autopsies were placed in ambient water in small containers that were incompletely closed and the water was changed weekly. The samples were macerated for several weeks until complete separation from the remaining soft tissue had been achieved. Several atherosclerotic calcifications were retrieved in each soft tissue extraction. Ultimately, the recovered calcifications were dried at ambient temperature.

The remaining 173 calcifications were collected from 12 skeletons in the CAL Milano Cemetery Skeletal Collection (Cattaneo et al., 2018), a modern and documented osteological collection housed and under study at the Laboratorio di Antropologia e Odontologia Forense (LABANOF), in the University of Milan, Italy. The collection is both contemporary (comprising individuals who lived and died in the twentieth century) and documented (each individual is associated with documentation and diagnoses performed by modern medical doctors). The individuals had been buried in coffins in the largest cemetery of Milan (Cimitero Maggiore) for at least 15 years before being exhumed by cemetery workers. Once completely skeletonised, and if unclaimed by relatives, they could be accessioned into the collection, in accordance with Article 43 of the Italian National Police Mortuary Regulation

Table 13.1 Details of the study sample.

	No. of cases	No. of calcifications	No. of males	No. of females	Mean age (years)	Minimum age (years)	Maximum age (years)
Autopsied individuals	60	200	39	21	74.4[*]	58[*]	89[*]
Cemetery skeletons	12	173	6	6	83.4	69	102

[*] Data based on the seven individuals for which age at death was available at the time of the study.

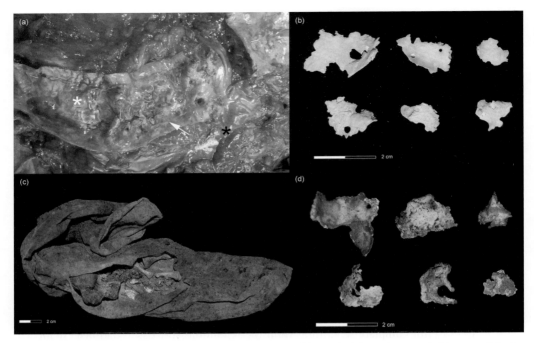

Figure 13.1 Atherosclerotic plaques found in situ. (a) A calcifying atheroma (white arrow) in the open aorta (white asterisk) in a well-preserved cadaver taken during an autopsy at the Medico-Legal Institute of Milan (black asterisk shows the diaphragm). (b) Details of atherosclerotic calcifications following maceration of an atheroma and complete separation of the soft tissue. (c) Atherosclerotic calcifications found in the sock of an individual from the CAL Milano Cemetery Skeletal Collection under study at the LABANOF (University of Milan), exhumed after 15 years of burial in a cemetery of Milan. (d) Details of atherosclerotic calcifications recovered with skeletal remains. (A black and white version of this figure will appear in some formats. For the colour version, please refer to the plate section.)

(10 September 1990, no. 285). Each individual in the collection is associated with documentation that includes demographic data as well as a death certificate that specifies the cause of death and any additional condition related to it (Cattaneo et al., 2018). Thus, 12 individuals from the CAL Milano Cemetery Skeletal Collection were selected based on their associated documentation and, in particular, their ante-mortem clinical diagnosis of vasculopathy (a general term used to describe any disease affecting blood vessels) or atherosclerosis. Six individuals were female and six were males, with age at death ranging from 69 to 102 years and a mean age at death of 83 years. All the individuals died of natural causes following cardiac or pulmonary complications. The calcifications were collected after careful and meticulous sieving of the associated remains (soil and dirt collected with the remains during exhumations) using a 1.5-mm woven wire sieve, the content of the cranial vault (when the state of preservation was good) and that of clothing such as tights or socks. The calcifications were identified by morphological comparison with autopsy calcifications, as reported in a previous study (Biehler-Gomez et al., 2018a).

Macroscopic analysis of the calcifications consisted of recording multiple specific characteristics, including shape, dimensions (measured with vernier callipers) and colour.

Histological analysis was performed on undecalcified and decalcified sections, following previous studies (Biehler-Gomez et al., 2018b). Ten atherosclerotic calcifications were processed for undecalcified histological analysis, including three extracted from autopsies and seven from the cemetery skeletons (Table 13.2). Samples were submitted to a horizontal grindstone (Struers DAP-7) with abrasive discs (Buehler micro cut discs, grains of 180, 320, 500, 1200, 2400, and 4000) used progressively. The sections obtained were then fixed in Pertex (mounting medium for light microscopy; Histolab, Göteborg, Sweden) and left to solidify for 72 hours at ambient temperature before observation with an optical microscope.

Eight atherosclerotic calcifications were subject to decalcified analysis, four extracted from autopsies and four from cemetery skeletons (Table 13.2). The plaques were first fixed in formalin (pH 7–7.6, ratio 20 : 1 v/v) for 24 hours and decalcified at room temperature in 14 per cent hydrochloric acid (Decalc; Histo-Line Laboratories, Milan). Each section was then rinsed in tap water for 24 hours, dehydrated in alcohol (the tissues were processed using increasing concentrations of alcohol, with 70% alcohol usually employed as the first solution and 100% as the last solution) and embedded in paraffin. The blocks were stained with haematoxylin and eosin (H&E) and 5-μm sections were cut for observation under the microscope.

In addition, scanning electron microscopy/energy dispersive spectrometry (SEM-EDS) was performed on three atherosclerotic calcifications from autopsied individuals and two from the cemetery (Table 13.2). This was undertaken using a Cambridge Stereoscan 360 with an electron gun, vacuum pump, and detector from 138 eV to 5.9 keV, along with image acquisition software (Oxford Link Pentafet, Oxford, UK). This process allowed the structural and elemental composition of the vascular calcifications to be determined.

13.3 Results

One of the advantages of recovering atherosclerotic calcifications from autopsied cadavers is the unequivocal knowledge of their original location in the body. Thus, of the 60 atheromatous samples (one per individual), 51 originated in the aorta, 5 in the iliac arteries, 2 in the carotid arteries, 1 in the pulmonary artery and 1 in the basilar artery. In comparison, the exact original location of the atherosclerotic calcifications from the cemetery skeletons remains unknown. Nonetheless, some were found in situ; this was the case of a plaque attached to dried soft tissue remains on the left side of a lower lumbar vertebra, suggesting the abdominal aorta (Biehler-Gomez et al., 2018b). Despite this variation in the quantity and quality of all three analyses of the calcifications (macroscopic, histological and SEM-EDS), they provided similar and complementary results regardless of their original location in the body.

Table 13.2 Distribution of the samples per type of analysis.

		Histological analysis		
	Morphological analysis	Undecalcified protocol	Decalcified protocol	SEM-EDS
Autopsied individuals	200	3	4	3
Cemetery skeletons	173	7	4	2

13.3.1 Macroscopic Analysis

Atherosclerotic calcifications were stratified convex–concave plaques, with dimensions of 1–4 mm thick and 5–34 mm long. When extracted from well-preserved cadavers and macerated in tap water until they were completely separated from the soft tissue, they appeared pale yellow. However, in the buried (cemetery) individuals the plaques ranged in colour from yellow to brown due to taphonomic alterations, including the physicochemical effects of decomposition and the characteristics of soil (Figure 13.2).

These vascular calcifications presented two surfaces: concave and convex. The concave surface, which faces the lumen of the artery, is even and smooth textured, modelled by the continuous passage of blood (Figure 13.2a). The convex surface, adjacent to the middle layer of the artery, or tunica media, is rough to the touch. It is also multilayered due to successive calcification processes that give the plaques their stratified appearance (Figure 13.2b). This multi-layered surface is consistent with the pathogenesis of atherosclerotic plaques, which develop over time in an outward direction (Libby, 2003). When forming, atheromas take on the shape of the artery affected, which gives them their concave–convex or half-cylindrical shape that is represented in the resulting calcifications (Figure 13.2c).

13.3.2 Histological Analysis

On the one hand, histological sections of semi-thin decalcified plaque samples from both autopsied and cemetery individuals and stained with H&E show a clear stratification within the calcifications: the arterial layers (tunica adventitia and tunica media) are identifiable and surround a core of extracellular lipids and cholesterol crystals, as well as some macrophage (foam) cells that were identified as 'ghost' elements (Figures 13.3 and 13.4). In some cases, it was even possible to observe a medial calcification core (Figure 13.3d, e, dark purple staining). These observations highlight the stratified nature of atherosclerotic calcifications and corroborate the aetiology of atherosclerotic plaques. Indeed, they are formed in the tunica intima of large and medium-sized arteries by the deposition of macrophages and lipoproteins

Diagnosis of Cardiovascular Disease in Skeletal Remains 235

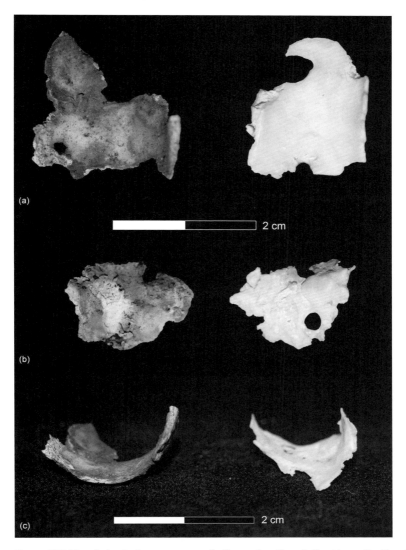

Figure 13.2 Morphological appearance of atherosclerotic calcifications. On the right are atherosclerotic calcifications after extraction from well-preserved cadavers during autopsies at the Medico-Legal Institute of Milan and after maceration for several weeks (until the soft tissue was completely separated); note the pale-yellow coloration of the plaques. On the left are atherosclerotic calcifications collected with skeletal remains of an individual from the identified CAL Milano Cemetery Skeletal Collection (under study at the LABANOF, University of Milan); note the coloration of the plaques, which ranges from yellow to brown. (a) View from the interior of the artery: Note the smooth and even concave surface of the plaque. (b) View from the exterior of the arterial wall: Note the multilayered convex surface of the plaque. (c) Cross-sectional view: Note the convex–concave or half-cylindrical shape of the calcifications. (A black and white version of this figure will appear in some formats. For the colour version, please refer to the plate section.)

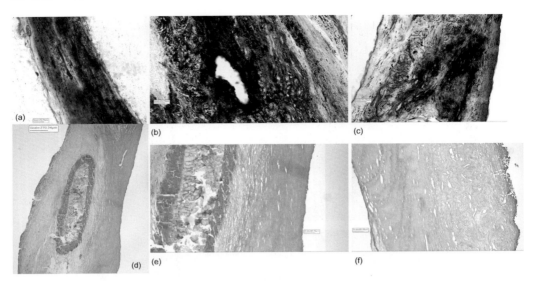

Figure 13.3 Histological comparison of undecalcified (a–c) and decalcified (d–f) sections of atherosclerotic calcifications extracted from well-preserved cadavers. Undecalcified sections illustrate the stratified structure of atherosclerotic plaques; original magnification ×2.5 (a), ×10 (b), ×10 (c). Decalcified sections from the same autopsy plaque, semi-thin sample stained with H&E showing 'ghosts' of macrophages (foam) cells and a calcified core (d and e, dark purple); original magnification ×2.5 (d), ×10 (e), ×10 (f). (A black and white version of this figure will appear in some formats. For the colour version, please refer to the plate section.)

decaying in a necrotic core. The initial atheromatous lesion is then covered by smooth muscle cells that have migrated from the tunica media of the artery, forming a fibrous plaque (Lusis, 2000; Glass & Witztum, 2001; Libby, 2003; Falk, 2006). Additionally, these histological results suggest a continuum between the tunica intima and the atherosclerotic plaque. On the other hand, undecalcified histological sections of atherosclerotic plaques present a rather homogeneous consistency with darker elements and margins. However, the structure of the calcified atheroma is still observable (Figures 13.3 and 13.4) and the 'ghost' of the calcification core may be identified (Figure 13.3b).

13.3.3 Scanning Electron Microscopy and Energy Dispersive Spectrometry

Scanning electron microscopy images of atherosclerotic calcifications confirmed their stratified nature at a higher resolution, observable in cross-sectional view, but no other structures could be identified using this technique (Figure 13.5). SEM coupled with EDS provided details of the chemical composition of the plaques; they appeared to be formed mostly of carbon, calcium and phosphorus, compatible with a calcified material, and occasional traces of magnesium and sodium.

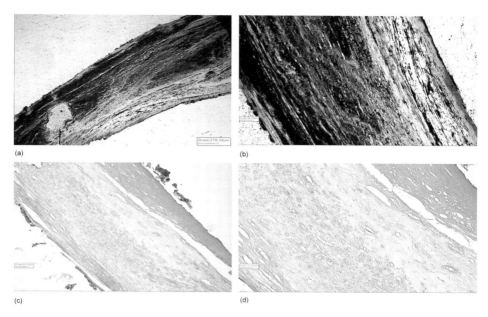

Figure 13.4 Histological comparison of undecalcified (a, b) and decalcified (c, d) sections of atherosclerotic calcifications collected with skeletal remains of an individual from the CAL Milano Cemetery Skeletal Collection (Milan, Italy). Undecalcified sections: original magnification ×2.5 (a), ×10 (b). Decalcified sections of the same calcification stained with H&E, with post-mortem contamination (c, brown staining) and 'ghosts' of macrophages (foam) cells; original magnification ×10 (c), ×20 (d). (A black and white version of this figure will appear in some formats. For the colour version, please refer to the plate section.)

13.4 Discussion

13.4.1 Macroscopic Analysis

Although there is a profusion of published data on atherogenesis (Lusis, 2000; Glass & Witztum, 2001; Libby, 2003; Falk, 2006) and calcified atherosclerosis in the medical literature (Sangiorgi et al., 1998; Fayad & Fuster, 2001; Jang et al., 2002; Becker et al., 2003; Rudd et al., 2010; Yang et al., 2017), there is a regrettable lack of information on how these atherosclerotic plaques can be recognised macroscopically. In fact, information from the literature is exclusively palaeopathological and can be summarised as follows: plaques suspected to be atherosclerotic calcifications are irregular, oval-shaped or flattened, with a hard texture and a semicircular outline (Aufderheide & Rodríguez-Martín, 1998: 79; Binder & Roberts, 2014), appearing as 'calcified flakes varying in length from a few millimetres up to 2 cm long' (Aufderheide & Rodríguez-Martín, 1998: 79).

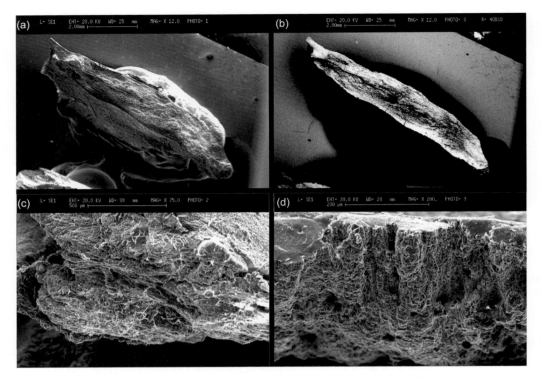

Figure 13.5 Scanning electron microscope images of atherosclerotic calcifications (magnifications ×12, ×75 and ×200). (a, b) Atherosclerotic calcifications from the same autopsy (b, back-scatter detector). (c, d) Images of a single atherosclerotic plaque from an individual in the CAL Milano Cemetery Skeletal Collection (University of Milan, Italy).

Following the analysis of 373 atherosclerotic calcifications from known and documented individuals, we can now describe these vascular plaques. Atherosclerotic calcifications are stratified convex–concave plaques with a yellow to brown coloration, depending on taphonomic alterations. They present a smooth concave luminal surface modelled by the continuous passage of the blood, and a multilayered convex external surface that gives them their stratified structure. This is the result of a successive calcification process over time, consistent with the pathogenesis of atherosclerotic calcifications progressing in an outward direction (Libby, 2003).

Calcifications in the body may be classified into six categories (Table 13.3). Macroscopically, these can be differentiated from atherosclerotic calcifications based on morphological characteristics.

When considering differential diagnoses, this 'convex–concave plaque' shape is distinguishable from the round/oval mass of hydatid and ovarian cysts, gallstones, leiomyomas, lithopaedions, calcified lymph nodes and ovaries, but also from the small mass of psammoma bodies, aortic valve calcifications, phleboliths and mesenteric cysts. Similarly, the irregular shape of urinary calculi or heterotopic calcifications

Table 13.3 Concretions/calcifications that may be confused with atherosclerotic calcifications.

Type of calcification		Morphology	Reference	Archaeological (A)/clinical (C) reference
Trauma	Heterotopic calcification	Irregular shape, smooth outer cortex; various sizes (a few millimetres to a few centimetres)	DiMaio & Francis (2001)	C
Neoplasia	Leiomyoma	Ovoid mass with smooth irregular surface	Baud & Kramar (1991)	A
	ovarian cyst	Round mass; may show vascular impressions	Komar & Buikstra (2003); Özdemir et al. (2015)	A
	Mesenteric cyst	Relatively small ovoid mass	Komar & Buikstra (2003); Özdemir et al. (2015)	A
Infection	Calcified lymph node	Ovoid mass with numerous perforations and eggshell-like calcification	Baud & Kramar (1991); Komar and Buikstra (2003)	A
	Hydatid cyst	Ovoid and hollow mass with irregular external surface and smooth internal surface	Baud & Kramar (1991)	A
Stones	Gallstone	Ovoid mass with cross-sectional surface showing cholesterol crystals, concentric layers or amorphous filling	Biehler-Gomez et al. (2019); Kim et al. (2003)	C
	Urinary stone	Small hard mass of irregular shape	Abboud (2008)	C
Vascular	Aortic valve calcification	Small nodules	Demer & Tintut (2008)	C
	Tunica media calcification	Long and thin cylindrical calcification (not obstructing the lumen of the artery)	Biehler-Gomez et al. (2018a)	A/C
	Phlebolith	Small round mass	Armentano et al. (2012)	A
Other	Calcified pleural plaque	Large, hard and flat plaque with an irregular surface	Baud & Kramar (1991)	A
	Non-neoplastic cysts (e.g. ovaries)	Ovoid mass; may show vascular impressions	Komar & Buikstra (2003)	A
	Psammoma body	Size of a grain of sand	Komar & Buikstra (2003); Özdemir et al. (2015)	A
	Lithopaedion	Ovoid mass; may show vascular impressions	Komar & Buikstra (2003)	A

allow for differentiation from intimal artery calcifications. Differentiation from calcified pleural plaques and tunica media calcifications is more challenging, especially if the calcification is fragmented. Nonetheless, the flat shape of calcified pleural plaques and the thin single-layer structure of calcifications of the tunica media contrast with the multilayered convex–concave shape of atherosclerotic calcifications.

13.4.2 Histological Analysis

The microscopic analysis of 18 atherosclerotic calcifications from autopsied cadavers and cemetery skeletons (buried for at least 15 years) illustrates characteristic features of vascular plaques, including a calcified lipid cholesterol core, successive fibrous layers and the 'ghosts' of macrophage (foam) cells. These findings are consistent with the literature describing soft-tissue samples (Stary et al., 1995; Virmani et al., 2000; Van Engelen et al., 2013; Ababneh et al., 2014; Torii et al., 2019) and with the pathogenesis of the plaques (Lusis, 2000; Glass & Witztum, 2001; Libby, 2003; Falk, 2006).

In both undecalcified and decalcified histological analyses, atherosclerotic calcifications show a clearly stratified structure in the form of successive layers deposited one on top of the other (Figures 13.3 and 13.4). This multilayered structure is consistent with their pathogenesis and morphological characteristics (Figure 13.2). In addition, these findings reflect the clinical description of soft-tissue samples (Stary et al., 1995; Virmani et al., 2000; Van Engelen et al., 2013; Ababneh et al., 2014). However, this stratified structure is not specific to atherosclerotic calcifications as other biological calcifications may be constituted of successive layers, such as gallstones and urinary stones (Steinbock, 1990a, 1990b; Biehler-Gomez et al., 2019), cysts (Charatsi et al., 2015), phleboliths (Gouvêa Lima et al., 2015) and psammoma bodies (Das, 2009). However, these are distinct pathological entities that can be clearly distinguished macroscopically (Table 13.3) and histologically from intimal artery calcifications.

While these microscopic findings present considerable value for the recognition of atherosclerotic plaques in samples with a post-mortem interval of up to 15 years (hence, in forensic contexts), could they be identified in archaeological human remains? To the best of our knowledge, no histological studies have been performed on archaeological atherosclerotic calcifications. Nonetheless, the 'ghosts' of macrophage (foam) cells in fibrous layers should be observable even after very long post-mortem intervals (such as archaeological time frames). In fact, they can be seen on thin sections of mummified remains from the seventeenth century (Kim et al., 2015; Gaeta et al., 2019). The lipid cholesterol core may not be visible due to degradation phenomena but could be transformed into cholesterol crystals (in a cleft) as documented by Gaeta et al., (2019) in mummies (see also Chapter 3).

The microscopic study of histological sections of intravascular calcifications stained with H&E can provide valuable information concerning the composition and detailed structure of atherosclerotic plaques. In fact, it has also been shown that their composition and size influence the likelihood of rupture of the plaque, which can result in life-threatening cardiovascular and cerebrovascular events (Shah, 2003; Libby et al., 2011).

Diagnosis of Cardiovascular Disease in Skeletal Remains **241**

Moreover, microscopic analysis can provide the ability to differentiate vascular calcifications of the arteries. According to clinical literature (Towler, 2008), there are at least two types of pathologically induced calcium phosphate deposition in arterial walls: intimal calcification and medial calcification, also named Mönckeberg's mediasclerosis or Mönckeberg's mediacalcinosis (Mönckeberg, 1903). Intimal (tunica intima) artery calcifications can be found in any large or medium-sized artery (Falk, 2006), whereas medial (tunica media) artery calcifications are more commonly encountered in the abdominal aorta, aortic arch, popliteal and peroneal arteries as well as the tibial and femoral arteries (Mönckeberg, 1903). Medial or Mönckeberg's calcifications are considered aetiologically different from intimal artery calcifications. In the latter, calcium phosphate crystals are located within the cholesterol-rich lesions characteristic of atherosclerosis, and monocytes, macrophages and lipids are found in the tunica media, while they are absent in the pathogenesis of medial artery calcifications (Yoshida et al., 2011). Consequently, histological analyses can give a clearer picture of the origin of calcifications formed in the tunica intima, tunica media or both. As such, histological support has been considered essential in clarifying diagnoses based on clinical imaging (such as CT; Charlier et al., 2014).

As outlined above, calcifications found associated with skeletal remains are not restricted to atherosclerosis; other conditions may lead to similar pathological changes. A histological assessment provides a clearer picture of the pathogenesis of these calcifications and the arterial layering, allowing the differentiation of atherosclerotic calcifications from other calcification or ossification mechanisms. For this reason, morphological analyses supported by histological observations are recommended for accurate evaluation of these structures.

13.4.3 Scanning Electron Microscopy and Energy Dispersive Spectrometry

Like morphological and histological analyses, SEM images illustrated the stratified structure of atherosclerotic plaques, corroborating SEM findings in the clinical literature (Schembri et al., 2008; Curtze et al., 2016). In addition, EDS analysis provided the chemical composition of the plaque, which was consistent with calcified material. By comparison with classic microscopy, while the SEM multilayered shape cannot be considered diagnostic of atherosclerotic calcifications, histological thin sections provided characteristic details of the vascular calcifications, including cores of extracellular lipids and the 'ghosts' of macrophage (foam) cells. These features may be directly related to the intimal atherosclerotic process and may thus be useful in the identification of atherosclerotic calcifications.

13.4.4 Recovery and Significance

Diagnosing atherosclerosis in archaeological skeletons relies on the recovery and identification of atherosclerotic calcifications, which act as surrogate markers of cardiovascular disease. However, due to the absence of training for those who may come across them, most are unaware of these fragile structures that may be found in archaeological excavations or in forensic settings.

The prerequisite for a potential diagnosis is their recovery. The finding of atherosclerotic calcifications requires careful and meticulous excavation as well as sieving of the associated soil, any dried soft tissue and the contents of clothing. While external factors may lead to rapid recovery situations, finding calcifications demands patience and care.

In living individuals, well-preserved cadavers and mummified remains from archaeological contexts, atherosclerosis is recognised through characteristics such as luminal narrowing, thickening of an arterial wall and atheromatous plaque findings, which is made easier by the presence of the arteries and the imaging of atheromas and calcifications within their walls (Figure 13.1a, b). In skeletonised individuals, the soft tissues of the body, including arteries, have undergone decomposition. Therefore, the true in-situ position of vascular calcifications can be altered. Despite this difficulty, some situations may aid in overcoming this issue.

In skeletonised individuals from forensic contexts, dried soft tissue may be found associated with the bones. For example, following 15 years of burial a cemetery individual had an atherosclerotic calcification embedded in dried soft tissue still attached to the anterior side of the body of a lower thoracic vertebra. In addition, the presence of clothing can be common in decomposing and skeletonised individuals in forensic situations. Clothing can protect the fragile structure of atherosclerotic plaques from taphonomic processes and this can aid in their identification (Subirana-Domènech et al., 2012). Atherosclerotic calcifications may be recovered in socks and tights even after several years of burial (Biehler-Gomez et al., 2018a), as demonstrated in the present study (Figure 13.1c, d). However, although clothing can preserve the integrity of these delicate cardiovascular disease-related structures and provide an additional argument for their identification, it cannot prevent their separation from their original anatomical position. For instance, in the case of tights, an atherosclerotic calcification originating from the abdominal aorta and localised in the pelvic area could be found all the way down the legs to the feet because of movement during the handling of the skeletal remains. Thus, care is needed when making assumptions about the anatomical site of origin of atherosclerotic plaques based on their recovery location.

Assuming one is able to recover and identify atherosclerotic calcifications with skeletal remains, what are the implications of such a discovery? What does it mean? In an archaeological context, it demonstrates that, contrary to popular belief, the lack of evidence of atherosclerosis in the archaeological record is no proof of the absence of the disease in ancient populations. As established with the analysis of ancient mummies, atherosclerosis did affect people in ancient times and evidence of the disease should therefore also be found with skeletal remains.

However, regardless of the setting, whether archaeological or forensic, the identification of atherosclerotic calcifications is fundamental for the construction of a precise and informative biological profile or osteobiography. The aim of the profile is to describe the characteristics of an individual's life from the study of their skeletal remains, or indeed their preserved body. A diagnosis of atherosclerosis would add specific information about the health of the person, including identifying or arguing for potential risk factors that could have caused cardiovascular disease.

While the core aim of bioarchaeology is to understand the lives and deaths of our ancestors through their remains, the stakes are higher in forensic anthropology. This is particularly the case for unknown deceased people or victims of mass catastrophes where the analysis of human remains should provide as much information as possible to help identify the individual(s). In this context, atherosclerotic calcifications, as unique skeletal features that can distinguish one individual from another, can be used for individualisation (Cunha, 2006). For instance, if ante-mortem medical images or reports of atherosclerosis are available, a match specific to a single individual may be obtained by superimposing the exact location and morphological characteristics of atherosclerotic calcifications in the deceased with the location and shape of the calcifications from the ante-mortem imaging/reports, thus providing a strong argument in favour of a positive identification of the individual.

13.5 Conclusions

Atherosclerotic calcifications are the direct product of atherosclerosis and, as a result, they can act as surrogate markers for the vascular condition. The diagnosis of cardiovascular disease from skeletal remains thus solely depends on the recovery and recognition of these fragile markers of pathological change. Nonetheless, reports of the diagnosis of this condition in the forensic and archaeological literature are scarce. Careful and meticulous recovery of calcified structures associated with skeletonised remains and preserved bodies, as well as a knowledge of what to expect (e.g. morphology, size, location), could help forensic anthropologists and bioarchaeologists better recognise and identify atherosclerotic calcifications.

References

Ababneh, B., Rejjal, L., Pokharel, Y., et al. (2014). Distribution of calcification in carotid endarterectomy tissues: comparison of micro-computed tomography imaging with histology. *Vascular Medicine*, 19, 343–50.

Abboud, I. A. (2008). Mineralogy and chemistry of urinary stones: Patients from North Jordan. *Environmental Geochemistry and Health*, 30, 445–63.

Armentano, N., Subirana, M., Isidro, A., Escala, O. and Malgosa, A. (2012). An ovarian teratoma of late Roman age. *International Journal of Paleopathology*, 2, 236–9.

Aufderheide, A. C. and Rodríguez-Martín, C. (1998). *The Cambridge Encyclopedia of Human Paleopathology*. Cambridge: Cambridge University Press.

Baud, C.-A. and Kramar, C. (1991). Soft tissue calcifications in paleopathology. In D. J. Ortner and A. C. Aufderheide, eds., *Human Paleopathology: Current Syntheses and Future Options*. Washington, DC: Smithsonian Institution Press, pp. 257–60.

Becker, C. R., Nikolaou, K., Muders, M., et al. (2003). Ex vivo coronary atherosclerotic plaque characterization with multi-detector-row CT. *European Radiology*, 13, 2094–8.

Biehler-Gomez, L., Cappella, A., Castoldi, E., Martrille, L. and Cattaneo, C. (2018a). Survival of atherosclerotic calcifications in skeletonized material: Forensic and pathological implications. *Journal of Forensic Sciences*, 63, 386–94.

Biehler-Gomez, L., Maderna, E., Brescia, G., et al. (2018b). Distinguishing atherosclerotic calcifications in dry bone: implications for forensic identification. *Journal of Forensic Sciences*, 64, 839–44.

Biehler-Gomez, L., Maderna, E., Brescia, G., et al. (2019). 'Aged' autopsy gallstones simulating dry bone context: a morphological, histological and SEM-EDS analysis. *International Journal of Paleopathology*, 24, 60–5.

Binder, M. and Roberts, C. A. (2014). Calcified structures associated with human skeletal remains: Possible atherosclerosis affecting the population buried at Amara West, Sudan (1300–800 BC). *International Journal of Paleopathology*, 6, 20–9.

Cattaneo, C., Mazzarelli, D., Cappella, A., et al. (2018). A modern documented Italian identified skeletal collection of 2127 skeletons: The CAL Milano Cemetery Skeletal Collection. *Forensic Science International*, 287, 219.e1–e5.

Charatsi, D. I., Kotsopoulos, I. C., Xirou, P., Valeri, R. M. and Kaplanis, K. (2015). Synchronous adenocarcinoma and echinococcosis in the same ovary: A rare clinical entity. *Hippokratia*, 19, 88.

Charlier, P., Wils, P., Froment, A. and Huynh-Charlier, I. (2014). Arterial calcifications from mummified materials: Use of micro-CT-scan for histological differential diagnosis. *Forensic Science, Medicine and Pathology*, 10, 461–5.

Cunha, E. (2006). Pathology as a factor of personal identity in forensic anthropology. In A. Schmitt, E. Cunha and J. Pinheiro, eds., *Forensic Anthropology and Medicine*. Totowa, NJ: Humana Press, pp. 333–58.

Curtze, S. C., Kratz, M., Steinert, M. and Vogt, S. (2016). Step down vascular calcification analysis using state-of-the-art nanoanalysis techniques. *Scientific Reports*, 6, 23285.

Das, D. K. (2009). Psammoma body: A product of dystrophic calcification or of a biologically active process that aims at limiting the growth and spread of tumor? *Diagnostic Cytopathology*, 37, 534–41.

Decreto di Polizia Mortuaria. (1990). *Decreto del Presidente della Repubblica*, n. 285, 10 settembre 1990. Regolamento di Polizia Mortuaria. https://presidenza.governo.it/USRI/ufficio_studi/normativa/D.P.R .%2010%20settembre%201990,%20n.%20285.pdf

Demer, L. L. and Tintut, Y. (2008). Vascular calcification: Pathobiology of a multifaceted disease. *Circulation*, 117, 2938–48.

DiMaio, V. J. M. and Francis, J. R. (2001). Heterotopic ossification in unidentified skeletal remains. *American Journal of Forensic Medicine and Pathology*, 22, 160–4.

Doherty, T. M., Asotra, K., Fitzpatrick, L. A., et al. (2003). Calcification in atherosclerosis: Bone biology and chronic inflammation at the arterial crossroads. *Proceedings of the National Academy of Sciences USA*, 100(20), 11201–6.

Falk, E. (2006). Pathogenesis of atherosclerosis. *Journal of the American College of Cardiology*, 47(8 Suppl), C7–C12.

Fayad, Z. A. and Fuster, V. (2001). Clinical imaging of the high-risk or vulnerable atherosclerotic plaque. *Circulation Research*, 89, 305–16.

Gaeta, R., Fornaciari, A., Izzetti, R., Caramella, D. and Giuffra, V. (2019). Severe atherosclerosis in the natural mummy of Girolamo Macchi (1648–1734), 'major writer' of Santa Maria della Scala Hospital in Siena (Italy). *Atherosclerosis*, 280, 66–74.

Glass, C. K. and Witztum, J. L. (2001). Atherosclerosis: The road ahead. *Cell*, 104, 503–16.

Gouvêa Lima, G. de M., Moraes, R. M., Cavalcante, A. S. R., Carvalho, Y. R. and Anbinder, A. L. (2015). An isolated phlebolith on the lip: An unusual case and review of the literature. *Case Reports in Pathology*, 2015, 507840.

Jang, I.-K., Bouma, B. E., Kang, D.-H., et al. (2002). Visualization of coronary atherosclerotic plaques in patients using optical coherence tomography: Comparison with intravascular ultrasound. *Journal of the American College of Cardiology*, 39, 604–9.

Kim, I. S., Myung, S. J., Lee, S. S., Lee, S. K. and Kim, M. H. (2003). Classification and nomenclature of gallstones revisited. *Yonsei Medical Journal*, 44, 561–70.

Kim, M. J., Kim, Y. S., Oh, C. S., et al. (2015). Anatomical confirmation of computed tomography-based diagnosis of the atherosclerosis discovered in seventeenth century Korean mummy. *PLoS One*, 10, e0119474.

Komar, D. A. and Buikstra, J. E. (2003). Differential diagnosis of a prehistoric biological object from the Koster (Illinois) Site. *International Journal of Osteoarchaeology*, 13, 157–64.

Libby, P. (2003). Vascular biology of atherosclerosis: Overview and state of the art. *American Journal of Cardiology*, 91(3A), 3A–6A.

Libby, P., Ridker, P. M. and Hansson, G. K. (2011). Progress and challenges in translating the biology of atherosclerosis. *Nature*, 473, 317–25.

Lusis, A. J. (2000). Atherosclerosis. *Nature*, 407, 233–41.

Mönckeberg, J. G. (1903). Über die reine Mediaverkalkung der Extremitätenarterien und ihr Verhalten zur Arteriosklerose. *Virchows Archiv für pathologische Anatomie und Physiologie und für klinische Medizin*, 171, 141–67.

Özdemir, K., Akyol, A. A. and Erdal, Y. S. (2015). A case of ancient bladder stones from Oluz Höyük, Amasya, Turkey. *International Journal of Osteoarchaeology*, 25, 827–37.

Rudd, J. H. F., Narula, J., Strauss, H. W., et al. (2010). Imaging atherosclerotic plaque inflammation by fluorodeoxyglucose with positron emission tomography. *Journal of the American College of Cardiology*, 55, 2527–35.

Sangiorgi, G., Rumberger, J. A., Severson, A., et al. (1998). Arterial calcification and not lumen stenosis is highly correlated with atherosclerotic plaque burden in humans: A histologic study of 723 coronary artery segments using nondecalcifying methodology. *Journal of the American College of Cardiology*, 31, 126–33.

Schembri, L., Congiu, T., Tozzi, M., et al. (2008). Scanning electron microscopy examination and elemental analysis of atherosclerotic calcifications in a human carotid plaque. *Circulation*, 117, e479–e480.

Shah, P. K. (2003). Mechanisms of plaque vulnerability and rupture. *Journal of the American College of Cardiology*, 41(4 Suppl S), 15S–22S.

Stary, H. C., Chandler, A. B., Dinsmore, R. E., et al. (1995). A definition of advanced types of atherosclerotic lesions and a histological classification of atherosclerosis. A report from the Committee on Vascular Lesions of the Council on Arteriosclerosis, American Heart Association. *Circulation*, 92, 1355–74.

Steinbock, R. T. (1990a). Studies in ancient calcified soft tissues and organic concretions. II: Urolithiasis (renal and urinary bladder stone disease). *Journal of Paleopathology*, 3, 39–59.

Steinbock, R. T. (1990b). Studies in ancient calcified soft tissues and organic concretions. III: Gallstones (cholelithiasis). *Journal of Paleopathology*, 3, 95–106.

Subirana-Domènech, M., Borondo-Alcázar, J. C., Armentano-Oller, N., et al. (2012). Arteriosclerosis in paleopathology: Are macroscopic findings well known? *International Journal of Paleopathology*, 2, 246–8.

Torii, S., Mustapha, J. A., Narula, J., et al. (2019). Histopathologic characterization of peripheral arteries in subjects with abundant risk factors: Correlating imaging with pathology. *Journal of the American College of Cardiology Cardiovascular Imaging*, 12, 1501–13.

Towler, D. A. (2008). Vascular calcification: A perspective on an imminent disease epidemic. *IBMS Bonekey*, 5, 41–58.

Van Engelen, A., Niessen, W. J., Klein, S., et al. (2013). Automated segmentation of atherosclerotic histology based on pattern classification. *Journal of Pathology Informatics* 4(Suppl), S3.

Virmani, R., Kolodgie, F. D., Burke, A. P., Farb, A. and Schwartz, S. M. (2000). Lessons from sudden coronary death: A comprehensive morphological classification scheme for atherosclerotic lesions. *Arteriosclerosis, Thrombosis and Vascular Biology*, 20, 1262–75.

Wexler, L., Brundage, B., Crouse, J., et al. (1996). Coronary artery calcification: Pathophysiology, epidemiology, imaging methods, and clinical implications. A statement for health professionals from the American Heart Association Writing Group. *Circulation*, 94(5), 1175–92.

Yang, W., Wong, K. and Chen, X. (2017). Intracranial atherosclerosis: From microscopy to high-resolution magnetic resonance imaging. *Journal of Stroke*, 19, 249–60.

Yoshida, H., Yokoyama, K., Yaginuma, T., et al. (2011). Difference in coronary artery intima and media calcification in autopsied patients with chronic kidney disease. *Clinical Nephrology*, 75, 1–7.

14 Atherosclerosis in Indigenous Tsimane

A Contemporary Perspective

Randall C. Thompson, Gregory S. Thomas, Angela D. Neunuebel, Ashna Mahadev, Benjamin C. Trumble, Edmond Seabright, Daniel K. Cummings, Jonathan Stieglitz, Michael Gurven and Hillard Kaplan[*]

14.1 Introduction

The Horus and other research teams have found that atherosclerosis is not uncommon in ancient people through the study of their mummified remains (Murphy et al., 2003; Allam et al., 2009, 2011; Thompson et al., 2013, 2014). However, some have postulated that traditional hunter-gatherers are in some ways healthier than modern people and that they had very little atherosclerotic disease (O'Keefe et al., 2010). The aim of this study was to evaluate the burden of atherosclerosis in a population alive today but living a traditional lifestyle similar to that experienced by past populations. This led to the Tsimane Health and Life History Project Team (THLHP) (Gurven et al., 2017) and the Horus Study Team combining efforts to evaluate the prevalence and extent of coronary atherosclerosis in the Tsimane of Bolivia (Kaplan et al., 2017).

14.2 The Tsimane of Bolivia

The Tsimane are forager-horticulturalists in the Bolivian Amazon region. They are an isolated population of approximately 16 000, inhabiting more than 90 villages along the Maniqui, Quiquibey and Mato Rivers in lowland Bolivia (Gurven et al., 2017). Most villages lack running water and electricity and have limited access to market goods. Poling a canoe or raft on a river or walking are their traditional forms of transportation. Recently, small outboard motors have become widely available and can be placed on canoes to shorten the duration of trips to the market town of San Borja.

The Tsimane economy is based on small-scale cultivation of produce including plantains, sweet manioc, rice and corn, as well as fishing, hunting and gathering fruits and honey. Figure 14.1 illustrates some of their lifestyles. The surrounding

---

[*] For the Horus and Tsimane Health and Life History Project Teams. *Horus study team members*: Adel H. Allam, Ibrahim Badr, Emily M. Clarke, Caleb E. Finch, Klaus O. Fritsch, Bruno Frohlich, Samantha I. King, Guido P. Lombardi, Gomaa Abd el-Maksoud, David E. Michalik, Michael I. Miyamoto, Jagat Narula, Frances M. Neunuebel, Abd el-Halim Nur el-Din, Chris J. Rowan, Muhammad Al-Tohamy Soliman, James D. Sutherland, Ian G. Thomas, Adam M. Thompson and L. Samuel Wann.

Tsimane Health and Life History Project team members and other collaborators: Juan Copajira Adrian, Sarah Alami, Giuseppe Barisano, Bret Beheim, Angela R. Garcia, Andrei Irimia, Margaret Gatz, Raul Quispe Gutierrez and Daniel Eid Rodriguez.

Figure 14.1 Images of Tsimane lifestyle: (a) Tsimane individual crossing the Maniqui River at sunrise; (b) Tsimane dwellings; (c) inside a Tsimane dwelling; (d) woman crushing dried corn; (e) Tsimane woman retrieving water from a nearby stream; (f) two Tsimane hunters in the forest. Sources: (a) Ben Trumble; (b–d) Jonathan Stieglitz; (e, f) Michael Gurven. (A black and white version of this figure will appear in some formats. For the colour version, please refer to the plate section.)

rivers offer a variety of fish and nearby arable land for cultivation. Arrows, hooks and line, or nets are used for freshwater fishing. Depending on the wild game density around the village, hunting plays an important role in many communities. Guns or bows and arrows are used in hunting neotropical mammals such as the collared peccary, grey brocket deer, the Brazilian tapir and the howler monkey, sometimes with the help of hunting dogs or machetes. The corn, manioc, plantains and rice are high in fibre and low in saturated fats and simple sugars (Gurven et al., 2017).

The Tsimane diet lacks artificial *trans* fats (created by adding hydrogen to liquid vegetable oils to make them more soluble) and people's daily food intake on average contains 11 g saturated fat, 14 g monounsaturated fat and 8 g polyunsaturated fat (Martin et al., 2012). Diets differ from village to village, but a typical Tsimane diet consists of 72 per cent carbohydrates, 14 per cent protein and 14 per cent fat (Martin et al., 2012). In comparison, the typical modern US diet comprises 50 per cent carbohydrates, 16 per cent protein and 34 per cent fat, 11 per cent of which is saturated (see Kris-Etherton et al., 2012 and Figure 14.2). Tsimane days mostly consist of hunting, farming, cooking, parenting, grandparenting and socialising. Hunts often last more than eight hours and cover many kilometres (Trumble et al., 2014). Clearing of fields for horticulture requires heavy chopping of forests with axes (Trumble et al., 2013). A recent increase in access to the market town of San Borja and to intermittent wage labor have, however, been changing the Tsimane diet (Kraft et al., 2018). Men and women spend on average six to seven and four to six hours, respectively, per day carrying out physical activity. Only 10 per cent of the Tsimane waking hours are spent in a sedentary manner (Gurven et al., 2013) compared with

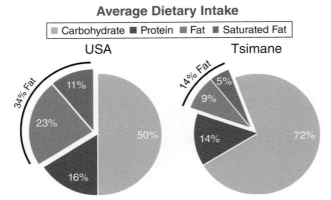

Figure 14.2 Comparison of major dietary components of US and Tsimane populations. (A black and white version of this figure will appear in some formats. For the colour version, please refer to the plate section.)

approximately 54 per cent in industrial populations (Matthews et al., 2008). This high level of physical activity has rather obvious implications for cardiovascular health (Lee et al., 2012). The THLHP and Horus cardiovascular studies aimed to determine if this population with traditional human lifestyles, but high rates of infection, have low or high rates of atherosclerotic disease.

14.3 Material and Methods

The Tsimane Health and Life History Project began in 2002, and combines biomedical surveillance of health with the anthropology of everyday life to analyse the impacts of ecology and society on the human life cycle. The Tsimane people of Bolivia are a remote-living Amerindian tribe with traditional lifestyles, very high levels of physical activity and limited access to market goods. The THLHP and Horus study teams collaborated in a study involving 705 adult Tsimane men and women who were transported from their villages to the clinics and computed tomography (CT) scanner at the German Busch Hospital in the regional capital of Trinidad, Bolivia between 2014 and 2017 (Kaplan et al., 2017). To reach the city, they typically journeyed one to two days by river to the roads originating from San Borja, followed by six hours in a taxi or bus. The composition of the Tsimane group studied was selected randomly by computer to achieve a cross-sectional study population. Voluntary participation in the study was high (92 per cent) among the Tsimane given the trust that THLHP had engendered over many years. The Tsimane who travelled to Trinidad were also provided with free access to medical care, including medical specialists. Individuals were compensated for their time and travel with subsistence goods. To evaluate coronary atherosclerosis, CT and coronary artery calcium scoring were utilised as sensitive measures of preclinical coronary atherosclerosis. Deposits of coronary hydroxyapatite (a component of atherosclerotic plaque) can be detected on CT scans and are diagnostic of atherosclerosis (Stary et al., 1995). These calcified deposits occur prior to the development of symptoms, such as those associated with myocardial infarction or angina pectoris (Agatston et al., 1990). The degree of calcification is scored by the number and density of CT pixels that are over a threshold density of 130 HU using the Agatston method, with higher numbers correlating with more extensive coronary atherosclerosis (Agatston et al., 1990).

14.4 Results

The Tsimane were found to have a very low prevalence of coronary atherosclerosis, as measured by coronary artery calcification (CAC). The vast majority (596 of 705; 85 per cent) of participants had no CAC. A small number had mild coronary calcifications, with scores lower than 100 ($n = 89$; 13 per cent), and only 20 individuals (3 per cent) had CAC of 100 or higher (Figure 14.3) (Kaplan et al., 2017). These results were compared with published calcification scores of general population-based studies in industrialised countries (Schmermund et al., 2002; Budoff et al., 2013). The Tsimane have less CAC than any other population ever described, including two major comparative studies: the cross-sectional population of the US Multiethnic Study of Atherosclerosis (MESA) and the European cross-sectional population of the German Heinz Nixdorf Recall (HNR) study (Schmermund et al., 2002; Budoff et al., 2013). The differences in CAC were further analysed by age across broad categories (Figure 14.3).

Using CAC as a metric for arterial age, the Tsimane have an average arterial age that is about 28 years younger than matched Americans (Figure 14.4). The difference in arterial age is best shown by using the MESA arterial age calculator. Figure 14.4 displays the predicted arterial age of the Tsimane by their actual chronological age, and the difference between the MESA arterial age calculator scores for the Tsimane and their true chronological age. By the age of 80, the estimated arterial age is 52 years for women and 51 years for men. For a Tsimane over the age of 75 years, the mean difference between chronological and arterial age was 33 and 28 years for females and males, respectively.

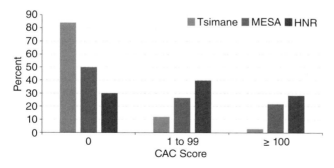

Figure 14.3 Percentage of Tsimane CAC scores in three risk categories compared with the general cross-sectional population-based participants from the MESA study (Budoff et al., 2013) and the Heinz Nixdorf Recall (HNR) study (Schmermund et al., 2002). (A black and white version of this figure will appear in some formats. For the colour version, please refer to the plate section.)

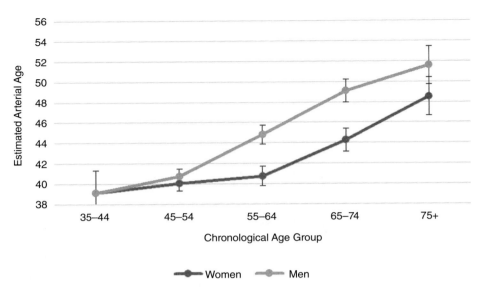

Figure 14.4 Arterial age versus chronological age for Tsimane women and men.

14.5 Discussion

14.5.1 Why Do Tsimane Have So Little Coronary Atherosclerosis?

The most obvious explanation for the reason why the Tsimane population has such little coronary calcium and subsequent coronary atherosclerosis is related to their optimal coronary risk factor profile (Yusuf et al., 2004); in other words, the paucity of traditional cardiovascular risk factors. Genes, the presence of inflammation and immune regulation represent three other possible explanations. The Tsimane subsistence lifestyle meets all four of the lifestyle factors that the American Heart Association lists as goals: no or minimal smoking, body mass index (BMI) less than 30 kg/m^2, a healthy diet and moderate or greater physical activity (Lichtenstein et al., 2006) Although some Tsimane smoke lightly, and they are not particularly lean (almost one-quarter of adults qualify as being overweight according to their BMI), almost all Tsimane meet the goals of the American Heart Association and often greatly exceed them. Their subsistence lifestyle includes a very low saturated fat diet and substantial daily physical activity. As a result, there is little obesity, hypertension or peripheral arterial disease, and their mean low-density lipoprotein (LDL), or 'bad' cholesterol, is quite low. Lifetime LDL is estimated to be 72 mg/dL (Kaplan et al., 2017). Among the 705 Tsimane in this study, mean fasting glucose was 79 mg/dL (desirable <100 mg/dL) and none had diabetes. Figure 14.5 serves as a summary of this discussion. It should be noted that the Tsimane and other indigenous people in South America and Africa are experiencing a rapid change in some of these metrics, as progressive access to market goods increases lipid levels, body weight and rates of diabetes.

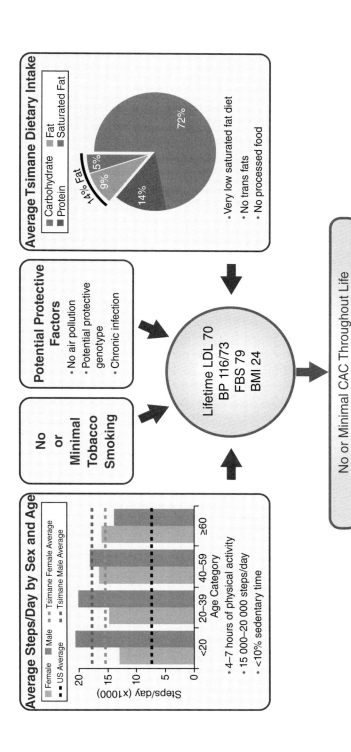

Figure 14.5 Concepts of how multiple factors contribute to the remarkably low rates of coronary arterial calcification in the Tsimane. (A black and white version of this figure will appear in some formats. For the colour version, please refer to the plate section.)

The Tsimane also have potential atheroprotective factors within their environment, including no industrial air pollution (although they cook over an open fire), and the presence of chronic helminthic infections, which some theorise may induce beneficial modulation of the immune system (Gurven et al., 2016 and see below). As the Tsimane have recently experienced increasing levels of cholesterol with advances in acculturation, a genetic predisposition to low cholesterol seems an unlikely cause of their benign lipid levels (Kaplan et al., 2017). If the genetic constitution of the Tsimane is similar to that of other North and South Americans, their subsistence lifestyle and high levels of physical activity, and resultant optimal cardiovascular risk factor profile, set a new standard of achievable metrics when discussing potential preventative measures for avoiding atherosclerosis.

However, the Tsimane live without modern sanitation and have high rates of infection and markers of inflammation. Blood markers of inflammation such as white blood cell count (WBC), high–sensitivity C-reactive protein (hsCRP) and erythrocyte sedimentation rate (ESR) are frequently elevated (Zebrack & Anderson, 2002). In particular, the hs-CRP test measures the level of inflammation and can be used to assess risk for heart disease/stroke (Ridker et al., 2009). The ESR measures how quickly red blood cells move to the bottom of a test tube; if a person has inflammation, their cells may settle at a fast rate.

Infection and inflammation, particularly periodontal disease and elevated hsCRP, have been found to be associated with atherosclerosis in industrialised societies (Chistiakov et al., 2016). However, there is reason to hypothesise that chronic infections of the lungs and skin do not promote atherosclerosis, and other infections, especially those caused by helminths, could be protective against atherosclerosis, especially when a person has low LDL in their cholesterol (Gurven et al., 2009, 2018). For example, intestinal helminths draw metabolic resources from their host, including blood lipids and glucose, and modulate immune function towards greater T_H2 (anti-inflammatory) polarisation. These helminth-induced alterations may be factors in slowing atheroma progression and diminishing the possibility of atherosclerotic plaque rupture, in which a sudden blood thrombosis forms over the rupture causing a heart attack or stroke (Gurven et al., 2016).

14.5.2 Studies of Cardiovascular Disease and Risk Factors in Other Subsistence Populations

Studies of individuals from cultures living a subsistence lifestyle have found similarly low blood pressure and LDL cholesterol levels, as documented in four reports. Firstly, in 1975 Oliver and colleagues reported a study of 506 men and women out of approximately 15 000 from the Yanomamo tribe in the tropical rainforest of northern Brazil and southern Venezuela (Oliver et al., 1975). Without access to markets, the Yanomamo people farm, hunt, fish and gather their food. While blood pressure in industrialised cultures gradually increases over adult life, the blood pressure of Yanomamo men was 108/69 mmHg during their twenties but remained stable thereafter through adult life. Blood pressure in Yanomamo women in their twenties was 100/64 mmHg, again without increasing thereafter. LDL levels were obtained and reported in 1990. Mean LDL among 34 men was 68 mg/dL and was 78 mg/dL among 14 women (Mancilha-Carvalho & Crews, 1990). This compares favourably to what is considered desirable (<100 mg/dL) and to the mean in general population-based studies of Westerners (e.g. 132 mg/dL in the PESA study; Fernandez-Friera et al., 2015). Secondly, two cultures in southeastern India living a subsistence lifestyle had mean LDL cholesterol levels similar to those of the Tsimane and Yanomamo. The Kandha tribe of the Eastern Ghat mountains (n = 97) who hunt, gather and practice slash-and-burn agriculture, and the Naulia fishermen of the Coromandel coast (n = 93) both had mean adult LDL values of 71 mg/dL (Mandal et al., 1994). Thirdly, the long-standing subsistence culture of the Parkateje of northern Brazil experienced a change over a 20-year period in which they gained access to market food and motorised vehicles. While mean blood pressure remained low in a sample of 90 individuals studied (111/73 and 107/70 mmHg for men and women, respectively), LDL was higher than in cultures prior to acculturation (the Tsimane and Yanomamo) at 90 and 93 mg/dL for male and female Parkateje, respectively (Tavas et al., 2003).

Finally, a frequently cited study explored risk factors for cardiovascular disease in a Melanesian population from the Trobriand Islands, Papua New Guinea (Kitava) and compared them with those of a healthy Swedish population (Lindeberg et al., 1994). This study focused on horticulturalists who were thought to have been free from ischaemic heart disease or strokes. A total of 220 people were studied, 151 male and 69 female between the ages of 14 and 87 years. These people maintained a traditional horticulturist lifestyle and had not been uninfluenced by Westernised diets. Instead, fruits, fish, tubers and coconut were their main foods. The investigators measured blood pressure, height, weight and BMI, and waist, pelvis and upper arm circumference. They also measured serum total cholesterol, high-density lipoprotein (HDL), LDL and the lipid subfractions apolipoprotein B and A1. BMI, diastolic blood pressure and triceps skinfold thickness measurements were all lower in the Islanders compared to the Swedes. Systolic blood pressure was lower in women over age 60 and men over age 20. The authors attributed the very low rates of stroke and ischaemic heart disease to lower blood pressure and lean body weight among the Islanders relative to modern-day Swedish people. The authors believed this difference could be explained by the considerable difference in diet between the two cultures, especially less salt and saturated fat and more soluble fibre in the Trobrianders. However, relative physical activity may have a part to play here, although Lindeberg et al.'s (2014) study was focused on dietary factors.

These studies of the Yanomamo, Kadha, Naulia, Parkateje and Trobriand Islanders are consistent in showing healthy cardiovascular risk factor metrics and apparently low rates of cardiovascular disease, findings similar to those of the Tsimane. All represent physically active populations who consume diets low in Western food items and have a very low burden of risk factors for heart disease.

14.5.3 How Do We Reconcile the Absence of Atherosclerosis among the Tsimane with Its Apparent Prevalence among Ancient People?

The Horus study found atherosclerosis among Egyptian mummies as well as pre-Columbian Peruvians, Aleutian Islanders and Ancestral Puebloan Native Americans of the southwestern USA (see Chapter 4). While Egyptian mummies tend to be of people who were elite in life, the two latter cultures lived a subsistence lifestyle that may have been similar to that of the Tsimane. The ancient Egyptian lifestyle (and to a lesser extent the ancient Peruvian) was more hierarchical and even urbanised. In addition, the elite Egyptians were artificially mummified in a costly 40-day process, whereas the human remains analysed in the other cultures were preserved naturally through desiccation (Peruvians and Native Americans of the southeastern USA) or very cold environments (Aleutian Islanders). The Egyptians who were mummified were particularly of the higher social classes, especially in the older dynastic periods (David, 2010). They likely ate a rich diet, in many ways similar to moderns (David, 2010), and were not physically active in life. This may have contributed to the occurrence of atherosclerosis in these people. One study of pathological bone conditions on CT scans of Egyptian mummies revealed numerous examples of joint disease in the bones of the knees, hips and spine, but ankle osteoarthritis was relatively rare (Fritsch et al., 2015). This finding led the investigators to conclude that these Egyptians in life likely did not commonly walk on irregular surfaces because of their high status, which could have resulted in ankle injuries (Fritsch et al., 2015).

The heart is typically not well preserved after either artificial or natural mummification and, in the case of the Egyptians, was sometimes removed. This makes coronary artery calcification particularly difficult to evaluate in such studies. Thus, the presence of atherosclerosis in mummies has usually focused on extra-coronary atherosclerosis. Extra-coronary atherosclerotic calcifications, such as calcium in the thoracic aorta, abdominal aorta and the iliac, femoral and carotid arteries, is known to occur earlier than in the coronary arteries (Allam et al., 2018) and is fairly easy to identify on the CT scan of a reasonably well-preserved mummy. For example, Allam and colleagues have pioneered the study of whole-body calcifications using whole-body CT scanning to investigate extra-coronary atherosclerosis in living people (Allam et al., 2018), with 154 Egyptian patients studied as part of this project. They underwent clinically indicated nuclear cardiology stress testing (myocardial perfusion imaging), but their scans showed no evidence of lack of blood flow caused by coronary artery heart disease. The investigators found that calcification was frequently present in the iliac and femoral arteries of the legs and the abdominal and thoracic aorta. However, calcification in the coronary and carotid arteries was typically seen only in older individuals. As coronary and carotid atherosclerosis result, respectively, in myocardial infarctions and strokes (Kaptoge et al., 2019), they can be termed 'event-related arteries'. The investigators thus proposed that atherosclerosis moves in a 'south to north fashion' with age (Allam et al., 2018), occurring first in the iliac and femoral arteries, then the aorta and then arteries to the head. Based on these findings, whole-body CT scanning in the Tsimane would likely reveal more atherosclerosis in more 'southern' arterial beds than was seen in the coronary arteries. Extra-coronary atherosclerosis has not yet been fully evaluated in the Tsimane, but thoracic aortic calcium has been observed to be more prevalent than coronary calcification (Thompson et al., 2018). Thus, it is not really possible to say whether ancient people had more atherosclerosis than the Tsimane. However, what can certainly be said is that atherosclerosis has been present in humankind for a very long time. It is also clear that cultures where people are very physically active and eat a lean diet have much less atherosclerosis than people who live in modern Western cultures.

14.6 Conclusions

The findings of atherosclerosis in multiple diverse ancient cultures demonstrates a natural human tendency to develop atherosclerosis, the primary cause of cardio-vascular death and the number one cause of death in the modern-day world (Yusuf et al., 2015). Finding that the Tsimane experience minimal coronary atherosclerosis demonstrates that coronary disease can be dramatically reduced with a very low fat diet and high levels of low to moderate activity. These two variables appear to produce low LDL cholesterol, low blood pressure, minimal obesity and an avoid-ance of diabetes. While this lifestyle and diet is not always realistic in contempor-ary urban populations, it sets a standard of what can be achieved to slow the modern-day scourge of atherosclerosis. The study of the bioarcheology of athero-sclerosis has added substantially to our understanding of this very common human disease.

Acknowledgments

We thank Tsimane participants and their communities, and the Tsimane Health and Life History Project field team (including San Borja office staff, physicians, biochem-ists, and anthropologists), whose support, expertise, and commitment made this work possible. We also thank the National Institutes of Health for their support of the Tsimane Health and Life History Project, namely awards R01AG024119, R56AG024119, and RF1AG054442. JS acknowledges IAST funding from the French National Research Agency under the Investments for the Future (Investissements d'Avenir) program, grant ANR-17-EURE-0010.

References

Agatston, A. S., Janowitz, W. R., Hildner, F. J., et al. (1990). Quantification of coronary artery calcium using ultrafast computed tomography. *Journal of the American College of Cardiology*, 15, 827–32.

Allam, A. H., Thompson, R. C., Wann, L. S., Miyamoto, M. I. and Thomas, G. S. (2009). Computed tomographic assessment of atherosclerosis in ancient Egyptian mummies. *Journal of the American Medical Association*, 302, 2091–4.

Allam, A. H., Thompson, R. C., Wann, L. S., et al. (2011). Atherosclerosis in ancient Egyptian mummies: The Horus study. *Journal of the American College of Cardiology Cardiovascular Imaging*, 4, 315–27.

Allam, A. H., Thompson, R. C., Eskander, M. A., et al. (2018). Is coronary calcium scoring too late? Total body arterial calcium burden in patients without known CAD and normal MPI. *Journal of Nuclear Cardiology*, 25, 1990–8.

Budoff, M. J., Young, R., Lopez, V. A., et al. (2013). Progression of coronary calcium and incident coronary heart disease events: MESA (Multi-Ethnic Study of Atherosclerosis). *Journal of the American College of Cardiology*, 61, 1231–39.

Chistiakov, D. A., Orekhov, A. N. and Bobryshev, Y. V. (2016). Links between atherosclerotic and periodontal disease. *Experimental and Molecular Pathology*, 100(1), 220–35.

David, R. (2010). The art of medicine: Atherosclerosis and diet in ancient Egypt. *Lancet*, 175, 718–19.

Fernandez-Friera, L., Penalvo, J. L., Fernandez-Ortiz, A., et al. (2015). Prevalence, vascular distribution, and multiterritorial extent of subclinical atherosclerosis in a middle-aged cohort. The PESA (progression of early subclinical atherosclerosis) study. *Circulation*, 131, 2104–13.

Fritsch, K. O., Hamoud, H., Allam, A. H., et al. (2015). The orthopedic diseases of ancient Egypt: Findings on CT scans of 52 mummies. *Anatomical Record*, 298(6), 1036–46.

Gurven, M. D., Kaplan, H., Winking, J., et al. (2009). Inflammation and infection do not promote arterial aging and cardiovascular disease risk factors among lean horticulturalists. *PLoS One*, 4(8), e6590.

Gurven, M. D., Jaeggi, A. V., Kaplan, H. and Cummings, D. (2013). Physical activity and modernization among Bolivian Amerindians. *PLoS One*, 8, e55679.

Gurven, M. D., Trumble, B. C., Stieglitz, J., et al. (2016). Cardiovascular disease and type 2 diabetes in evolutionary perspective: A critical role for helminths? *Evolution, Medicine and Public Health*, 2016(1), 338–57.

Gurven, M. D., Stieglitz, J., Trumble, B. C., et al. (2017). The Tsimane Health and Life History Project: integrating anthropology and biomedicine. *Evolutionary Anthropology*, 26(2), 54–73.

Gurven, M. D., Finch, C. E. and Wann, L. S. (2018). Are intestinal worms nature's anti-atherosclerosis vaccine? *European Heart Journal*, 39, 1653.

Kaplan, H., Thompson, R. C., Trumble, B. C., et al. (2017). Coronary atherosclerosis in indigenous South American Tsimane: A cross-sectional cohort study. *Lancet*, 389, 1730–9.

Kaptoge, S., Pennells, L., De Bacquer, D., et al. (2019). World Health Organization cardiovascular disease risk charts: revised models to estimate risk in 21 global regions. *Lancet Global Health*, 7(10), e1332–e1345.

Kraft, T., Stieglitz, J., Trumble, B., et al. (2018). Nutrition transition in two lowland Bolivian subsistence populations. *American Journal of Clinical Nutrition*, 108(6), 1183–95.

Kris-Etherton, P. M., Lefevre, M., Mensink, R. P., et al. (2012). Trans fatty acid intakes and food sources in the U.S. population: NHANES 1999–2002. *Lipids*, 47, 931–40.

Lee, I. M., Shiroma, E. J., Lobelo, F., et al. (2012). Effect of physical inactivity on major non-communicable diseases worldwide: An analysis of burden of disease and life expectancy. *Lancet*, 380, 219–29.

Lichtenstein, A. H., Appel, L. J., Brands, M., et al. (2006). Diet and lifestyle recommendations revision 2006: A scientific statement from the American Heart Association Nutrition Committee. *Circulation*, 114, 82–96.

Lindeberg, S., Nilsson-Ehle, P., Terent, A., et al. (1994). Cardiovascular risk factors in a Melanesian population apparently free from stroke and ischemic heart disease: The Kitava study. *Journal of Internal Medicine*, 236(3), 331–40.

Mancilha-Carvalho, J. J. and Crews, D. E. (1990). Lipid profiles of Yanomamo Indians of Brazil. *Preventive Medicine*, 19, 66–75.

Mandal, S., Das, S., Mohanty, B. K. and Sahu, C. S. (1994). Effects of ethnic origin, dietary and life-style habits on plasma lipid profiles: A study of three population groups. *Journal of Nutritional Medicine*, 4, 141–8.

Martin, M. A., Lassek, W. D., Gaulin, S. J., et al. (2012). Fatty acid composition in the mature milk of Bolivian forager-horticulturalists: Controlled comparisons with a US sample. *Maternal and Child Nutrition*, 8, 404–18.

Matthews, C. E., Chen, K. Y., Freedson, P. S., et al. (2008). Amount of time spent in sedentary behaviors in the United States, 2003–2004. *American Journal of Epidemiology*, 167, 875–81.

Murphy, W. A. Jr, zur Nedden Dz, D., Gostner, P., et al. (2003). The Iceman: Discovery and imaging. *Radiology*, 226, 614–29.

O'Keefe, J. H., Vogel, R., Lavie, C. J. and Cordain, L. (2010). Achieving hunter-gatherer fitness in the twenty-first century: back to the future. *American Journal of Medicine*, 123, 1082–6.

Oliver, W. J., Cohen, E. L. and Neel, J. V. (1975). Blood pressure, sodium intake, and sodium related hormones in the Yanomamo Indians, a 'No Salt' culture. *Circulation*, 52, 146–51.

Ridker, P. M., Danielson, E., Fonseca, F.A., et al. (2009). Reduction in C-reactive protein and LDL cholesterol and cardiovascular event rates after initiation of rosuvastatin: A prospective study of the JUPITER trial. *Lancet*, 373(9670), 1175–82.

Schmermund, A., Möhlenkamp, S., Stang, A., et al. (2002). Assessment of clinically silent atherosclerotic disease and established and novel risk factors for predicting myocardial infarction and cardiac death in healthy middle-aged subjects: Rationale and design of the Heinz Nixdorf RECALL Study. Risk factors, evaluation of coronary calcium and lifestyle. *American Heart Journal*, 144, 212–18.

Stary, H. C., Chandler, A. B., Dinsmore, R. E., et al. (1995). A definition of advanced types of atherosclerotic lesions and a histological classification of atherosclerosis. A report from the Committee on Vascular Lesions of the Council on Atherosclerosis, American Heart Association. *Circulation*, 92, 1355–74.

Tavas, E. F., Viera-Filho, J. P. B., Andriolo, A., et al. (2003). Metabolic profiles and cardiovascular risk patterns of an Indian tribe living in the Amazon region of Brazil. *Human Biology*, 75(1), 31–46.

Thompson, R. C., Allam, A. H., Lombardi, G. P., et al. (2013). Atherosclerosis across 4000 years of human history: The Horus study of four ancient populations. *Lancet*, 381, 1211–22.

Thompson, R. C., Allam, A. H., Zink, A., et al. (2014). Computed tomographic evidence of atherosclerosis in the mummified remains of humans from around the world. *Global Heart*, 9(2), 187–96.

Thompson, R. C., Trumble, B., Neunuebel, F., et al. (2018). Atherosclerosis as manifest by thoracic aorta calcium: Insights from a remote native population with extremely low levels of coronary atheroscler-osis and traditional CV risk factors (Abstract). *Journal of the American College of Cardiology*, 71(11 Suppl), A1685.

Trumble, B. C., Cummings, D. K., O'Connor, K. A., et al. (2013). Age-independent increases in male salivary testosterone during horticultural activity among Tsimane forager-farmers. *Evolution and Human Behavior*, 34, 350–7.

Trumble, B. C., Smith, E. A., O'Connor, K. A., et al. (2014). Successful hunting increases testosterone and cortisol in a subsistence population. *Proceedings of the Royal Society B, Biological Sciences*, 281(1776), 20132876.

Yusuf, S., Hawken, S., Ôunpuu, S., et al. (2004). Effect of potentially modifiable risk factors associated with myocardial infarction in 52 countries (the INTERHEART study): Case–control study. *Lancet*, 364, 937–52.

Yusuf, S., Wood, D., Ralston, J., et al. (2015). The World Heart Federation's vision for worldwide cardiovascular disease prevention. *Lancet*, 386(9991), 399–402.

Zebrack, J. S. and Anderson, J. L. (2002). The role of inflammation and infection in the pathogenesis and evolution of coronary artery disease. *Current Cardiology Reports*, 4, 278–88.

15 Reflections on Cardiovascular Disease

The Heart of the Matter

Charlotte A. Roberts, Michaela Binder and Daniel Antoine

Cardiovascular diseases (CVDs) are the leading cause of death globally, accounting for around one-third of all deaths overall in 2019 (17.9 million; World Health Organization, 2021). Since then, we have also learnt that there are worse outcomes for people with underlying CVD comorbidities who contract COVID-19: they have an increased risk of death (Nishiga et al., 2020). CVDs are still challenging to manage in populations worldwide, and their continuing presence resonates with many of the United Nations' Sustainable Development Goals, not least good health and well-being. Yet, while perceptions persist that CVDs are essentially a modern phenomenon, we are also starting to realise that human populations have experienced CVD for much longer than was once thought, as seen in this volume. It is clear that the evolution of the cardiovascular system has a four-billion-year history (Danziger, 2016). It originated in invertebrate animals, with subsequent evolution in amphibians and reptiles, with the most developed cardiovascular system found in mammals, including humans. The question is why CVDs are such a challenge to human populations today. It has been suggested to be the result of new selective forces – lifestyle factors in particular – that are being placed on a system not adapted to coping with them.

The antiquity of CVDs has been identified through palaeopathological studies of human remains from archaeological sites with direct evidence of CVDs, and from historical documents and illustrations, including knowledge of the cardiovascular system by past writers on medicine and surgery (see Barr, 2014). This includes Greek physicians like Hippocrates, who dates to the fifth century BCE (Katz & Katz, 1962). According to Cheng (2001: 182), Hippocrates 'truly accomplished a remarkable task in describing the various disorders of the heart and blood vessels'. It has also become apparent that, in spite of the albeit scarce primary evidence from human remains, CVDs can also be inferred from the presence of other pathological conditions whose complications include CVDs. When we organised a symposium on this subject in 2014, and have now produced a subsequent volume of studies by a multitude of authors, we could not have anticipated how insightful these submissions would be.

Palaeopathology, as a subdiscipline of bioarchaeology, has a long evolutionary history, starting with individual studies of non-human remains and moving on to human mummies and skeletons (Buikstra & Roberts, 2012). Some of the early work did find evidence of CVDs in mummified remains (Ruffer, 1911), but this type of evidence has never been prominent in the palaeopathological literature. This is likely because (1) burial contexts with skeletons provide most of the evidence of disease from archaeological human remains, although graves (see Chapter 8) and vascular impressions on the skeleton (see Chapter 10) can and do preserve evidence of CVDs; and (2) relatively few mummified or preserved bodies have been studied and published compared with skeletal remains from archaeological contexts. Nevertheless, while pathological conditions such as joint and dental diseases may be macroscopically evidenced with greater frequency through the study of human remains, there are indirect ways of accessing information related to the impact of CVDs on past populations (see Chapter 2).

When trying to identify CVDs, bioarchaeologists could be accused of not 'seeing the wood for the trees' (a proverb by John Heywood, the English writer, *c.* 1497 to *c.* 1580), particularly because when compared with other pathological conditions in human remains, evidence for CVDs is not common. Bioarchaeologists are also acutely aware of the osteological paradox, whereby most diseases do not affect the skeleton and, when they do, only a small percentage of individuals are affected or live long enough for pathological changes to involve the skeleton (Wood et al., 1992; Wright & Yoder, 2003; DeWitte & Stojanowski, 2015). The CVDs per se are a group of conditions that are usually seen only in preserved bodies, particularly in their soft tissues such as the blood vessels and heart. One could therefore begin to think that CVDs were uncommon in the past, and consequently bioarchaeologists might not even consider the possibility of finding evidence of CVDs if they are analysing a skeleton. However, they may be puzzled when finding 'objects' in a grave context (i.e. atheromas) that they do not easily recognise or cannot identify due to the object's disassociation with blood vessels, owing to the lack of preservation of such soft tissues (see Subirana-Domenech et al., 2012; Binder & Roberts, 2014). Yet, if one looks at the bigger picture, the potential for more evidence is clear. Further, taking a contextual approach relevant to CVDs – where archaeological and historical information is used to interpret collected data to answer specific questions – may help in providing more nuanced data. For example, we need to ask questions such as the following. Were the foodstuffs being consumed conducive to causing high blood pressure and CVDs (e.g. high cholesterol)? Did people have diabetes or drink high levels of alcohol? How much physical activity were people engaged in? Was obesity a factor to consider? Was air pollution a problem in their environments? Did ethnicity or an inherited predisposition influence CVD development? Was poor oral health, often found in archaeological populations, a driver of CVDs (see Chapter 6).

In considering the chapters in this volume, the majority of the evidence comes from mummies that span five continents and date from the fourth millennium BCE to the twentieth century, with CVD evidence associated with skeletons contributing further examples that are more recent in date. Macroscopic, histological, DNA and CT analyses are all used to explore the evidence. It is of course likely that, in the future, new analytical methods will be developed that will produce more nuanced data. Furthermore, studies of CVDs at the individual and population levels that make use of a range of methods from a variety of disciplines ought to provide more informative and nuanced data than data not produced in this way.

15.1 Take-Home CVD Messages

- CVDs have a long history, as seen through a variety of evidence. They are not just a modern phenomenon, and neither is the evidence necessarily only found within preserved bodies.
- The evidence of CVDs in the past is an important and insightful contribution to medicine today in terms of evolution of disease.
- As yet, the evidence from and with human remains is currently scarce for a variety of reasons that likely related to their initial identification on archaeological sites; mummies have produced more evidence than skeletons.
- The environment of the site being excavated is important to consider. Is it more likely than not to preserve CVD evidence?
- Identifying CVDs starts at excavation. Excavators of skeletons should be CVD aware, that is they should know what to look for (sizes and shapes of calcifications of the cardiovascular system) and be familiar with the anatomy of a human skeleton, particularly the distribution of blood vessels. Training is important.
- If calcifications are found, detailed recording of their position in relation to the bones of the skeleton is important for final identification in relation to the blood vessels affected.
- Soil samples from graves are helpful for recovering calcified tissues and, in this case, atheromas that may be missed during excavation.
- When lifting skeletons, excavators should package any CVD evidence carefully prior to processing (cleaning) the human remains.
- When the excavated skeleton is being cleaned, attention to what is being cleaned and its relative fragility are important when seeking evidence of CVD such as calcifications.
- Calcifications should be carefully stored alongside the skeleton with which they were found.
- In areas where bones and vessels come into close contact, the vascular system can leave impressions on the skeleton that allow the investigation of vessel variations and pathological changes long after the loss of any soft tissues (e.g., aneurysms).
- Studies of preserved bodies using CT scanning is essential for detecting CVDs but the limitations of single-energy CT may skew prevalence data. Dual-energy CT appears to allow a better understanding of what organs and vessels remain, as well as identifying atheromas.
- In mummified remains, embalming practices are likely to affect the available evidence, particularly the prevalence of vessels and atheromas. A more systematic approach that accounts for vessel presence (whether or not affected by atherosclerosis) should offer a clearer assessment of the past prevalence of CVD and enable like-for-like comparisons across studies.
- Conditions linked to CVDs should also be systematically recorded, including poor oral health, as the latter has been shown to increase the risk of developing atherosclerosis via several pathways (Joshipura et al., 2009; Carrizales-Sepúlveda et al., 2018).

- Ancient DNA analysis of human remains may detect genes that predisposed people to CVDs. However, it is important to explore both genes and the environment in thinking about underlying causes for CVDs.
- Bioarchaeologists should think outside the box and not dismiss the idea of the presence of CVDs in antiquity. CVD as a complication of other diseases that affected the body also needs to be considered.
- Finally, context is important in any bioarchaeological study. Were the people buried in the cemetery more predisposed to CVDs, for whatever reason? Use of archaeological and, where available, historical data needs to be considered.

As a result of the content of the chapters in this volume, we anticipate much more evidence will be forthcoming. This will allow for a fuller story of the origin, evolution and history of CVDs. We also hope that these studies will be conducted in an ethical manner, and that the results will be communicated not only to relevant disciplines in the academic world, including medicine, but also to wider audiences. Many of the general public are invested in learning about the past, and especially when stories provide insights relevant to who we are today. Finally, research would benefit from the creation of a central repository for evidence of CVDs, from archaeological/ forensic contexts, including images and prevalence data. This would help produce synthetic studies, and allow for the integration of new finds with extant data.

References

Barr, J. (2014). Vascular medicine and surgery in ancient Egypt. *Journal of Vascular Surgery*, 60(1), 260–3.

Binder, M. and Roberts, C. A. (2014). Calcified structures associated with human skeletal remains: Possible atherosclerosis affecting the population buried at Amara West, Sudan (1300–800 BC). *International Journal of Paleopathology*, 6, 20–9.

Buikstra, J. E. and Roberts, C. A. (eds.) (2012). *A Global History of Paleopathology: Pioneers and Prospects.* New York: Oxford University Press.

Carrizales-Sepúlveda, E. F., Ordaz-Farías, A., Vera-Pineda, R. and Flores-Ramírez, R. (2018). Periodontal disease, systemic inflammation and the risk of cardiovascular disease. *Heart, Lung and Circulation*, 27 (11), 1327–34.

Cheng, T. O. (2001). Hippocrates and cardiology. *American Heart Journal,* 141, 173–83.

Danziger, R. S. (2016). Evolutionary imprints on cardiovascular physiology and pathophysiology. In A. Avergne, C. Jenkinson and C. Faurie, eds., *Evolutionary Thinking in Medicine: From Research to Policy and Practice.* Cham, Switzerland: Springer, pp. 155–63.

DeWitte, S. N. and Stojanowski, C. M. (2015). The osteological paradox twenty years later: Past perspectives, future directions. *Journal of Archaeological Research*, 23, 397–450.

Joshipura, K., Zevallos, J. C. and Ritchie, C. S. (2009). Strength of evidence relating periodontal disease and atherosclerotic disease. *Compendium of Continuing Education in Dentistry*, 30(7), 430–9.

Katz, A. M. and Katz, P. B. (1962). Diseases of the heart in the works of Hippocrates. *British Heart Journal,* 13(4), 423–37.

Nishiga, M., Wang, D. W. and Han, Y., et al. (2020). COVID-19 and cardiovascular disease: From basic mechanisms to clinical perspectives. *Nature Reviews Cardiology*, 17, 543–58.

Ruffer, M. A. (1911). On arterial lesions found in Egyptian mummies. *Journal of Pathology and Bacteriology*, 15, 453–62.

Subirana-Domenech, M., Borondo-Alcazar, J.-C., Armentano-Oller, N., et al. (2012). Arteriosclerosis in palaeopathology: are macroscopic findings well known? *International Journal of Paleopathology*, 2, 246–8.

Wood, J. W., Milner, G. R., Harpending, H. C. and Weiss, K. M. (1992). The osteological paradox: Problems of inferring health from skeletal samples. *Current Anthropology*, 33(4), 343–70.

World Health Organization. (2021). Cardiovascular diseases (CVDs). www.who.int/news-room/fact-sheets/detail/cardiovascular-diseases-(cvds)

Wright, L. E. and Yoder, C. J. (2003). Recent progress in bioarchaeology: Approaches to the osteological paradox. *Journal of Archaeological Research*, 11(1), 43–70.

Index

acromegaly 28–9
Africa 44, 56, 217, 250
age (as a risk factor) 9, 41, 56, 171, 180
air pollution 21, 27, 157, 169, 252
Alaska 47–8, 57
alcohol 9, 19, 24, 138–9, 233
Aleutian Islands 47, 57, 68–74, 254
American Heart Association 250
aneurysm 5, 12, 20, 24, 77, 174–5, 179, 185, 205
angina pectoris 77, 249
ankylosing spondylitis 23
aorta 7, 11–12, 20, 23, 41–2, 44–5, 47–8, 50, 53, 56, 59, 67, 69–70, 73–4, 85, 89, 106, 133–5, 155, 172, 204–5, 233, 241–2, 254
aortic dissection 52, 76
archaeozoological analysis 170
artery
    basilar 233
    carotid 41, 44, 52, 59, 67, 69–70, 76, 89, 106–7, 110, 113, 116, 118, 132, 136, 138, 142, 164, 166, 219, 223, 233, 254
    coronary 41–2, 47–50, 59, 67, 69, 76, 85, 89, 106, 133–4, 138, 254
    femoral 49, 59, 69, 106, 110, 113, 118, 132, 138, 156, 223, 254
    iliac 48, 59, 69–70, 106, 132, 138, 155, 223, 233, 254
    iliofemoral 69
    meningeal 208–9, 211
    peripheral 59, 106, 116, 118
    popliteal 67, 106, 132, 138
    pulmonary 233
    renal 47, 156, 223
    subclavian 44, 59, 155
    tibial 47, 69, 106, 138
    vertebral 174–5
Asia 44, 51, 56

asthma 9
Australia 21, 105, 178
Austria 11, 202–3
autopsy 21, 42, 44, 47–50, 53, 72, 74, 85, 105, 132, 140, 203, 205, 207–10, 231–2

biological sex (as a risk factor) 41, 56, 67, 74, 76, 183
Blackfriars 164
blood pressure 9, 13, 21–2, 24, 29, 84, 252–3, 255
Bolivia 246–55
Brazil 252
British Museum 1, 98–123, 150, 188
bronchopneumonia *see: disease, respiratory*
Bronze Age 26

cancer 9–10, 53, 157
Chile 50–1
China 49, 51
cholesterol 9–10, 21, 41, 48, 50, 52–3, 72, 100, 118, 120, 122, 138, 234, 240, 250, 252–3, 255
coca leaves 51
computed tomography 42, 50, 53, 59, 63, 66–78, 98–123, 131, 248
    dual energy 98–123
congenital anomalies *see disease, congenital*

dental disease 22, 25, 60, 118–21, 153, 158
    calculus 25–8, 61, 151, 169
    caries 12, 60, 110, 115, 118, 169
    periapical lesion 110, 113, 115, 118
    periodontal disease 12, 27–8, 60, 74, 118–21, 151, 169, 252
dental wear 26, 104, 110, 113, 115, 158

diabetes 9–10, 13, 19, 21–2, 24, 29, 31, 33, 41, 43, 49, 56, 72, 159, 169, 215, 250, 255
diet 41–2, 57, 70, 72, 88, 138, 247, 250
    fish 138, 170
    meat 46, 53–4, 69, 139, 170
    Mediterranean 138
disease
    cerebrovascular 7
    congenital heart 7
    coronary artery 7, 21, 24, 28, 42, 50, 59, 67, 73, 76–7, 130, 138
    coronary heart 138
    degenerative disc 178, 180
    degenerative joint 22, 29, 46, 187, 254
    endocrine 29
    infectious 42, 60, 140, 158, 248
    ischaemic heart 51, 256
    non-communicable 7
    Paget 28–9
    parasitic 49
    peripheral artery 7, 21, 250
    renal 28–9, 43, 47, 159
    respiratory 9–10, 27, 48, 150, 153, 156–7, 252
    rheumatic heart 7
    rheumatoid 19, 28, 73
DISH 12, 22–3, 185
Down syndrome 19–20

East Asia 50
Egypt 3, 11, 13, 22, 44, 47, 49, 56, 66–78, 82, 84, 91, 98–124, 126, 159, 174, 186, 254
El Salvador 51
embolism 7
England 23
Enterobius vermicularis 49
epidemiological transition, second 9
ethnicity 9

264 Index

Europe 44, 56
  Eastern 51
evolutionary medicine 1, 3, 30
excavation 211, 242

farming *see subsistence strategy*
France 174

genetic predisposition 41, 50–1, 59,
    83, 85, 159
Germany 27
globalisation 9
goitre 51, 56
gout 21, 24, 167
Greenland 84

Hamann–Todd collection 179
Harvey, William 11
heart
  aortic valve 134–5
  mitral annulus 133
  mitral valve 49
Heinz Nixdorf Recall Study 249
Helicobacter pylori 81
helminths 252
heritability *see genetic*
    predisposition
Hippocrates 11, 258
histology 43–4, 47–9, 52–3, 59, 70,
    84, 150, 165, 233
Horus study 6, 57, 66–78
hyperlipidaemia 9, 119
hypertension 41, 49, 52, 56, 72, 119,
    139, 156, 250
hypertrophic osteoarthropathy 19
hypothyroidism 51, 56

Iceman 12, 25, 28, 70, 73, 81–2, 84,
    86–90
India 253
industrialisation 9
Industrial Revolution 60
infection
  bacterial 73
  helminthic 252
  parasitic 73
ischaemia 197
Islamic period 26
Italy 52

Japan 174

Kandha 253
Korea 70

Latin America 51
Leonardo da Vinci 14, 42, 215
Lithuania 130–1
London Bills of Mortality 14, 214
lupus erythematosus 73

Marfan syndrome 19–20, 174
maxillary sinusitis 28, 35
medial vascular calcification 220,
    223
medieval period 16, 53, 98, 141,
    164, 174, 184–6
metabolic syndrome 14, 22–4,
    30
military 28
Mongolians 70
myocardial infarction 42, 49–50, 52,
    59, 74, 76–7, 229, 231, 249

Native American 57
Natural History Museum Vienna
    202–3
Naulia 253
Neolithic 13, 28, 61, 89–90, 115
neoplastic disease *see cancer*
North America 37, 44, 57, 84, 252

obesity 8, 22, 25, 41, 49, 56, 118,
    121, 138–9, 156, 170, 250, 255
osteoarthritis 21–2, 104, 149, 153,
    167, 186, 188, 194, 254
osteoporosis 22, 29, 167, 218
Ötzi *see Iceman*

Pacific Islands 24
palaeobotanical analysis 87
palaeogenetics 59, 81
palaeoproteomic analysis 88
Papyrus
  Ebers 11, 22, 77, 147
Parkateje 253
pericarditis 19, 24, 29, 206–7
Peru 47, 50, 68–74, 82, 254
physical activity 138, 248, 250
physical exercise *see physical*
    activity
Poland 26
Portugal 23

pseudoaneurysm 182
Pueblans 68–74, 254
pulp stone 25

radiography 150
radiology 43, 50–1, 84
rheumatoid arthritis *see disease,*
    rheumatoid
Rokitansky, Carl von 205
Ruffer, Marc Armand 66

scanning electron microscopy 5,
    150–1, 233, 236, 241
Schistosoma haematobium 74
Schistosoma japonicum 49
sedentary life *see physical activity*
Sicily 21, 36, 130–1, 141
sieving 211, 221, 224, 232
single nucleotide polymorphism 50,
    83–5
smoke
  biomass fuel 28, 74, 90, 139,
    156–7
  tobacco 28, 41, 61, 90, 156–7,
    250
smoking *see smoke; tobacco*
social status 57, 67, 73, 137–8, 170,
    254
South America 44, 56–7, 84, 250
South Korea 49, 85
stable isotope analysis
  carbon/nitrogen 53–4, 139
  strontium 87, 150
stroke 7, 9, 13, 15, 22, 24, 27, 42,
    51–2, 76, 90, 118, 171, 184,
    205, 229, 252–3
subsistence strategy 51, 69, 255
Sudan 1, 3, 5, 12–13, 20, 22, 28,
    98–123, 175, 188
  Amara West 1–2, 5, 12, 22, 28,
    147–60
Sweden 164, 253
syphilis 13, 169, 202
Syria 26

taphonomy 215–19, 242
three-dimensional modelling 1,
    150
thrombosis 7, 119, 138, 157, 229,
    252
Tinea spp. 74

trauma 48, 183, 187
Trichinella spiralis 74
Trichuris trichiura 49
Trobriand 253
Tsimané 246–55
tuberculosis 16, 20, 22, 81, 83, 140, 157–8, 169, 202, 218

Unangans 57
United Kingdom 174, 184
US Multiethnic Study of Atherosclerosis (MESA) 249
USA 180

Venezuela 252

vitamin D deficiency 24

Withering, William 14

Yanomamo 252